Forgotten Reformer

Robert McClaughry and Criminal Justice Reform in Nineteenth-Century America

Frank Morn

UNIVERSITY PRESS OF AMERICA, ® INC.
Lanham • Boulder • New York • Toronto • Plymouth, UK

University Press of America,® Inc.
4501 Forbes Boulevard
Suite 200
Lanham, Maryland 20706
UPA Acquisitions Department (301) 459-3366

Estover Road
Plymouth PL6 7PY
United Kingdom

Printed in the United States of America
British Library Cataloging in Publication Information Available

Library of Congress Control Number: 2010931099
ISBN: 978-0-7618-5300-8 (paperback : alk. paper)
eISBN: 978-0-7618-5301-5

∞™ The paper used in this publication meets the minimum requirements of American National Standard for Information Sciences—Permanence of Paper for Printed Library Materials, ANSI Z39.48-1992

For Vergie and Betty
Mothers to all

Contents

Preface

". . . we are doing something very wrong."

Most people today think that American criminal justice—the police, courts, and prisons—is in a shambles. Police are racist, brutal, corrupt and ineffective. Courts—with overcrowded dockets, politicized judges, ill prepared lawyers, and arbitrary juries—do not measure out justice. Worst of all, perhaps, prisons are overfilled with hostile, idle, conspiring criminals likely to get out too soon and return too quickly. Recent figures show that one out of one hundred adult Americans is incarcerated. The United States continues to be one of the most unforgiving penal countries in the world. Try as it might, America has not found the formula to deal with its more recalcitrant populations. If it is true that "A nation is known by how it deals with those it hates the most," America has lost sight of its historic mission to be the "city on the hill."

Such angst and disillusionment go back two hundred years. There have been many waves of disgust with the system and desires to reform it. But history indicates two things. First, reform tends not to stick. The adhesive gives away exposing persistent sores underneath. Second, reform often has unintended consequences that are corrupt and counter effective. Apparently, many reformers are "nearsighted visionaries."[1]

This book tells the story of a justice system of a bygone era that resonates to this day. Much of the hullabaloo directed at probation, parole, and prison regimes toady is the product of well-intentioned reforms in the nineteenth century.

It also tells the story of a man named Robert McClaughry, who was in the midst of these attempts to reform an antiquated and ineffective system and who gave us what we enjoy condemning. Though an interesting and important figure, McClaughry is largely forgotten today. Profoundly religious, he was a blend of old stock Puritanism and evangelical Christianity. An intellectual trained in the classics, he taught in a small Midwestern college for a year before bringing his thoughtful consideration to managing a prison. Gifted as an eloquent speaker, often called upon to give speeches before citizen groups, criminal justice professionals, and politicians, he operated in a world of working class lingo and criminal cant. Finally, McClaughry was a bureaucrat caught up in an era of nepotism and politics. His ability to manage men and resources in an age when Americans were bumbling their way through criminal justice bureaucracies made him a rare find for conservative legislatures. Thanks to these attributes, McClaughry is an apt person through whom to explore the story of crime, prisons, policing, and criminal justice reforms in the last decades of the nineteenth and opening ones of the twentieth centuries.

This story has taken on increased importance today. Cries have come from the halls of power in Washington D.C. to study and reform criminal justice, particularly the area of corrections. Reforms initiated and defended by Robert McClaughry—such as indeterminate sentencing, probation, parole, and rehabilitation in prison—are problematic. Today America imprisons 756 inmates per 100,000 residents, a rate five times the world's average. "Either we are the most evil people on earth or we are doing something very wrong," argues one United States Senator as he calls for a national commission to "fix our prisons."[2] Of course, that fix, its progress and success, depends upon what we know of its history, a history in which Robert McClaughry was closely connected.

NOTES

1. Alas, I wish I had coined that phrase but I owe it to Adam Gopnik, *Angels and Ages: A Short Book About Darwin and Lincoln, and Modern Life* (New York: Alfred A Knopf, 2009), p. 19.
2. See Senator Jim Webb, "What's Wrong With Our Prisons?" in *Parade Magazine*, March 29, 2009, pp. 4-5

Introduction

"... the tragedy was long remembered ..."

In October, 1857, the governor of Illinois gave permission to negotiate. The warden would have none of it, and instead gave the order to rush the cell door. Behind it stood John Hall, a crazed inmate of the Illinois State Penitentiary at Alton, Illinois. Hall, an outdoors man from Champaign County, had gone insane and held a guard, C.C. Crabb, hostage. Cells in Alton were configured oddly. All cell doors were made of solid oak with iron straps as reinforcement. Inmate bunk beds, hung up during the day, were situated in such a way that when down they obstructed the door which opened inward. One night the guard was called into the cell on the pretense of inmate sickness. Once inside the guard was bound and held hostage for two and a half days. Ignoring the governor, officials at Alton broke down the door, and filled the air with gunshots and knife slashes. In the end Hall was dead and Crabb severely wounded. Crabb recovered to become a guard at the new facility being constructed at Joliet, Illinois, but the Hall "tragedy was long remembered in Alton and throughout the state."[1] That same year of 1857, the state legislature introduced a bill to abandon Alton and construct another prison closer to Chicago, for such contests of prison authority were not supposed to happen in America's young prison system.

By the last third of the nineteenth century, when McClaughry hit the scene, America's experiment with criminal justice reform had fallen on hard times. The "New Nation" that emerged after the revolution had promised to move away from the cruel and harsh colonial system based initially on the Bible and British dictates. As in any revolution, fresh starts were in order. This desire was helped as a new criminology coincided with the Revolutionary era.

Most explanations for why a person committed a crime had until then been along the lines of "the Devil made him do it." Such explanations had stymied much criminal justice development. Though there was some movement in the law, particularly something called the Common Law, much early legal precedent had emerged from the Old Testament. The definition of crime and how to respond to it was derived from the first five books of the Bible. Consequently in Colonial America all kinds of corporal and capital punishments, also prescribed by the Bible, were meted out. Temporary lockups existed–from stocks and pillories to informal gaols–but these were merely way-stations for the miscreant before the real punishment. Banishment, the first choice, owed its origins to the biblical examples of Adam and Eve (and later their murderous son, Cain), banished for their ancient crimes. Of course, such exile was more painful in sparsely populated and presumably more dangerous places. As the colonies filled up, banishment, still practiced by England with its transportation of criminals first to America and later to Australia, no longer had the desired sting in the new world.[2]

Banishment could be supplemented with branding or maiming the body. Not only were such punishments painful, they also labeled people as criminals. Furthermore, if carried out with some thought physical disfigurement could be a specific deterrent. It is hard for a pick pocket to do his job missing a hand. Spies without eyes would be useless. Adulteresses with an "A" burnt upon their breast might be less desirable. God knows how a rapist might cope.

The types of capital punishment were legion. With the exception of some witch burnings and pressings, most of these executions were done by hanging. Sometimes such a horrid practice could border on the ludicrous, as was the case with Thomas Graunger who at 16 became the first juvenile to be executed in Colonial America. He was hanged in 1642 for having gentile copulation with a mare, a cow, two goats, five sheep, two calves and a turkey. The animals were executed as well as dictated by Leviticus 20:15. Most often these punishment ceremonies were public affairs with hundreds in attendance expecting some morality play to be presented. The condemned person was supposed to be contrite and confessional. By admitting guilt the criminal solidified and validated community support for the rules and perhaps could hope for the gates of heaven to admit him too.

With such an ideology little extra was needed in terms of criminal justice; after all, entire communities were to be on watch for deviance during the day and a small number of roundsmen watched at night.[3] The unequivocal nature of common law and Biblical models presented little need for elaborated legal codes, except perhaps in the case of debtors. Thankfully, much of this type of superstitious/ religious criminal justice ended with the Revolution.

An intellectual revolution occurred slightly before the military one. Cesare Beccaria in Italy and Jeremy Bentham in England articulated a new criminology, one that found a compatible home in the new nation. Beccaria suggested that people chose to commit or not commit crime based upon a "hedonistic calculus." Free choice became the standard. If the pleasure of a criminal act was greater than the potential pain the crime would be committed. Conversely, if the likely pain were greater the person would be deterred. Choice in a country espousing freedom and independence seemed a natural fit. Yet some basic principles were still necessary, claimed Beccaria in his essay *On Crimes and Punishment (1764)*. The old barbaric (biblical) laws should be applied only to issues of pure vice or morality, in general matters to do with one's soul and afterlife. Things of this world, went the argument, needed to be dealt with practically. Laws should be written down so that ignorance could not be used as an excuse. The trick, of course, was to calibrate the law. Punishments should be severe enough to deter but not so bad as never to be enforced. Punishment should be certain and not arbitrary. Finally, there should be celerity: punishment should occur close in time to the commission of the crime to best be appreciated by both the public and the person being punished. In response to these intellectual and political revolutions, what followed in the early decades of the new nation were a series of "republican codes."

After independence most former colonies, now states began to write their own criminal codes. From a Beccarian point of view this was logical. Having the law written down, especially articulated by representatives of the people–duly elected legislators in state legislatures–made sense to these thinkers in the new nation. Even though illiteracy was common, oral traditions were such that ignorance of the law was a less compelling argument. Furthermore, it generally took the Bible out of the arena. Of course, many so called "Blue Laws" still existed but most would wither away over time. That left the Common law with which to contend. Such judge-made law had a long precedent in Anglo-Saxon history. Medieval judges roamed a circuit resolving disputes, with their rulings becoming precedents for similar cases. For many in the new United States, however, law made by a small number of elites seemed undemocratic. The creation of the Supreme Court, and other appellate courts, especially after John Marshall flexed its muscle, flew in the face of the more liberal elements of the founding fathers. Statutory law, which was what the republican codes were, became a counter weight against the persistence of common law in the democratic republic.

Thomas Jefferson made some early moves in Virginia,[4] but it was Pennsylvania that really led the way in developing a criminal code. In 1786 it eliminated death for robbery and burglary. In 1791 it abolished death for accused witches and branding as a punishment for adultery and fornication. Pennsylvania was the first state (in 1794) to divide murder into two categories. First degree murder warranted the death penalty and was characterized by lying in wait or poisoning or some other demonstrated deliberate premeditation. Second degree murder consisted of all other killing, and imprisonment rather than death was the punishment. Virginia followed in accepting this categorization in 1796. Ohio (1824), Missouri (1835), Michigan (1846) were the first of a majority of states who then joined the republican code movement.[5]

Yet if one reduced so many capital offenses and eliminated so much corporal punishment, how were criminals to be punished?

Some experiments in incarceration had occurred early in the new nation period. At the Walnut Street Jail in Philadelphia and the Newgate Prison in New York City wide ranges of people were piled together in an attempt to implement Beccarian criminological thinking. The system was pretty much a failure from the start. The old jail soon overflowed with criminals. Men and women, and sometimes children too, were forced to reside in dungeon-like spaces whose horrific conditions led to only more crime and criminals. Some new concept needed to be invented.

At first, this revolutionary generation remained perplexed. Free from the cruel dictates of England and antiquated Biblical ideas, why did crime continue and even increase in the United States? Those who looked hard saw two things: First, they observed the loosening of family ties. In the quest to get ahead, adults left children behind. With time, the House of Refuge movement arose in an attempt to clean the streets of the growing number of kids living on cities' door stoops. Second, they observed that many people were just not ready for the freedom and liberty of this new country.

In the 1820s, frustrated by earlier experiments and still flush with revolutionary fervor, two new institutions were invented in America: solitary confinement and silence. Together they ushered in the U.S. penitentiary movement.

Pennsylvania was the first to institute the silent and solitary system in its Walnut Street Jail.[6] It failed immediately, raising the need for a new prison architecture, from which were born Western Pennsylvania Penitentiary, in Pittsburgh, finished in 1826, and Eastern Pennsylvania Penitentiary, in Philadelphia, that opened three years later. Both were strictly solitary confinements. Quaker ideas of silence and meditation were behind these institutions. Prisoners, under a fixed sentence, had little human contact for the duration of their stay. At first, enforced idleness was the rule but over time small scale craftsman work was introduced. The idea here was to make work a pleasurable activity, a reprieve from the burden of idle solitude. Away from others' criminal influence and able to contemplate one's own misbehavior, prisoners would reform, one thought. Religious materials were provided to inspire repentance as well. Such a monastic environment was intended to bring about reform and redemption, but because humans are innately gregarious and ill equipped for such cloistered environments, many inmates slipped into various degrees of mental disease. They may or may not come out cured of crime but many moved from one asylum, the penitentiary, to another, the mental asylum.[7]

Failure at Newgate inspired a counter model at Auburn, New York. This penitentiary believed in silence too. Prisoners were to live in solitary cells at night but would come together to march and work in silent congregations during the day. The famous lock step was invented to minimize communication in the marching lines. Whereas Pennsylvanians claimed their penitentiaries as economical–a criteria esteemed by parsimonious state legislatures–because it took less personnel to watch over such confined people, New Yorkers touted their economic advantage because they had more of a factory model for work in penitentiaries. More products meant greater profits and less of a strain in the state capital. In the argument and tussle for place in America's growing penitentiary industry, the prisoners were largely forgotten.[8] As the Auburn system gained prominence in America, the Pennsylvania system spread to Europe. Within a generation of their creation both systems had failed.

But other forces and institutions had their impact. Certainly, after the 1840s the demographic picture began to change. The Potato Famine in Ireland prompted a flood of immigrants to America and cities such as Boston, New York City, Philadelphia, and Chicago gained sizable Irish populations. Boston, for example, had less than 4000 Irish in 1840. Ten years later there were 35,000. By 1855 the number had grown to 50,000.[9] On one day—April 10th 1847—1000 immigrants landed in Boston.[10] America had always been xenophobic and anti Catholic. Now these two sentiments found a single target among "paddies," the Irish. However, prejudice was not simply casual. In the 1850s various local patriotic organizations formed the American Party to protect the nation from the "insidious wiles of foreigners." Largely a secret organization, members were urged when questioned about their meetings to respond: "I know nothing."[11] The governor of Massachusetts and most state officials were members of this Know Nothing party.[12] So was the mayor of Chicago, Levi Boone.

On the "crooked ladder of success" in America, with most means of moving up the social and economic scale closed to them, ethnic groups had limited options. Though there was considerable menial labor for the Irish, three other alternatives were available: the Church, sports, and crime. The Irish thus began to predominate in Catholicism by mid nineteenth century.[13] As for sports, with one exception these developed later. The exception was prize fighting. For example, John Morressey, an Irish street thug and ballot box bully, proved his skills as a fighter. Convinced of his athletic abilities he took up fighting defeating Yankee Sullivan to become one of the earliest "World Champions." Turning that reputation to politics he became a Congressman and then gambling kingpin in New York City and Saratoga Springs. As for crime: this new disposable immigrant people was seen as the criminal class. Soon, large percentages of inmates in the prisons, particularly in New York and Illinois, were Irish born. If prisons could not reform, reasoned those in power, at least they could be warehouses filled with those most hated in society. Their numbers grew not only because of the tremendous rise in immigration but also because the modern police force had been invented.

For over two hundred years the police of America consisted of a day time constabulary and a night time watch. The more rural areas, especially in the south, had a sheriff system. All three were made up of untrained citizens who often avoided their duties. Each of these systems lasted a long time, and though none was particularly effective, resistance to establishing a more professional police remained strong. European models suggested the possibility of a police state, but even the newly created English model, the London Metropolitan Police, seemed overbearing to Americans. Besides, with the memories of two recent wars, England was not looked upon favorably.

By the 1840s many cities were experiencing challenges which village institutions were incapable of handling. Crime increased but public disorder became most vexing. New York City might be a useful example. By the early nineteenth century the middle class had established itself firmly. Criminal justice, in this instance the police, is an invention of the middle class. Business and professional people wanted order and tranquility to carry out the day to day activity of conducting commerce. Tired of the disruptive presence of street ruffians, the middle class demanded a new police. New York was becoming heterogeneous with a mix of people with different values and practices. Those more xenophobic wanted a better police to control the "under class." From loitering street roughs to out-and-out mob activities there was enough disorder to prompt concern. Certain sensational crimes occurred exposing the inadequacies of the constable/ night watch system. The murder of Helen Jewett, a notorious prostitute, caused quite a stir.[14] More important was the murder of Mary Rogers, a cigar sales girl known for her beauty, which was chronicled by a young writer by the name of Edgar Allen Poe. In both instances journalists were more capable investigators than were existing constables. Finally, there was the rise of the (corrupt) political machine, in New York City called Tammany Hall. Political bosses relying on a patronage system called "spoils" could garner and maintain support by doling out jobs.

Expansion of urban agencies, in this instance a police department, would add up to over one thousand patronage positions. Consequently, in 1845, New York City created America's first modern police force. In the next ten to fifteen years most cities in America did likewise. A "pebble-in-the pond" effected resulted. The more police and the more active they were, the more criminals there were in the courts and in prisons.

Overcrowded, the prisons of America lost any pretense of maintaining the penitentiary ideology of a generation earlier. On one hand there was no attempt to reform or modify the system. That was because the political ideology of the spoils system had a vested interest in keeping that system, no matter its failings. Also, these prisons became warehouses for a disposable people. For example, in New York during the 1850s "foreigners" made up two thirds of the prison population. Most of these were illiterate and intemperate.[15] And most of them were Irish.

That is not to say that the penal and police systems were totally bankrupt. There were some reformers who strove to change the system. Large societal forces were at work as well. In order to appreciate Robert McClaughry's contribution, these reformers and forces need to be understood better.

REGIONALISM

The United States of America have not always been united. From the beginning regional differences shaped the nature and character of America. Long before the South thought of it, New England contemplated seceding from the union. One of the most devastating wars in American history, the Civil War, was based upon regional differences. Well into the twentieth century Presidential and Congressional politics was drawn along regional lines. The interests of the South and the West frequently clashed with Eastern politicians.

The earliest immigrants—those through the colonial, New Nation and Jacksonian periods—had profound impacts upon the character of the nation. At first they were simply categorized and homogenized as English. In actuality, they came from distinct places and had differing attitudes towards culture. America's numerous folkways—its patterns of speech, its cooking, its views on gender relations, its notions of governance—were due to four main migrations and settlements from England. Each provided a different set of lenses through which to see issues of crime, law, order, and punishment.[16]

Britons coming to New England originated largely from East Anglia, the nine eastern counties of England. These Puritans were mostly middle-class folks who believed they were a chosen people. That belief system affected crime and criminal justice for generations. To them the world was a battle ground. The forces of good and evil were constantly engaged. In this understanding, events in Salem, Massachusetts, for example, were merely a small battle in a larger war in their cosmology. Being a "city on the hill" demanded order and unity so that other nations (and God) could look upon them with favor. Righteous display and deportment were critical in the scripts they wrote for themselves. Individual liberty was to be sacrificed for the sake of community order. As put by one Puritan minister, John Norton, it was "better an innocent and a good man should suffer than order; for that preserves the whole." Child rearing practices dictated that the "willful" be broken for it was a small step from toddler to trouble maker when it came to discipline. Similarly, time was most precious and not to be wasted. "Lost time is never found," was a Puritan proverb that shaped their views on incarceration.[17]

Those coming to the tidewater regions of the South originated in southwestern England and had more elitist notions of society. These "Cavaliers", more royalist and Anglican then those in New England, created an aristocratic culture emphasizing leisure, sport, and military arts over work. Being elitist the "topping families," the upper ranks of society, suffered less harsh punishments than the "lowly sorts." The medieval notion of "benefit of clergy" was used more often in Virginia than any other colony. This legal loophole allowed for lighter punishments if literacy was proven. Reading Psalm 51, called the "neck verse," was mitigating proof. In the name of personal honor many disputes among the planter classes were settled by duels. Even the development of the sheriff system, as opposed to New England's more democratic constable-night watch, was strictly controlled by the planter classes.

Once again child rearing practices may be suggestive of how society as a whole was imagined. Rather than breaking the will, these Southerners wanted to bend it. One's individuality was respected as long as it did not challenge the hierarchical culture. But if a child (or criminal) went against larger societal norms, punishment could be severe. Lastly, liberty to these enslavers had a particular twist. While vigorously defending their liberty ("give me liberty or give me death," one of them said) they unabashedly withheld it from others.[18]

Settlers from the North Midlands of England came to the Delaware River regions of West Jersey, Pennsylvania, and North Delaware. Quakers dominated here and their beliefs in the "inner light" emphasized contemplation and reform. Since everyone had this touch of the Divine, Quakers had greater tolerance for ethnic pluralism. Unlike the puritan quest for unity and homogeneity, and the Virginia desire for hierarchy, the Quaker strove for peace and harmony. Liberty and individuality were important (these are the people who would build Independence Hall and make the Liberty Bell) and reciprocal. More than any other colony, the Quakers lived and loved the "Golden Rule." Work, to them, was a form of worship, idleness a deadly sin. They respected and sought a life of austerity, or "plain living" they called it. Once again, if child rearing can be indicative of how to deal with the intractable the Quakers were permissive, more inclined to entice with rewards than threats of punishment. By 1690, Pennsylvania Quakers had softened many of the English punishments and eliminated most capital offenses.[19]

A fourth group came from the borderlands of England. Northern Ireland, Western Scotland, and Northern England supplied the people for this migration. They came to America in increasing numbers between 1717 and 1775. Seen as prideful and pugnacious, they were shooed away to the borderlands and backcountry of western Pennsylvania, Maryland, Virginia, and the Carolinas. Coming from violent and volatile places in England they settled in similar locations in America. Among them, the warrior ethic was strong and citizens were expected to be involved as soldiers and keepers of the social order. It was in the backcountry of South Carolina where the Regulator [Vigilante] Movement started. Later, in Virginia and South Carolina, Captain William Lynch opened his court and etched his name in American history by his excessive use of hanging. The presidential personification of this culture would be Andrew Jackson. As a boy his mother gave him advice that sums up the backcountry ethos. "Andrew never tell a lie, nor take what is not your own, nor sue anybody for slander, assault and battery. Always settle them cases yourself." If anywhere *lex talionis* existed it was in the backcountry of colonial America.[20]

RELIGION

The impact of religion and religious values upon crime and punishment cannot be overestimated.[21] Semantically, many of the words connected to punishment—cell, penitentiary, reformation, capital punishment—have religious origins. These American Protestants needed to reconcile Christian teachings and values with punishment—the depriving of liberty, the imposing of discomfort, and even possibly the taking of life. At least two streams came together in nineteenth century penology.

Colonial Puritanism did not entirely end with the revolution. It manifested and maintained itself in conservative wings of Presbyterianism and Congregationalism. These Puritans and Neo Puritans looked to the Bible for inspiration. Not only did they believe in harsh, and now antiquated punishments, they also believed in a close tie between the state and religion. The state, they thought, should be harsh, repressive, and disciplinarian, for all humans were estranged from God and those who committed misdeeds needed to feel the wrath of God. Compelling obedience did not seem strange to their patriarchal way of thinking. Nor did the notion that all social activity should have an aspect of economic viability. Such a Puritan work ethic demanded the "lowly sorts" be forced to work and fit better into a robust capitalist economy.[22] Such Calvinist preachers of Colonial New England as Cotton and Increase Mather were two outspoken proponents of the Puritan theology. Increase, besides his numerous execution sermons, was particularly well known for his role in the Salem witch hysteria.[23] Cotton was particularly active sermonizing at executions of pirates.[24] Those of their Puritanical bent found no twinge of conscience in inflicting pain and discomfort. To them, punishment was an end in and of itself. Any personal or positive outcomes were not expected from punishment, the larger societal benefit being simply of having despicable characters taken away from the "saints."

Such a harsh outlook did not go unchallenged. The Great Awakening of the eighteenth century, particularly the work of Jonathan Edwards, watered down strict Puritanism. This religious revival rekindled with the Second Great Awakening of the 1820s. Numerous denominations emerged as waves of religious revival swept the countryside. Religion became more personal and emotional, with conversion being the measure of having saved a lost soul. Missionary work now became important as a means to save the heathen or the lost Christian.

It was this evangelical Christianity that was present at the creation of the penitentiary.[25] A host of individuals and various societies took on this mission. Along with the aforementioned Quakers of Pennsylvania, arose a more specific institution, The Philadelphia Society for the Alleviating the Miseries of Public Prisons, formed in 1776. Quakers like Richard Vaux were critical in creating the Pennsylvania system of penitentiaries.[26] Fearful of large gatherings of prisoners, institutions such as chapel and Sunday Schools did not make their appearance in the Pennsylvania type of penitentiaries. Of course, religious instruction was still emphasized but it was on a personal level rather than a congregational one.[27]

Similar changes happened elsewhere. The Prison Association of New York and the Boston Prison Discipline Society were filled with religious activists who mixed "old light" Puritanism with "new light" evangelicalism to create the Auburn system. Louis Dwight, a man of pure Puritan stock, was a proponent of the Auburn system and single handedly pioneered the adoption of that model in Maine, New Hampshire, Vermont, Connecticut, Washington DC, Virginia, Tennessee, Louisiana, Mississippi, Illinois, and Ohio.[28] Enoch Wines—first a Congregational and then Presbyterian minister—was in the vanguard of the new evangelical approach as a member of the Boston Prison Discipline Society. So were John Luckey, Chaplain at Sing Sing, and Zebulon Brockway, head of the House of Correction in Detroit.[29]

PHILOSOPHY

However, another stream in the development of the early prison system was a bit more perplexing. Granted, the new nation was built upon the ideological foundations of liberty and freedom, and religion was still an important part of those. Yet many of the founding personalities of the nation were Deist and had more philosophical views and concerns than the Evangelicals. That shrewd observer Alexis de Tocqueville noted that, "While society in the United States gives the example of the most extended liberty, the prisons of the same country offer the spectacle of the most complete despotism."[30] The Revolutionary generation was obsessively against oppressive concentrated power given that the bedrock of the new nation was liberty and freedom. But such notions were intoxicating and liberty could and did turn to license. Consequently, those living in the first third of the nineteenth century were faced with a problem: how to instill and justify patriarchy in a land of liberty.

Philosophically, the post-revolutionary generation subscribed to John Locke's notion of a social contract. All humans had natural rights, Locke would say and Thomas Jefferson reiterate, and these rights guaranteed life, liberty, and the pursuit of happiness. Fundamental to these rights, however, was public order. In order to get this liberty, other liberties had to be voluntarily surrendered to the state. Apparently public order trumped liberty. Utilitarian philosophers such as Jeremy Bentham taught that private happiness was to be subordinated to public happiness.[31]

To understand why some should be chosen to lose their liberty, one needs to know how the revolutionary generation distinguished between a "good citizen" and a "bad citizen." This new "good" American was to have self discipline resisting base instincts and passions. Though tolerant, the ideal American was to play by the rules, and resist corruption and violence.[32] The bad, or potentially bad, citizen was youthful, unmarried, idle, and lustful.[33] Depriving certain persons of liberty in a liberty-loving country was intended to cure criminals of their excessive passions and insure the safety and tranquility of the good citizens. Philosophically, it was necessary to take away some liberty in order to preserve it. This became more important as villages turned into cities.

URBANIZATION

It was clear to those living in the first and second generations of the New Nation that cities were growing at a rapid rate. Urban populations increased over 700 percent in those years before the Civil War. For example, Philadelphia went from 161,000 in 1830 to over 500,000 thirty years later, Boston from 61,000 to 133,000, and New York City from 200,000 to 800,000. In the Midwest, laced with rivers and canals, river towns like Pittsburgh, Cincinnati, Louisville, Memphis, and St. Louis became cities. This was true for Detroit, Milwaukee, and Chicago too. In 1830 Chicago was not much more than a fort. Thirty years later there were over 100,000 Chicagoans. Immigrants streamed in to these places precipitating low rent, slum areas, and general urban disorder. More than 200 major gang wars occurred in New York City in the decade from 1834 to 1844. Angst increased among the middle class as they saw their old cities come apart, and an anti-urban ideology began to form. Cities, with all their artificiality, temptations, and anonymity were a threat to an orderly life. Numerous institutions arose to reinstitute village values in these heterogeneous cities, but with limited success. The penitentiaries and prisons dotted throughout the landscape mirrored concerns over urban America. Often placed in bucolic environments, prisons were to be Puritan villages—places of order, work, continuity, and predictability—that attempted to remold recalcitrant urbanites. The prison managers, like McClaughry would become, were moral reformers who reflected the concerns and agendas of the reformers of the cities.[34]

BUREAUCRACY

Another stream affecting the penitentiary/prison system was management. Prison managers had to implement reform ideals in a real world of uncooperative prisoners. Few models were in place to help them achieve this. Organizations and organizational theory were in their infancy, and criminal justice systems remained highly politicized for decades. Nonetheless, managers had to learn to play several of such games in order to survive. Certainly *empire building*—making oneself too indispensable to lose—was one of these. Of course, after their creation prisons were intrinsically indispensable. With so many political hacks hungry for jobs a young bureaucrat needed to become personally indispensible. Another game is national *reputation building,* for becoming nationally famous might stall local or state politicians from eliminating one's position. In addition, in order to warrant more money for one's institution in the next fiscal cycle, it was essential for the nineteenth century warden to end each year *in the black.* State legislatures wanted a self-sustaining prison that made few demands on the public coffers. Another game played was *crisis management.* Everyday there would be a crisis in the nineteenth century prison. Not only did the warden and his staff have to respond to these crises once they happened, they also had to anticipate them. As the prisons became more complex filled with various amenities—mass dining, recreational yard activities, and bustling workshops—wardens had to assume any breakdown was inmate inspired. This increasing complexity demanded staff with special skills.

The earliest model for prison management came from the military. In this regard, the career and professional style of Elam Lynds has become notorious.

Lynds had been an army captain before entering the world of penology. A battle field promotion during the War of 1812 attested to his brave and gritty character. In 1817 he became a staff member at Auburn penitentiary eventually working his way up to administrative head. The severe discipline he imposed at Auburn met considerable opposition from state politicians and general public. Much noise, he would confide to two French visitors, was made about tyranny. And tyranny there was as he beat prisoners, encouraged guards to be brutal, shaved inmate's heads to mimic the look of slaves, and introduced not only the striped uniform but also the lock-step and ball-and-chain. But he turned a profit, making the penitentiary self sustaining. In a very short time he became something of a state-wide hero. Consequently, in 1825 he was called upon to construct a new prison north of New York City on the Hudson River, to be called Sing Sing. About 100 prisoners were taken from Auburn and, under the watchful eyes of guards and a leather whip in Lynd's hand, the new prison was built in three years. He became its first warden and started what some considered a reign of terror. When de Beaumont and de Tocqueville visited they were shocked. "One cannot see the prison of Sing Sing and the system of Labour which is there established without being struck by astonishment and fear." They predicted catastrophe.[35]

On their tour of America, Gustave de Beaumont and Alexis de Tocqueville interviewed Lynds. By the time they got to him he had fallen on hard times and been dismissed from Sing Sing. His political support, so strong for so long because he ran a self-sustaining prison, eroded quickly when it was discovered it actually cost the tax payers $35,000 a year. Found running a hardware store, Lynds consented to an interview lasting several hours. Probably still bridling from his dismissal but also reflecting his true character, Lynds revealed himself to the French travelers. America was too much a slave to public opinion, he felt. The head of a prison needed total and absolute control. To be good, a warden had to be practical when it came to leading men. All of the religious/charity types did not truly understand the character of the criminals. "I consider it impossible to govern a large prison," he declared, "without a whip." Twenty five percent of those in Sing Sing were foreigners and incapable of reform, Lynds felt. Perhaps showing his New England Puritan side, he insisted that his wards needed to be restrained and disciplined.[36] Now, with the passage of time, Elam Lynds is known as the antithesis of a good warden.

But there were other views on the ideal warden, largely forged by members of various religious organizations. Criminals were immature, they said, arrested in their development, and they therefore needed a father figure that was both stern and sympathetic. A series of character qualities began to emerge and become ideal employment criteria. The warden was to be understanding, cool tempered, equitable, benevolent, firm, dignified, mild, and patient. Above all else he (and until the twentieth century it was always a man who was warden) was to love and strive for order.[37]

This was the environment in criminal justice leading up to the Civil War. In the meantime, in Central Illinois, a man completely from outside the mid-nineteenth-century criminal justice systems was developing, one who would revolutionize prisons and reformatories for the next thirty years. That man was Robert McClaughry. This man from Illinois would add new insight into the matrix of reformers. Many reformers were idealists who would change the world but have little experience in it. Religious and philosophical ideals propelled them. Then there were those practitioners who desired to make more efficient the work they do. Political and bureaucratic ideals engaged them. There was a third group—admittedly small—who had a foot in both camps. These practitioners saw the larger ramifications of tinkering with their work. They saw that reforming the individual and reforming the institution were connected. Robert McClaughry falls into this group. The mystery, however, is where this particular impulse came from. To explore that, we turn to mid-nineteenth-century central Illinois and the critical years of McClaughry's development

NOTES

1. W.T. Norton, "An Old Time Tragedy in the State Penitentiary at Alton," *Journal of the Illinois State Historical Society*, 6 (1913) pp. 242-245.
2. For a good place to start understanding Colonial misbehavior, see Kai Erikson's *Wayward Puritans: A Study of the Sociology of Deviance* (New York: Wiley & Son, 1966).
3. See Douglas Greenberg's, *Crime and Law Enforcement in the Colony of New York, 1691-1776* (Ithaca: Cornell University Press, 1974).
4. Kathryn Preyer, "Crime, the Criminal Law and Reform in Post Revolutionary Virginia," *Law and History Review* Vol. 1 No. 1, 1983, pp. 53-85.
5. Bradly Chapin, "Felony Law Reform in the Early Republic," *The Pennsylvania Magazine of History and Biography* Vol. 113 No. 2 (April 1989), pp. 163-183. William Nelson, "Emerging Notions of Modern Criminal Law in the Revolutionary Era: An Historical Perspective," *New York University Law Review* Vol. 42 (May 1967), pp. 450-482.
6. LeRoy B. DePuy, "The Walnut Street Prison: Pennsylvania's First Penitentiary," *Pennsylvania History* 18 (April), pp. 130-144.

7. David J. Rothman, *The Discovery of the Asylum: Social Order and Disorder in the New Republic* (Boston: Little, Brown and Company, 1971), pp. 94-95.

8. *Ibid.*, pp. 95-108, 240-264.

9. Oscar Handlin, *Boston's Immigrants: A Study in Acculturation* (Cambridge, Mass.: Harvard University Press, 1959), p. 52.

10. Thomas H. O'Connor, *Bibles, Brahmins and Bosses: A Short History of Boston* (Boston, Mass.: Trustees of the Public Library of the City of Boston, 1984), p. 114.

11. See Dale T. Knobel, *Paddy and the Republic: Ethnicity and Nationality in Antebellum America* (Middletown, Connecticut: Wesleyan University Press, 1986) and his *"America For Americans": The Nativist Movement in the United States* (New York: Twayne Publishers, 1996).

12. Ibid., p. 115.

13. See Jay Dolan's *The Immigrant Church: New York's Irish and German Catholics, 1815-1867* (Baltimore: Johns Hopkins University Press, 1975).

14. See Patricia Cline Cohen's masterful, *The Murder of Helen Jewett* (New York: Vintage Books, 1999).

15. Robert Ernst, *Immigrant Life in New York City, 1825-1863* (New York: King's Crown Press, 1949) p. 202.

16. For an important discussion of these folkways see David Hackett Fischer's *Albion's Seed: Four British Folkways in America* (New York and Oxford: Oxford University Press, 1989), pp. 3-6.

17. *Ibid.,* pp. 31, 50, 97-103, 189-196.

18. *Ibid.*, pp. 225, 240, 311-320, 398, 410.

19. *Ibid.,* pp. 426-427, 430, 556, 584, 595.

20. *Ibid.,* pp. 606, 613,637, 642, 676, 765 [quote of mother] -771.

21. Andrew Skotnicki, *Religion and the Development of the American Penal System* (Lanham, Maryland: University Press of America, 2000), p. 142.

22. Ibid., pp. 12, 71, 73, 80

23. See Eve LaPlante's *Salem Witch Judge: The Life and Repentance of Samuel Sewall* (New York: Harper One, 2007), pp. 140, 169, 171,175, 177.

24. David Cordingly, *Under the Black Flag: The Romance and the Reality of Life Among the Pirates* (Orlando, Florida: The Harvest Book, a subdivision of Harcourt Brace, 1995), pp. 236-239.

25. Skotnicki, pp. 19, 23, 34, 68.

26. Ibid., pp. 103-105.

27. See Michael Cassidy, *Warden Cassidy on Prisons and Convicts* (Philadelphia: Patterson & White, 1897), pp. 49-54.

28. Ibid., pp. 44, 95-96.

29. Skotnicki, pp. 97, 110-111, 115.

30. Quoted in Mark E. Kann, *Punishment, Prisons and Patriarchy: Liberty and Power in the Early American Republic* (New York: New York University Press, 2005), p. 14.

31. Ibid., pp. 23-26.

32. Ibid., pp. 28-29.

33. Ibid., pp. 67, 81.

34. Paul Boyer, Urban Masses and Moral Order in America, 1820-1920 (Cambridge: Mass.: Harvard University Press, 1978), pp.65-84.

35. Denis Brian, *Sing Sing: The Inside Story of a Notorious Prison* (Amherst, NY: Prometheus Books, 2005), pp. 16-22, quotation on p. 28.

36. Gustave de Beaumont and Alexis de Tocqueville, *On the Penitentiary System in the United States and Its Application in France* (Carbondale and Edwardsville, IL: Southern Illinois University Press, 1964), pp. 161-165.

37. Kann, p. 162.

Part One

MCCLAUGHRY AND HIS MIDDLE BORDER BEGINNINGS

Chapter One

Matters of Place

"First settlers . . . fix the character of a settlement."

Who we are and what we become is largely based upon the molding forces of our youth. Robert McClaughry was no exception. His life and career were built upon the foundations laid during his childhood and early adult years in rural Illinois. While many things shape a person's character, a few always stand out as most significant. The region in which he grew up, his particular Protestant religion of the mid nineteenth century, his college experiences, the Civil War, and his business and political activities after the war particularly shaped McClaughry.

McClaughry was a product of the nineteenth-century Middle Border, those Midwestern states of Illinois, Iowa and Indiana. He was of Scotch-Irish ancestry going back generations. Scotch-Irish denotes those Scots forced by the British to move to Ireland in hopes that their Protestantism would blunt the influence of Irish Catholicism. They had little love for the English for such a policy that uprooted them from their home land. His great-grandfather, Richard McClaughry, consequently migrated to New York from Ireland in 1765 and fought in the American Revolution serving in Alexander Webb's regiment of New York militia. He was there at the capture of the British army under Burgoyne, and took part in the battle of Bennington in Vermont.[1]

Robert's father, Matthew, was born in Delaware County, New York, in 1803. His first wife, Margaret Seal, died in New York in 1833. One daughter resulted from that union. Matthew migrated to Fountain Green in Hancock County, Illinois in 1837. Robert would be born there.

Hancock County, named for the famed signer of the Constitution, was on the western edge of Illinois bordered by the Mississippi river. Population growth had been great in Illinois at that time, the population in Hancock

County expanding from 483 people in 1830 to 9,946 ten years later.[2] The town of Carthage was named county seat in 1833. Such growth was common for the entire state. Between 1820 and 1840 the population of Illinois trebled each decade. The largest concentration of this new settlement was in west central Illinois bounded by Peoria County on the north, Macon County (Decatur) on the east, and Marion County (Centralia) on the south. Both Adams and Hancock counties were part of the Illinois Military Bounty Tract, a slice of land between the Illinois and Mississippi rivers set aside by Congress for the veterans of the War of 1812.[3] These counties became centers of settlement and land speculation after they were opened up to general settlement in the late 1830s and early1840s.

Illinois had two distinct migration patterns in this early period. A northward movement from the south was the earliest with Virginia and Kentucky models dominating the formative period of the government's organization. The first six governors of Illinois were transplanted southerners. A southward movement from the north occurred in the late 1830s and 1840s. Central Illinois became a clash point as these two cultural groups moved in and confronted each other.[4] Thomas Ford, governor of Illinois in the 1840s, had strong views about Hancock County, a place that tarnished his administration and place in history. Later he would write:

> I had a good opportunity to know the early settlers of Hancock County. I had attended the circuit courts there as State's Attorney, from 1830, when the county was organized, up to the year 1834; and to my certain knowledge the early settlers, with some honorable exceptions, were, in popular language, hard cases.[5]

As he vented his anger over the Mormon problem in Hancock County Ford would philosophize later that,

> having passed my whole life on the frontiers . . . I have frequently seen that a few first settlers would fix the character of a settlement for good or for bad, for many years after its commencement. . . . Rogues will find each other out, and so will honest men.[6]

If Ford were correct then Hancock County was a violent place in this early period. Though past crime statistics are slippery, historian Susan Sessions Rugh has created a sense of crime rates for the county. The rates are per 1000 residents.

The township of Fountain Green resembled the rest of the county in settlement patterns. Four distinct migrations occurred: First, those of southern origin, generally from Tennessee and Kentucky, begun by Ut Perkins in 1826. He settled an area called Crooked Creek, a meandering stream mak-

Table 1.1. Crime Rates for Hancock County

Years	Population	Murder Rate	Violent Crime
1833–39	9,946	4.3	14.4
1840–49	14,652	5.7	28.4
1850–59	29,061	4.1	29.3*

*See Susan Sessions Rugh, "Civilizing the Countryside: Class, Gender, and Crime in Nineteenth-Century Rural Illinois," *Agricultural History* 76 (2002).

ing the area one of the best watered in the township. Shortly after the first group, another cluster of southerners, distinct from the earlier ones because of their Catholicism, came from western Kentucky. By 1832, the St. Simon the Apostle Church was established attended by thirty Catholic families. Both of these southern groups scattered their farmsteads on the land in the open country pattern of farmers from the southern back country. They brought a typical southern backwoods way of life to Illinois, building cabins out of timber, hunting small game, and cultivating corn. These families were often linked by marriage extending for several generations. For example, the 1830 census showed eighty-seven households, with 5.6 persons in each, with 31 percent of the surnames shared by two or more households.[7]

A third group came to Fountain Green from the north, particularly New York. The first settler of this migration was Jabey Beebe from Hinsdale, Cattaraugus County, in southwestern New York. He settled in Horse Lick Grove, named for its swampy area fed by underground springs that provided livestock with abundant water, and there opened a tavern or inn. Following the New England tradition of town building, the village of Fountain Green, named after a spring that bubbled up out of the prairie, was established on June 8th, 1835. As one student of the town observed:

> Just as the southerners distributed themselves on the land in patterns learned from the past, the New Yorkers perpetuated the Puritan ideal of the town as a nucleus of social and commercial ties that bound the community together.[8]

By 1837, the town was advertised in *Peck's Gazetteer* as a "flourishing settlement" ten miles northeast of Carthage. "Any laboring man with reasonable industry and economy with a family, may arrive here without any capital, and in a half dozen years be the owner of a good farm, with stock in abundance," easterners were told.[9] Jabey Beebe became the postmaster.

The fourth group also came from the north, in this case the Cumberland Valley area of Pennsylvania. Led by Thomas Geddes these settlers specialized in cultivating wheat.[10] These Pennsylvania settlers quickly set up a Presbyterian congregation. Although the McClaughrys were from New York they shared the Scottish-Irish heritage of these Pennsylvanians and were part of the founding members of the congregation.[11]

Fountain Green township was part of the Illinois Military Tract and formal entry was forbidden by the national government until 1835. However, considerable informal squatting occurred. People simply took land and continued to improve it under squatting laws until they could afford to purchase it. Southerners moved to the southern parts near Perkins settlement along Crooked Creek. Northerners clustered around Fountain Green and the upper two-thirds of the township. The New Yorkers tended to be wealthier or more ambitious and took larger parcels of land than the other groups. For example, Matthew McClaughry purchased the northwest quarter of Section 22 in July 1836 and a year later acquired title to two more quarters in the same section.[12]

Matthew married again in 1838, this time Mary Hume, the daughter of Robert Hume, a Scotsman who traced his ancestry back to the "Lord Hume" of whom Sir Walter Scott spoke in one of his poems. Three children, two of whom survived, resulted from that marriage before Mary died in 1852 at the age of thirty-nine. Of these, Robert was born in a log house at Fountain Green on July 22, 1839. He spent his youth on his father's farm there, attending school in the winter months and doing agricultural chores in the summer. Farm labor was scarce so children were a valuable force. Two men and a boy could handle 100 acres of corn or 25 of wheat, it was believed.[13] The average size of the farm in Hancock County was 150 acres.[14] Some claimed the McClaughry place as being a "prosperous farm."[15]

Comfortable or not, young Robert did not escape the dangers of living on the Middle Border. For example, according to family lore, when he was thirteen years old he got lost in a snow storm on the prairie. He spent the night fighting off a pack of wolves in defense of his horses.[16] This wide open, and somewhat wild nature of the Illinois prairie remained imprinted on the minds of at least one pioneer. Charles C. Tyler, who owned a store with Matthew McClaughry, in 1912 reminisced about early Fountain Green. The town and surrounding countryside "was all open, few fences were necessary, except on the line of the creeks where stock of all kinds ranged." He went on:

> One might as well have been a navigator at sea without a compass as to have been out in the open country during one of those old time storms, there being no fences all traces of a road would become obliterated and one was liable to get out of true course, become turned around and arrive at the place of beginning.[17]

In the meantime, Matthew continued to prosper and so did young Robert. In the mid 1840s Matthew joined up with Charles C. Tyler to establish Tyler & McClaughry, merchants,[18] a general store. Yardage and sewing supplies were abundant there as of course wives created family clothing and supplemented incomes by clothes making, but all kinds of readymade clothes and shoes were available too. The store stocked household items such as coffee, sugar, and saleratus or bicarbonate of soda, along with farm tools, rifles, brandy, whiskey, tobacco, tea, and snuff. Purchases were made in an interlocking system of credit. A farmer might bring in a quantity of homemade axe handles to credit his account. Women might bring in butter, eggs, knit socks, or linen woven from home-grown flax to earn credits towards purchases of other items.[19]

By 1856, after Tyler committed suicide, Matthew had sole ownership of the store. At purchase time he had $10,000 in property and was an economic force in the community.[20] Later Tyler's son would join and then buy out McClaughry. Such commercial activity developed the business and organizational skills of young Robert, who not only worked the farm but was expected to clerk in the store as well.

Family prosperity and prominence in the area were such that in 1849, Matthew McClaughry, John Fonda, and George Edmunds were appointed by the County Court to lay out and divide the county into townships.[21] This duty was all the more important because a sizable portion of the County's population, the Mormons, had just been forced to leave. In 1855 Matthew was the first local resident appointed to collect private subscriptions for a proposed railroad to link Fountain Green to Chicago.[22] When Matthew died in 1879 a local paper said of him that:

> Mr. McClaughry was a man of great industry and energy, but his manners were always quiet and unobtrusive. . . . He was widely known among the old settlers, and was prominent in Mormon times, as a staunch, reliable, but discreet opponent of Mormon aggressions. In his intercourse with his fellow-men he was always on the side of religion and morality; charitable, but unostentatious in his charities. He was the friend of the deserving poor, and was ever ready to help those who were willing to help themselves. He was a good man in all the relations of life, and set an example in his daily work and in his intercourse with his neighbors, that young men would do well to follow.[23]

It is in that environment that Robert McClaughry was born and raised. Robert spent his youth in a cauldron of political activity and religious upheavals. To be sure, these political and economic issues were critical, but like so often religion became an excuse to vent other underlying tensions.

NOTES

1. See James G. Leyburn, *The Scotch Irish: A Social History* (Chapel Hill, North Carolina: University of North Carolina Press, 1962), pp. 157-316. Also Jeff Biggers, *The United States of Appalachia: How Southern Mountainers Brought Independence, Culture and Enlightenment to America* (Shoemaker Hoard, no place given, 2006).

2. Newton Bateman, Paul Selby and J. Seymour Currey, *Historical Encyclopedia of Illinois and History of Hancock County*, ed. Charles Scofield. Vol. 2. (Chicago: Munsell Publication Vo., 1921), p. 744.

3. Robert Bruce Flanders, *Nauvoo: Kingdom on the Mississippi* (Urbana: University of Illinois Press, 1965), p. 16.

4. *Ibid.*, p. 15. {**CHECK UPA House style; some publishers no longer accept ibid., op.cit., idem., but instead on subsequent mentions want author's last name, short title, and page. UG]

5. Quoted in *Ibid.*, p. 21.

6. Quoted in *Ibid.*, p. 22.

7. Susan S. Rugh, "Creating a Farm Community: Fountain Green Township, 1825-1840," *Western Illinois Regional Studies* 13 (1990), pp. 8-9.

8. *Ibid.*, p. 10.

9. Susan S. Rugh, *Our Common Country: Family Farming, Culture, and Community in the Nineteenth-Century Midwest* (Indiana University Press: Bloomington, Ind. 2001), p. 7.

10. *Ibid.*, p. 18.

Table 1.2. A regional breakdown of the families between 1825 and 1840

South	*South (Catholic)*	*New York*	*Pennsylvania*
Brewer	Berry	Alton	Duffy
Cox	Carrico	Beebe	Geddes
Dill	Cambron	Ferris	Glass
Duff	Gittings	Hobart	Huston
Duncan	Hardy	Leal	McConnell
Perkins	Lincoln	McClaughry	Miller
Renshaw	Mudd	Mull	Spangler
Roberts	Riley	Ostrander	Walker
Sayers	Shipley	Tyler	Witherow
Williams	Yeager	White	Yetter

11. *Ibid.*, p. 15.

12. *Ibid.,* p. 14.

13. Rugh, *Our Common Country*, pp. 17-18.

14. *Ibid.*, p. 59.

15. *Pontiac Illinois Daily Leader*, November 11, 1920.

16. *Ibid.*

17. Quoted in Rugh, *Our Common Country*, p. 79.

18. T. H. Gregg, *History of Hancock County, Illinois (*Chicago: Chas Chapman & Co., 1880), pp. 422, 820, 837.

19. Rugh, pp. 17-18.

20. Rugh, *Our Common Country* p. 83.

21. Gregg, p. 471.

22. Rugh, *Our Common Country*, p. 95.

23. Quoted in Gregg, p. 728.

Chapter Two

Matters of Faith

"CITY ON THE HILL"

Robert McClaughry's ancestry—and as we shall see later his college education as well—was decidedly Presbyterian, the name given to Protestant movements coming from Scotland and England. Presbyterians have their roots in John Calvin's *Institutes of Christian Religion* (1559). Calvin's ideology was taken to Scotland by John Knox, a Scottish student/cleric residing in Geneva, who created the Scottish Reformed Presbyterian Church, called Puritans by the English.

Though Puritanism would be more closely linked to the development of Congregationalism, the Presbyterian mind set was very close to those who held sway in Colonial New England. By the time of the Revolution the Presbyterians were one of the largest religious groups in America. They had come in different waves, the first being made up of those called New England Puritans. Together with the Congregational churches they dominated much of New England religious history and established popular stereotypes that persist to this day. It was a matter of church organization rather than ideology that separated the Presbyterians and the Congregationalists. Presbyterians believed in the priesthood of all believers, meaning that every Christian shared in the leadership of the church. They stressed uniformity, universality, and democracy, and so ministers and elected laity (elders and deacons) together governed at all levels. The second group was made up of the Irish (more properly the Scots Irish) who settled in the middle colonies such as New York, New Jersey, and Pennsylvania. They accounted for the remarkable growth of the Presbyterian denomination in the eighteenth century; by 1788 the church had two hundred congregations organized into sixteen Presbyteries divided among four synods. They became so well established that by the Revolution most of the leaders worshiped at Presbyterian churches. Several Presidents around McClaughry's time—James Buchanan and Abraham Lincoln to name two—attended Presbyterian churches. It became the faith of the established, the bourgeois.[1]

Church meetings for young McClaughry were a social and learning experience. They were also arduous. Sabbath services were long and exhausting. The meeting opened with the singing of a psalm and saying of a prayer, supplications that could last nearly half an hour. A Bible selection ranging from a few verses to an entire chapter was then read and explained. The main event, the minister's sermon, went on for up to an hour. Another song closed the morning meeting that had by this time lasted for nearly two hours. After a luncheon another similar meeting, required attendance for all, consumed the afternoon.[2]

Presbyterian preachers had a message that fitted in perfectly with the emerging country: Be frugal, work hard, save money and you will be successful. Personal honor and social responsibility were key to Presbyterians' thinking, and these were expressed in ambition, achievement, riches, and philanthropy or stewardship. By the mid nineteenth century much old style Puritanism had been softened by the two Great Awakenings that later gave rise to evangelicalism. Consequently, though the Puritan Ethic was deeply ingrained in McClaughry, so was the evangelical sense of mission. Finding and redeeming the fallen became important in newly emerging Methodist and Baptist faiths. It found room in Presbyterianism too, in what was referred to as "old light" and "new light" developments. Robert McClaughry was clearly leaning to the "new light" in his faith and his world view.[3]

Into this rural environment came a group of people whose religious collectivism, authoritarian politics, and questionable religious practices seemed un-American to mainstream Protestants: they were members of the Church of Jesus Christ of Latter-Day Saints, or Mormons. Robert was just a youngster when the Mormon wars broke out but he could not help but be influenced by the flurry of activity that went on around him as a result. Hancock County will go down in history for its intolerable mob practices and dubious judicial process.

Admittedly, not all of Hancock County was Presbyterian. Besides the large numbers of Anglicans, Methodists, and Baptists, the presence of a large number of Catholics, during this heyday of nativistic anti Catholicism, suggests that there was a reasonable amount of religious toleration there. If Robert's father's obituary was any indication, many Presbyterians had a wait-and-see attitude towards more bizarre religions. Since the Mormons were a theocratic community it is easy to lay everything at the feet of religious hysteria. Yet the Mormons, here and elsewhere, also represented values antithetical to the agrarian ideals of Hancock County. Whereas the right to own private property, to trade in a free market economy, to participate in local government, and to exercise patriarchal control of one's family were articles of faith held dearly by most Americans, the Mormons violated those values at every turn.[4] While religious differences between the Mormons and others were important, it was these more secular values that particularly caused friction.

THE MORMON WARS

Joseph Smith's revelations and presentations of a new Church and canon of scripture in New York State soon found explosive impact in the West, particularly Ohio, Missouri, and Illinois. Smith believed that the native peoples of the Western Hemisphere were descendants of migrants from the Biblical lands who had come to Central and South America two thousand years before the birth of Jesus Christ. The religion of these people paralleled those of ancient Israel, and Christ visited and set up a church organization in the new world shortly after his crucifixion, according to Smith. Records of these people and the visit of Christ were recorded and deposited in the hills of New York a thousand years before their discovery, translation, and publication by Joseph Smith as the *Book of Mormon*. He and his small sect moved from Palmyra, New York, to Kirkland, Ohio, then to Independence and Far West, Missouri and finally in Smith's lifetime to Commerce, Illinois, Hancock County, which he renamed Nauvoo. In each place he set up a theocracy, a tightly organized and unified religious state with himself as prophet-leader guided by modern day revelation.

On the one hand, the people of central Illinois openly welcome the followers of Joseph Smith and the Church of Jesus Christ of Latter Day Saints because they contributed to the demographic and economic growth of the area. The enormous land speculation that had been underway earlier had been interrupted by an economic downturn in the late 1830s, and the prosperity of the state was linked to population growth. Soon Nauvoo became the largest city in the state (for a time even surpassing Chicago), challenging Carthage, the county seat, and another river town named Warsaw. Before long, Nauvoo had nine lawyers, three physicians, three newspapers, and several professional teachers. Thirty-five general stores turned the riverside community into a thriving commercial presence,[5] and indeed even quite a tourist attraction. For example, Eudocia Baldwin Marsh, a young resident of Warsaw, remembered:

> During this time of Mormon prosperity, whilest Nauvoo was growing rapidly filling up with people from all parts of the world and becoming a place of considerable importance, many excursions and pleasure parties were gotten up to visit the city.[6]

On the other hand, the Mormons represented something held in suspicion by Midwest inhabitants: group settlement. When the *Illinois Advocate and State Register* heard of one New England association planning a group move, it wrote that no man should come "if he were so strongly imbued with the peculiar manners, notions, and ways of thought of . . . home, as to be unable to shake them off and adopt those of the adopted country."[7] Old inhabitants began to despair as they saw this "kingdom on the Mississippi" grow to five thousand by 1839. By 1842, there were ten thousand Mormons in Nauvoo and another six thousand in the surrounding communities. For example, in 1840 the Mormons established a town called Ramos. Its name would be changed to Macedonia in 1843 (then Webster in 1869). Prior to the Mormon exodus, Ramos (Macedonia) had 600 people and promised to become quite a center of population and trade. It was one mile west of Fountain Green, the home of the McClaughry family.[8] In fact, soon Fountain Green itself had a significant number of Mormons.[9]

The Mormons became an important political presence as well. Throughout the 1830s there had been a statewide trend toward the Democratic Party. Remnants of the Whig Party were barely hanging on. Disliking their treatment by democratic governors in Missouri, the Mormons arrived as Whigs. Soon their numbers would allow them to dominate the Whig party of Hancock County. Old Whig settlers feared and resented the potential takeover of their party by Mormons, and Democrats resented the Mormons for assuring a Whig dominance. Nonetheless, at first, all politicians, particularly young ambitious men like Steven Douglas, courted the political boss, Joseph Smith.[10] Eventually, Smith would be so emboldened by his economic and political power that he would even announce his candidacy for the presidency of the United States.

Anti-Mormonism grew rapidly in the early 1840s. Largely, this was based upon the threatening political and economic power of the group. But there were other concerns. For example, Nauvoo, Carthage, and Warsaw competed for pre-eminence in the county, a contest easily won by Nauvoo for that Mormon city had its own charter, law enforcement apparatus, criminal justice system, and militia. It appeared to be a city-state independent of outside control. Non-Mormon rural residents by 1843 had little law enforcement except that provided by Mormon or anti-Mormon posses, or by vigilante action.[11] Furthermore, though there was considerable religious tolerance, news began to leak out of Nauvoo of certain bizarre beliefs such as the practice of having plural wives. In fact, these issues forced some Mormons to criticize Smith and to leave the community. A virtual civil war was imminent as Mormon and anti-Mormon armies threatened conflict. Governor Ford arrived and forged a rough peace on condition that Smith and a few of his prominent leaders go to the Carthage jail for their own protection. But with the Governor's attention briefly distracted by a visit to Nauvoo a mob of two hundred stormed the Carthage jail on June 27, 1844 killing Joseph and Hyrum Smith and seriously wounding another. There is no evidence that any McClaughrys were present at the jail. However, Thomas Callister—a Mormon immigrant recently arrived from England—claimed to have infiltrated one anti-Mormon crowd and have heard Matt McCleary [sic.] swear he would drive the Mormons out.[12] But there was, in some popular sovereignty way, widespread agreement by the non-Mormons in the mob action. At first, however, Hancock County was shocked into peace for a time as the Mormon community slowly transferred power to Brigham Young.

The Circuit Court of the fifth judicial circuit, comprising the ten western counties of Illinois, came to Carthage twice each year on the third Mondays of May and October. It would hold two weeklong sessions which became a circus-like event for the entire county.[13] Carthage was the geographical center of the county, there being from it no more than a fifteen-mile radius for most residents to walk, ride a horse, or drive a wagon to it.[14] The courthouse was new and the residents of Hancock County were justifiably proud. In the previous court session, the first in the new courthouse, the people of Hancock County had seen the trial of the only person to date who would be executed for murder. William Fraim, a twenty-one year old Irish river boat sailor had killed a man in a drunken brawl. Abraham Lincoln of Sangamon County had unsuccessfully defended him. The trial had taken one day and the execution followed three weeks later. It had been a sensation.[15]

But this Mormon murder case proved to be even more exciting because in no small way the entire county was complicit. Five prominent men were indicted for the assassination of the two Smith brothers, Joseph and Hyrum. In May 1845, the suspected assassins went on trial. Several of the county's most prominent citizens were charged as well. A state senator, a colonel, a major, and two captains in the local militia, and the region's most eminent newspaper editor were defendants.[16]

Earlier, because of their political power and the fact that they made up half of the population of the county at the time of the trial, the Mormons would have dominated the proceedings. But anti-Mormon feeling was so high that the "Saints" were systematically eliminated from participation. To no one's surprise, the defendants Thomas Sharp, Mark Aldrich, Jacob Davis, William Grover, and Levi Williams were acquitted. In fact, most went on to have prominent, productive, and prosperous lives in the county.[17]

Most non-Mormons believed that the sect would self-destruct after the death of Joseph Smith, but it did not. Consequently, anti-Mormonism arose again in the next several months resulting in some more conflict and destruction labeled the "Mormon War." Mobs roamed the countryside intimidating outlying Mormon communities and threatening an attack on Nauvoo. Civil war began anew in Hancock County. Finally, on April 9th 1847, a "pioneer band" of 150 Mormons headed by Brigham Young left Nauvoo and started a westward trek that would end in the settlement of Salt Lake City. Hancock County was finally at peace but at a price dearly paid. With the Mormons gone, local residents quickly took over their lands. Matt McClaughry added to his holdings this way. But he and his family's role in religion was not over yet.

On the eve of the Civil War, men dominated the Presbyterian Church. In September, 1859, three women left the established church and founded a new one, the United Presbyterian Church on the south west corner of the McClaughry farm. One of those women was Eliza McClaughry, the third wife of Matthew McClaughry. Eliza had recently arrived from New York and was not about to sit idly by and be ruled by men. The new church was noteworthy for giving women a larger say in the governing of the congregation. Eventually it took one third of the members from the original church.[18] Such was the environment in which young Robert McClaughry spent his earliest years.[19]

NOTES

1. For a survey see Sydney E. Ahlstrom's *A Religious History of the American People* (New Haven: Yale University Press, 1972), and Martin E. Marty's *Righteous Empire: the Protestant Experience in America* (New York: Dial Press, 1970).

2. William B. Bynum, "'The Genuine Presbyterian Whine' Presbyterian Worship in the Eighteenth Century," *Journal of Presbyterian History* 74 (1996), pp. 157-169. Also see Jon Meacham's *American Lion: Andrew Jackson in the White House* (New York: Random House, 2008), pp. 16-17.

3. See Martin Marty, *Protestantism* (New York: Holt, Reinhart and Winston, 1972), p. 31. And Martin Marty, "American Presbyterians: Bicentennial Reflections," *American Presbyterian: Journal of Presbyterian History* Vol. 66 no. 3 (1988), p. 144.

4. Rugh, *Our Common Country*, p. 31.

5. Roger D. Launius and F. Mark McKiernen, *Joseph Smith Jr.'s Red Brick Store*, (Macomb, Illinois: Western Illinois Monograph Series, 5, Western Illinois University Press, 1985), pp. 9, 11.

6. Eudocia Baldwin Marsh, "Mormons in Hancock County: A Reminiscence," *Journal of the Illinois State Historical Society* 64 (1971) pp. 36, 38.

7. Quoted in Robert Bruce Flanders, p. 20.

8. Newton Bateman, Paul Selby, and J. Seymour Currey, *Historical Encyclopedia of Illinois and History of Hancock County* ed. Charles Scofield, Vol. 2. (Chicago: Munsell Pub Co., 1921), p. 1077.

9. Dallin H Oaks and Marvin Hill, *Carthage Conspiracy: The Trial of the Accused Assassins of Joseph Smith* (Urbana: University of Illinois Press, 1975), p. 47.

10. Flanders, pp. 217, 220-221, 222, 224.

11. Ibid., p. 307. Also "The Boys of 1861", p. 406-407.

12. Rugh, *Our Common Country*, pp. 50 and 220 fn. 127. This was from some "Autobiographical Notes" later written in Salt Lake City that are in the Church of Latter Day Saints Archives

13. For a good description of this see Dallin H. Oaks and Marvin S. Hill, pp. 1-2.

14. *Ibid.* pp. 3, 75.

15. *Ibid.*, p.3.

16. *Ibid.*, pp. 51-59.

17. *Ibid.*, pp.53-57, 185, 217-218.

18. Rugh, *Our Common Country,* pp. 89-90.

19. For the western movement of the Mormons see Ray Allen Billington, *The Far Western Frontier, 1830-1860 (*New York: Harper & Brothers, 1956), pp. 193-217. Also Robert F. Riegal and Robert G. Athearn *America Moves West* (New York: Holt and Winston, 1964), pp. 389-404.

Chapter Three

Matters of the Mind

THE GREAT COLLEGE DEBATE

Robert attended the local schools. State law requiring tax-supported public schools would not be enacted until 1855, two years after he had left the school for college. So the fact that he attended school attests to his family's economic position and his commitment to education as a means of upward mobility. The old school he attended was small, 24 by 30 feet and 12 feet high. Inside students sat on benches, boys on one side girls on the other. A central stove provided heat; a bucket of water, with a common gourd, provided drinking water. Outside a hitching rack allowed one to tie up one's horse. Outhouses were located at each back corner of the yard. Students began attending at age five or six, but most were ten to fourteen. By fifteen, many quit to work the family farm or to move on to a local college.[1]

Robert was a young teenager when his mother died. He and one of his two sisters survived their mother's death. It was when his father remarried in 1853 that Robert, just fourteen years old, went to live with relatives in Macomb, Illinois, and then three years later moved to Monmouth alone where he entered college. There is no evidence of tension with the stepmother, simply that young Robert struck out on his own as the family constellation changed.

Monmouth College was an example of the growing presence of the denominational experiment in higher education. Already in the 1820s, several church academies had been founded in Illinois. The Baptists had moved their Rock Spring Seminary to Alton in 1827 and renamed it Shurtleff College. McKendree College was begun by Methodists in Lebanon in 1823. A cooperative effort by Congregationalist and Presbyterians led to the founding of Illinois College in Jacksonville the following year, and within the next thirty years many more such colleges opened. For example, in 1840 there were nine colleges in Illinois, ten years later there were twelve, and by 1860, that number had grown to thirty-six, most of which were denominational. In the 1830s and 1840s, Monticello Seminary for Young Ladies opened in Godfrey (1835). Canton College in Canton (1836), McDonough College in Macomb (1836) Knox College in Galesburg (1837), Jubilee College near Peoria (1841), and MacMurray in Jacksonville (1846) are other examples. In the 1850s over two dozen more were added, and Monmouth was one of them.[2]

Monmouth, Illinois, some thirty miles north east of Fountain Green, was settled largely by Presbyterians. In 1853, the Illinois Associated Reformed Presbyterian Church opened Monmouth Academy. In September, 1856, it was elevated to college status and moved into a new brick structure, forty by eighty feet and two stories high. David Alexander Wallace, an avid abolitionist from Miami University of Ohio, was president and was aided by two faculty members, Brown and Morrison. When McClaughry arrived, the new building had a chapel seating three hundred, and eight classrooms. Heat was furnished by stoves and fireplaces. The downtown college campus (it will not move to "college hill" until 1863) probably was the main feature of the settlement; Monmouth was as yet not really a town. The arrival of the Chicago, Burlington, and Quincy Railroad in 1855 promised a lively future, but when McClaughry came to school the streets were still muddy lanes or dusty trails depending upon the weather. There were very few sidewalks, no street lights, and cows and chickens provided most of the traffic jams.[3] Students could chose between the classical department, which McClaughry did, and the English department. The classical department charged $8 per semester. The English curriculum cost $6 per semester. Upon graduation in 1861, McClaughry remained for a short time teaching classics.[4]

As the politics of the late 1850s heated up, the town of Monmouth and the college became sharply divided between Steven Douglas and Abraham Lincoln. President Wallace did not want the students to be too involved in the Democratic/Republican politics because he felt it might hamper their job opportunities after graduation. Consequently, when the Lincoln/Douglas debates occurred Monmouth would not allow a real face-to-face debate. Douglas soap-boxed on one corner and Lincoln on another. But the students of Monmouth, perhaps jealous of their counterparts at Knox College who did host a debate, staged their own. It was publicized widely in the countryside, but not the town for fear that President Wallace would interfere. The student debate between Daniel Harris for Lincoln and Robert McClaughry for Douglas drew large crowds. Surprised at the attention, the students became stage-shy and stumbled through the program. It was noted that McClaughry did not do particularly well[5]—a poor start for a man who would later be known for his ability as a public speaker.

After a few months of teaching at Monmouth, illness—something that would plague him for much of his young adult life—forced McClaughry home to recuperate. At this same time he met Elizabeth C. Madden, the eldest daughter of a prominent lawyer of Monmouth. He would marry Elizabeth in June, 1861. After his recovery McClaughry changed careers, entering the law offices of John J. Glenn to apprentice.[6] But again due to ill health and another career change, McClaughry moved back to Carthage in the summer of 1861 to purchase with a brother-in-law, Dr. Andrew Griffith, the *Carthage Republican.* The newspaper had been run earlier by pro-Confederate Democrats and was on the verge of bankruptcy. McClaughry was adamantly opposed to the Republican Party and promised "to publish a thorough Democratic journal."[7] Politics still sharply divided Hancock County. In the 1861 election 52 percent of the total Hancock County voters supported Stephen Douglas. Strangely enough, and against the tide, Fountain Green township went for Lincoln by 170 to 152 votes. Even support for any war was split in Hancock County as the Democrats—despite prompting by Stephen Douglas to support the conflict—were critical and tentative. Many communities in the county were reluctant to raise the money to pay bounties to encourage enlistment in the army. When it came to raising troops, the Democratic Party leadership dragged its feet, not forming the 118th Regiment until 1862. As we will see, McClaughry would join that regiment.[8] At this time McClaughry remained an ardent Stephen Douglas Democrat and for the short time he ran the paper called to crush the rebellion. As long as there was a rebellion, McClaughry thought, there could be but two parties: patriots and traitors."[9]

NOTES

1. Rugh, *Our Common Country*, p. 100.
2. John V. Bergen, "College Towns and Campus Sites in Western Illinois,' *Western Illinois Regional Studies*, Vol. 134 no. 2 (1990), pp. 48, 64.
3. F. Garvin Davenport, "The Pioneers of Monmouth College," *Journal of the Illinois State Historical Society* Vol. 46 (1953), pp. 45-59.
4. *Ibid.*
5. William Urban, "Monmouth College in the Civil War," *Journal of the Illinois State Historical Society*, Vol. 71 (1978), p. 14.
6. *The United States Biographical Dictionary and Portrait Gallery of Eminent and Self-Made Men: Illinois Volume* (Chicago: American Biographical Publication Co., 1876), pp. 150-151.
7. *Carthage Republican*, August 1, 1861.
8. Susan Session Rugh, "'Awful Calamities Now Upon Us': The Civil War in Fountain Green, Illinois," *Journal of the Illinois State Historical Society*, Vol. 93 no. 1 (2000), p. 16
9. Gregg, p. 728.

Chapter Four

Matters of War

"THE BOYS OF '61"

As the Civil War approached, Republicans called upon Democrat McClaughry to use his newspaper to help recruit volunteers for the military companies springing up in central Illinois. This favor would be returned to him after the war. Since he had been a prominent figure in the small denominational colleges in Central Illinois, McClaughry targeted these schools. Although some colleges resisted encouraging their students to enlist, others became openly involved. President Burgess of Eureka College became the first captain of a company made up of his students. President Hovey of the Illinois State Normal College commanded the thirty-third Illinois Infantry; its roster had so many faculty and students that it became known as the "Normal Regiment."[1] McClaughry helped raise the 2nd Illinois Calvary, the 7th Missouri Calvary, and the 78th, 84th and 118th Illinois Infantries. Then in August, 15, 1862, he enlisted himself as a private in Company B, 118th Illinois volunteers, filled with "boys from the shops and farms of central Illinois," he would later remember.[2]

As was the custom during the early years of the war, most of these companies were geographically based, made up of friends and neighbors. In a matter of three months private Robert McClaughry was elected Captain and then Major, a military title by which he would be known for the rest of his life.[3] Actually, he was the commander of Company "B", forty-seven of the seventy-seven men being from Carthage. The fact that he was elected so easily, in a company not made up of his hometown friends suggests that some politics were responsible. McClaughry had married into a prominent family that probably helped him in military politics. Company "A", commanded by Thomas Campbell, was largely made up of young men from Fountain Green,

McClaughry's home town. Fifty-seven of the eighty-six soldiers in Company "A" were from Fountain Green. Company "C" under Arthur Marsh was predominately from Warsaw. The command staff of the 118th Illinois would eventually be Colonel John G. Fonda, Lt. Colonel, Thomas Logan, and Major Robert McClaughry. John Barnes and Huddlestone Sleater were the adjutants. William Davidson was quartermaster while John Boude and Vaughn Corey were the assistant surgeons. William Underwood was the chaplain. A total of 490 men from Hancock County served in the 118th.[4]

McClaughry's war experiences were typically heroic and arduous. His rank may explain his subsequent and successful career as a prison warden. After all, two of the most bureaucratic settings in America, then and now, are the military and the prison. Military officers of rank during the Civil War formed two large groupings. First, there were the professional soldiers, those trained at West Point, who looked upon other officers with disdain. Then there were the "political generals," those made officers because they had friends in high places or to meet the necessities of a war that took so many professional soldiers to the Confederacy. There was no love lost between these two groups on the generalship level.[5] After the war many generals, both professional and political, were elected to high office. For example, U.S. Grant was a West Point graduate who became president. Rutherford Hayes, a Major General, represents the political general as president. So did James Garfield. Arthur and Cleveland did not serve in the military during the war, but Benjamin Harrison had been a brigadier general. William McKinley, like McClaughry, had been a major.

What exactly did a nineteenth century major in the army do? In the command structure a major is just above a captain and below a lieutenant colonel. This is an important distinction. As to officers of rank, those who have direct influence on the enlisted men are second lieutenant, first lieutenant, and captain. McClaughry had been elected captain earlier and had considerable clout with his men. As a major, however, he moved into a middle ground. Along with Lieutenant Colonels and Colonels, these officers have less direct influence on and contact with their men. Unlike the next group up—brigadier general, major general, and general, who have strategy and planning responsibilities—the major, according to a military scholar of the nineteenth century, saw to the drill and equipment needs of his regiment. He would be a mounted officer to the rear in all parades and action.[6] So on the one hand, McClaughry's early experience with the rank and file showed him the noblest and the vilest of human nature. Then on the other, when promoted to the rank of Major he saw less of the "boys of sixty-one" and more of the political tensions between the professional and political soldiers of rank. These war experiences would prepare him for the post-war prisons of Illinois.

Though he rose quickly in the command structure, he thought of himself as a common soldier, as a representative "everyman" speaking to and for all of the "boys of 1861." Fortunately, he left behind a thinly disguised autobiographical picture of his initial experiences in a speech delivered thirty years later. "The Boys of 1861," he remembered," signed their three month's enlistment service amid the cheers of his fellow-citizens and envious blushes of all the pretty girls in the neighborhood." He continued,

> Little did the boy of 1861 think when signing that enlistment paper that each of those three months would lengthen into a year, and to their sum yet another year would be added, before he would see the end of the great war.[7]

Sisters, cousins, and aunts gathered around to give advice on individual health care. Mothers prepared stores of bandages, and Perry Davis' Pain Killer. Country doctors gave daily lectures on the nature and treatment of gunshot wounds.

> The result proved that the mothers were wiser than the doctors, for more of the first enlisted men fell before green apples, green corn, and unripe water melons than by the bullets of the foe.[8]

Ladies' societies made red flannel shirts to act as temporary uniforms. Then, before moving off to training camp, there was the slipping away from father, mother, sister, through the back gate and across lots to his best girl, his Beth, to make eternal pledges and promises of returning from war and having an everlasting love.[9]

"NO LADY IS SAFE FROM INSULT . . . "

For McClaughry's "Boys of 1861," the first great shock was the training camp at Fort Butler in Springfield, Illinois. Earlier the camp had been at Camp Yates on the west side of the town but complaints about the rowdy soldiers forced a move to a new place on Clear Lake.[10] Even the new location angered many.

> No lady is safe from insult the moment she steps forth from the quiet retirement of her household. In what direction soever she moves her ears are compelled to listen to the ribald jests and profanities in which the maudlin children of the camp are want to indulge. At night matters are still worse. At every corner, in front of or in the vicinity of the multitudinous grog shops, they group together in squads of four, five and upwards, and interfere with and annoy quiet citizens whose business summons them abroad.[11]

In June, 1862, John G. Fonda, previously a Major with the 12th Illinois Calvary, took over camp administration. Later he would be made Commander of the 118th Illinois, McClaughry's unit. By the fall of 1862 there were 10,000 recruits housed on a forty acre space. Sometimes ethnic tensions erupted. For example, in August a riot broke out between German soldiers of Colonel Frederich Hecker and the men of Colonel Henry Day. It had to be put down by other soldiers with fixed bayonets.[12]

Basic training lasted thirty to forty days with different groups arriving between September and December 1862. Another trauma was being turned over "to the tender mercies of the most exasperating and yet most useful institution of the early army, The German Drill Sergeant." Here could be heard roared out: "Eyes vront!,""Leetle finger mit de seam de bantaloon!," "Vy shtand you like some—hay shtack?" and the ever present assessment that "You neffer make a soldier!"[13]Although most of these recruits knew they were going to war to fight African slavery, they had no idea that in the process they were to be subjected first to the slavery of a German master.

Along with the basic training, McClaughry and his fellow soldiers acted as guards at the prison for Confederate prisoners of war. There were four Civil War prisons in Illinois. Alton, on the Mississippi River just north of St. Louis, was the smallest. Camp Butler, in the Springfield area, initially had two thousand Confederates who had been taken at Fort Donelson, Tennessee. Numbers grew with the capture of Island N. 10, in Missouri. Over 850 Confederate soldiers are buried at Camp Butler. Camp Douglas, near Chicago, had eight thousand prisoners who had been taken at Fort Donelson, Tennessee. Finally, the Rock Island Prison in northwestern Illinois was the most notorious. Eventually, almost two thousand Confederate soldiers would be buried there.[14] In part, this short exposure to the idea of incarceration and the security of large numbers of prisoners prepared him for his career as a warden later on.

After basic training McClaughry's regiment moved south to take part in a series of campaigns with the Army of the Mississippi that would ultimately lead to Vicksburg. If basic training at Butler was a trauma, now ordinary camp life became a rigorous factor shaping the character of the soldier.

"THE SWEARING ESPECIALLY IS TERRIFIC."

For the most part, McClaughry's "boys of 1861" were rural people. Initially, they were shocked and excited over the congregations of thousands of men, more people in one place than they had ever seen. Soon the camps became more than training places for war; they became schools of corruption. One of the most common evils to shock these prairie Protestants was profanity. One soldier from Chicago reported that, "The swearing especially is terrific, and even to a man accustomed to hear bad language, and with sensibilities not very easily shocked, it is really disgusting."[15] Next was the problem of gambling, particularly just after payday when soldiers wanted to multiply their earnings.[16] Card playing, especially poker (commonly called "bluff") was the favorite. Crap shooting, horse racing, and cock fighting were other diversions.[17] Excessive drinking was so common that in response many regiments created temperance associations to stem the tide. Stealing from fellow soldiers was prevalent too. One soldier felt "it will be a great wonder, indeed, if the army does not turn out hundreds of men perfectly irresponsible and thievish, not to speak of uncontrollable licentiousness, who before the war were not bad men."[18] Prostitution was always a problem as camp followers formed brothels just outside of camps, but it was a greater menace nearer cities.

Attempts were made to combat these vices, the most prominent being the recruiting of chaplains, generally one for each regiment. Most of the soldiers were pious Protestants: Baptists, Methodists, and Presbyterians. Some Catholics made up the eastern regiments. Though the chaplain was to help the soldier withstand the temptations of vice, more often than not, he was simply looked down upon. The most common complaint was that the chaplain neglected his work, going off to nearby cities to get the mail, or that he was battle shy, or gave poor sermons. An Illinois private wrote home that, "our minister is no account. He will get up and praise himself and tell the lord what he [sic.] must do."[19] Officers and men alike complained that chaplains did not give adequate attention to their spiritual duties. This lack of esteem toward chaplains was manifest in a variety of nicknames. One chaplain, who had preached and pledged to be with the men throughout the battles yet disappeared when things got dangerous, was called the "great thunderer." Another charged a penny for each letter he carried for the soldiers and was referred to as "One cent by God." Another who always dwelt on the uncertainty of life was called "Death on a Pale Horse."[20]

To be sure there were some chaplains who the troops liked. These "Holy Joes" were respected for their down to earth relations with the soldiers. One chaplain gave up his horse to an ailing soldier, another went into the thick of battle to pray for the wounded and comfort the dying. Being available for the individual troubled soldier was also important, but so were the chaplain's corporate worship responsibilities. Attendance was required and generally resented. Of course, as battle neared mini-revivals occurred and those attending were more receptive. Among most Protestant denominations there was the singing of songs. Favorites were "All Hail the Power of Jesus' Name," "Blest Be the Tie That Binds," "Jesus Lover of my Soul," "Rock of Ages," and "Sweet Hour of Prayer." The core of the Sunday service was the sermon. The favorite texts stressed homely virtues, warned against the evils of camp life, gave assurances about the transforming power of Divine grace, called attention to the precariousness of life, and threatened sinners with eternal damnation.[21]

"SPAT, SPAT OF THE BULLETS"

A series of reports from "our army correspondence" began appearing in the *Carthage Republican.* Though the reports were signed with a variety of names, most likely they were penned by McClaughry himself to his brother-in-law at the paper. One, signed simply by The Private, told of the trip from St. Louis down the river:

> Our noble steamer, with her precious burden of loyal soldiers, plowed her way proudly over the bosom of the "Mighty Father of Waters;" that is, I suppose she would have done so, had she not stalled every few miles. I do think, we found every sand bar in the river. The river is at such a miserably low stage that it was nothing but drag, drag; stick stuck, all the way down. The boat was so much crowded, that many of the men suffered severely from cold and exposure, We reached here on the morning of the 11th inst., and right glad were we to get upon "Terra Ferm"[sic.] again.

Later the correspondent would talk of the first encampment:

> We are encamped about three miles from the city of Memphis, in a beautiful grove, upon the banks of the Wolf River, a muddy little stream, whose water we have to use. It is cloudy and rainy for some four days; making it very disagreeable for us raw recruits. All last night the rain poured down in torrents, and many a poor fellow was aroused from his slumbers upon the cold ground to find himself and bed in a pond of water. This was rather a cool introduction to camp life.[22]

McClaughry's 118th Illinois was in the Army of the Mississippi under Major General John A. McClernand—Black Hawk War veteran, Springfield neighbor of Abraham Lincoln, and former Democratic congressman from Illinois—who was more of a politician than a military man. In fact, McClernand was at considerable odds with the "West Pointers," who he thought were trying to undermine his authority. Letters to Grant and Lincoln complaining of mis-communications and machinations were common. The 118th was under Colonel Fonda and belonged to the Second Division under Brigadier General Peter Osterhaus.[23] The troops pushed down the Mississippi towards Vicksburg where McClaughry had his first taste of battle with Sherman's unsuccessful winter campaign against this Confederate citadel.

Vicksburg was critical in controlling the Mississippi River. After a year of fighting, much of the Mississippi was under Union control, from the mouth of the Ohio to below Memphis, and from the Gulf of Mexico to north of Baton Rouge. By the fall of 1862, only two Confederate strongholds remained: Port Huron, Louisiana, and Vicksburg, Mississippi. Geography was crucial. This prosperous town of 4,500 was on bluffs two hundred feet high overlooking the river. Federal soldiers, accustomed to fighting on the rolling plains of Tennessee, would have difficulty with the steep gullies and minor precipices. An important east-west railroad junction was there adding to the town's strategic value. President Jefferson Davis thought it so important that it was heavily fortified and referred to as "the Gibraltar of America." Nine massive forts, some with walls twenty feet thick, covered the six wagon roads and one railroad that approached the city. Swampy ground to the north protected the town from that direction, as McClaughry would soon see. Powerful batteries along the river guarded the shore against naval attack. Lt. General John C. Pemberton commanded the 50,000 Confederate troops in Mississippi. Many Southerners distrusted this native Pennsylvanian but Jefferson Davis had confidence in him. Both felt that the defense of Vicksburg was critical. Pemberton was in charge of the entire state but his superior, General Joseph E. Johnson, was in charge of the Confederate armies of the west. He did not agree with Davis and Pemberton. From his headquarters in Tennessee, Johnson favored a mobile rather than a static defense strategy. Such differences in military strategy were to bode ill for the defenders.[24]

Major General Ulysses S. Grant was in charge of the Union attack. Grant's earliest attempts to take Vicksburg failed. In December 1862, Grant moved 40,000 troops south from Tennessee through Mississippi. He was forced to turn back due to rebel Calvary raids that disrupted supply lines. At the same time, in this the last week of the year, Major William T. Sherman with the young recruit Robert McClaughry, approached Vicksburg by the river. Crowded and horrible conditions on the boats caused many to come down with measles.[25] Sherman attacked the city's northern defenses by going through the marshy bottom lands fronting Chickasaw Bayou and Walnut Hills about five miles northeast of Vicksburg. The terrible swampy conditions resulted in Union soldiers falling prey to malaria and snake and insect bites. Union losses were 191 killed, 982 wounded, and 765 missing. The Confederate losses were low with 63 dead, 134, wounded and ten missing.[26] It was in these campaigns that McClaughry took part from afar. One regiment from each division was allocated to guard the boats and thus the Illinois 118th stayed out of the major fighting. Shortly after this failed campaign he was to go to Arkansas Post.[27]

One historian has labeled the Arkansas Post campaign the "Wild Goose Chase."[28] But for young soldiers like McClaughry it was to be the first taste of battle, that experience from which all things would forever be measured. As his first combat neared (the precursor of a battle was the scurrying around of the Calvary and "those little wizards of the camp, the orderlies, [who] begin to flit about with mysterious messages and airs of the greatest importance,"[29]) like many around him, McClaughry began to review some survivor statistics. For example, in the evening before battle foot soldiers would receive forty rounds of ammunition. McClaughry assured loved ones at home that when his regiment's 40,000 cartridges hit into Confederate lines—not even counting the other Northern fire power—the war would be about over. To further diminish pre battle jitters the camp rumor mill reported army surgeons had calculated that sixteen pounds of lead was fired for every man killed in battle, and the Confederacy was short on lead.[30]

At first McClaughry's company became a "reconnaissance force" during which he witnessed skirmishes chiefly by the Calvary. Then came the day for battle. After a hasty breakfast, he recalled, they marched through the timbers passing by "ambulances that seemed to be waiting for business,"[31] and doctors' instruments laid out at the ready on tree stumps and fallen timbers. Beyond this, they came upon a thin line of skirmishers, which soon gave way to another line, and another, and another. McClaughry was at war:

> As the skirmishing grows heavier the "spat," "spat" of the bullets is heard as they fall around . . . .With occasional expression of pain from the lips of a comrade that tells its own story, there is borne . . . the awful realization that the war is actually on and [I am] actually in it.[32]

At the siege many were wounded but five thousand Confederate prisoners were taken. After Arkansas Post was captured, the troops moved up to Young Point, Louisiana, opposite Vicksburg, for a winter encampment. They would be there from January to March, 1863. Conditions were terrible and McClaughry remembered this time as "the Valley Forge of our experiences."[33] He did feel moved to write home to the *Carthage Republican* to dispel rumors that his men were not adequately provided for at this time.[34]

Then in May and June he was in a series of attacks on Vicksburg. For example, the Battle of Thompson's Hill on May 1st lasted sixteen hours. Union soldiers were outnumbered three to one and they suffered casualties of one hundred thirty dead and over seven hundred wounded. The Confederates, however, lost 68 dead and 380 wounded. Things were not going well.

On May 16th at the Battle of Champion Hills, the ground was so broken with gullies and rocks that artillery was useless. Sixty thousand Rebels engaged 40,000 Union troops in a long and bloody battle. Six thousand prisoners were taken. Rebel dead were nearly twice that of the Union, fifteen hundred to eight hundred.

Next day, May 17th, Black River Bridge twelve miles east of Vicksburg was attacked and five thousand prisoners taken. The fleeing Confederate troops were demoralized and ran wildly for cover of the city. Two very close friends of McClaughry from Fountain Green—Captain A.W. Geddes and Lieutenant Thomas White—were killed here.

Two days after that, Vicksburg was surrounded and attacked. Several failed bloody assaults resulted before a general state of siege was established. For over six weeks the contending armies faced each other across battle lines barely six hundred yards apart. As the siege continued, the Union troops dug a series of tunnel-trenches that gradually brought the opposing lines within yards of each other. In such situations considerable fraternizing and exchange of amenities occurred. During the forty-seven-day standoff, the residents of the city meanwhile lived virtually underground.[35] Vicksburg would fall on July 4th, 1863, and Pemberton would surrender over thirty thousand Confederate soldiers.[36] The blow was devastating and the South would never recover. That same week the Confederacy suffered another defeat in Pennsylvania at Gettysburg. The war was turning on all fronts.

It was during the Vicksburg campaign that an incident occurred that was indicative of McClaughry's personality, an event that perhaps presaged his future behavior as a warden. Two of McClaughry's men had left camp without passes and against orders to see some new artillery in a nearby battalion. The major general, John McClernand, ordered that they be punished in the standard way, that is, hung by their thumbs for an agonizing period of time. McClaughry was outraged, and against orders he went up to the two men and cut them down. Then he and the major general yelled at each other before the startled eyes of the troops. Threats of court martial could be heard but McClaughry stood his ground and won the admiration of the troops. Thereafter his men knew that their major was for the common soldier.[37] To McClaughry, punishment for punishment's sake seemed cruel and senseless. It also pointed up the issue of familiarity. Clearly, McClernand was well known to his major and McClaughry was not intimidated. Furthermore, the politician, McClernand, was not liked by the professional soldiers and West Pointers. There were plenty of men who would have come to the defense of this insubordinate major against his general.

But animosity and revenge will have its way. Shortly after this incident, in July and August of 1863 McClaughry was ordered to Jackson, Mississippi, to serve under General Sherman, and from there, to Port Hudson and New Orleans. Raids and small skirmishes in southern Mississippi and Louisiana preoccupied the 118th for the remainder of the war.[38]

But McClaughry's fragile constitution and arduous work ethic had undermined his health. Early in 1864 he went home to recruit soldiers and then for the remainder of the war he was assigned to the paymaster corps at Springfield, Illinois. The 118th Illinois was officially mustered out of service in October, 1865. It had taken part in one hundred battles and skirmishes, traveled over four hundred miles by train, three thousand by boat, and walked another two thousand. A total of twenty-seven young Hancock County men had died, most of disease. Sixty three remained missing. Nearly three hundred had to be discharged due to a wound or other disabilities.[39] Such a war—such a slaughter—would affect all of America for generations to come. As they did for so many, those four years transformed Robert McClaughry. Henceforth, he would always be known as the Major.[40]

NOTES

1. Bill Irvin Wiley, *The Life of Billy Yank: The Common Soldier of the Union* (Garden City, NY: Doubleday, 1952), p. 19.

2. Robert McClaughry, "The Soldier," *In Memoria: Madison Reece, M.D. [a booklet of remembrance at his dying]* (Abingdon, Illinois: Enterprise Press, 1894), pp. 14-15. Madison Reece was a medical officer for the 118th Illinois Volunteer Infantry during much of the time McClaughry fought in the Civil War.

3. Gregg, p. 728.

4. Judith L Kammerer, *Hancock County, Illinois in the Civil War, "Reflections".* (Carthage, Illinois: Journal Printing Co., 1988), p. 175.

5. See Thomas J. Goss, *The War Within The Union High Command: Politics and Generalship During the Civil War* (Lawrence, Kansas: University Press of Kansas, 2003).

6. Edward S. Farrow, *Farrow's Military Encyclopedia: A Dictionary of Military Knowledge* (New York City: By the Author, 1885), Vol. 2. p. 252.

7. Robery McClaughry, "The Boys of 1861—and Their Boys," a speech read in June 10, 1897 and reproduced in *Military Essays and Recollections*, vol. 3 pp. 400, 401.

8. *Ibid.*, p. 401.

9. *Ibid.*

10. For town views on army camps, see E. B. Long's "Camp Douglas: 'A Hellish Den?'" *Chicago History* Vol. 1 [new series] (1970), pp. 83-95.

11. *Ibid.* Also see Camilla A. Quinn, "Soldiers on Our Streets: The Effects of a Civil War Military Camp on the Springfield Community," *Illinois Historical Journal* 86 (1993), 247-248.

12. William Peterson, "A History of Camp Butler, 1861-1866," *Illinois Historical Journal* Vol. 82 (1989), pp. 74-92.

13. *Ibid.*, p. 402.

14. Victor Hicken, *Illinois Camps, Posts, and Prisons, Illinois Civil War Sketches*, No 9 (Springfield: Illinois State Historical Library for the Civil War Centennial Commission of Illinois. [1965]).

15. Wiley, p. 248.

16. *Ibid.*, p. 249.
17. *Ibid.*, p. 250.
18. *Ibid.*, pp. 254-255.
19. *Ibid.*, p. 265.
20. *Ibid.*, p.266.
21. *Ibid.*, p. 269.
22. Quoted from the *Cartage Republican* in Kammerer, p. 188.
23. Edwin Cole Bearss, *The Campaign for Vicksburg, Vol 1, Vicksburg is the Key* (Dayton, Ohio: Morningside House, nd.), p. 356.
24. For accounts of the battle see Richard Wheeler, *The Siege of Vicksburg* (New York: Thomas Y. Crowell, Co. 1978).
25. Robert McClaughry, "The Soldier" *In Memoria*, p. 15.
26. Kammerer, p. 171.
27. Bearss, p. 166.
28. *Ibid.* p. 349.
29. "The Boys of 1861," p. 408.
30. *Ibid.*, pp. 406-407.
31. *Ibid.*, p.408.
32. *Ibid.*, p. 409.
33. Robert McClaughry, "The Soldier", *In Memoria*, p. 15.
34. Susan Sessions Rugh, "`Awful Calamities Now Upon Us': The Civil War in Fountain Green, Illinois," *Journal of the Illinois State Historical Society*, 93 (Spring 2000), p. 41.
35. G. Randall and David Donald, *The Civil War and Reconstruction* (Boston: D.C. Heath and Company, 1961), pp. 409-412.
36. Gregg, pp. 483, 728-729.
37. *Kansas City Star*, May 1913.
38. Kemmerer, p. 172.
39. Susan Sessions Rugh, "'Awful Calamities Now Upon Us'" 'p. 24.
40. See Drew Gilpin Faust's *This Republic of Suffering: Death and the American Civil War* (New York: Alfred A Knopf, 2008).

Chapter Five

Matters of Business

"... this debt of honor."

POLITICS AS USUAL

McClaughry's reputation and rank of major became useful after the war in rural Illinois. For the next five years he was active in business and political circles. Although McClaughry had started the war as a Democrat, the success of the Union and the assassination of Lincoln edged him into the Republican Party—although actually it becomes difficult to determine his political attachments. On one hand, he remained identified as a Democrat. But his closeness to the Republicans could not be denied. As early as 1864 he ran for Clerk of the County Court but lost to Melancton Carey 2,643 to 2,957. The next year he won against Francis Corby 2,659 to 2,458. His local and state-wide status now was such that he was chosen to be one of the celebrity marchers in the funeral procession of the slain president when Lincoln's body was taken from the State House in Springfield to Oak Ridge Cemetery. McClaughry was prominent enough that he helped set up a college in town, Carthage College.[1]

The impact of Lincoln on the nation—his election, administration, and death—had been tremendous. Yes, Lincoln made McClaughry a quasi-Republican, but more interestingly he shaped McClaughry's speaking style. McClaughry had been thrust into public speaking while in college. His subsequent career—as a businessman, politician and criminal justice administrator—was to force him into situations that called for speeches and interviews. Now he modeled his public speaking on Lincoln. Whether as prairie lawyer or President, Lincoln had been a storyteller. He told stories strategically—to win a case, make a point, and alleviate tension. He learned that a humorous story could disarm opponents and steer the conversation—as he often did in Cabinet meetings.[2] From this point on an important part of McClaughry's speaking and interviewing style was the story as parable. Such growth in his public discourse, however, could not always sustain his political career. He would serve as County Clerk until December 1869 at which time he lost the election to George Rogers by a vote of 3,353 to 3,074.[3] Frustrated with politics McClaughry turned his attention to a business career.

BUSINESS AS USUAL

The Major had a good business role model, his father. By 1870, Matt McClaughry was worth $23,000, this at a time when the value of the average farm was three thousand dollars.[4] At the end of the war the state legislature passed a special act to organize the Hancock County Bridge Company. McClaughry was one of nine authorized to build a bridge over the Mississippi,[5] supplying stone for the construction of a bridge across the Mississippi River between Keokuk, Iowa and Hamilton, Illinois. He quickly became involved in politics even in this situation, going up against the powerful railroad lobbyists who wanted this bridge to be restricted to trains. McClaughry fought hard to ensure that the bridge would be large enough for foot and wagon traffic as well. He was not successful.

At the same time McClaughry began work with William Patterson and Gary Wells of Keokuk, Iowa, furnishing stone both for the new Illinois State House at Springfield, and the one at Des Moines, Iowa. The stone for the state prison at Fort Madison, Iowa, came from his quarry as well, as did that for many other projects all over the Midwest. Such quarrying and transport of stone would come in handy later as new prisons were being constructed. In the meantime, his business was flourishing. Sensing that the post-war boom could be better exploited from a big city McClaughry moved to St Louis in 1871 but ill health shortly forced his return to central Illinois.[6] Then came the panic of 1873 and his business failed leaving him with a huge debt of $25,000. He would spend the next thirty eight years paying off his debts. At the age of seventy-four he said, "I would rather have died and been buried by the county in the potter's field than to have failed to pay this debt of honor."[7] He was in these economic and political doldrums when a call came for him to head up the new prison at Joliet.

NOTES

1. See Drew Gilpin Faust's *This Republic of Suffering: Death and the American Civil War* (New York: Alfred A Knopf, 2008), p. 439.

2. See the remarkable book by Doris Kerns Goodwin, *Team of Rivals: The Political Genius of Abraham Lincoln* (New York: Simon & Schuster, 2005), pp. 8, 18, 50, 88-89, 103, 119-120, 127, 137, 140, 151-152, 166, 281, 375, 436-437, 511, 630, 675, 710, 713.

3. Gregg, p. 456.

4. Rugh, *Our Common Country*, pp. 169, 171.

5. Charles J. Scofield, *Historical Encyclopedia of Illinois and History of Hancock County*, v. 2 (Chicago: Munsell Publishing, 1921), p. 874.

6. Gregg, p. 730; Also "Robert Wilson McClaughry, 1839-1920," *Journal of the Illinois State Historical Society* 13 (1920), pp. 598-600.

7. *Ibid.*

Part Two

CRIME AND PUNISHMENT IN POST-CIVIL WAR ILLINOIS

Chapter Six

Crime

"... bullies, strumpets, vagrants and sneak thieves."

America was transformed after the Civil War. Immigration increased and changed, with the majority of immigrants now coming from southern and eastern as opposed to northern Europe. More and more people lived in and changed the face of large cities. Ethnic ghettoes became quite common in places like New York City, Boston, Philadelphia, Detroit, and Chicago. The more important visible change came from industrialization, specifically the huge factories that enterprising businessmen, pejoratively called "robber barons," built all over the landscape. Lost in harsh work environments, workers tried to find an identity in the organized labor movement, which for their part many businessmen thought un-American in that they threatened their hegemony. Strikes led to conflicts between both public and private police and workers. One year after the centennial celebration, the nation was threatened with a general railroad strike, the kind of strike that was always a precursor to revolution in Europe. And then there were those impersonal capitalistic forces that caused boom times and hard times, the cyclical recessions seen as disrupting the quest for profit. Cheap and reliable labor forces were a necessity, one that might be found in abundance perhaps at a nearby prison.

Crime and disorder increased rapidly across the country after the Civil War, with many blaming the war for being a school for violence and vice. "Defalcations, embezzlements, frauds, murders, swindles, violence, riots and thefts are and have been the order of the day," lamented the *Chicago Tribune* in 1875. Chicago, indeed, a city so large and diversified, would become the center of crime and disorder. Things became so bad in the 1870s, particularly after the railroad strikes of 1877, that many Chicagoans began carrying concealed pistols for self protection. This prompted an ordinance forbidding the possession of a gun without an official permit.[1] Yet it was also "plebeian" leisure activities that shaped violence, not just the pressures of recession or the habits of wartime. Much homicide involved young, poor, unmarried men who killed one another in barroom brawls and street fights. Sailors, ashore from barge work on the lake, got drunk and fought, often prompted by something as minor as refusing a fellow drinker's treat.

Yet by the 1880s barroom murders had decreased as bedroom ones increased.[2] Forty-two year old James Cunningham stabbed his wife to death in 1881, noting later that he had beat her often but no more than most in his neighborhood. One man rebuffed the police for interfering in a family quarrel. "We've got a right to fight; we're married," he claimed. Shortly afterwards, he shot her four times. Three groups in Chicago–Germans, Italians, and African Americans–have been studied most when it comes to domestic murder. The differences in the underlying motives for their violence are informative. When German immigrants killed at home with a gun it typically ended up as a murder/suicide connected to the husband's loss of gender authority. Italian immigrants did not kill wives or children but brothers, fathers, or others in honor killings. African Americans–though fewer in number compared to Germans and Italians–had both a homicide and a family homicide rate five times higher than the overall population. Most African American domestic murder occurred as a result of a spouse threatening to leave and break up the family.[3]

Contrary to popular myths about the virtues of village life, downstate Illinois had its own share of violence and disorder. The history of America is often the story of rural unrest,[4] yet small town living, particularly people knowing each other, did deter misbehavior. There were small town temptations aplenty, as we can see from statistics of neighboring Indiana, which in 1879 document 374 houses of ill fame, 2277 prostitutes, 3060 pimps, 4760 "deadbeats", and 2895 drunkards statewide.[5] Much the same could be said of Iowa as well.[6] Hancock County, from which McClaughry originally came, had a murder rate of 4.0 per 100,000 in the 1860s. Other violent crime was 34.5 per 100,000. There was a drop in the 1870s to a 2.5 murder rate and a 25.8 violent crime rate. The drop continued in the 1880s but the influx of tramps and of traveling circus and carnival shows kept concerns and crime figures high.[7] It is significant that Illinois' second prison, at Chester, was built and opened in 1877-78. Springfield, the state capital, was overrun by "bullies, strumpets, vagrants and sneak thieves," it was claimed. Cairo, Illinois, had at least one murder per week throughout this period. In the late 1870s one eighth of the males between 18 and 45 in rural White County were in jail, a majority for larceny and other property crimes. A feud between two families in Williamson County resulted in 27 murders, making that county notorious throughout the state.[8]

Among the high profile murders in rural Illinois we read about the following: William W. Lee owned a whore house, called the "Gunboat," in East Burlington, Illinois along the Mississippi river. In a fit of rage in 1876 he beat to death one of his "girls", Jessie McCarty, and was hung in June.[9] Logan County, a central Illinois area north of Springfield, had over 270 cases of physical violence, typically the result of domestic fights, in the last thirty five years of the nineteenth century,[10] twenty-six of which were murder. A German farmer, Charles Herberk, left his house and took up residence in a hotel in 1879. After fuming for a week he returned home and shot his wife in the back as she ironed. Then he shot himself. Julia Etta Worth, Mary Ann Osborn, and Narcissa Barger were all indicted for infanticide in the 1870s. Two old enemies, Henry Talbott and Shepard S. Bell, met on New Year's Day in 1879. A scuffle broke out ending in Talbott's death.[11] Five years later John Holland Hall–who would die in prison while McClaughry was warden–William Ferris, and Belle Hall were indicted for a triple murder in Mt. Pulaski, a small town in Logan County.[12] When Aaron Goodfield of McLean County was murdered in 1879, the *Bloomington Daily Pantagraph* lamented that the

> [h]orrible suicides and murders within the last few years have given the city and county a name for violence and crime which is not easy to be obliterated unless the community undergoes a great change, regarding the moral conduct of a certain class of lawless hoodlums, whose deeds of crime are becoming too numerous for the safety and welfare of our citizens.[13]

In Clinton,Illinois, Patsey Devine was convicted of murder. Shortly before his execution a cell mate, Charles Pierce, was snatched by a mob and lynched.[14]

Grave robbing became epidemic throughout the United States in the last third of the nineteenth century. Of course, there was the famous attempt to steal Abraham Lincoln's body for ransom from Springfield in 1876.[15] But most body snatching was connected to medical students needing to study cadavers for anatomy. One such medical college was in Keokuk, Iowa, just across the border from Illinois. At first individual students stole fresh bodies for anatomical studies. Shortly, it became a criminal business. Across the river in western Illinois a large number of ghouls arose to steal and sell bodies to the doctors. For example, in 1878 the grave of John Douglas was robbed in Warsaw, Illinois. Caught in the act, one of the robbers, John Brown from nearby Alexander, Missouri, claimed he had been stealing bodies for nearly a decade. His wife reported "he had often crossed the river at night, to steal from Oakland Cemetery (at Warsaw); that he would bring them to the house at night, and the following night would take them to the medical college at Keokuk; that sometimes they were so far advanced in decomposition that she could not remain in the house."[16] It became such a problem that for several months friends of the deceased would post night guards at cemeteries, giving rise to the notion of the "graveyard shift." By the end of the century medical colleges had other means of acquiring and the practice of autopsy became more prevalent, but until then grave robbing in rural America was a pesky problem. Like most states, Illinois sloughed off old puritan ways of punishment when it became a state. Corporal and capital punishments were abolished or greatly reduced in the new criminal code drawn up by the state legislature. As crime increased new ways had to be found. As in other states Illinois created its own penitentiary.

NOTES

1. *Chicago Tribune*, August 4, 1877.
2. Jeffrey S. Adler, "'On the Border of Snakeland': Evolutionary Psychology and Plebeian Violence in Industrial Chicago, 1875-1920," *Journal of Social History* 36 (2003), pp. 541-60. Also Jeffrey S. Adler, "'Mother-in-law is to Blame, But I'll Walk On Her Neck Yet': Homicide in Late Nineteenth Century Chicago," *Journal of Social History* 31 (1997) pp. 253-75.
3. Jeffrey S. Adler, "'We've Got a Right to Fight; We're Married ': Domestic Homicide in Chicago, 1875-1920," *Journal of Interdisciplinary* History 34 (2003), pp. 27-48. Jeffrey S. Adler "'If We Can't Live in Peace, We Might As Well Die,': Homicide-Suicide in Chicago, 1875-1910," *Journal of Urban History* 26 (1999), pp. 3-21.
4. Catherine McNicol Stock, *Rural Radicals: From Bacon's Rebellion to the Oklahoma City Bombing* (New York: Penguin Books, 1997), pp. 79, 137.
5. Richard J. Jensen, *The Winning of the Midwest: Social and Political Conflict, 1888-1896* (Chicago: University of Chicago Press, 1971), pp. 181-182.
6. See Sharon E. Wood, *The Freedom of the Streets: Work, Citizenship, and Sexuality in a Gilded Age City* (Chapel Hill, North Carolina: The University of North Carolina Press, 2005), pp. 79-101,132-57.
7. Susan Sessions Rugh, "Civilizing the Countryside: Class, Gender, and Crime in Nineteenth-Century Rural Illinois," *Agricultural History* 76 (2002), pp. 67, 71, 73.
8. Ernest Ludlow Bogart and Charles Manfield Thompson, *The Centennial History of Illinois, Vol. 4: The Industrial State, 1870-1893* (Springfield, Illinois: Illinois Centennial Commission, 1920), pp. 28-29. Richard J. Jensen, *Illinois: A Bicentennial History* (New York: W.W. Norton, 1978), 73. Also see Paul Angle's *Bloody Williamson: A Chapter in Lawlessness* (Urbana: University of Illinois Press, 1952, 1988).
9. John Lee Allamen, "The Crime, Trial, and Execution of William W. Lee of East Burlington, Illinois," *Western Illinois Regional Studies* 6 (1983), pp. 49-66.
10. Beverly A. Smith, "Murder in a Rural Setting: Logan County Homicides, 1865-1900," *Western Illinois Regional Studies* 13 (1990), pp. 61-79.

11. *Ibid.* And Beverly Smith, "Homicide in a Nineteenth-Century Rural Community: The Talbott/Bell Case of 1879," *Deviant Behavior* 11 (1990), pp. 17-43. See also Beverly A. Smith, "The Murder of Zura Burns, 1883: A Case Study of Homicide in Lincoln," *Illinois Historical Journal* 44 (1991), pp. 218-34.

12. Beverly A. Smith, "'Mt. Pulaski's Horror', 1882: Murder and the Rural Underclass," *Journal of Illinois History* 4 (Winter 2001), pp. 271-90.

13. *Bloomington Daily Pantagraph*, August 5, 1879. Quoted in Beverly A. Smith, "'Divine is Doomed. AND SO ARE HIGH PRICES': The Hanging of Patsey Devine in Clinton, 1882," *Illinois Historical Journal* 91 (1998), pp. 21-40. Quotation found on page 22.

14. *Ibid.*, pp. 30-31.

15. *Chicago Tribune*, November 8 and 18, 1876.

16. Quoted in John E. Hallwas, *Western Illinois Heritage* (Macomb, Illinois: Illinois Heritage Press, 1983), pp. 137-43.

Chapter Seven

Punishment at Alton

"no outlay of money can convert this prison into a . . . durable establishment."

Before the 1830s, the chief form of punishment in Illinois had been heavy fines and flogging. This was in keeping with the practices of most states, going back to the Colonial era in American history. Stocks and pillories, a variety of corporal inflictions and capital punishments, were the common penology for much of the earlier history.

Then in 1827, like many states in the Union, there was a reform of the criminal code in Illinois. Capital crimes and flogging still persisted but at a decreased rate, and some of the older puritanical punishments—such as branding and standing in the pillories—were abandoned. Instead, imprisonment became the typical punishment.[1] Construction of the Alton, Illinois prison began in 1827 and was opened in 1834, Wilson Hess from Greene County, its first inmate, having to be housed temporarily in the Alton jail to await formal opening on August 29th, 1834.[2]

Problems emerged almost immediately. The prison, poorly built on uneven ground, had walls that tended to topple down. Those that stood, held in the dampness during summer and turned to ice in the winter. One prison doctor protested that the blankets and beds of inmates actually froze during cold snaps.[3] Access to water was limited, as well, and became critically short as the inmate population increased. Soon the initial twenty-four cells were crowded. When prison reformer Dorothea Dix visited in 1846 she found inmates chained to the passage way walls. All inmates were forced to eat standing up since neither tables nor chairs were available.[4] In her statement to the state legislature in 1847, Dix warned politicians that "no outlay of money can convert this prison into a secure, commodious, or durable establishment."[5] Even expansion did not save the day and by 1858 there were 256 cells housing 600 men.

Administrative roles at the prison were political appointments. At first, the warden was elected by the State's General Assembly and re-elected every other session. A Board of Inspectors was set up to assist the warden and act as a check on his power. In 1837, the office of warden was abolished and the Board of Inspectors took over completely. Subsequently, wardens really denoted those businessmen who had won a business contract from the state to use inmate labor.

Then there was the problem of work. The early penologists were only partially concerned with the rehabilitative nature of labor. Most wanted to minimize costs of incarceration and maximize profits for the state. Consequently, in 1839 the prison at Alton went to a lease system of work. The state simply sold its prisoners as slave labor to private individuals or contractors, in return for which the contractor promised to feed, clothe, and care for the inmates. All profits went to the contractor. At first, the prisoners performed their work anywhere the contractor desired. Soon free workers in the various work areas complained about the "unfair competition," and by the mid 1840s—although the workers remained under contract—they were confined to the prison grounds.

By the 1850s considerable dissatisfaction with Alton emerged. Faced with growing expenses the State tried to maintain low costs by cutting back on services and amenities. Conditions became deplorable. The site had never been the best and now the city of Alton was growing so quickly that the prison stood in the way of development. In addition, other reforms in criminal justice were having an impact. With the creation of the Chicago police, in 1855, the new police caught more criminals and thereby added more people to the courts and prisons. Consequently, prison populations rapidly grew, forcing at least two persons to a cell. Under the old penitentiary ideology of silence and solitude this double occupancy flew in the face of any pretense of reforming the convicts. Clearly a larger facility was needed. Also, it was becoming obvious that the Illinois population was going to be weighted northward, nearer to the new booming village called Chicago. Finally, prison administration continued to be mired in politics. Fearing the power of the Board of Inspectors, the governor abolished the Board and set up a Superintendent in 1857.

With such overcrowding discipline became a problem. At first, solitary confinement was the main way to control inmate behavior. A throwback to the more monastic Pennsylvania system, such solitude was considered by officials to be less a punishment and more an opportunity to reflect and repent. Yet by taking a prisoner and further imprisoning him in the midst of an existing prison, solitary confinement became perceived as punishment. Conditions in solitary cells were worse than those for the general population and few inmates survived with good health. Besides, prisoners were needed for labor, and one more prisoner in solitary meant one less for the labor force. Soon, alongside cold baths, whipping took over as one of two favored forms of discipline. This had been a common punishment for other people: sailors in the navy and slaves on plantations. Abusing the guards warranted twenty-five stripes of the whip. Attempts at escape and any fighting earned the inmate fifteen stripes. Destroying property resulted in ten blows. The cold bath, first used to discourage prisoners from feigning illness to avoid work, also grew to be a disciplinary devise. The form of the machine resembled that of the common stocks of Colonial America. The offender was stripped and seated with feet and hands locked in place. From a reservoir eighteen inches above a stream of water struck the head of the convict. When the reservoir was full, the force of the blow upon the head equaled a column of water seventy-two inches in height.[6]

Escapes were to be expected and it was estimated that in the 1830s one third of the prisoners at Alton escaped.[7] From 1864 to 1874, 120 escapes occurred.[8] Then there was the infamous John Hall case in 1857, (the "tragedy long remembered,") discussed earlier, that acted as the final straw. That same year legislation was introduced to abandon Alton entirely and construct another prison nearer to Chicago. During the Civil War, Alton would be converted into a prisoner of war camp for captured Confederate soldiers. In the meantime, construction was started at Joliet, Illinois.

NOTES

1. For an excellent general account of this see Rothman, pp. 79-108. Also McKelvey, pp. 45-46.
2. Sidney W. Wetmore, *Behind the Bars at Joliet* (1892), p. 20.
3. Robert S. Johnston. "Early Crime and Punishment in Illinois," *Illinois State Genealogical Society Quarterly* 18 (1986), p. 4.
4. *Ibid.*
5. D.L. Dix, "Memorial of Miss D.L. Dix in Relation to the Illinois Penitentiary," Illinois Legislature 15th Assembly 1st sess. (February 5, 1847), p. 5. See also Thomas J. Brown, Dorothea Dix: New England Reformer (Cambridge, Mass.: Harvard University Press, 1998), p. 142.
6. See Wiley Britton Sanders, The History and Administration of the State Prisons of Illinois (unpublished dissertation at the University of Chicago, 1929), pp.221, 313.
7. Johnston, p. 4.
8. Henry Douglas Kamerling, "Too Much Time For the Crime I Done": Race, Ethnicity, and the Politics of Punishment in Illinois and South Carolina, 1865 to 1900. Unpublished Doctoral Dissertation, University of Illinois, Urbana, Illinois, 1998, p. 279.

Chapter Eight

Early Joliet

"the curious thing . . . is that the prisoners are made so comfortable."

Legislation, in 1857, placed the new state prison at Joliet, Illinois, about fifty miles south of Chicago. The site was closer to larger urban centers, increasingly the major source of prisoners. In addition, the area weather was healthier. Good drainage, a more reliable water supply, better availability to building materials, and easier access to markets were reasons for the selection. Construction began at the turn of the decade but slowed because of the Civil War and was not finished until 1869.

The new penitentiary was erected on a solid rock foundation,[1] with a square prison yard of fifteen acres, enclosed by stone walls eight hundred feet long on each side. The wall was twenty-five feet high, six feet thick at the bottom and three feet thick at the top. At the four corners were large turrets, twenty feet in diameter and sixty feet high, for the rifle toting sentinels. Inside, for male prisoners east and west wings—260 feet long and fifty-four feet wide—ran from the warden's residence. The east wing contained four tiers of cells, for a total of four hundred, the west five tiers and five hundred cells. Cells were built running down the center of each wing, fourteen feet from the walls on either side, each cell four by seven by seven feet high. Half of the cells faced south and the other half faced north. Ventilation tubes extended from each cell to the roof to provide some fresh air without risking security. Iron grated doors admitted some light, air, and heat. Seventy-eight gas burners in each wing provided some light but for the most part cells depended upon candle power for illumination. Furnishings were spartan: an iron bedstead, straw mattress, pillow, woolen blanket, a stool, tin cup, and a toiletry bucket.[2] Also, there might be found a variety of food items, such as salt and vinegar, because meals were eaten in the cell. Inside the main prison yard, with its own encircling wall, was the female department.[3]

From 1857 to 1873 conditions were chaotic, for prisoners transplanted from Alton did much of the construction. The first prisoners from Alton left the old prison May 5th, 1858, meaning that until July 24th, 1860 both the old and the new prisons were open.[4] In the meantime, the men were literally building the prison up around themselves causing all kinds of security problems.

Aside from the unusual conditions as building their own prisons, there continued to be two main systems of work in American penitentiaries: state managed and the lease system. In the former, the warden leased out contracts to entrepreneurs. The state still furnished all supplies, controlled the prisoner-workers, and received a substantial share of the profits. Most prisons had this system by the 1860s. On the other hand, there were those with pure "lessee systems." In such cases the entire prison was leased out to a man, or company of businessmen, who took over most of the management of the institution. The state received a fee from the contractor who thereafter assumed all the risks and profits. Illinois favored this latter system throughout the antebellum period. In 1863 the Illinois General Assembly leased Joliet to James Pitman for a six year period. One administrator, S.A. Buckmaster, came from Alton where he had been warden since 1838. As warden he and his "company"—S.A. Buckmaster & Co.—dominated this leasing system.[5] In many regards Joliet was a private prison. Businessman got the lease for a fee and ran the prison as they saw fit. By 1866 control of Joliet was in the hands of the Illinois Manufacturing Company. The next year the company dropped its lease and—catching the state completely off guard—turned it all back to the state. The company took most of its capital investment leaving the state destitute and panicky. In 1867 the lease system was abolished altogether. From 1867 to 1871 the state directly controlled the prison and its industry and lost over $547,000.[6]

In response, the contract labor system of work was introduced and would predominate for the next fifteen years. Work would still be contracted with outside businesses but prisoners and oversight of their work would remain on the prison grounds. This gave the warden considerably more power and responsibility. At Joliet, a shoe department was set up where 325 men worked for 65 cents each a day. Then came a stone department (employing 225 at 81 cents each per day), cooper department (working 165 men at 70 cents), cigar works (with 150 men at 55 cents), and a harness department (with 40 men). The sixteen female prisoners at Joliet made underclothing. Apparently there was considerable corruption among prison officials, and some political jealously too, so that the governor fired the warden and commissioners in 1873.[7]

The chaplain of Joliet at this time, S. G. Lathrop, has left a revealing account of prison life in the late 1860s. According to Lathrop, when a prisoner arrived as a so-called "fresh fish," he was immediately taken to the bath house to bathe and receive an exchange of clothes. The prison uniform was white and black striped woolen outfits of coat, vest and pants. The new inmate would get two pair of socks a year. Under garments could be exchanged every two weeks.[8] In the summer they wore a straw hat, half of which were colored red. Such uniforms not only identified but stigmatized the inmates; as Chaplain Lathrop recalled, "A lady who visited her husband here, told me that his appearance reminded her of a clown in a circus, and for weeks she could not get the strange image from her mind."[9] A visit to the barber occurred next at which the face was shaven clean and the hair cut short. Besides the obvious hygienic reasons for such a practice, since the prevailing styles on the outside were long head and facial hair, this increased the prisoner's stigma. For internal control purposes a thorough description of the inmate was recorded at this time. Then the prisoner was assigned to the work most suitable to his experience and skills.[10]

A dining room, capable of seating one thousand men, was under construction at the time of Lathrop's remembrances, but until it was finished all inmates dined in their cells. Yet eventually, this new dining hall became such a security problem that mass dining was abolished by 1890.[11] The diet emphasized meat (usually beef), bread, and seasonal vegetables. Coffee was served twice a day and soup once a week. On Sundays there was pudding for desert.[12] The convicts were allowed to eat all they wanted. By 1890, it was estimated that the average cost of feeding the convicts was about eleven cents per man per day. After supper, each was given a candle to light his cell and could read until 8pm when they were to retire. They could write letters once every eight weeks and receive mail whenever it arrived. All correspondence was read by the warden and censored if necessary. Convicts were allowed one bath and shave per week, as well. Some weeks before their release they were allowed to grow their hair and beards so as to be less marked as ex-cons.[13] All of this led one visitor, a British Member of Parliament named W. E. Price, to comment in 1869 that

> the curious thing in the Illinois Penitentiary is that the prisoners are made so comfortable. They work together, are allowed to talk, and provided with tobacco by the State, have meat twice a day, are encouraged to read, have a candle in their cells every night, and, when well behaved, are allowed to work overtime and earn money, which they spend on books.[14]

Such comments and observations are as revealing about the nature of English prisons as much as they are about American ones.

As Price's visit indicates, up until 1865 the practice of penitentiaries being tourist spots was quite prevalent in America. Any one, for the fee of twenty-five cents, could tour the Joliet prison. This practice was stopped in 1865 but started up again shortly after.[15] Criminals had always been a fascination to the law abiding public. Earlier, thousands would travel miles to watch a public execution. With the building of the penitentiaries the socially conscious and the plain curious wanted to enter the walls to gawk at those in a free society who had been deprived of their freedom. And when the visitors came they saw a wide variety of inmates.

The demographics of the prison population at this time are revealing. Of the 586 inmates in the late 1860s 356 (or about 60 percent) were incarcerated for larceny. Forty-nine were burglars and thirty robbers. Thirty-three had committed manslaughter and nineteen murder. Most prisoners were in their early twenties. Ninety six were under twenty, two of them were ten years old, and eleven were seventeen. One hundred eighty six were from twenty-one to twenty-six; 127 were from twenty-six to thirty-one years old. By October, 1866 there were thirty-nine guards, or one guard for every fifteen inmates. Prison populations grew so rapidly that a new prison, Southern Illinois Penitentiary, was opened at Chester, Illinois, in 1870. With such prison population growth managerial control became very important. Of course, there was oppression and intimidation. But another way was to offer incentives like early release.

According to a "good time" law passed in 1863, these inmates could be released early due to good behavior. If well behaved the first month, one day would be taken off the inmate's sentence. If the second month was one of good behavior, another two days were subtracted. A third month of good living and obedience brought an additional three days off. And each month thereafter brought five additional days off. Chaplain Lathrop had mixed views on this release policy. On one hand, he felt,

> The law promotes a most powerful motive to good conduct, and has a strong influence in promoting obedience to prison rules.

On the other hand,

> If a convict has once broken a prison rule, he can never thereafter secure any advantage from the law. He has no encouragement from it, to good conduct after one transgression. It makes a man's citizenship depend upon less than a crime, the simple violation of a prison rule.[16]

Between 1871 and 1873 prison administration was done by three commissioners and one warden. The governors appointed the commissioners for six-year terms. They could not have any business interest in the prison. They were to meet at Joliet once a month to determine broad policies regarding food (quality and quantity) and work contracts. Once a year they were to present an annual report to the governor. The warden, appointed for a three-year term by the governor, was to implement the policies of the commissioners.[17]

Because of politics tenure for wardens was short, leaving very little continuous leadership and managerial culture. Up until the arrival of McClaughry the Joliet penitentiary experienced three distinct stages of prison administration. From 1857 to 1866, the governor appointed a superintendent who was directly responsible to the chief executive of the state. From 1861 to 1867, three commissioners were appointed by the governor along with a lease warden, a person in charge of prison contracts. From 1867 to 1871, when the so-called lease system of prison industry was abolished, the governor selected three commissioners and they in turn selected the warden.

The first warden was Samuel Casey from 1858 to 1863. He was briefly followed by Captain J. M. Pitman and then until 1866 Colonel Sam Buckmaster, the former warden at Alton. In quick succession Gilbert Simons, Ben Dornblazer, and George Perkins followed. Elmer Washburn would be warden from 1870 to 1872 to be followed in quick succession by A.W. Edwards, Jack Smith, (who lost his life in the Sag bridge disaster on the Alton railroad only three months into his administration) and Joseph Wham. In 1874 McClaughry would take over and remain warden for nearly fifteen years, the longest and most successful wardenship to date.[18]

The Joseph Wham story is indicative of the politics of prison administration. Wham, like McClaughry, had been a major during the Civil War and carried that title proudly for the rest of his life. He took over the job from Jack Smith, the former mayor of Springfield. Wham had been warden only for a short time when there was a scandal. Allegations of mismanagement of funds were leveled at the commissioners and the warden. Quickly the local very partisan papers took sides. The *Joliet Republican* wanted all officials removed. The *Joliet Sun* wanted to keep them. The *Joliet Signal* had a wait-and-see position. Investigations indicated some "irregularities," but no fraud.[19]

Another incident aroused more concerns for the governor. In December 1873, convict Henry Williams died undergoing the "bath," a form of water torture for refusing work. Good discipline, as manifested in working, was essential both to these nineteenth-century penologists and to current and potential contractors who demanded a stable workforce. Williams was 25 at the time of his death and serving a four year term for stealing horses. The *Chicago Times* investigated and laid the responsibility on deputy warden, Captain J.P. Hall, and assistant warden J.F. Sleeper. They in turn claimed they were only carrying out the wishes of the warden and commissioners. The *Times* and the *Joliet Signal* concluded the real culprits to be the warden and commissioners.[20]

With suspicions aroused, Governor Beveridge removed the entire Board of Prison Commissioners and Warden Wham. However, Wham was a relative of Jack "Black Jack" Logan, a political powerhouse in Illinois, and he threatened the governor with career-ending repercussions. Logan, himself a Union general, would become the U.S. Senator from Illinois for 18 years and a vice presidential candidate under James G. Blaine. Apparently Wham's friends in high places put pressure on the governor and demanded that Wham keep the warden ship or be given the presidency of the new Board of Commissioners. So in a move that outraged many critics, Beveridge named a new Board, one of whom was the former warden. Not surprisingly, the *Signal* declared all to be "professed politicians."[21]

Also caught up in the turmoil were assistant warden J.P. Hall and his assistant J.F. Sleeper. In the prison hierarchy Hall was in charge of discipline. He had been around for years going back to Washburn's administration, and was given credit locally for the financial condition of the prison. Sleeper had been at the prison for thirteen years. Both men were fired. Hall and Sleeper blamed the commissioners for obsessive concern over prison contracts and for their willingness to punish those who refused to work. A petition was circulated and signed by most of the guards requesting that Hall be placed back in office. Both were exonerated and rehired by the new warden Robert McClaughry.[22]

Boss politics and fragile business conditions in a recession era made being a prison warden difficult. Not only were there an increasing number of inmates but also growing demands by state politicians to run a self sufficient prison. For a man with no prison experience and a failed business career such a venture seemed impossible. Such was the environment awaiting Robert McClaughry.

NOTES

1. Wetmore, p. 20.
2. S. G. Lathrop, *Crime and Its Punishment and Life in the Penitentiary* (Joliet, Illinois: S. Lathrop, 1866), pp. 220-21.
3. Saunders, pp. 322-23, 373.
4. Lathrop, p. 214.
5. Lathrop, pp. 241, 243.
6. Kamerling, pp. 91-92.
7. *Ibid.*, pp. 240-42, 259, 266.

8. Wetmore, p. 49.
9. Lathrop, p. 247.
10. Ibid. p. 249. At the time of Lathrop's writing the men were distributed thus:
    Machine shop 15
    Stone cutters/masons . . . 80
    Blacksmith shop . . . 31
    Laborers/quarrymen . . . 312
    Wagon shop . . . 19
    Dinning room/kitchen . . . 45
    Cooper shop . . . 264
    House waiters . . . 6
    Cigar shop . . . 44
    Invalids/unemployed . . . 34
    Harness shop . . . 1
    Hospitalized . . . 5
    Tailor shop . . . 10
    Paint shop . . . 7
    Shoe shop . . . 103
11. Wetmore, p. 33.
12. Wetmore, p. 208. A typical bill of fare for a week would be
    Monday—Breakfast=beef stew, boiled potatoes. bread, coffee.
        Dinner= boiled ham, beans, bread and water
        Supper= Bread and tea
    Tuesday—Breakfast= Corned Beef hash, bread, coffee
        Dinner= Vegetable soup, boiled beef, bread
        Supper= Bread and tea
    Wednesday—Breakfast=Fried Sausage, potatoes, bread and coffee
        Dinner=Boiled bologna, bread pudding, bread and water
        Supper=Bread and Tea
    Thursday—Breakfast=Hash, potatoes, bread and coffee
        Dinner=Same as Tuesday
        Supper=Bread and Tea
    Friday—Breakfast=Stewed cod fish, potatoes, bread and coffee
        Dinner=corned beef, potatoes, turnips or beets, bread
        Supper=Bread and Tea
    Saturday—Breakfast=Same as Tuesday
        Dinner=Irish stew or pork and beans
        Supper=Bread and Tea
    Sunday—Breakfast=Butter, molasses, bread, coffee.
        Dinner=Roast pork or beef, mashed potatoes and gravy, apples or onions, bread and coffee.
13. *Ibid.* pp. 247-51.
14. Philip M. Price, *America After Sixty Years: The Travel Diaries of Two Generations of Englishmen* (London: George Allen, 1936), p. 26.
15. Lathrop, p. 225.

16. *Ibid.*, p. 254.
17. Sanders ,pp. 225, 230, 236-37.
18. Wetmore, p. 24.
19. The *Joliet Signal,* April 22, 1873.
20. *Ibid.*, December 23, 1873 and January 6, 1874.
21. *Ibid.*, May 13, 1873.
22. *Ibid.*, August 25, and September 8, 1874.

Chapter Nine

McClaughry at Joliet

"He will study the work . . . with the care of a philosopher."

Robert McClaughry's tenure at the Illinois State Penitentiary is revealing at several levels. His career at Joliet highlights the political nature of prison administration in the nineteenth century. Also, we can see more clearly the emerging inmate culture and inmates' relationships to correctional officials–particularly with McClaughry. A guard culture becomes more visible and the relationship of the warden and his numerous subordinates becomes complicated. Finally, the nature of criminal justice reform began to have two quite different audiences in mind. On one level, McClaughry, as a Puritan/evangelical, is genuinely interested in the welfare of the prisoners, particularly first offenders. On another level, his reforms are aimed at the profession, its practices and practitioners.

Of course, being new to the job these issues were not obvious at once, they evolved and developed over time, as did McClaughry's response to them. But under McCaughry's direction the Illinois State Penitentiary will become one of the best run prisons in America. This was no mean task as Chicago continued to send floods of obstreperous people to live in this bucolic setting. Though Chicago loomed large to the north, McClaughry's first prison experience was in small town America.

The town of Joliet underwent a transformation during McClaughry's tenure as warden. Established in 1852 the "stone city," so called for its abundance of limestone, grew to be a bustling place just thirty-eight miles south of Chicago. By the late 1870s, when the McClaughrys arrived, the population was just over fifteen thousand. An Opera House and street car system had been built in 1873, and telephone service had been introduced in 1880.

Concern over public health led to the building of the "pest house" on "quarantine hill." In typical boosterism of the era, the sixty-five miles of graded streets were touted. So were the sixteen school houses, eight clothing stores, ten dry goods stores, six boot and shoe stores, four daily and five weekly newspapers, thirteen drug stores, sixty grocery stores, four harness shops, eight hardware stores, six ladies shops, five jewel stores, five dentists, three greenhouses, along with two national banks and four private ones. Twenty-nine stone companies, nine wire mills, the largest rail mill in the world, a stove foundry, and numerous gravel and sand pits made this town a vital place for these folk from rural Illinois. Two fire stations existed equipped with the latest technology. Citizens were thrilled to see the fire wagon pulled by eight horses race about town. The chief was paid eight hundred dollars a year. The police department had a chief, who made twelve hundred dollars per year, and fourteen patrolmen. A patrol wagon, with two big gongs, escorted rascals to a ten-cell jail.

There was a dark side to Joliet as well. One hundred twenty-five saloons spread along Collins Street, dubbed by the locals as Whiskey Row. Beginning in 1882, licensing fees were increased from fifty to five hundred dollars, which closed sixty-five saloons. The next year the fee was doubled again to one thousand dollars and forty-five more closed. But the saloon street would continue to be a city problem—dominating the crime rates with daily beatings, fights, and robberies–and a source of consternation for puritanical reformers like McClaughry.[1] Though he might wag his finger at the seamier sorts of the town, McClaughry's primary responsibility was to keep control of his institutions. There might be politics outside the walls but there were ample political challenges within them too.

POLITICS

With his recruitment speeches during the Civil War and some work for the Republican Party, a waffling political conversion recently occurring during the war, Robert McClaughry impressed several people in Illinois politics. Even while still in the army, McClaughry spent 1864 campaigning for Lincoln's reelection. Since he had been an adamant Stephen Douglas Democrat before 1860, the war and the presidential assassination profoundly affected McClaughry, as it did many soldiers. So by the 1870s he became something of a political favorite of the Republican Party. In fact, his friends pressured him to run for Congress in 1874, but just then the offer arrived from Joliet.[2] Appointed to be the warden in 1874 by the new governor, John Beveridge, McClaughry would hold that job for the next fifteen years.[3] In terms of regional politics the appointment of McClaughry was praised as good for central Illinois. David Wallace, president of Monmouth College, had known McClaughry for eighteen years and wrote to the governor, promising that McClaughry would "study the work under his supervision with the care of a philosopher."[4] McClaughry was to become a case study of an intellectual in a very practical world. He was to be a Puritan in Babylon.

McClaughry's appointment was for a three year renewable term. As recent history had shown the likelihood of surviving that period was slim. Relations with the Board of Commissioners were critical. Although, they themselves were creatures of the politics of the state capital, the Board and the warden had closest contact. Historically, the three Commissioners were appointed by the governor for six year terms. Once a month they would hold a meeting at the prison to discuss issues and ultimately compile an annual report for the governor.[5] The importance of warden-commissioner relations was highlighted earlier when, in 1872, the Board fired Elmer Washburn. At no time, the Board contended, did the warden make income equal expenses. Furthermore, in a statement reflecting the politics of penology, Washburn acted "too independent" of the Board and had to go. Washburn fought back but the Commissioners prevailed.[6]

The Commissioners were watched closely by the opposing party and its newspapers. For example, rumors of impropriety surfaced in 1879. The Joliet *Signal*, a partisan Democratic paper, chided the Commissioners for overspending their travel allowance.[7] All requests for money and new buildings, and all annual reports went to and were eventually published over the signature of the Board. Generally, the commissioners were seen as a rubber stamp to McClaughry.

Prison conditions had been so deplorable before McClaughry's arrival that the Board was eager to have a honeymoon from the constant interventions. Surprisingly—given the lack of previous experience—McClaughry proved to be a capable warden. Either naturally or through wartime experience, he took charge with a strong hand and it looked like the turbulent previous ten years were at an end.

Relations with the state capital—both with the governor and legislature—were critical as well. This was made easier with McClaughry's transformation to Republicanism. The "land of Lincoln," especially downstate, will be Republican. For his entire tenure at Joliet the state governorship was in the hands of Republicans. John Beveridge, the governor at the time of McClaughry's appointment, in many ways was like McClaughry. Born in New York State of Scotch and Scotch-Irish decent he was a strict Presbyterian. Moving to Illinois he taught for a short time, studied law, became involved in a failed business venture, and formed a Calvary unit when the war started.

He led the 8th Illinois Calvary at Gettysburg and then returned to the Midwest to form the 17th Illinois Calvary that watched over Confederate prisoners at Alton. Cold and unsociable, his temperance positions made him an enemy of the saloon interest and political bosses of Chicago. He served as a sheriff for two years and state senator for four more when he was elected lieutenant governor with Richard Oglesby heading the ticket. Eleven days after the election Oglesby appointed himself U.S. Senator and Beveridge became an "accidental governor," the third and last Civil War general to become governor of Illinois. His administration was plagued with the revival of the Democratic Party (it won control of the legislature) a growing lawlessness in southern Illinois, and the economic depression starting in 1873.[8] Even though Beveridge wanted to run for re-election, the Republicans went for Shelby Cullom.[9]

For most of McClaughry's years as warden at Joliet the governor was Shelby Cullom. McClaughry and Cullom had much in common also. This conservative governor was from a rural background in central Illinois and was a strict Methodist, having gone to the Rock River Seminary. Like McClaughry, Cullom had a history of illnesses and had to leave the Seminary before finishing. He moved to Springfield, Illinois, to study law under Abraham Lincoln—he looked remarkably similar to Lincoln, which endeared him to many—but his mentor became so busy that Cullom left to join Stuart & Edwards until illness drove him back home. A series of political machinations got him elected to Congress, a position he held until becoming governor in 1877. He regarded state government as a business enterprise with emphasis on preserving order, enforcing the law, punishing criminals, caring for the poor, and educating the young. At the end of his first term he was able to declare that for the first time in twenty-five years the state was debt free. Most of his tenure as governor was plagued with the economic depression. He left in 1883 to become United States Senator. Before he left office, however, Cullom was a supporter of McClaughry.[10] Such friends in the state capital made McClaughry's job a bit easier. In addition, some of the initial and essential work, building up the physical plant and procedures of the prison, had the full support of the governor.

BUILDING THE INSTITUTION

Although the prison was reasonably new when McClaughry arrived, its physical plant needed numerous additions and improvements. In part this was due to the natural, but intensive, wear-and-tear of over 1,500 men living at the place. But in part it was also due to the generally parsimonious attitude of the state legislature. Even the governor, but certainly other state politicos, expected the prison to be largely secure and self-sustaining.[11] Speaking to an assembly of prison administrators, McClaughry summed up his feelings on prison architecture. "Our prison," he confided to those nodding in agreement, "was built on the old plan of ornamenting the outside and leaving the inside rather inconvenient."[12] Various building projects were started. In his first two years McClaughry oversaw the laying of sewage pipes, steam heat pipes, the digging of a reservoir, putting a new slate roof on the foundry, and building water closets in two of the shops.[13]

Even though the financial depression of the early 1870s took its toll even on the prison, by 1877 McClaughry had built new shops for Selz & Company, a contractor employing fifty inmates in the making of boots and shoes. A blacksmith shop was added as well. In addition, a new boiler house was constructed, a railroad platform built, drilling for a new artisan well started, and the deepening of the ice pond continued. Apparently, the souls of the inmates were not as important as their labor. The chaplain's request for a chapel was turned down because of lack of funds.[14] Of course, in the name of labor the health of the prisoner was important.

One building project, completed in 1884, particularly affected the prisoners. Health was always a problem particularly with periodic epidemics. Bathing had been difficult to coordinate by the administrators and widely hated by the prisoners. It is more than coincidental that the term for the most dreaded punishment in prison was "shower bath." Generally two or more (sometimes many more) prisoners bathed in the same tub at the same time. In 1884, however, a new bath system with 60 tubs allowed for individual bathing.[15] Joliet became recognized as a nationwide pioneer in the area of bathing and other prisons soon followed. Showers would not become the norm until introduced in Clinton, New York in 1892.[16] Besides hygiene, essential to a healthy work force was food.

Feeding so many prisoners was an enormous task. In 1876, it was estimated that every day thirteen hundred pounds of meat, thirteen barrels of flour, fifty pounds of coffee, and thirty bushels of potatoes were consumed.[17] Not only feeding but the management of feeding was a critical task. One visitor remembered vividly when

> The whistle blew for dinner, and the men came marching from various parts of the yard in lock step, with the hand of the hinder man resting on the right shoulder of the one in front. As they passed to the floor where their cells are situated one of the waiter convicts held out a large pile of bread and the taker was allowed to make his own ration. He might take one piece or five, but whatever he took had either to be eaten or returned without being soiled. The returned bread is then laid out to dry, covered so as to protect it from flies, and every Thursday an immense bread pudding is made of which they eagerly partake. Beside the

> ration of bread one of meat and potatoes stewed together was given. As each one received his ration he hurried to his cell door and stood there awaiting the signal to enter.[18]

All the amenities—be they a workable and secure physical plant, some health care and wholesome food—were essential to maintaining a compliant and productive inmate. Prisoners had their own way at looking at things, further complicating the administrative skills of McClaughry.

NOTES

1. Much of this is taken from John Whiteside's The History of Joliet at http://suburbanchicagonews.com/hearldnews/history/chapters.
2. *Joliet Illustrated, 1897* [published by the *Joliet Daily Republican*] pp. 72-74.
3. Thomas Gregg, *History of Hancock County, Illinois,* p. 730.
4. David Wallace to Governor Albert Beveridge, August 10, 1874 in the Albert Beveridge Papers, Illinois State Archives.
5. Sanders, pp. 241-42.
6. Casper Butz to Governor John Palmer June 14, 15 and 20, 1872 in the John McAuley Palmer Papers, Illinois State Archives.
7. *Joliet Signal* March 25, 1879.
8. See Paul M. Angle, *Bloody Williamson: A Chapter in American Lawlessness* (Urbana, Il: University of Illinois Press, 1992).
9. Robert P. Howard, *Mostly Good and Competent Men: Illinois Governors, 1818-1988* (Springfield, Illinois: Illinois Issues, Sangamon State University and Illinois State Historical Society, 1988), pp. 157-61.
10. *Ibid.* , pp. 163-73
11. *Report of the Commissioners, 1877*, p.384.
12. *National Prison Association Proceedings, 1886*, pp. 47-48.
13. *Ibid,* 1875, p. 535.
14. *Ibid.,* 1877, pp. 382-83.
15. *Ibid.*, 1885, p. 5.
16. McKelvey, pp.180-81.
17. *Joliet Sun* January 13, 1876.
18. Huntingdon [Pa.] *Globe*, November 22, 1888.

Chapter Ten

The Prisoners

"the number of men here . . . being greater than in any prison."

INMATE CULTURE

When McClaughry assumed duty at Joliet there were 1,350 prisoners, 15 of whom were females. These women included Mollie Trussel, Thresa Sturlatta, Nellie Price, Mary Jane Brown, Minnie Daley, and "Midget" Miller.[1] Twenty-five percent of the total prison population came from Cook County and the Chicago area. One hundred and sixty five were "colored". Most (554) were in lock up for larceny. One hundred and seventy two were burglars and 179 were killers.[2] The youngest prisoner in the history of Joliet came in 1879. He was Dickey Bradshaw, a twelve-year old black boy who had killed a playmate for a nickel and had received a twenty-year sentence.[3] McClaughry would claim with some exaggeration that "the number of men here confined being greater than in any prison on this continent, if not in the world."[4] The numbers would increase over McClaughry's fifteen years at Joliet but the proportions remained the same.

No matter their demographics or crime, every prisoner had an interesting human story, but some were historic in nature and achieved nationwide notoriety. In November 1876, a plot was hatched in a Chicago tavern called The Hub.[5] Although it was not a crime, (there was no law on the books outlawing it yet) grave robbing had become increasingly common and annoying. Overly excited delinquents and aspiring medical students stole bodies for fun and education. The scheme at The Hub, though, was different: they wanted to steal the body of Abraham Lincoln. "Big Jim" Kinealy planned to hold the body for a $200,000 ransom and the release from Joliet of one of his friends, a master counterfeiter named Ben Boyd. Kinealy got Terrence Mullen, (owner of The Hub), John Hughes and Lewis Swegles, (pushers or passers of bogus money for the gang) to help plot the theft. None of the conspirators knew that Swegles was actually employed by Patrick D. Tyrrell, head of the Chicago District's Secret Service, who was trying to get Hughes on counterfeiting charges. When Hughes, Mullen, and Swegles left by train for Springfield, Tyrrell was on board with several detectives. Tyrrell brought along several Pinkerton detectives as well. The three broke into the monument easily and were carrying the casket out when the detectives closed in. A gun fight broke out and the two escaped to Chicago only to be arrested there a few days later. Lincoln was once again laid to rest but this time virtually encased in concrete. Since there was no law against grave robbery—that would come shortly—Hughes and Mullen were sent to Joliet for stealing a casket.[6] Though their sentence was short—only one year for casket stealing—they were immediate prison celebrities when they arrived in June, 1877. And when they arrived at Joliet they found a wide range of prisoners forming an inmate culture in which they were quickly incorporate.

Modern day anthropologist could profit from a study of this emerging prisoner culture of the nineteenth century American prison. Probably beginning earlier, but certainly evident now, new lingo developed. In a place that stripped people of their identities, inmates developed a long list of colorful alias. There was Stiff-necked Tom, Stuttering Bob, Memphis Bill, Pockmarked Frank, Antonio the Dago, Pretty Tom, The Spider, Lame Sam, Glass-Eyed Dick, Jew Jake, Frenchy, Little Dave, Bad Jimmie, Speckled Ed. Gopher Jim, Black Tom, Piano Charley, to name a few.[7] Besides names, a new language emerged. As prison gangs, called "flashmen," developed a new vernacular, "flash language," arose. Such convict cant was important to disguise communication from the guards. Pickpockets and sneak-thieves used it mostly but it trickled down to ordinary criminals. Such terms as "stall," "beef," "thug," "graft," "gun," "shadow," were common to all classes of criminals. A "night-worker" was a burglar or house-breaker. A "gopher-man" was a safe blower. A "knuck," "wire," "dip," or "tool" were names for a pickpocket. A "hoister" or "shop-lifter" stole from stores. A "moll-wire" was a pickpocket who targets women. To "nick a bloke" is to pick a pocket of a man. A "fence" was a receiver of stolen goods. The "hole" was the prison's punishment cell. "Climb racket" or "climber" is to climb porches to rob second story rooms. To be "settled" is to be convicted and sent to prison. "Grand Quay" or "Quod" or "stir" means the state prison. The "cooler" was the jail. A "stretch" meant one year in prison. "Fly copper" was a detective, while "flatty" was an ordinary officer. This was just a small sample of an extensive sub-culture language that had emerged in the late nineteenth century.[8]

Besides the marking off of an "us v. them" mentality, it was an attempt to befuddle the prison staff. McClaughry and his men had to learn a new language to better control the inmates.

Some inmates were really desperate people causing continual crises for the prison staff. Frank Rande had killed sixteen people, mostly law enforcement officers. He was a classic western desperado. While serving a life sentence, he attacked and nearly killed the deputy warden. Eventually, he hung himself.[9] Mollie Brown tried to escape but miscalculated the height of her building and fell almost to her death.[10] Mike Mooney stabbed his cell mate, John Anderson, thirty three times.[11] Joe Kinsley tried to escape but was trapped in some plumbing and died. His body was not discovered until the stench became terrible.[12] Frank Koch, a German barber, became despondent and sharpened his dinner knife to open up a vein in his leg; he was dead before anyone could come.[13] Pluck Whalen had been reprimanded by the foreman of the harness shop. Later Whalen got the foreman to come over to his work place to inspect his work. While scrutinizing the harnesses, Whalen attacked and nearly killed the foreman.[14] These furious inmates, many of whom certainly had the same qualities outside the walls, were driven to the edge by the day-to-day tedium of prison life.

Daily routine was well established and any disruption caused an institutional crisis. At 5:45 AM the wake up bell sounded. By 6:00 AM the guards had taken their rifles and mounted the sentry boxes. Then the shop guards—fifty of them—took their heavy canes, the only weapons allowed inside the walls, and opened the cells. The inmates then lock stepped into the yard and marched to the sewer openings to empty their "cell buckets." Then they shuffled to the "rations table" to pick up a quart of coffee and as much bread as they wanted and a pan of hash. Back to their cells they marched to eat their breakfast. At 6:45 AM bells rang summoning them to work.

The hardest labor was in the quarries; the easiest caning a chair seat. Keepers sat on high stools and watched every man in the shop. Talking was not allowed at the work station. Prisoners' eyes had to be riveted to their work. At noon they marched to dinner and had forty minutes to eat in their cells. Then back to work until supper. After evening meal each man stood before his cell door with his right hand clutching the bars and was counted. The count, an administrative device to keep track of all inmates, was an enormously important procedure. If in the entire population one inmate was missing—either due to escape or victimization by other inmates or miscounting—everything stopped for a recount. Guards gave the count on a slip of paper to the deputy warden who entered it in a daily count book. After the count, inmates were left alone to rest or read until the morning bell rang once again.[15] Either intended or unintended, the inmate was reduced to a number. They wore a number on their clothing and now they were reduced to another in the count. To be sure there was a policy of humiliation. But also it was a bureaucratic necessity as the prison population exploded.

Not even a decade old, the prison was already overcrowded. In 1876 the prison physician noted that, "common humanity towards those unfortunates incarcerated here, requires a prompt and immediate remedy of these evils. The remedy can only be found in an increase of cell capacity, even at the expense, if necessary, of building an additional cell house."[16] According to a report of the warden, things were no better twenty years later:

> What excuse the Great State of Illinois can offer for compelling the management of this Penitentiary to so deal with men who are required by law to serve sentences here, that they must eat, rest and sleep in quarters so contracted, so repellent, so utterly unfit for the purpose, that their very existence is a disgrace to the State that permits it.[17]

Indeed, life in Joliet was hard. One prison official later summed up the general "keeper's" attitude toward his charges: "A convict is like a rubber ball; he will stay as long as you press him down, but he flies up the instant the pressure is removed. He must feel the pressure all the time."[18] Inmate number 10,001 remembered his existence at Joliet and his coping strategies like this: "I thought of this upon one occasion and resolved to live a dual life during all the term of my imprisonment: to annihilate the mind and the soul in the workshop, to annihilate the physical self and its environments when in the cell."[19]

Other prisoners tried to find expression and identity by tattooing their bodies. For this reason, one prison official thought it an interesting sight to witness the disrobing of a gang of convicts in the bathroom:

> Now is the opportunity to observe the work that has been executed by various India-ink artists. On the white bodies of many of these criminals are pricked almost every design imaginable—some of the designs are finely executed, and are drawn in various color inks.[20]

Billy Forrester, one of the "best marked criminals in America," must have been some sort of patriot because he had a Goddess of Liberty on his right arm, an eagle and the stars and stripes on the same arm, an Indian queen seated on the back of a flying eagle on his left hip, a fully rigged ship on his chest, the coat of arms of the United States on his left arm, and bracelets of red and blue on his wrists. Perhaps the most popular tattoo at Joliet was that of a weeping willow tree and tombstone, with the words "In memory of my Mother."[21]

Others tried to find their identity in some dark humor in their situation. For example "Hawkshaw" saw through the pretentious nature of the Robber Baron era. If one stole

$1,000.000—it was called genius
100,000—shortage
50,000—litigation
25,000—insolvency
10,000—irregularity
5,000—defalcation
1,000—corruption
500—embezzlement
100—dishonesty
50—stealing
25—total depravity
one ham—war on society[22]

As Hawkshaw's insight suggests, during the Gilded Age society was conflicted over business practices. When were capitalists simply shrewd business men and when were they unethical, even criminal. "Robber Baron," the term used to describe the business classes of America, suggest a felonious connection. Of course, McClaughry was a child of the business world and would disagree with Hawkshaw. Very much like those businessmen who six days a week could exploit workers and consumers and then teach a Sunday school class on the Sabbath, McClaughry mixed his devilish duties with an angelic philosophy. He recognized the arduous conditions of prison life and was committed to making it more humane.[23] Prisoners still wore stripes and walked around in lock-step, a clear reminder of the Auburn system of an earlier generation. The night bucket remained a deplorable feature as well. It was not until 1899, in Maryland, that running water toilets, the "crapper," would become a feature.[24] Adequate ventilation was likewise a problem. It was not until the 1890s that another Illinois prison, Chester, would provide ducts to ventilate the interior. McClaughry believed that the prisoner got only one-third of the space and fresh air needed for good health, and that this led to the constant health crisis. Every year a few prisoners "went up the hill," or died, and were buried by the state on the prison grounds. McClaughry would declare that, "The destruction of the health or constitution of a convict, is far from being a part of the requirements of the law which imposes confinement and hard labor for a term of years."[25] Coal stoves and kerosene lamps provided not only most of the heat and light but also the pollution. McClaughry implemented steam heat, but candles continued to light America's prisons until Elmira introduced incandescent bulbs in 1892.[26]

In spite of McClaughry's efforts inmates complained about their lot at Joliet. At least one inmate, convict #4776, took other inmates, and us, on an excursion of the prisons of America with a long poem. This prison poet told his fellow inmates to:

Take your Medicine Like a Man
I'll show you lots of prisons that are worse
than Joliet.
You never heard the Auburn boys tell how
they shriek and groan
When they swing them on the "pulley," just
under "Copper John."
You never heard the Clinton men say how
they gasp and choke,
While standing underneath the beam they
call the shoulder "yoke."
You ought to hear the yells that make the
rafters ring
When they put the boys upon the boat that "paddles"
in Sing Sing.
You think you're walking, mate, in a hard and
thorny path
You ought to try Columbus and the icy "shower-
bath."
Come West to Kansas, if you want to see a fearful
kind of hole
Where out at Leavenworth the prisoners are put to
digging coal.
Go further West, to Canon City, and get some crook
to tell
Of "Sixteen-shooter Maggie," beside the sulphur-
well.
You ought to hear the story a forger told me,
Of "Dead Man's gulch," outside the wall of the pen
at Laramie.
You ask about San Quentin; now, mate, I can not
say,
I don't know many crooked men in California.
You ought to go to Baton Rouge, where the keepers
yell with glee
When some poor nigger gets a shock on the galvanic
battery.
If you think the officers at Joliet are tough and
mean,
You ought to see some "Tie camp" guards in Mississippi
I've seen.

Would you like to change our deputy for "Alabama
Jack?"
Cell-mate, you'd very soon wish you had the Captain
back.
I know men out of Chester, and often have heard
them tell
They don't like Deputy Starkweather, down there, a
bit too well,
Just ask some Chicago shop-mate to tell the little
tale
Of Bridewell-Keeper Felton and "thumb-string"
piggy Gale.
There are lots of convicts in the States would gladly
change you bet,
And finish their remaining "bits" in the Grand at
Joliet.[27]

Of course the inmate population of those prisons convict #4776 poetically described were males. Throughout America, and Joliet too, the main prisoners were men. But there were some female prisoners too. Out of the fifteen hundred prisoners at Joliet fifty were women. What might be called the "sisters keepers" movement—the distinct women's prison facility—would not flourish for another thirty years. Compared to males, the percentage of female prisoners in the United States had doubled in thirty years. In 1850 women represented 2.5 percent of the total prison population; in 1880 it was 4.6 percent. Between 1880 and 1890 the total number of women in prison went from 4,518 to 6,169.[28] Most of the female inmates had been sneak thieves or shop lifters. A small number were murderers, predominantly of their husbands and children. One woman, a Swiss immigrant, had tortured her son so that he became a cripple. The boy had been beaten repeatedly until his back was covered with sores. Then his hands had been held upon a hot stove burning off the flesh. Finally, he was strapped to the floor and left uncovered one freezing night so as to eventually lose both feet.[29] This "loving" mother would serve two years in Joliet.

The women's section was completely isolated from the male population. They spent all day sewing and darning socks. Largely because they were seen as nonviolent they slept in a dormitory rather than cells. Their uniforms were gowns made of blue and white gingham, "of a pattern popular for kitchen aprons among all classes of women." Each woman had three dresses, one saved for Sunday. Their life style in prison was one of forced domesticity.[30] Largely, women in prison were not dangerous, something that could not be said of the men.

Life in prison, for inmates and staff, was dangerous. Within months of McClaughry's arrival an incident occurred which reflected upon the character of the new warden and his relations with prisoners. It became part of McClaughry family legend, recounted probably with some exaggeration over and over again in later years. Allegedly, one day McClaughry was at his desk while most personnel were out to lunch. William Ritchie, a cop killer from a small town in Illinois, broke into the administrative offices carrying a long knife. Threatening McClaughry, he began his escape. The warden stalled for time and slowly reached for an army service revolver in his desk. Even when McClaughry got the drop on him, Ritchie would not back off because he feared the other prisoners' ridicule when they found out about the botched escape attempt. Fearing the prison culture more than the keepers, he would rather die than back down. McClaughry promised that no one would ever hear the story from his lips, a pledge he kept for over thirty years. Ritchie was astonished to meet a man with such courage and integrity and served the rest of his sentence as a model prisoner.[31]

On another occasion shortly after McClaughry arrived at Joliet, an escape plot was discovered. Apparently, up to 250 men were in on the scheme, which was to occur in the chapel. A sham fight was to bring the guards to the center of the room where they were to be killed. Women and children visiting and attending church services were to be used as shields against gun fire. A rush on the gates and a mass escape would then occur. McClaughry got wind of the plot and on the day of the planned escape when the inmates reached chapel they found the warden sitting in a cage high above the general seating. He held a repeater rifle pointed at the spot where the fight was to occur. Services were not held that day and instead a dozen ringleaders were arrested. In their pockets were found large stones and other prison-made weaponry.[32]

Such an incident indicates the state of affairs when McClaughry arrived. The new warden, as all before and after him, was being tested. In the previous ten to fifteen years before McClaughry arrived, prisoners often literally walked away from the prison. One observer believed that by 1890 several hundred prisoners who had escaped between 1860 and 1870 were still at large. But after McClaughry arrived escapes declined.

> Escapes? There have been very few of late years—and under the present state of perfect discipline there is no chance for mutinies or outbreaks, such as characterized the prison along in the early seventies. At that time there was no discipline, the convicts ran the prison to suit themselves. They worked when they felt like it, and pleased themselves as to when they should play, fight, turn on the guards or plot to get away.[33]

At first, in order to get some control, McClaughry divided the prison in to three parts. A high wall or stockade was built directly through the center of the prison yard. All the really tough and unruly inmates under heavy security were placed in what was called the north wing. To try to prevent the spread of their bad influence, they were also deliberately kept away from the newly arrived prisoners. After about four years McClaughry, always uneasy with the punitive messages sent out by the architecture, tore down the stockade. Besides such security oriented buildings, inmate compliance to the prison life could be eased in other ways. One way to deal with recalcitrant prisoners is to exhaust them. Besides sustaining the prison economically, work became critical in controlling the inmate.

WORK

When McClaughry first took over at Joliet, the contract work system was what sustained the prison, making it essentially "a vast manufacturing establishment."[34] Prison work was important to nineteenth-century prison officials and politicians, for they saw it as critical in the rehabilitation of the prisoner. Society considered that criminals had flaunted middle-class values of self-discipline, hard work, frugality, dependability, and having essential job skills. How better to prepare for respectable outside life than to drill inmates in those values inside prison? Of course such work was also seen as essential to the economic well being of the prison. Prison labor was the only source of revenue for the institution.[35] Morris Selz & Co., shoemakers from Chicago, was the largest employer at the prison throughout the 1870s and 80s. In 1871, 250 prisoners worked for sixty-five cents per day. Four years later the number had grown to 375. By 1887, 452 prisoners were making shoes. Over half of Selz's production force worked at Joliet.[36]

Such prison industry was dependent upon the national economy. In 1873 the nation underwent a general economic slump that slid into a depression. Many companies could not keep up their part of the bargain by supplying raw materials, so when he arrived, McClaughry was forced to cancel several contracts which meant idling inmates. Short & Brayton, for example, had contracted the prison to make harnesses and saddles but they became $6,735 in arrears. The contract was canceled and 40 inmates were out of work. Reed, Jones & Co., cigar makers, lost their contract as well. Stone cutters working for William Richardson also became idle.[37] It was the custom for these contracts to be made for five to eight years. Consequently a few contractors asked to lock up their convicts and pay for their labor though not working them because the company could not afford to buy raw materials.[38] In 1878, the stone department, employing over 200 inmates and the main anchor of the contract system at Joliet, was in trouble as the contractor went $8,000 in debt.[39] By 1880 things were better so that the prison was soon out of debt, but the institution still lived "from hand to mouth."[40] Within two years, however, improvement was so good that McClaughry predicted that the prison would be self-sustaining shortly.[41] His estimates suggested that between 1,400 and 1,500 inmates had to be under work contract to achieve this goal.[42]

The whole notion of prison-made products became an issue in the early 1880s. Some of a more radical persuasion saw convict labor more than a money-making proposition, it was a way to punish organized labor. For example, in 1877 26.4 percent of entering prisoners at Joliet were shoemakers. In 1880 that percentage went down to 10.8 percent. But on the outside only 3 percent of skilled workers in Chicago were shoemakers. In 1880 2 percent of the skilled workers in Chicago were cigar makers, but 8.7 percent of those in prison were cigar makers. Both occupations were heavily unionized. In addition, in 1880, 76 percent of the shoemakers and 63 percent of the cigar makers were foreign born.[43]America had always been xenophobic. Now this angst joined up with anti-union prejudices. The prison became a dumping ground for others besides criminals.

For some all organized labor was bad. But in reality there were two large labor ideologies. One represented all that was fearful for the business classes. These were the more radical groups led by the anarchists. Then there was a more conservative less threatening movement led by Samuel Gompers and the American Federation of Labor. Pressure from the more conservative movement mounted against prison-made products. The anti-prison labor movement began in Chicago in 1886 when the National Anti Contract Labor Association met. The year after McClaughry left Joliet, the Illinois State legislature forbade contract labor and moved to a state account system.[44] Under this system those things made in the prison by inmates had to be used only in other state institutions. Prison made products, especially if sold in open market and competing with those made by union labor, will remain a political issue for years. Restrictions on prison labor led to piled up inventories and idle inmates. Without work to fill their days prisoner discipline became even more important.

DISCIPLINE

Part of McClaughry's puritan character was the importance of self discipline. Criminals lacked self control, it had to be imposed upon them. Proper conduct could be rationalized by setting forth "rules for the government of convicts," he felt. A rule booklet came out in 1876 showing his penal philosophy. The foremost duty of a prisoner was obedience. As a throwback to earlier days, McClaughry required strict silence.[45] Such clear cut statements of expected behavior had an effect on the guards and other prison staff as well. By 1877 the Commissioners could report that, "The morale of the prison is excellent, and we think was never better. Dissensions and jealousies among its officers, keepers and guards, once so common and so detrimental to good discipline, have disappeared." This was largely due to McClaughry whom they called "our very competent and efficient warden."[46] Of course such silence—among inmates and guards alike—may have been muffled resentment.

Discipline would be a constant problem confronting McClaughry. The types of punishment common prior to his arrival increased rather than decreased disciplinary problems, punishments such as flogging and the "Cold Bath," which were quite common up to 1867. In the latter case a person was forced to soak in cold water for prolonged periods of time. It was replaced by "hydrotherapy" or cold water dunking. Often the dunk was prolonged enough to resemble drowning. This practice caused a problem in 1873 which in part initiated a shakeup bringing McClaughry into the prison.[47]

Solitary confinement took the place of flogging. In its early days, solitary confinement was accompanied with cuffing to the wall or carrying around the cell a fifty pound sand bag. McClaughry did away with both the cell cuffs and the sand bag treatment in 1874.[48] Minor infractions were handled by taking away the inmate's allowance of candles or tobacco. Some years later he would reflect:

> My idea of punishment is to restrict the man from further wrong doing without inflicting pain upon him or doing anything in the nature of retribution, but at the same time to grip him with a sufficiently firm hold to let him know that he is in the hands of the law.[49]

However, apparently McClaughry was not above some physical torture when he deemed it necessary. The more recalcitrant prisoners at Joliet, the noted reformer and superintendent of the Elmira Reformatory Zebulon Brockway revealed, were subjected to "fumes of burning turpentine—a ball of candle-wick saturated and ignited that produced a sense of suffocation."[50] Although McClaughry and Brockway were like minded as reformers, the tone of such revelations suggests some one-upmanship might have been going on. In many respects these two reformers were competing for top spot in the reform movement. And, indeed, as we will see later, McClaughry was a reformer. While his main concern at Joliet was the prisoner, organizing the physical and psychological environment of inmates in humane and disciplined ways, there was another key group to deal with, his subordinates.

NOTES

1. Wetmore, p. 46.
2. "Report of the Commissioners of the Penitentiary" in *Illinois Reports to the General Assembly, 1875,* Vol. 1, p. 537.
3. *Joliet Republican,* May 10, 1879.
4. *Ibid.*, p. 539.
5. See Thomas J. Craughwell's *Stealing Lincoln's Body* (Cambridge, Massachusetts: Harvard University Press, 2007).
6. See Bonnie Stahlman Speer's *The Great Abraham Lincoln Hijack* (Normon, OK.: Reliance Press, 1990.)
7. Wetmore, p. 154.
8. *Ibid.*, pp. 201-203.
9. Wetmore, pp. 108-09.
10. *Ibid.*, pp. 110-12.
11. *Ibid.*, pp. 131-32.
12. *Ibid.*, pp. 142-44.
13. *Joliet Sun* January 13, 1876.
14. *Joliet Republican.* October 4, 1879.
15. *Ibid.* pp. 30-34.
16. *Report, Illinois State Penitentiary*, 1876, p. 31.
17. *Ibid.*, 1898, p. 14.
18. Wetmore, p. 33.
19. *Ibid.*, p. 51.
20. *Ibid.*, p. 170.
21. *Ibid.*, pp. 170-171.
22. *Ibid.*, pp. 188.
23. *Ibid.* p. 538.
24. McKelvey, p. 181.
25. *Report of the Commissioners, 1877,* p. 381.
26. *Ibid.*, p,182.
27. Quoted in Wetmore, pp. 167-69.
28. L. Mara Dodge, " 'Her Life Has Been An Improper One': Women, Crime, and Prisons in Illinois, 1835-1933'' (unpublished dissertation at University of Illinois at Chicago, 1998), p. 150.
29. *Ibid.*, p. 45.
30. Wetmore, pp. 42-45.
31. Kansas City *Star*, May, 1913
32. This story was told by Rev. W. T. Meloy and it appeared in the Huntingdon, Pa. *Globe*, November 22, 1888.
33. Wetmore p. 90.
34. *Ibid.*, 1877, p. 373.
35. *Ibid.*, p. 374.
36. Margaret Dorsey Phelps, "Idle Outside, Over Worked Inside: The Political Economy of Prison Labor During the Depressions in Chicago, 1871-1897," Unpublished dissertation at University of Iowa, 1992, pp.217, 222.

37. *Ibid.*, pp. 376-77.
38. *Ibid.*, p 374.
39. *Ibid.*, 1879, p.3.
40. *Ibid.*, 1881, p.12.
41. *Ibid.*, 1885. p, 5.
42. *Ibid.*, 1889, p. 5.
43. Phelps, pp. 320-23.
44. "Biannual Message of Richard J. Oglesby, Governor of Illinois to 36th General Assembly, January 9, 1889", in *Illinois Reports to the General Assembly 1889,* vol. 1 p. 7.
45. 1. The first duty is *obedience* to all rules and regulations and the orders of the officer under whose charge you may be placed.

2. You must observe strict silence while at your work or marching. No conversation allowed except by permission of the officer in charge. In the evening in your cell, you are permitted to converse in a low tone with your cell mate, until the 9 o'clock bell rings, but conversation with prisoners in adjoining cells is strictly forbidden.

3. You must not speak to any visitor, or give to, or receive from a visitor, anything except by permission of the warden or deputy. You must not gaze at visitors or strangers passing through the prison, but at all times during working hours, give your undivided attention to your work. You are expected to apply yourself faithfully and diligently to whatever labor you are assigned; and after reasonable teaching, to perform the same amount of labor as would be required of you outside.

4. At the ringing of the morning bell you must turn out, dress, make up your bed neatly, and be ready for marching out. At the signal, open the door, step out and close the same—holding on until the bar is closed—and stand erect until ordered to march.

5. At every signal to 'fall in' for marching, you must take your place in the line promptly, march lock-step, with your right hand upon the shoulder of the man in advance, incline your face toward the officer, attend to and promptly obey his orders. In passing through the yard with other convicts, you must walk in file, never abreast.

6. On returning to cell house, stand at cell with your right hand on the door. At the signal, open the door, step in, close the same, *without slamming*, keep it firmly closed until the second signal is given and the bar thrown, and remain standing with your hand upon the door until the count is made. In case of miscount, resume your position at the door until the count is correct.

7. You must not leave the line or your place of employment without permission. If sick or unable to work, make it known to the officer in charge and act as he may direct.

8. You must keep your cell and furniture in good order. No marking, scratching the walls, or spitting on the floor will be allowed. You must not make any alteration in your clothing or cell furniture. If your clothing needs repair, report the fact to your cell keeper.

9. At the ringing of the bell at 9 o'clock P.M., you must put out your light, undress and retire. If you have occasion to call the night officer give the signal by rapping on your cell door.

10. You must not carry knives, tools of any kind, pencils, paper, or any material whatever, from your shop to your cell, without permission in writing, of the warden

or deputy. Finding such things in your possession will be considered proof that you have disobeyed this rule. Writing notes to other convicts, or carrying notes from one convict to another is strictly forbidden.

11. You must approach an officer in a respectful manner— always touching your cap or forehead before speaking. You must confine your conversation with him strictly to the business at hand. You must not address an officer on matters outside the prison. Insolence in any form, to an officer, foreman, or even another convict, will not be tolerated.

12. On entering the warden's house, or the office of the commissioners, warden or deputy, you must remove your cap, unless your duties are such that you have special permission to remain covered.

13. You are required to attend religious services on Sunday, unless sick or excused by the warden or deputy. In chapel, you must sit with arms folded, and silence must be observed. No reading will be allowed. Strict attention must be given to the service. Spitting upon the floor, shuffling of the feet or any unnecessary noise is strictly forbidden.

14. You are required to bathe once a week in summer, and once in two weeks in winter, unless excused by the physician, warden or deputy.

15. On entering the prison you will receive four tickets which will entitle you—so long as you obey strictly the foregoing rules—to the following privileges, viz.:

1. One ration of tobacco each week.
2. One ration of candles each week.
3. Permission to write once in five weeks.
4. Permission to see friends once in eight weeks.

You are permitted to receive such weekly papers as the warden may approve. In case of special letters, written permission must be obtained from the warden or deputy. All letters written or received,must first be examined at the office, under the direction of the warden, before being sent or delivered.

All the above privileges depend upon your good behavior, and you will be deprived of one or all of them for bad conduct. The use of library books depends upon the care you take to keep them scrupulously neat and clean.

16. This card must be preserved in good condition. If you deface, alter or injure it, you will be immediately reported and severely punished.

(signed) R.W. McClaughry

46. *Ibid.*, 1877, p. 393.

47. Sanders, p. 311-12.

48. *Ibid.*, p. 313.

49. "The Warden's Story: Recollections by Robert McClaughry" *Kansas City Star*, May 11, 1913.

50. Zebulon R. Brockway, *Fifty Years of Prison Service* (New York: Charities Publications, 1912), p. 190.

Chapter Eleven

Prison Workers

"... almost as confined as are the prisoners."

ADMINISTRATIVE SUBORDINATES

Managing a nineteenth-century prison was complex and multi-layered. First, there was the administrative corps, the warden and various assistants. That there had been three wardens in the two years prior to McClaughry's arrival at Joliet, indicates the precarious position McClaughry was entering. This was a profession in embryo. No training schools for such jobs existed and—as we will see in a subsequent chapter—a professional association was only in its infancy. Of course, there had been wardens before in the nearly 50 years since the creation of the penitentiary system. But those wardens then—and many still in the period under consideration—were political hacks or religious/charitable people. A major part of McClaughry's career would be about creating the professional wardenship. In doing so he would become very active outside Illinois.

In some respects such visibility abroad blurred his position at home. On one hand, he was becoming so famous in warden circles that it would be unwise for a so-minded governor to dismiss him. By the end of his tenure at Joliet, McClaughry was arguably one of the most famous wardens in America. If politicians did tinker with his position, he knew there would be numerous colleagues throughout the United States ready to offer him alternative jobs. On the other hand, since he was one of the most sought after wardens, thoroughly mixed up in the national criminal justice scene, he was in real danger of becoming lax in taking care of his own backyard, leaving prison subordinates to go their own way.

Of course McClaughry was a product of his times. In some respects he had vision, in other ways he was stumbling throughout the century little better than other prison administrators. This was especially true when it came to nepotism. McClaughry put a senile uncle in charge of the prison library; on his death, the memorial plaque placed on the library wall read:

> At the earnest request of a large number of prisoners, this tablet is placed here to perpetuate the memory of one whose constant aid and unwearied kindness to them gave him the well deserved title of The Prisoner's Friend.[1]

Likewise, Robert McClaughry's sons would begin career paths based upon their father's positions and prestige. Matthew Wilson McClaughry was born in St Louis in 1871, amidst his father tumultuous and failing business career. His education would follow his father's career moves. At first, he was educated at the Joliet schools. Later, after his father moved to the reformatory in Pennsylvania, he attended Dickinson College at Carlisle, Pennsylvania, and then, following another family move, the University School in Chicago. In the meantime, in1886, at the age of 15, he started working at the Joliet prison eventually taking over the criminal identification process called the Bertillon System at the prison.

Robert's eldest son, Charles, likewise worked at various prison jobs under his father. Born in Carthage, Illinois, in April 1863, Charles was educated in St. Louis and Monmouth schools. After graduating from Knox College at Galesburg in 1885 he immediately became the chief engineer at the Joliet prison. Later he would be assistant superintendent at the Allegheny County Workhouse at Hoboken, Pennsylvania; Deputy Superintendent of the Chicago House of Correction, Deputy Warden of the Indiana State Prison at Michigan City; Warden of the Wisconsin State Prison at Waupon; Deputy Warden of the U.S. Penitentiary at Atlanta; and Superintendent of the Missouri Training School for Boys at Boonville. He would become the Warden of the Men's Reformatory in Anamosa, Iowa, in 1912, and in 1918 Warden of the Connecticut State Prison at Wethersfield, before ending his career as Warden of the District of Columbia Workhouse. Another son, Arthur, became a broker in Chicago. A daughter, Emma, would marry a military man, James Buchanan Henry, and move to San Antonio, Texas.

Yet it was not only his sons that he nurtured. McClaughry had an eye for talent in general and brought along many of his subordinates. Take Moses Luke, for example. Luke, a rural farm boy from central Illinois served in the 17th Illinois Cavalry under General, and then Governor, John Beveridge, guarding POWs in Alton. In 1877 he became a guard at Joliet and within a year became captain of the night watch. In 1878 he was made receiving and discharge officer. Luke became the first officer in America to handle the instruments for taking Bertillon measurements for criminal identification. He become the assistant deputy warden and eventually followed McClaughry to Pontiac.[2]

Some of Moses Luke's subordinates succeeded him at the prison. Albert Garvin had been connected to the prison for several years as guard keeper. When the deputy warden, Meyhew, was forced to resign, Garvin became McClaughry's deputy. When the Major left, Garvin was appointed Warden.

Yet at times McClaughry was over protective of his executive staff. Take Benjamin Mayhew for example. Mayhew, born in Dennyville, Maine in 1822, had been a guard at Charlestown [Mass.] Penitentiary for thirteen years. He came to Joliet in 1869 working his way up from guard to deputy warden. He had been deputy warden earlier under Elmer Washburn. When Washburn was fired Mayhew was kept but the Commissioners understood he had to be "properly controlled."[3] Because Mayhew had proved himself a trusted subordinate, McClaughry helped him move up the professional ladder with a wardenship in Indiana State Penitentiary at Michigan City. Politics there forced Mayhew's resignation and he returned to Joliet as deputy warden again. The solitary cell death problems, to be discussed later, were laid at his door and tarnished Mayhew's career. Certainly he was facing termination when he died suddenly and unexpectedly of "consumption" at the age of 57.[4]

TREATMENT STAFF

In addition to the prison management personnel, there were also what were known as treatment people, such as doctors, chaplains, and work supervisors. During McClaughry's administration there was one chaplain and one doctor. Owing to the many religious origins of incarceration, chaplains were quickly on the prison grounds. It was believed that if any change of heart was to occur it had to come from the soul of the inmate. Many of our early accounts of any prison come from the writings of chaplains. Certainly, some inmates "found Jesus" in prison and went on to productive lives. But many played the "con-game" and simply acted religious when it was to their advantage. Any interpretation of their sincerity was left in the hands of the chaplain. For their part a chaplain's sincerity (or not), as had been the case during the Civil War, was quite understood by the inmates.

Large numbers of people living in such unhealthy environments demanded the presence of a doctor. Medical science was limited, though there had been a post Civil War bump in medical knowledge. Just as many prisoners pretended religion, many also tried to con the doctor to get out of work. Unlike the chaplain who was at the prison full time, doctors at first showed up only periodically at the gates. Before long, however, they became a regular fixture.

Depending upon one's perspectives, these treatment personnel were either essential or a liability. On one hand they were there to care for the soul and body of the inmates. On the other hand they might be the most overworked and most easily duped of the personnel. The number of prisoners feigning illness each day stretched the energy and resources of medical people. Not surprisingly, these doctors would be some of the first to adopt new criminological ideas in the late 1880s, regarding their inmate populations with "scientific" eyes as born criminals. Assorted others—master machinists, hospital stewards, stewards of the warden's house, wagon masters, storekeepers, and janitors—filled out this level of subordinates. Yet those most closely associated with the prisoners were the guards.

GUARDS

Like the prisoners a guard culture became evident in nineteen century prisons too. Due to the political "spoils system" the job of guarding prisoners was always precarious. Occasionally, at the expense of their jobs, some conflicts between the guard corps and wardens at Joliet arose earlier. For example, in 1869, forty-two guards went to the commissioners complaining that the warden was "tyrannical" and required duties and discipline guards considered to be "outrageous." Many guards refused to go to work, forcing the inmates to be in their cells for twenty-four hour periods. Twenty-six "good guards" remained but the rest walked out. The commissioners stood behind the warden, and denounced "the 'strikers' [as] the worst element of our guarding force, and we think their leaving is 'good riddance.'"[5] There place was quickly filled by more compliant officers.

By 1870, the guard corps had been divided into two categories. First-class guards were those who were in the shops, at the gate, in the cell houses, posted at the warden's house, and mingling in the yard. Their pay was thirty-five dollars per month for the first six months. That thirty-five dollars in 1870 had the purchasing power of about $500 in today's dollars.[6] It was raised to forty dollars per month for the second six months; forty-five dollars for the third six months and fifty dollars thereafter. The second-class guards were posted on the walls, front gates and at the quarry. They were paid twenty-five dollars per month for the first six months and thirty dollars per month thereafter.[7] By some comparison, the highest paid janitor at the local public school made fifty dollars per month, the lowest-paid teacher in the Joliet schools thirty dollars.[8]

According to City Directories, in 1873, two years before McClaughry arrived, there were twenty-seven guards and twenty-nine "keepers." for a total of fifty-six. That latter category denotes those who were a step up from ordinary guards and probably were a remnant of the first-class category of a few years earlier. In 1875, when McClaughry was in office and older categories were reestablished, there were forty-one first-class guards (the designation keeper had been dropped) and fourteen second class, for a total of fifty-five. Only fifteen of the 1873 pre-McClaughry group were still on duty. Around 70 percent of the old guard force had disappeared, apparently the result of a political blood bath. This meant several things for McClaughry: First, he had fresh people with no previous attachments who could consequently be tied more closely to him. Second, it meant he had rookies, inexperienced people who had to learn the job on the job. Since there was no official training school this meant that the fifteen carry-overs were important in transferring a guard culture to the new men. Third, it also meant that these pre-McClaughry guards had their own "keeper culture" and thought they knew best how to do things. Their occupational memories extended to before McClaughry's arrival and changes in policy would typically cause some foot dragging among them. For example, one guard—Isaac Park—was already entrenched at Joliet when McClaughry arrived. He was caught sleeping on his post. Several other problems against "good order" were charged against him. McClaughry asked him to leave but allowed some face saving by accepting his resignation. This tension or adjustment, between old guards and the new warden was, as we will see, a dangerous situation.[9]

From his largely removed perch McClaughry could be both magnanimous and condescending. Guards, however, saw the prisoners, up close and personal, day-in and day-out. The prisoner/guard ratio, with around one officer per nineteen inmates, compared to modern times, was reasonable.[10] Chances for rehabilitation and/ or resentment most probably were ignited by prisoner/ guard relationships. Noting the variety of con games, prisoner posturing to gain favor or power over the guard, gave rise to an attitude of suspicion. During the day, when inmates were in the shops, guards would go into the cells and search for illegal goods and signs of escape plans. The doors were the point of attack and compromise favored by most prisoners, who would cut or saw part way through the bars, then use moist bread or soap to disguise the cut, leaving the final break through until the night of escape. One longtime observer recounted how guards checked for work on the doors by listening for a sound signature:

> The cell-house keeper strikes a blow with a hammer upon each door, and if all is right the result will be a clear, sharp, ringing sound—and will show that the

> doors have not been tampered with; but if the blow brings forth a dull, dead sound the watchful guard notes it at once and hunts for the cause.[11]

One guard, Jack Allen, in the following poem tells the guard's side of the story and also reveals the ingenuity of prisoners when it came to "The Convict's Telephone," or how the wicked convicts bother the guard. The poem also suggests the "institutional crisis" that any new technology introduced:

> If you'll listen to my tale, my troubles I'll relate,
> I am a prisoner officer, in the service of the state,
> To guard convicted felons doing penance in the
> pen.
> The cell-house is my charge, and a gang of
> basement men.
> Now, when I first came to this place, the men would
> read at night
> Their books and papers and the like, in their cells
> by candle light.
> On Sundays on the galleries, the guards went round
> to see
> That each man got his "tallow dips," and never
> bothered me.
> But when the news was told to me that the State
> would put in gas,
> I little dreamt the trouble that would shortly come
> to pass.
> You see, the pipes were first put in, and ran from
> tier to tier,
> Then in the cells and galleries strange noises I
> would hear.
> I puzzled long to understand, until the truth was
> known
> That the tricky convicts had invented a gas-pipe
> telephone.
> You know the law on talking, so it's no use to tell
> That it's against the rules to chin and talk from cell
> to cell.
> But these sly dogs, instead of talking through the
> iron door,
> Would get up to the gas-pipe and through it would
> roar.
> Of course I tried to catch them, but that was
> mighty hard.

For, along the pipe a warning ran, "Look out!
here comes the guard!"
But one day, climbing on the tier from the gallery
down below,
I caught a convict "dead to rights," just as he
bawled "hello!"
You bet I horsed that convict out, and led him down
the hall,
And stood him underneath the stairs, with his nose
against the wall.
No doubt, that rascal thought his "hello!" very
queer and droll,
But he got a chance to halloa in a different kind
of "hole."
Now, when the gas was ready, and the burners were
put in,
Of course that put a stop to the telephone din.
I thought that then, at least, my troubles would be
o'er.
By Jove! The gas was worse than I had ever
known before.
For every day when I went round (according to the
law)
Examining the iron doors for marks of file or saw,
In every cell I came to there was a slate upon the
bed.
I'd pick it up and read it, and this is what it said:
"Oh, cell-house guard! the gas won't burn," or else
"The burner's gone."
The gas is a bigger nuisance than the gas-pipe
telephone;
But when the day is o'er, I go up the warden's stair,
And rush into the chaplain's room and kneel me
down in prayer.
I then beseech forgiveness for the wickedness I've
shown
And for the curses that I've cast at the convicts'
telephone.
When the evening shades draw nigh, and the
chaplain by me stands
And says the benediction, and stretches out his
hands,
I mingle with the mourners that stand around the
throne,

> And pray for the wicked convicts and their gas pipe
> telephone.[12]

Not all guards were as thoughtful or literate as Jack Allen. Most were working class men thankful for any job in these economic topsy-turvy times of late nineteenth century. When times got rough in the state capital layoffs and salary cuts were likely, In 1876, for example, there was a 20 percent reduction of salaries for the guards. The *Joliet Republican*, an anti penitentiary newspaper, claimed the prison was "on the ragged edge." Guard life was hard, it reported. The guard

> is almost as confined as are the prisoners, although in a different manner and for a different purpose. Many bought houses in the city paying half their salary a month for it. This leaves them with $16 to $20 per month to support families.
>
> The feeling among the employes [sic.] is one of suppressed indignation, but they are obliged to submit. If they don't like it, they have the privilege of resigning and seeking employment elsewhere, and this, in the circumstances in which some of them find themselves, is not an easy matter. Half a loaf, in these times, is better than idleness, and if they cannot get what they should have, they must be satisfied with whatever is allowed them.[13]

In many ways the guard was "as confined as . . . the prisoners." Fear that their off duty behavior would impact work day performance, the guards were watched closely. Joliet was a small enough community that guards could not avoid being watched. The *Joliet Sun* had a reporter/informant, who called himself "Capacity" (because he had held every job in the prison except warden), posted weekly "prison news." One keeper, H. Wolfer, complained over a report that he had broken the Sabbath by playing baseball. He announced to "Capacity" that the story was a lie.[14] This prompted "Capacity" to state:

> Much depends on the character of guards and officers in successfully applying means most conducive to general results of good [behavior]in prison. The class of guards and keepers now at the prison is much higher in every respect than in former years. As a class they are moral, sober, intelligent and industrious. In fact, the prison, in every particular, [sic.]it is gratifying to notice, is improving rapidly, an effect caused by the fact that its authorities are deeply and earnestly interested in applying the best methods for successful management.[15]

Most likely "Capacity" was Benjamin Mayhew. His correspondence to the newspaper suddenly came to an end coinciding with his departure for Indiana and another "informant" appeared in the paper.

Mayhew's leaving was orchestrated by McClaughry. Either to help his favorites or remove troublesome characters, the Major could encourage them to leave. Like any administrator of a large organization, however, McClaughry did not always control his subordinates. Since he was so busy building the profession outside his particular prison, the opportunity for employee misconduct at home in Joliet was great. Furthermore, as is true with most leaders, he was always tempted to make unseemly events go away or at least protect himself from being caught up in them and brought down. An example of this came to light in 1878 when one inmate, Gus Reid, died in solitary confinement due to a beating by officer Stephen Reed. The guard had been at Joliet for eight years; he was one of the few holdovers from pre-McClaughry days. An investigation resulted that shed light on punishment places, processes, and personnel under McClaughry.

What the investigation found was that in spite of reforms put in place by McClaughry, there remained some harsh punishments at Joliet. The solitary cells—those prisons within the prison–were still heavily used. The typical solitary cell was twelve to fourteen feet long, seven to eight feet wide, and ten to twelve feet high, and of course isolated the inmate from the general population. Solitary was isolated from central offices too; much could occur there without the warden knowing. The deputy warden had his office in the building housing the solitary unit but at a considerable distance from the warden's office. Each cell in solitary had two doors. The outside door was solid hard wood. Ten inches inside the outer door was another one but it was grated. Therefore a guard could open the outer door and confront the prisoner and still be protected from close contact.

For those who were troublesome in solitary—making excessive noise, not keeping themselves clean, attacking guards—there were additional punishments, such as cuffing the inmate to the door using a device called a "Bull ring," thus forcing the person to stand for several hours. Officially, this form of torture had been abandoned by McClaughry when he arrived. But it was clear that the practice continued in these isolated cells. Generally, there were two such rings on each door, and which one was used depended on the individual prisoner's height. One guard testified that, "I try to not put a man's hands higher than his chin," because the pain would be excruciating and possibly lethal. John Brown was one such prisoner who was still cuffed. Brown had assaulted his work foreman, nearly killing him, and had then he assaulted his guard. He was a big strong man, like a "wild bull" it was said, and it took three men to hold and subdue him. Brown was cuffed at his door for two days and two nights. He was let down three times a day— once in the morning, again at noon, and finally at night. But when released from solitary he caused such a commotion that a platoon of officers was necessary to bring him under control.

There were other brutal punishments. Prisoners making excessive noise in solitary were gagged. Controlling noise was very important to prison officials;

McClaughry deemed silence as most essential in the matter of discipline. "If noises were permitted on the cell houses the men would take advantage of the confusion thereby created to work up their plans for escape," he claimed. E.A. Beaty, Keeper of the north cell house, felt there to be no more important thing than controlling noise and that there was no better device than the gag. Here is how the gag was explained in an investigation:

> The gag is about 3/4 of an inch thick, and about 4 1/2 inches long. The strap is twenty inches long and half an inch wide, and there is a buckle in the long strap about four inches from the gag. The gag is placed in the man's mouth, and the strap is passed around the back part of his neck through the ring in one end of the gag, and through the buckle.

One prisoner, Michael Ryan, had been gagged in just this way in November 1877. He passed out and extraordinary effort was used to revive him. He did come back for a short time but after he was placed in his cell he died. Guards in the solitary unit became more hesitant to use the gag after that.

Whipping, or "strapping, "as it was called then, was another disciplinary tool. Pants were pulled down and shirt pushed up to expose the prisoner to the strap. Frequently the prison doctor's prescription was "strap him five or six or seven or eight times a day." The strap was two feet long and one inch wide. Fastened to a sixteen-inch long wooden handle, it was stored in a bucket of water to stay pliable. Sometimes the wooden stick was used to strike the head of the inmate. Thomas Carroll died of head injuries due to such a beating. Stephen Reed, the guard who would later be investigated for other excessive uses of force, whipped another inmate named Thomas Harris six times a day for keeping his cell filthy and dirtying his face with his own feces. Dr. Heise told Reed to continue to beat Harris if necessary. According to the doctor this was a "test case" to see if Harris was truly insane. Reed claimed that the deputy warden had ordered it and said that, "I don't care a damn whether he comes out head first or feet first." Reed testified:

> I don't think I ever struck him higher than the shoulder blades. One day he ducked his head down, and I struck him by accident on the head, I struck him most of the time on the legs above the knee, and on his rump and back.

When McClaughry heard that such strapping was so pervasive in solitary he was surprised:

> I wish to say in relation to the strapping that I never heard and never dreamed until it came out in Mr. Reeds [sic] testimony that a strap or whip of any kind had been used on any convict in this prison under any circumstances during my term as warden.

Gus Reid was considered to be the most troublesome person in Joliet. He had been put into solitary for fighting in his cell. While in solitary Reid was defiant and troublesome being noisy and refusing to change into clean clothes. He had been strapped on numerous occasions but to no avail. On this occasion, May 7th, 1878, he was gagged. But the gag slipped off and the guard, Reed, beat him. Gus Reid died shortly after, prompting an investigation.

The Board of Commissioners, with McClaughry sitting in, conducted the inquiry. The commissioners, all political appointees, had to deflect any possible criticism by conducting an investigation. McClaughry, significantly away on prison business at the time of the incident, needed to be deeply involved so as to free himself from any culpability. The incident also shows the guard culture on several levels. Obviously, guards warred on inmates. But now treatment and administrative people were implicated too. On one hand, those involved claimed they were under orders, that their superiors had ordered the particular punishments. In addition, the guards showed that they had considerable discretion in deciding the number of "stripes" given and how often they beat a person. Furthermore, the inquiry revealed cover ups, that fellow guards were reluctant to expose others and their practices.

There was another layer, a more important one of complicity. The deputy warden, Benjamin Mayhew, seemed deeply involved. Mayhew's immediate predecessor had been James Hall. As deputy warden Hall was signing punishment orders and not reporting them to McClaughry. Tension developed between warden and his deputy. McClaughry explained that "Captain Hall felt that I was interfering with his prerogative. He thought he ought to manage the punishments himself." The deputy warden's office was in the same building as the solitary cells, far from central administration. It was a penal satrap unto itself. Hall was quickly replaced by Mayhew. Officer Reed claimed that Mayhew had ordered the beating. In his own defense Meyhew said that the order to whip came from headquarters, by implication the warden's office.

Another group of men involved were the doctors and medical orderlies. Dr. Heise had been in service for several years. The main problem from the doctor's point of view was insanity among prisoners—or at least faked insanity. What were the manifestations of this insanity? First, there was the problem of aggressive behavior. Most of those who ended up in solitary were there due to fighting with other prisoners or attacking the guards. Second, there was poor personal hygiene. Numerous inmates refused to wash themselves or to change their clothes. Yet they tended to deteriorate even more once placed in solitary and away from any prisoner peer pressure. Now their lack of hygiene became a defiant cause. Third, there was bizarre behavior. Perhaps an inmate would begin to howl and act like a caged animal. The problem was that these medical people did not know if that inmate was truly insane. Their treatment, therefore, was a test of sanity. Such a problem in the past several years had prompted McClaughry to advocate for a place for the criminally insane. Interestingly enough, as the Reed/Reid beating was going on, McClaughry was away helping design an asylum for the criminally insane.

As the inquiry progressed, it transpired that Reed had beaten inmates before who had acted crazy. It became apparent that the warden, despite all of his talk of reform, was far removed from his subordinates. Although ultimately his administration could be questioned for allowing this to happen, he was more a part of the investigation than being investigated. On numerous occasions he asked questions of the witnesses, always trying to see how extensive these beating practices were. But those questions were also an attempt to exonerate himself:

> Having the fiscal affairs as well as the disciplining affairs of the Institution upon me, I am compelled to leave the men while in punishment the greater part of the time to the supervision of the deputy. He is my executive officer in that respect. It is entirely possible for the deputy warden to keep a man in severe punishment a good many hours without my knowing it.

The Major was busy, traveling extensively across the state and even the nation, but such quotes are self serving. Ultimately, he must be held accountable for the actions of his subordinates. Still, views about appropriate punishment differed up and down the administrative ladder. Unlike many of his staff McClaughry brought to prison management a mixture of puritan sternness and evangelical humaneness. McClaughry categorized punishments into two areas: minor crimes resulted in taking away certain privileges such as tobacco or candles. More serious problems meant being sent to solitary where reduction of diet, chaining to the cell door, and gagging took place. The more severe punishments that could end in death supposedly were not allowed. Doctor Heise testified to McClaughry's attempts to regulate the severity of punishments. But isolated away in the solitary cells prison personnel could go too far. Several layers of administrative and treatment people knew of such goings on. Deputy warden Benjamin Mayhew knew. The accused, Stephen A. Reed, claimed that he "had orders from the Deputy Warden to strap the man [Reid], or at least to strap him when he disturbed the solitary—to strap him when he made a noise." So did doctors C. T. Dripps and Heise. Captain Isaac Sawyer, former captain of the night watch, another pre-McClaughry guard, apparently had been demoted because in the investigation records he was identified as a guard. While he had been connected to the solitary unit, up to forty inmates had come there. At the conclusion of the investigation, Mayhew conveniently died before he could be fired. Guard Reed was dismissed and the tempest subsided. But the Reid/Reed incident was more than example of brutality; it was a crisis in management that reflected badly on McClaughry.

As the Reed incident indicates, guards—for good or ill—were key to any well-run prison and even more so to one that hoped to reform the inmates. The guard had the closest and most persistent contact with the prisoners. Unfortunately, guards were picked for their politics and not their professionalism. After years of dealing with guards and how their political connections often got them their jobs, McClaughry, speaking to an assemblage of prison administrators, highlighted the importance of the guard:

> They who are the hands, eyes, ears and mouth of the reformatory prison work, must be attracted to and retained in the service, because of natural taste for and adaptation to this line of work, and must cease to be mere party followers who are receiving pay for former political or other service. The officers, from the highest to the lowest, should be models on which the reformation of the prisoner is attempted. The habit of imitation is largely responsible for the making of criminals and can be largely used for their betterment . . . .
>
> Enlistment in prison service should, in some respects, resemble enlistment in military service–for definite periods, under definite requirements, with re-enlistment, veterans service pay, and with honorable retirement on certain conditions of age and physical disability. The service should be honorable, and appointees should always be men who will honor the service.
>
> The way to obtain intelligent officers and teachers is to obtain the recognition of prison work as a profession of skilled intelligence, and to make intelligence and fitness the requirements necessary to appointment as a prison officer.[16]

Increasingly, McClaughry was becoming a reformer—not just of the inmates, but also an agent for change of the system as a whole. In this regard, he was not all that different from those who created the penitentiary in the first place. This first generation of reformers believed in the power of institutions, their architecture and regimen, in transforming human behavior. So for him Joliet was something of an experimental lab., a place to create and try out elements of reform.

NOTES

1. This placard is on display at the Joliet Area History Museum, Joliet, Illinois. The author is indebted to the staff of the museum for calling his attention to the artifact.
2. *Joliet Illustrated, 1897*, p. 74.
3. Casper Butz to Governor John McAuley Palmer June 16, 1872, in John McAuley Palmer Papers, in Illinois State Archives.

4. *Joliet Republican* August 16, 1879.

5. Andrew Shuman to Governor Palmer, November 12, 1869 and Warden Perkins to Governor Palmer November 13, 1869 in John McAuley Palmer Papers, Illinois State Archives.

6. For this calculation see John J. McCusker, "Comparing the Purchase Power of Money in the US (or Colonies) from 1650 to any other year including the Present" Economic History Series, 2004. URL http://WWW.eh.net/hmit/ppowerusd/

7. "Proclamation" by Warden George Perkins, June 23, 1870 in the John McAuley Palmer papers, Illinois State Archives.

8. *Joliet Signal*, May 19, 1874.

9. This analysis was carried out by studying the City Directories of Joliet for 1873 and 1875 at the Joliet Public Library.

10. See the *Joliet Sun*, September 30, 1875 for the numbers. For modern-day rations, which are 40 prisoners to one officer, see George Cole and Todd Clear, *American Corrections* 3rd edition (Belmont, CA, Wadsworth, 1994), p. 327.

11. Wetmore, p. 23.

12. *Ibid.*, pp. 218-20.

13. *Joliet Republican* April 12, 1876

14. *Joliet Sun*, October 21, 1875.

15. *Ibid,* December 2, 1875.

16. *National Prison Association, 1898*, pp. 90-91.

Chapter Twelve

McClaughry and Reform

"We believe that the prisons may become reformatory institutions."

McClaughry's Civil War experiences with vast assemblies of men–both common soldiers and POWs–together with his religious convictions, shaped his notions of human behavior and how best to redeem the fallen. At first he still subscribed to the old asylum ideology forged in the 1820s and 1830s, an ideology in keeping with his puritan heritage. This ideology placed emphasis upon silence and solitude (the Pennsylvania model) or control of large groups working and marching in silence (the Auburn model). Such silence, it was felt, would keep old time criminals from educating the newer ones. It would also allow people time to meditate upon their wrongdoings and to reform themselves. Coming from a Scotch-Irish background, he was endowed with ideals of the Protestant Ethic. Individual responsibility, hard work, and perfectibility of the soul were implicit in his character. His war experiences were crucial in shifting his belief structure. Living and fighting with and commanding groups of men in chaotic situations gave him a sense of the good and the bad qualities of humans.

In addition, he was slowly becoming an advocate of the newly developing "reformatory ideology," which emerged after the Civil War with the work of Zebulon Brockway and a declaration of principles made at gathering of reformers in 1870 called the Cincinnati Congress. Brockway had worked at the Detroit House of Correction from 1862 to 1872. While there he became angered over the prevailing lock-up system of the city and his inability to stimulate behavioral change in the inmates. The Cincinnati conference of the National Congress of Penitentiaries and Reformatories (the real beginning of the National Prison Association) declared a set of principles which would guide penologists for several generations.

We have already seen that one of the more important rehabilitative regimes implicit in the old asylum movement was silence and solitude. Of course, in the Pennsylvania model this was carried to extremes by keeping everyone utterly separate. More realistically, the Auburn model allowed some silent congregation to exist for work. Nonetheless, the overcrowding of the prisons made such practices a sham. Other states—such as Michigan, Missouri, and Massachusetts—began to address this attempt at phony solitude. McClaughry revolutionized penal practices at Joliet when,

> On the Fourth of July, 1875, the prisoners were permitted—for the first time in the history of the prison—to have the freedom of their respective cell houses for a couple of hours on condition that they should not abuse the privilege. There they talked, laughed and sung, engaged in athletic sports and improvised minstrel performances to their heart's content, while the occasion was enlivened with instrumental music by the Wheaton cornet band, and splendid vocal music by Mr. and Mrs. D.P. Bliss of Chicago.
>
> So satisfactorily and seemingly productive of good was the experiment, that they were permitted to celebrate the Centennial Anniversary of Independence in the large car shops, which were cleared and prepared for the occasion . . . For more than two hours over fifteen hundred men, forgetting their 'stripes', mingled freely together, participated in all kinds of games and sports, and apparently enjoyed themselves as heartily as if the prison walls were not around them. The occasion was not marred by the slightest breach of propriety on the part of any prisoner.[1]

As a result of this success, other amenities were introduced as well. For example, in addition to the small library for the prisoners run by his senile uncle, in 1874, McClaughry began an officers' library to keep his personnel informed "in the progressive phases of Penology."[2] In his first two years at Joliet, two thousand volumes were added to the convicts' library and "the books are circulated freely among the convicts, and we believe more reading is done by them here than by four times the number of men of the same class outside."[3] We do not know much about the literacy of the guards and McClaughry probably assumed it to be higher than it really was. Besides, guards did have busy lives outside the prison so one can imagine inmate reading habits to be more extensive. It is doubtful, however, no matter the more time to read, that inmate literacy could be all that great.

The practice of allowing tourist access to the prison for a fee was revived. By the late 1880s, an average of four tour groups a day was escorted through the place. The twenty-five cent fee went to purchasing more books.[4] There were other changes too. Before McClaughry's arrival, prisoners had straw beds that were emptied and changed and blankets cleaned twice a year. In

1876 McClaughry introduced mattresses and sheets that were washed once a week.[5]

No matter his reforms within the institution, crime and convictions beyond the walls challenged the Major. Throughout McClaughry's tenure at Joliet, the years between 1874 and 1888, the number of prisoners steadily increased. There were 1,353 in 1874.[6] Four years later there was a record 1,900.[7] Sixteen percent of these were recidivist, he believed.[8] The growing number of prisoners and the total lack of support of the state legislature was a constant offense to McClaughry. It forced the prison very early to begin to double up its inmate population in their cells. "We believe that the prisons may become reformatory institutions, or very easily made schools of crime. One or the other they will be," he prophesied.[9] In 1880 he complained of the large number of short-term prisoners, those spending less than one year in Joliet. They were a drain on the small amount of money and the likelihood of any reformation was slight.[10] He advocated that no one be sent to the prison for less than two years and that the longest term not exceed thirty-three years.[11] Furthermore, he wanted a separation between older more committed criminals and the younger first offenders. This was in keeping with the reformatory movement with which he was joining. Although legislative committees had studied and called for the creation of an intermediary place for the less criminal types to be confined, nothing had been done. In 1884, McClaughry pleaded again for the creation of such "reformatories" to separate the young and older hardened prisoners:

> Let the law be so changed that courts may send prisoners of the former class to one of our penitentiaries, where they may be treated under the system pursued in the best reformatory of the country, while to the other penitentiary shall be sent those who properly belong to the 'crime class.'[12]

In addition, McClaughry was concerned over the irrational system of treating prisoners while incarcerated. As early as 1875 he called for the individualized treatment of the individual prisoner.[13] By 1877 a "graded system" was advocated. He declared in his 1878-1880 report that:

> Under our present system the prisoner who has been confined here for many years, and whose conduct during the entire period has been of the very best, has no privilege over a prisoner who is here for only a year and whose conduct is a continual source of annoyance and trouble.[14]

Under this new system, good prisoners would instead move up the grades and attain better food and conditions. The more obstreperous would stay fixed for all to recognize.[15] In addition, he felt the "congregate system"—that foundation stone of the old Auburn penal philosophy—"are more schools of crime than reformation."[16] Throughout the later 1870s and early 1880s McClaughry advocated the "reformatory system," and—admitting his tendency for experimenting—began to separate the housing of first offenders with recidivists.[17] Of course, many prisoners took advantage of this reforming ideology and "played the game." Listen to the doggerel by "Jimmie the Greek" when a singing reformer, Arabella Root, visited the prison:

> I'm trying to make up some excuse
> To get off working on these shoes;
> So I will try some "pious game"
> To interest this singing dame.
> And when they call the mourners out
> You'll here me raise my voice and shout
> "Look here!" I am a model man
> Reformed upon McClaughry's plan.
> O, yes, dear Miss, I'm glad to be
> Here in the penitentiary.[18]

He did get out but was quickly incarcerated in another state.

Another of McClaughry's concerns was for the discharged prisoner. On one level it was a practical administrative problem. In Illinois the discharged prisoner received $10, a suit of clothes, and a railroad ticket to the place of conviction. In 1881, McClaughry would complain that in the previous seven years 1,575 prisoners were released at an overall cost of $32,697, which he felt to be too much of a financial burden for the prison.[19] Other states, such as New York, had a "State Agency for Discharged Convicts," that offered help for two to three years upon release, but Illinois remained reluctant to give aid. McClaughry spent considerable time helping ex-cons to get work.[20]

The released prisoner posed another problem. Some would return to crime. These professional criminals—impervious to reform—needed to be traced and chased by law enforcement outside the prison. Though this was police work, McClaughry recognized he had the perfect laboratory for the emerging system of criminal identification called the Bertillon system.

NOTES

1. National Prison Association, 1898, p. 323.
2. *Ibid.*, p. 356.
3. *Report of the Commissioners, 1875* p. 539.
4. Wetmore p. 83.
5. *Ibid.,* p. 375.

6. *Report of the Commissioners, 1875*, p. 534.
7. *Ibid., 1879*, p. 24.
8. He estimated that percentage to be 10% in *Ibid, 1875*, p. 537. But by 1877 that percentage was 16%. *Ibid., 1877.* p.387.
9. *Ibid., 1877*, p. 391.
10. *Ibid., 1881,* pp. 6-8.
11. *Ibid., 1878.* p. 9.
12. *Ibid., 1885,* p. 8
13. *Ibid., 1875,* p. 538.
14. *Ibid., 1878-1880*, p. 18.
15. *Ibid., 1881,* pp. 17-18.
16. *Ibid., 1877*, p. 390.
17. *Ibid., 1884*, pp. 7-9.
18. Quoted in Wetmore p. 172-173.
19. *Ibid., 1881*, p.6.
20. *Ibid., 1881*, p.16.

Chapter Thirteen

The Bertillon System

"... a thousand means of avoiding the chances of being recognized."

A perplexing problem throughout history–but especially as societies became more populated and mobile–was that of identity. Even in the Judaic-Christian tradition the first murderer was given a "mark" to separate him out from others. Eventually the branding of criminals became commonplace to safeguard the larger society. One classic story, based upon real incidents in sixteenth-century France, illustrates the issue of questionable identity. A man claiming to be Martin Guerre returned to his village and family after a long absence. One hundred forty people testified in two separate trials. Thirty-five claimed him to be the long lost neighbor. Forty-five said he was not. The rest simply did not know. Apparently, a person's features and voice could change enough over time to confuse acquaintances and loved ones.[1]

All kinds of people floated across Europe causing suspicion and consternation. As nationhood arose richer people obtained letters of introduction and identity. In post-Revolutionary France identity papers, called passports, became common in 1792. This was an attempt to regulate both foreign and domestic travelers. Such devices worked in highly structured and regulated societies, as in Europe, but in an open country like the United States, declared Alexis de Tocqueville in 1833,

> [w]here passports do not exist, nothing is easier than to change one's name. If, therefore, a delivered convict commits a new crime under a fictitious name, he can very easily conceal his relapse, providing he is not brought back to the prison where he underwent his first punishment. There are, besides, a thousand means of avoiding the chances of being recognized. Nothing is easier than to pass from one state to another, the ties between the various states being strictly political, there is no central power to which the police officers might refer to

> obtain information respecting the previous life of an indicted person; so that the courts condemn, almost always, without knowing the true name of the criminal, and still less his previous life.[2]

Criminal identification was a major problem for criminal justice personnel in the nineteenth century. Highly mobile criminals would disappear into anonymity. Photography was still in its infancy and unreliable, because the slightest movement of the subject would distort the image. Some agencies had small rogues galleries but either guarded them jealously or used them—as Thomas Byrnes of the New York City police did—to further their career. In 1886 Byrnes published his gallery of pictures as *Professional Criminals*. In this book hundreds of images of men and women appeared with short descriptions of their crimes. As the number of pictures increased, there was information overload. An indexing system was needed to handle the chaos in most rogues galleries.[3]

Furthermore, criminals had a variety of picturesque names that belied their true identity. For example, there was Stiff-necked Tom, Stuttering Bob, Memphis Bill, Pockmarked Frank, Antonio the Dago, Glass-eyed Dick, Dublin Tricks, Jew Jake, Black Tom, to name just a few of the hundreds.[4] On one hand, such names were descriptive exaggerations of some personal quality of the criminal. Obviously, Stuttering Bob had an identifiable speech impediment. Pockmarked Frank had a skin problem, and so on. In many ways they were good identifiers. But, on the other hand, in terms of scientific style and fashion, such names were weak. Too many people had speech and skin problems. A more rational approach was needed.[5]

Into this vacuum stepped French anthropologist/criminologist, Alphonse Bertillon (1853-1914), who applied anthropometry or body measurement to the identification of criminals. He believed that the careful measurement and recording of certain bodily parts would provide a unique identifiable profile of a criminal. Such measurements should include:

1. Length and width of head
2. Length of the left hand's middle and little finger
3. Length of the left foot
4. Length of the left forearm
5. Length of the right ear
6. Height of the figure
7. Measurement of the outstretched arms
8. Measurement of the trunk (measurement from the bench to the top of the head of a person seated)
9. Other unique identifying marks such as scars etc.

Another aspect of bertillonage was photography. Each subject was photographed full-face and in profile; this was called *portrait parle*.[6] The Prefect of Police in Paris inaugurated the system in 1882, and by the following year had already positively identified 49 men as habitual criminals.

McClaughry did not come to bertillonage as a police officer. Yet from his base at Joliet prison he became the chief spokesman and proponent of bertillonage in the United States. As we shall see, his speeches before the National Prison Association throughout this period were advocacies and defenses of this system of identification. That American bertillonage came out of the prison system seems logical. Prison keepers could measure and categorize their populations in a leisurely way, whereas the police had to work in the fast and furious world of street crime and crime scenes. Bertillonage, the scientific measurement of persons, therefore first became the domain of prisons, and only later did a more police-friendly system come into being. Yet even in that arena McClaughry turned out to be a key player.

On one hand, it was part of his "reformatory" ideology. If you are going to let people out early on parole, another custodial check on them would be positive identification.[7] The collected wardens, at their Toronto meeting in 1887, adopted the Bertillon principle long before their brothers in policing.[8] And yet there was some resistance to the wardens, rather than the police or courts, taking the lead in this. Clearly, McClaughry disagreed. In some sort of nineteenth century notion of "total systems" analysis, he believed that the wardens and police together would be affected.[9] On the other hand, as head of a major prison, he saw the problem of recidivism—a word that entered into the English language in 1883, three years after the introduction of bertillonage in France.[10] Revolving door crooks were a constant source of consternation to the warden at Joliet.

The wardens felt that there were four main problems confronting America in the last third of the century. First, there had been a steady rise of the "confirmed criminal" classes. Second, transportation facilities allowing for greater mobility of criminals had occurred after the Civil War. Third, crafty crooks took advantage of the nominal sentences and generous release practices of the system. Fourth, many states—including Illinois—had Habitual Offender laws that gave rise to unattended consequences. The minimum sentence for a second offence was 15 years; conviction of a third offense brought a minimum of 20 years. Crooks wanting to avoid these automatic longer sentences would try to hide their identities. Bertillonage would catch them.[11] Although McClaughry was not in policing he felt that

> the imperfect police system, or more properly systems of this country are far from efficient in even seriously retarding the operations of this class. Isolated cases may afford the detective an opportunity to earn a reputation of shrewdness; but, from want of concerted action, and a uniform system of description as a means of identification, the entire burden of recognition necessarily rests upon the detec-

tive. His success is based upon his wits, not upon any fundamental rules for the identification of men; consequently the arrest and identification must not only prove a power in the pursuit and arrest of persons guilty of crime, but in the protection of the innocent, as well as in determining the just measure of punishment.[12]

The police were slow to adopt any identification system. Prisons, under the leadership of McClaughry, would take the lead. In February, 1888 a "well attended" school of instruction was held at Joliet. The plan was to put the Bertillon system into operation in ten to twelve prominent prisons in the United States. A central office at Joliet prison would be opened to collect and file all the measurements taken by the other prisons.[13] The next year the state General Assembly passed a law recommending the use of bertillonage in all Illinois prisons. McClaughry felt that it typically cost more to catch one runaway criminal then it would to set up and support a Bertillon system.[14] There were several distinct advantages to the introduction of Bertillonage. It would:

1. Give the courts a better knowledge of a person's real criminal record.
2. Help the police to have a greater concerted action across the country.
3. Concentrate information.
4. Simplify the interchange between police and penal institutions.
5. "It substitutes certainty for uncertainty—a thoroughly reliable identification for the shrewd guess of the detective, or the scarcely more reliable testimony of the photograph."[15]

As to those concerned over issues of privacy and the rights of the innocent McClaughry responded:

Suppose that one hundred and fifty or one hundred and seventy five of them are innocent or are not criminal, that is, they are first offenders, who have fallen into trouble and gotten into prison. The measurements and figures are taken, and the cards are filed away; and through all coming time that is a sealed book, unless the man himself opens it by committing another crime. Nobody can call for that measurement, or take it out, unless he has obtained it through the man's having lapsed into crime, and having been measured again. It is a protection to the innocent, as it is sure conviction to the guilty. It can do no harm. There is no stigma put upon him, any more than there is in having his name on the prison register, and dressing him in prison clothes.[16]

There were those concerned that more than one person might have the same measurements. McClaughry believed enough checks were in place to take care of such a likelihood:

We sometimes find four persons, each one having one measurement the same as the others; but there is enough difference in the measurements to prevent any

> confusion. Besides, the marks and scars would be different, and the photographs as well. There are two photographs of each person, one the full-face view, and the other in profile.[17]

Against some opposition which we will see unfold later, McClaughry was ushering in scientific procedure in the identifying and regulating of the career criminal classes. The Bertillon system of identification will be one of his major causes for much of his life. It would be, he contended, the most important reform in fighting the unreformed criminals. At the same time his interest in those who could be reformed, young first offenders, was leading him to the reformatory movement. It was time, after a long and successful tenure at Joliet, to move on.

NOTES

1. Simon A. Cole, *Suspect Identities: A History of Fingerprinting and Criminal Identification* (Cambridge, MA: Harvard University Press, 2001), pp. 1-10.
2. Quoted in *Ibid*., p. 17.
3. Christian Parenti, *The Soft Cage: Surveillance in America from Slave Passes to the War on Terror* (New York: Basic Books, 2003), pp. 33-42.
4. Wetmore, p. 153-54.
5. Actually this was a part of the general nineteenth century's desire to measure things. For example see Leila Zenderland's *Measuring Minds: Henry Herbert Goddard and the Origins of American Intelligence Testing* (Cambridge: Cambridge University Press, 1998).
6. For a discussion of this technique see Alphonse Bertillon, *Alphonse Bertillon's Instructions for Taking Descriptions for the Identification of Criminals and Others by the Means of Anthropometric Indications* (New York: AMS Press, 1977).
7. *National Prison Association Proceedings, 1887*, p. 111.
8. *Ibid*., 1888, p. 76.
9. Cole, p. 30.
10. *Ibid.*
11. *National Prison Associations Proceedings, 1887,* pp. 121-25.
12. *Ibid., 1888,* pp. 74-75.
13. *Ibid.,* p. 77.
14. *Ibid., 1887,* p. 100.
15. *Ibid., 1888,* p. 76.
16. *Ibid.,* p. 79.
17. *Ibid.*

Chapter Fourteen

Fond Farewells

" . . . another field of labor."

Although McClaughry had found a new cause—the Bertillon system, for which he would be America's chief spokesman for the rest of the century—he remained one of the new generation of penologists dedicated to the reformatory ideology. He was particularly interested in the young first offenders and their rehabilitation. Throughout his tenure at Joliet, he advocated the state's adoption of the reformatory principles for adult prisons. And indeed by 1891 the state politicians did pass a reformatory act but did not extend it to the adult prisons as he hoped. Instead, a new reformatory was to be made of an old reform school in Pontiac, Illinois. In the meantime a new reformatory was opening in Pennsylvania, the Industrial School at Huntingdon, and he left to head up that institution in 1888.

This was a big move for the growing McClaughry family. There were four living children, three boys and a girl. Their connection to central Illinois remained strong. On numerous occasions, Robert McClaughry had returned to his parent's home in Fountain Green. In 1880 he paid for the painting of his old church there. In fact, he was there when an incident occurred that would bring an old Fountain Green acquaintance to reside at the Joliet prison. In August a heated political debate occurred at the church. To everyone's surprise, including McClaughry who was visiting, an argument turned into a fight and then to murder on the steps of the church. Alvin Salisbury had said some angry things about local politics and local personalities and Thomas Duff took umbrage. Duff rushed Salisbury with a knife and murdered him before the eyes of the man who would be his keeper for years to come.[1]

McClaughry's departure from Joliet was cause for ceremony and politics of professional organizations. As will be discussed later, McClaughry had become increasingly active in the National Prison Association (NPA). For the past three years the NPA had split along east and west lines. A few central figures, such as Rutherford Hayes and Robert McClaughry, had held them together. So there were several reasons for a testimonial meeting at Joliet. First, to honor the man personally; he had after all reformed the prison to the brink of a reformatory. Second, it was an opportunity for a growing body of professionals to state their beliefs again. Third, there was work to be done to bridge gaps within the growing number of penologists. There were those representing the philanthropic and academic circles. These people had a long history of concern for the dependent and delinquent classes. Then there was the more practitioner group composed of those who shared the ideology but had to deal with the day-to-day administrative problems of running a prison. The lines between them were drawn geographically as well. The eastern wardens held themselves off from the western. So in McClaughry's transition, there was an opportunity to mend fences as well as honor a man who seemed to transcend the gaps.[2]

So a meeting of wardens was called for at Joliet on November 23rd, 1888. About 20 wardens came to Illinois.[3] Unfortunately, as a look at the attendance records shows, most were western wardens. Eastern penal administrators largely did not come, possibly due to the costs of travel, but more likely because there was not yet much sense of a profession in penology. Much work remained in making the National Prison Association truly "national," a topic for a later chapter.

Key to making the meeting important was the attendance of Rutherford B Hayes. Born in Delaware, Ohio in 1822, Hayes attended Kenyon College and then Harvard Law School before settling down to practice in Cincinnati. He served heroically during the Civil War—receiving several wounds that plagued him all his life—and emerged with the rank of major general. He left the army in 1864 to serve four years in Congress. In 1868 he started the first of three terms as governor of Ohio. Then in 1876 Hayes was elected President of the United States, a job he disliked. His election–one in which he lost in the popular vote–has been remembered in history as a theft of the presidency. Rather than being an instigator, he was himself duped and thereafter stigmatized unjustly even by modern day historians.[4]

The National Prison Association had weakened considerably by the early 1880s and Hayes was one of a few who revived it. He was named president of the association in 1883 and remained a highly visible leader for nearly a decade. Hayes, perhaps inadvertently recognizing the geographical divisions in the embryonic profession, would write:

> It gives me special pleasure to accept your kind invitation to attend the meeting of the wardens of the Western penitentiaries to present testimonials of their esteem to Major McClaughry, the warden of the prison at Joliet, on the occasion

of his leaving for another field of labor. Indeed, I have so high an appreciation of Major McClaughry that I prefer the privilege of uniting with you in testimonial instead of being present merely as your guest.

In my attendance on the meetings of the National Prison Association I have had an opportunity to know something of the value of the major's work as a practical manager of convicts, as a wise and intelligent penologist, and as an accomplished and estimable gentleman. Believing as I do, that the importance of the prison system and prison administration that shall be at once practical, wise, and humane, I think it an occasion of public importance when deserved honor is manifested in behalf of a man like our friend and associate Major McClaughry.[5]

McClaughry was given an album of wardens and superintendents of western prisons. It was a cushion-backed brown morocco album with hand-tooled bands and designs. Gilt-stamped lettering on front announced it was a "Testimonial to Robert Wilson McClaughry, Warden of the Illinois State Penitentiary, at Joliet, November 23, 1888." Twenty one cabinet size photos of participants included:

Rutherford B. Hayes
Frederick Wines
Joseph Nicolson, House of Correction in Detroit
Charles Felton, House of Correction in Chicago
Elyah G. Coffin, Warden of Ohio Penitentiary in Columbus
H. F. Hatch, Warden of Michigan State Prison
George W. Crosely, Warden of Iowa Penitentiary in Fort Madison
John Dean Scouller, Superintendent of Illinois State Reform School at Pontiac, Illinois
William Dickson Patterson, Superintendent of the Work House and House of Correction in Cleveland, Ohio
George W. Carter, Warden of Wisconsin State Prison
James Murdock, Warden of Indiana State Prison
D. W. Marmaduke, Warden of Missouri State Prison
Marques Barr, Warden of Penitentiary at Anamosa, Iowa
John B. Smith, Warden of Kansas State Penitentiary
James Massie, Warden of Central Prison of Toronto, Canada[6]

With such fanfare McClaughry went off to Pennsylvania to take up leadership of a new reformatory. His stay there would be short as in a year he would be back in Illinois, first as superintendent of police in Chicago (1891-1893), then as warden of the Pontiac Reformatory (1893-1897), and next to return to Joliet (1897-1899). Finally he would become warden of the new federal prison at Leavenworth, Kansas (1899-1913).

Major Robert McClaughry represents the second generation of penologists in America. The first, those involved in the "asylum movement" of the 1820s-1850s, pretty much set up the new prisons. But after the Civil War—due to the inherent weaknesses of the asylum ideology and the rise of crime in an urbanizing and industrializing America—the penitentiaries were found wanting. A new generation of reformers—those advocating reformatory ideas such as separating out of young first offenders from hardened criminals, creating more humane living regimens in prison, the use of indeterminate sentences, and parole—came to power in several prisons and leadership positions in the National Prison Association. In addition these hard-headed clear-eyed wardens brought administration in to the mix. To them (and McClaughry was a leader here), reforming the prisoner could not occur without reforming those institutions and procedures called to do that job. Their ideology and practices would dominate prison history for the next one hundred years.

NOTES

1. Rugh, p. 154.
2. Frederick Wines to Rutherford Hayes, December 16, 1889 in the Rutherford Hayes Presidential Library, Fremont, Ohio.
3. Fred Wines to Rutherford Hayes October 27, 1888 in the Rutherford Hayes Presidential Library.
4. See Roy Morris Jr. *Fraud of the Century: Rutherford B. Hayes, Samuel Tilden and the Stolen Election of 1876* (New York City: Simon & Schuster, 2003); and William H. Rehnquest, *Centennial Crisis: The Disputed Election of 1876* (New York City: Alfred A Knopf, 2004).
5. Rutherford B. Hayes to Charles Felton, reproduced in the *Diary and Letters of Rutherford Birchard Hayes* ed. Charles Richard Williams Vol. 4, 1881-1891,(Columbus, Ohio: Ohio State Archaeological and Historical Society, 1924), pp. 414-15.
6. At the Rutherford B. Hayes Presidential Library, Fremont, Ohio.

Part Three

MCCLAUGHRY AND THE REFORMATORY MOVEMENT

Chapter Fifteen

Youth Crime in Pennsylvania

"wild, reckless and semi-criminal lads."

By moving from Illinois to Pennsylvania (more importantly from an adult prison to a youth reformatory) McClaughry confronted a new group of inmates, the young first offender. Even at its centennial, in 1876, America remained a young country. The median age of Americans was a little over 20 years. One hundred years later it would be 28.[1] Consequently, as crime and disorder increased, it was very likely young people would get caught up in the criminal justice system. Even before its founding, young people were seen as problematic in the United States. Remember that the most sensational series of trials in colonial times, at Salem, Massachusetts, was set in motion by young girls. So was the "Negro Conspiracy" hysteria in New York City in 1749. Young boys and men had an even more felonious presence.

From its founding and formative periods, America held out the promise of freedom and independence to many unaccustomed to such an environment. Disorder and crime resulted—and so did the penitentiary system. But institutions caring for youthful offenders were nonexistent.

Particularly in the New Nation period (1776-1835), when villages turned into towns and then into cities, thousands streamed into new urban places. A boarding house culture developed for the countless young unmarried people flooding into Boston, New York, and Philadelphia. Expectations and concerns for young women were high and restrictive, though some "fell" to ply the streets for recreation and sustenance. Young men were expected to be risk takers, aggressive, and perhaps "sow some seed" before settling down. Living in rooming houses far from parents, these young men whose primary reference points were other young men, took to the streets for recreation and diversion. Entire industries, most notably vices such as saloons and brothels, flourished because of them. One of the most sensational crimes of the ante bellum period–the murder of Helen Jewett by Richard Robinson and the "youth culture" that followed the proceedings passionately–reflected on the growing power and perplexity of young people in New York City.[2]

Some young people, however, did not have jobs and boarding houses. These were the cast-offs of society. Either because conditions were so dismal or because they were kicked out of the house or because they were neglected to the point of running away, young nomads filled the streets disturbing the business classes. These were walking cities with middle-class people living and walking through areas filled with young "door stoop" children begging and stealing to exist. A variety of experiments such as Houses of Refuge arose as did private concerns over the young people of the streets.[3] Some, like Charles Loring Brace and various Children's Aid Societies, advocated sending these young people to the countryside to be raised up by righteous, and perhaps stern, farm families. Train loads of children, dubbed "Orphan Trains," went west for the therapeutic environment of farm life.[4] There was even a ship, the Mercury–filled with "wild, reckless, and semi-criminal lads"(256 of them at first) that sailed from New York City to St Thomas, Barbados, Rio de Janeiro, the Canary Islands and back to New York on a six month voyage. Conditions on this floating asylum were horrendous.[5]

Street culture reflected several aspects of the emerging nineteenth-century urban life. The lack of adequate housing forced people to take to the streets for respite from the weariness of tenement existence. In addition, particularly in the pre-Civil War period, there had been scant means to socialize and recreate. The quest for comradeship, seeking out those of your own ethnicity and class with whom to talk and drink, became all the more important. People wanted to joke and party with others in order to forget the obligations, commitments, and frustrations of daily life. Perhaps there was machismo too—displays of strength, virility, and risk taking to show autonomy and control. Such posturing was all the more important when they had little real economic and political control in a society "on the make" demanding the skill and fortitude some did not have. Frequently, a necessary ingredient was alcohol—either in a saloon or in a bucket of beer consumed on the sidewalks—providing a temporary lift in spirits, a sense of well being, a measure of one's masculinity, and a momentary amnesia of present conditions.

For those whose family had failed, a new one—the street gang—arose in the Jacksonian period (1835-1855). In New York City, Five Points became a battle ground for competing street gangs. Among them were the Plug Uglies, called such because they plugged their hats as helmet protection from blows to the head in street battles, arose in New York as an Irish gang. Then there were the Day Break Boys to be a member of which one had to kill someone as an initiation. Such rites make awful sense of the fact that in the one hundred rooms of the Old Brewery tenement, someone was murdered every 24 hours over a fifteen-year period.[6]

Not far away, Philadelphia by the mid nineteenth century had a well developed gang culture with gangs numbering over one hundred. A sampling of gang names in Philadelphia would include:

Bleeders
Blood Tubs
Blossoms
Bouncers
Buffers
Bugs
Bulldogs
Chesapeakes
Crockets
Darts
Deathfetchers
Dogs
The Forty Thieves
Garroters
Gumballs
Hyenas
Jack of Clubs
Jumpers
Keystone No. 2
Killers
Lancers
Neckers
Pickwick Club
Pluckers
Pots No. 2
Privateer Club No. 1
Rats
Rangers
Rebels
Red Roses
Reed Birds
Shifflers
Skinners
Smashers

Snakers
Snappers
Spiggots
Sporters
Tormentors[7]

Such gangs the Philadelphia newspapers divided into four types: street corner, theft, violent, and combat gangs. Street corner lounging was prevalent as a means to talk and maintain friendships, but because of public complaints, some of these groups rented rooms and created club houses. Others developed various hideouts and never went beyond the occasional pelting of citizens with snowballs and rocks to vent their anger. The Chesapeakes and Darts represent this type of gang. It was estimated that between 1840 and 1870 there were thirty-eight of these street corner gangs in Philadelphia.[8]

Nine gangs specialized in thievery. They liked to raid vacant buildings, those of families spending the summer in the countryside, or those recently vacated and for sale, and strip them of the metal fixtures and plumbing pipes. The Forty Thieves and Schuykill Rangers fall into this category.

Thirty-five violent gangs actively sought out victims—such as solitary pedestrians, street walkers, and any member of a despised ethnic group—to harm and terrorize. Their favorite armament was the slung shot, a ball of lead attached to a thong and chord that was swung and flung amidst a crowd. In the 1850s brass knuckles appeared and became a favorite tool of violent gangs such as the Turks, Tormentors, and Smashers.

Yet the most prevalent, numbering 55, were the combat gangs. They orchestrated street battles with rival gangs and night watchmen or police patrols. The Wildcats, Sporters, Garroters, and Bleeders were just a few of the combat gangs that gave notoriety to sections of towns called Battle Grounds.[9] Many of these gangs were associated with voluntary fire companies and every fire became an excuse for a clash. Though probably incorrigible many of these gang boys were going to filter into the penal system.

Crime increased as major cities like Philadelphia grew, and young people took part in a variety of street crimes. The favorite juvenile crime was till-tapping. Cash registers were nonexistent and merchants kept cash in a drawer under the counter. While other youngsters kept the proprietor busy the smallest boy would simply empty the drawer. Another merchandising technique helped the opportunistic youthful criminal. Businessmen would display their goods on tables in front of the store during business hours. Young crooks walked up to these displays to grab and run. When merchants replaced small windows with large plate glass display windows, the "smash and grab" technique became a favorite.[10] In days before credit or checks, most people carried cash. Anyone who looked well-to-do was a target of assault; one rare and therefore sure sign of affluence was the personal time piece. A favorite youthful ploy was to ask a passer-by for the time and then grab the watch when it came out of a pocket. Watch chains were a commercial response to such thieving practice but offered little deterrence.[11] So well before the late nineteenth century adults were quite aware of the problem of youth crime.

Popular culture fueled this growing adult angst toward young males. The popular adventure stories of young boys by Horatio Alger were one example. Born into a Unitarian family struggling in New England, Alger was able–with the help of an uncle–to attend Harvard. Studying under Henry Wadsworth Longfellow, Alger aspired to be a writer. At first unsuccessful he drifted into journalism before finally finding his voice and publishing 134 "dime novels." His most popular ones appeared in three series: Ragged Dick (1867-1870), Luck and Pluck (1869), and Tattered Tom (1871).

It was the Ragged Dick series that captured the attention of adventure starved boys and concerned adults. In that series there were six immensely popular books: *Ragged Dick*; *Fame and Fortune*; *Mark, the Match Boy*; *Rough and Ready*; *Rufus and Rose*; and *Ben, the Luggage Boy*. Each story told of a parentless street boy who due to a series of lucky breaks discovered his parents or at least better prospects. All six books were filled with kidnappings, robberies, detection, narrow escapes, and all of the adventures that appealed to young boys.[12]

On the one hand, these stories were optimistic and applauded by the adult population. The heroes were not troublemakers; indeed, Dick tells one of his street friends: "I'd like to be an office boy and learn business, and grow up 'spectable.'" Moreover, the stories emphasize the importance of proper parenting and the quest of these boy heroes to find lost parents or relatives. Failing that, a rich benefactor comes into their lives to save them. Success, whether due to pluck or luck, always depended upon being dependable, obeying orders, and serving others. So these books could in some ways be considered primers on how to function as a clerk or mechanic in a burgeoning industrial era.

On the other hand, those who read the series carefully–and indeed different people could get different meanings out of such literature–the Horatio Alger books were disturbing. These street boys had limited vision: they were concerned with day-to-day survival. If they had a job, they disliked it. To them the good life was one of consumption, immediate gratification, and adventure. Contrary to the Alger myth, claims a student of such popular culture, "Bootblacks rise by diving for the drowning son of a rich man, newsboys by foiling attempted robbery, match boys by the belated beneficence of a grandfather thousands of miles away. None ever attain eminence by diligent application; none are ever on a course of notable advancement before their big break."[13]

Of course youth committed crime beyond the borders of Pennsylvania and indeed achieved such national attention by it that it focused the public mind on juvenile criminals. Fourteen-year old Jesse Harding Pomeroy certainly did that. From December 1871 to September 1872 a series of sexual tortures of children occurred in Boston. Pomeroy was arrested, convicted, and sent to the Lyman School for Boys. Deemed reformed, he was released in 1874. Shortly afterwards, a girl and a boy were found tortured and murdered, and Pomeroy was arrested and convicted of these murders. Across the country people wondered how such a boy could do these horrendous things, how he was able to slip through the criminal justice system, and why the Lyman School for Boys had not done a better job at reforming him. There was considerable pressure, especially from women's groups, to execute Pomeroy. Murder was a capital offense in Massachusetts but only five juveniles had been executed, most of them in the Colonial period.[14] Instead, the judge sentenced Pomeroy to solitary confinement in prison. The "Boy Fiend" would spend forty-one years in solitary confinement, the longest such confinement in American history. Even after he was released to the general prison population, he was written up in the newspapers on a regular basis, and died in prison in 1932.[15] The case of Pomeroy highlighted many troublesome issues about youthful crime and punishment in nineteenth-century America.

Another such case ended differently. Charles Miller was a five-year old boy living in Manhattan when his mother died in 1880; the next year his father committed suicide leaving the remaining family destitute. Charley and his four siblings were cast into the New York orphanage system. The boy had severe problems and his constant bed wetting and masturbation practices put him on a circuit of foster care until he simply ran away and began a search for a brother living in Kansas. Even though he found his sibling, conditions were fragile enough that he "took to the rails," but thereafter referred to himself as "Kansas Charley." It was while he was tramping that he met and befriended two other boys, Waldo Emerson and Ross Fishbaugh from Nebraska, and they rode the trains into Wyoming. There in a box car Charley, now age fifteen, shot the two boys in the head while they slept. He was quickly caught, tried, and convicted. But Wyoming was not Massachusetts and Charley was sentenced to die. The nation waited anxiously for two years and then "Kansas Charley" went to the gallows in Cheyenne, Wyoming, in 1892.[16]

Charley Miller's story pointed up another problem that became an obsession in the last half of the nineteenth century: masturbation. This solitary sexual practice, with all the legends and lore around it, became the primary explanation for the problems with youth in Victorian America. Such practices had been condemned as sinful in the religious community going back to the biblical story of Onan.[17] In that incident Onan was commanded by his father to take his recently widowed sister-in-law and lie with her. He did so, but feeling guilty about it he practiced *coitus interruptus,* spilling his seed on the ground. God put him to death and condemned all those who wasted their procreative powers. This practice, its acceptance or condemnation, became a marker of monotheism's assault upon the pagans in the ancient world.[18]

Protestants suspected masturbation to be a widespread practice among the celibate Catholic priesthood, a suspicion fueled by the existing anti-Catholic bias, particularly in America. But masturbation was largely ignored—or at least not talked about—until the eighteenth-century publication in England of *Onania; Or the Heinous Sin of Self Pollution, and All Its Frightful Consequences in Both Sexes Considered.* Though Europeans became concerned, it was among Americans, particularly after the Civil War, that the response was hysterical. Several reasons account for this.

Particularly those Protestant faiths most closely related to the Puritan mind set had firm ideas on salvation, sex, and self-control. Those belief systems deemed sex to have three purposes: procreation, demonstrations of love and care, and pleasure, with pleasure firmly last in the list. Any sex without desire or expectation of pregnancy was considered sinful and a sign of character flaws. "Solitary sex" was regarded as pleasure without commitment and therefore irresponsible and selfish. Of course, such vices as prostitution were already the focus of moral crusades, but rarely did religious outrage against commercial sex reach the same heights as that against what one zealot, O.S. Fowler, called the "sin of sins, and vice of vices." In his widely popular lectures in the 1870s and 1880s Fowler, exhorting against masturbation, claimed that "Neither Christian nor heathendom suffers any evil at all to compare with this."[19]

In many ways Fowler represents another formula particularly relevant for nineteenth-century America. Masturbation not only caused eternal damnation in the next life but disease and dysfunction in this one. While independence and freedom were important, both American Christianity and capitalism demanded that workers exercise self control, the epitome of character. The chronic masturbator lacked that control. In his 1875 book, *Creative and Sexual Science, or Manhood, Womanhood and their Mutual Interrelations . . . as taught by Phrenology and Physiology*, Fowler expressed that masturbation "caused incomparably more sexual dilapidation, paralysis, and disease, as well as demoralization, than all the other sexual depravities combined."[20] Others of like mind chimed in. One observer in 1870 cautioned that "No words can describe the miseries it inflicts throughout your whole life down to death." Another, some 18 years later, thought "The sin of self-pollution is one of the vilest, the basest, the most degrading that a human being can commit. It is worse than beastly."[21]

The emerging middle class was an important factor in the growing concerns over both masturbation and a dissipated youth population. By the post-Civil War period a middle-class sexual ideology had developed. Three sexual views existed. There were those of a more promiscuous position that kept the brothels and houses of assignation flourishing. Many of these were married men who accentuated pleasure over propagation and fidelity. There were those that felt premarital and extra marital sex to be wrong but, with the rise of contraception and birth control, believed plentiful marital sex to be pleasurable and good. Then there were those who believed there should be no premarital sex and that marital sex ought to be exercised only in moderation. It was important to sublimate sexual energy into useful work.

Along with sex, the middle class also began to rethink the role of young people in society. Perhaps more than any other economic classes the American bourgeoisie segregated youth from adulthood. Childhood was extended as young middle-class kids attended the newly established school systems and so disappeared from the work place. Children were to be innocent, and sexual activity was to be a mark of adulthood. The education movement and its particular emphasis on sports must be seen as a quest to sublimate sexual urges of a newly discovered age category called adolescence.

But there were other reasons besides its spiritual and personal ramifications that so many people thought masturbation harmed a strongly emerging capitalist country like America in the post-Civil War period. It was said that masturbation diverted one's energies and attention from one's work and place in society. Those who masturbate "drivel away their existence on the outskirts of society," observed one commentator. "They are at once a dead weight, a sluggish, inert mass in the paths of this blustering life, having neither the will nor the capacity to take part in the general matters of life."[22]

The emerging sciences, particularly the medical and mental fields, also played their part in vilifying masturbation and its practitioners. A growing popular scientific notion, first propounded by a Swiss doctor named Samuel Tissot, was that semen was an "essential oil" that if wasted weakened the body. A one ounce loss of semen, Tissot insisted, weakened forty ounces of blood. For doctors perplexed over the causes and cures of physical diseases particularly among the poorer classes, the convenient answer seemed to be such sexual depravity. There was also a growing belief that masturbation caused insanity. Drawing on Lombrosian paradigms, proponents of this insanity theory suggested that signs of masturbatory insanity were a stooping gait, shifting eyes, and sunken chest.[23] Three reasons probably account for this belief. First, the notion of evil spirits and witchcraft had declined significantly by the Civil War and other explanations for evil occurrences were necessary. Second, the rise of medical science, particularly pathological anatomy, newly suggested bodily causes of insanity. Third, and most important, the rise of the asylum a generation earlier allowed keepers to see patients masturbating and draw hasty conclusions connecting insanity to masturbation.[24]

Although not mentioned in the academic literature the prison became a key venue for the practice of masturbation. By the end of the Civil War every northern state, and some southern ones too, had a penitentiary. Especially after overcrowding undermined the silent and solitary programs of earlier institutions, it was clear that opportunity for sexual misbehavior increased. Of course there was some rape but then as today the primary sexual outlet for prisoners was masturbation. Any examination of disciplinary actions in prisons such as Joliet makes it clear that many prisoners were "soiling themselves" with "disgusting practices." Young people not only needed to be protected from older predators but from their own sexual practices, felt these latter day puritans. These parental notions of protection and control gave rise to the reformatory movement.

NOTES

1. Historical Statistics of the United States: Colonial Times to 1970, Part 1 (Washington D.C.: US Department of Commerce, Bureau of Census, 1975), p. 19.

2. Patricia Cline Cohen, *The Murder of Helen Jewett: The Life and Death of a Prostitute in Nineteenth-Century New York* (Vintage Books, 1999).

3. See Robert Pickett, *House of Refuge: Origins of Juvenile Reform in New York State, 1815-1857* (Syracuse, New York: Syracuse University Press, 1969).

4. See See Miriam Z. Langsam, *Children West: A History of the Placing Out System of the New York Children's Aid Society, 1853-1890* (Madison, Wis.[**Please check what bibliog. style your publisher requires) University of Wisconsin Press, 1964), and Marilyn Irvin Holt, *The Orphan Trains: Placing Out in America* (Lincoln, Nebr., University of Nebraska Press, 1992).

5. See Timothy J. Gilfoyle, *A Pickpocket's Tale: the Underworld of Nineteenth-Century New York* (New York City: W.W, Norton, 2006), pp. 30-36,

6. See Timothy J. Gilfoyle, "Street-Rats and Gutter-Snipes: Child Pickpockets and Street Culture in New York City, 1850-1900," *Journal of Social History* 37 (2004), pp. 853-82.

7. David R. Johnson, *Policing the Urban Underworld: The Impact of Crime on the Development of the American Police, 1800-1887* (Philadelphia: Temple University Press, 1979), pp. 81, 189-91.

8. *Ibid.*, pp. 81-82.

9. *Ibid.*, pp. 82-84.

10. *Ibid.*, pp. 72, 76.

11. *Ibid.*, p. 77.

12. Michael Zuckerman, "The Nursery Tales of Horatio Alger," *American Quarterly* 24 (1972), pp. 191-209.

13. *Ibid.*, p. 201.

14. Victor L. Streib, *Death Penalty For Juveniles* (Bloomington, Indiana: Indiana University Press, 1987), pp. 197-98.

15. For example see *New York Times*, July 22, August 2, August 13, 1929 and *Boston Daily Globe*, September 30, 1932.

16. For a beautiful treatment of this boy killer see Joan Jacobs Brumberg, *Kansas Charley: The Boy Murderer* (New York City: Penguin Books, 2003).

17. Genesis 38 v. 9.

18. See Jonathan Kirsch's *God Against the Gods: The History of the War Between Monotheism and Polytheism* (New York City: Viking Compass, 2004).

19. Jean Stengers and Anna Van Neck, *Masturbation: The History of a Great Terror*, trans. by Kathryn A Hoffmann (New York: Palgrave Press, 2001), p. 107.

20. *Ibid.*

21. *Ibid.*, p. 106.

22. Quoted in Charles Rosenberg, "Sexuality, Class and Role in Nineteenth-Century America," *American Quarterly* Vol. 25 (1973), p. 146.

23. Joseph F. Kitt, "Adolescence and Youth in Nineteenth-Century America," *Journal of Interdisciplinary History* Vol. 2 (1971), pp. 283-98.

24. R. P. Neuman, "Masturbation, Madness, and the Concepts of Childhood and Adolescence," *Journal of Social History*, Vol. 8 (1975), pp. 2-3.

Chapter Sixteen

The Reformatory

"The Ideal of a True Prison System"

By the 1880s, when McClaughry assumed the superintendency of the Pennsylvania Reformatory, the Reformatory movement—with its cast of prominent characters, profound ideology and fledgling institutional development—was under way. It had been born due to the disillusionment with the penitentiary movement, that uniquely American bit of social engineering of the previous generation that had given rise to the silent system of Pennsylvania and the congregate one of New York. Even before the Civil War, penitentiary overcrowding had ended any hope of meaningful reform of inmates. After the Civil War, Americans thought they saw a tremendous increase in unrepentant criminality and clamored for reform.

Enoch Cobb Wines and Theodore Dwight, two religious activists convinced of the necessity and possibility of reforming criminals, conducted a study tour of penitentiaries and prisons of America as representatives of the New York system in the summer of 1865. They visited fifteen penitentiaries, sixteen reform schools, and many jails and Houses of Correction, and sent others an elaborate twenty-six-page questionnaire. A 570-page *Report on the Prisons and Reformatories of the United States and Canada* resulted in 1867. Wines and Dwight were generally disheartened with what they saw. They called for less sentence disparity and less profit-oriented prison labor, and for more emphasis on vocational and academic education. In addition, they advocated for more post-release supervision. Furthermore, they pressed for a new type of institution, an adult reformatory, to deal with the less hardened offenders. Some experiments along such lines had already occurred in New York. A House of Refuge had been created sometime earlier but it turned out to be essentially a children's prison run by the charitable sector rather than the public one. In any case, the governor of New York accepted the Wines-Dwight report and recommendations and set in motion the machinery for the creation of the reformatory at Elmira completed in 1876.

Through his travels and investigations, Wines was convinced that there were numerous like-minded individuals eager for reform. A mixture of Christianity and common sense motivated many of them. While he remained interested Theodore Dwight drifted into other fields. So did Rutherford B. Hayes, who eventually became president of the United States, but he came back to the program more often. In addition, people like Richard Vaux, Albert Byers, G. S. Griffith, Franklin Sanborn, Francis Wayland, Roeliff Brinkerhoff and Zebulon Brockway were part of this group.

One of the best-run penal institutions, according to Wines and Dwight, was the Detroit House of Correction under the leadership of Zebulon Brockway (1827-1920). He started his career as a clerk in Connecticut State Prison and worked his way up in a variety of positions, yet was disillusioned over the preachy quality of prison managers. In 1862 he became head of the Detroit House of Correction and stayed there for a decade. Present day penal policy continued to bother him, opinions he voiced in a paper, "The Ideal of a True Prison System of a State," at the 1870 meetings of the National Prison Association in Cincinnati. Out of that meeting a "reformatory" movement grew, one that aimed to rehabilitate young males. Three elements were necessary to do this: ideology, institution, and regimen.

The ideological underpinning of the reformatory movement was the belief in the possibility of reforming young first offenders, generally those 15 to 25 years old. The number of truly hardened career criminals was small, these reformers believed. Most people caught up in the criminal justice system, they believed, had simply made a mistake and could be set upon the proper paths to reformation and redemption. Placing young first offenders in a prison with career criminals could only result in them becoming hardened criminals. But some reforms were needed in the criminal justice system too. Historically the sentencing structures were flat with incarceration time fixed, no matter the inmate's progress toward reform. The reformatory advocates argued for an indeterminate sentence, a range of years from a minimum to a maximum to be spent institutionalized. In such away the ultimate decision as to the time of imprisonment was in the hands and behaviors of the inmates. A parole board, chaired by the head of the reformatory, would determine whether early release was justified and prudent, and establish conditions of behavior while a person was on parole. Even though the young person was released, he would still be supervised by correctional representatives called parole officers and could be sent back to the reformatory for violating any of the conditions established by the board. Of course, what the reformatory advocates did not say was that in the competitive world of criminal justice they were "empire building." Actually the administrators of the reformatory, and not the inmate nor the trial court judge, were the ones who determined release. The revocation of parole was in the hands of the parole officer and a reformatory based hearing.

To carry out this ideological perspective the state needed to create special institutions separated from the prisons. This in and of itself was no mean task. Most states demanded that their penitentiaries be self-sufficient. Many had just created reform schools for younger children. So the idea of an additional institution threatened to strain the budgets of state legislatures. Nonetheless, eighteen states created reformatories between 1876 and 1913,[1] the first being at Elmira, New York, under the leadership of Zebulon Brockway.

Elmira was set up to house young first offenders, generally the 16 to 31 year olds. Initially, there were 184 residents but that number grew quickly to one thousand. The institution was on an elevation on the western side of a valley about three miles from the town of Elmira. It embraced 280 acres of which fifteen were occupied by the institution, enclosed partly by buildings and partly by walls twenty feet high. The buildings were constructed out of blue stone and brick and commanded a view of twenty miles of woods and meadows. Every attempt was made for the reformatory to look different from the existing prisons of America.

Three categories of inmates were created and a distinct colored uniform identified and distinguished each group for the regimen that followed. Everyone came into the institution at an "intermediate" level, and their subsequent behavior placed them on a higher level with better conditions and the possibility of earlier release. Bad behavior put the inmate into a lower category with fewer amenities and a longer stay in the institution. The regime was calculated to instill middle-class views and habits. Inmates got up at 5:30 am, grade one going to breakfast first, grade three going last. Work was essential and was allocated according to the grade the inmate was in, the more arduous and less desirable tasks going to those in grade three. In the late 1880s, the Yates law came into effect severely limiting the distribution of prisoner-made goods to the outside market and shrinking the work opportunities in the institution. To take up this slack in things to do to keep busy, military exercises, particularly marching and drill, were put into place. The evening was reserved for music, notably a marching band, or sports. Military drill, marching band, and baseball all had a significant purpose for a middle-class capitalist society. They all emphasized individual performance in the context of a group effort and cooperation. One was to develop individual skills, whether it was playing a trombone or hitting a ball, but that talent was to be melded into a larger team effort.

It appeared that the reformatory had found the answer to a perplexing problem. By putting young first offenders in adult prisons they came out hardened criminals. In a special place—one more parental than punitive—the youth could be reformed, these reformatory advocates believed. Evidence from Elmira was promising. Brockway announced that 83 percent of his inmates never came back. As he left Joliet for Pennsylvania, McClaughry hoped he could do the same.

NOTE

1. They are:
   New York (Elmira, 1876)
   Michigan (Ionia, 1877)
   Massachusetts (Concord, 1884)
   Pennsylvania (Huntingdon, 1889)
   Minnesota (St Cloud, 1889)
   Colorado (Buena Vista, 1890)
   Illinois (Pontiac, 1891)
   Kansas (Hutchinson, 1895)
   Ohio (Mansfield, 1896)
   Indiana (Jeffersonville, 1897)
   Wisconsin (Green Bay, 1898)
   New Jersey (Rahway, 1901)
   Washington (Monroe, 1908-09)
   Oklahoma (Granite, 1910-11)
   Maine (Windham, 1912)
   Wyoming (Worland, 1912)
   Nebraska (Lincoln, 1912-13)
   Connecticut (Cheshire, 1913)

Chapter Seventeen

McClaughry at Huntingdon

"He must labor. He must study. He must practice self-control."

By the late 1880s the reformers and politicians of Pennsylvania wanted a "new departure" in penology. The state had always been in the forefront of reform, as early as 1821 creating the silent/solitary penitentiary system. By the Civil War that system had largely been displaced elsewhere, though it did remain for a while longer in Pennsylvania and various European countries. When Pennsylvania reformers visited Elmira and also attended the meetings of the National Prison Association, they became convinced that the growing problem of youthful disorder and crime could best be addressed by the creation of a reformatory. Their new prison was to be modeled after the work of Brockway in Elmira,[1] though with the acknowledgment that even there everything was just in an "experimental state" and would need to be tinkered with further. So it was that the board of managers—-Samuel McCamant from Tyron, J. Hay Brown from Lancaster, T. B. Patton from Altoona, W.W. Jennings from Harrisburg and Alexander Port from Huntingdon—-selected McClaughry as its first superintendent in August, 1888.

McClaughry's exposure to Brockway had made him a true believer in the reformatory movement. He reported to work on December 1st, 1888, convinced that the farewell testimonial at Joliet had paved the way for acceptance and success at Pennsylvania. He wrote to Rutherford Hayes "to say that the testimonial referred to, secured for me a cordiality of welcome here [Pennsylvania Industrial Reformatory] which, without it, would have been impossible."[2] And the feelings demonstrated toward his reforms at Joliet seemed to be sincere and widespread among the general population of that Illinois town as well. The people of Joliet were sorry to say farewell. "Among the many useful men and women in this community who have left us from time to time," wrote the press, "none leave with such marked manifestations of keen regret as that which the public shows over losing Major and Mrs. R. W. McClaughry."[3]

Soon after his arrival in Pennsylvania, McClaughry was called upon for his first public appearance and civic responsibility. The occasion was the presenting of the flag to the public schools of the area, an event filled with patriotic speeches. McClaughry's remarks were short but reflected the depth of his post-Civil War patriotism. In part he said that:

> The significance of this occasion is beyond the power of language to adequately portray. This emblem of liberty represents a national unity that can never be broken; that when a public question is settled by ballots it can never be defeated by bullets. It signifies that throughout all the lands of the earth this flag gave courage that hoped and prayed for universal freedom. And in proportion as we shall be faithful to the teaching that it represents just in that proposition may we hope God will bless this nation; and when kings shall realize that they are but men, and when men shall learn that they are all brethren.[4]

Everyone hoped to open the new facility at the first of the year but building problems delayed that event until February. The electric plant would not be finished until March.[5] In the meantime people had to be hired to act as guards and guardians. Eager for the economic opportunities, over 300 applicants for jobs came from the town folk.[6] McClaughry decided not to hire an assistant for several months and hoped "to manage the whole concern himself just as long as [I] can."[7]

On February 16th, the first inmate arrived and the number soon shot up to fifty. The age of the inmates clustered in the late teens, [8] with the average age of those in the reformatory in 1891 being 18.2.[9] Forty-nine were single and one was married. Five had never gone to school while forty-five had some schooling. Forty two were born in Pennsylvania. Illinois, New York, Virginia, North Carolina, Italy, and England provided one each, and Ohio two.[10] Their numbers swelled to 478 by March, 1891.[11]

As was done at Elmira, each new inmate was carefully examined by both the General Superintendent and the physician of the institution. McClaughry was interested in the inmate's birth, parentage, social relations, occupation, education, moral tendencies, and mental capacities hoping to find the causes for the present circumstances of the inmate and determine the best future action. McClaughry talked to each new inmate "endeavoring to find out what causes have led him into his present condition, and to carefully estimate what treatment will bring him out of it."[12] For his part, the physician was interested in the physical and mental condition of the young person. Finally, the inmate was turned over to a Moral Instructor, most likely the prison chaplain, to determine educational and religious acquirements and determine school assignment. All such interviews indicated a growing belief in the "scientific penology."

New inmates were given a gray suit and placed in Second or Neutral Grade. With any misbehaving the suit was changed to red and he became a common convict by entering the Third Grade or penal grade. In this category the inmate marched from place to place in lock step and ate in silence; in addition he was deprived of coffee at mealtime, of light in the cell in the evening, of library books and papers, and of the privilege of writing or receiving letters or visits from friends. Continued rebellion might lead to a transfer to a regular prison.

Inmates were closely watched and could earn marks: three for good conduct, three for labor, and three for study. If a perfect record were achieved for six consecutive months he would be promoted to First Grade and become a so-called trusty, now wearing a blue suit. Living arrangements now would be more commodious. This privileged position allowed for chatting during meals and movement within the institution without recourse to the lock step line march. If the trusty continued to demonstrate improvement, after two years the Parole Grade was available allowing a hearing with the Board of Managers and the possibility of a ticket-of-leave or conditional release.

If the Board of Managers thought the inmate ready and work had been obtained with a legitimate employer for at least a six-month commitment, the young person was released. Then the inmate had to:

1. Go immediately to the place of employment and remain there for at least 6 months.
2. Get permission from the Board of Managers through the Superintendent if he had to change work or residency.
3. On the first day of each month send a report to the superintendent about the job, pay and social experiences. In that report he must reveal what he has earned and expended. All of this must be verified by his employer.
4. Avoid bad company and obey the law.
5. Show up at place of employment as soon as possible.
6. Understand that he is still under custody of the Board of Managers.
7. That he might be taken back to the Reformatory for any cause as determined by the Board of Managers.[13]

If the released youngster got in trouble while out on a ticket-of-leave he would have to return to serve out the remainder of his term.[14]

Achieving reform of young people and their early release was the goal of the reformatory movement. Two key areas were critical to this plan: education and labor .When McClaughry arrived, only three of the nine school rooms had been furnished and were ready for students. Soon the rest were brought to order and the library supplied with two thousand books. These early reformers believed strongly in the need of education. The Board of Mangers would report to the governor that:

> The effect of the educational work of the institution as a reformatory agency, we are satisfied cannot be over estimated [sic], and we believe that the results of this work will prove that a thoroughly rigid system of ordinary common school education enforced in all our prisons, as a requisite to a release, will have an equally good effect, so far as reforming criminals is concerned, with the enforced system of labor, which all admit is necessary to reformation.[15]

McClaughry was a little more conservative. For example, asked about the reformatory while attending a Scotch-Irish Congress in Pittsburgh, he replied that "the institution is not more than a year old, and it will take some time to tell whether we are accomplishing much good or not."[16] A remarkably cautious statement for a man well on the road to being a true believer! In spite of McClaughry's apparent wait-and-see attitude, the procedures were in place.

Each inmate was required to attend school from six to eight o'clock in the evening. They were divided into twelve classes of 25 to 40 depending upon academic background and abilities. The lowest class had the illiterate while the highest classes had those who had attended some high school. Of course, most of these students were not academically inclined. J.H. Likens, the school director, understood that his students "think the world owes them a living, [and that] they mean to get it without the least possible effort." Consequently, Likens went on, "We aim to teach only the most essential facts of knowledge as bearing upon the individual in every day [sic.] business affairs of life."[17] Many of the courses taught were industrial trades such as chair making, shoe making, blacksmithing, carpentry, painting, baking, and laundry work.[18] Like in all penal institutions, underscoring middle-class values and working class-skills was the underlying agenda.

Students received marks for their academic performance. For example, three marks per month were available if the student got at least an 80 percent in class tests. If he fell below that percentage, somewhere in the 70 percent range, he would get two points. Only one point was given if the student fell below 60 percent.[19] McClaughry felt that the mark system taught profound lessons essential in a capitalist society. "His conduct report book, like the balance sheet of the businessman, sets before him, each month, a statement of gains and losses. Gains mean liberty. Losses mean lengthened bondage." He went on: "He must labor. He must study. He must practice self-control. When he has reached a point where the practice of these things has become habitual, who will dare to say that he is not less dangerous to the community than before."[20]

Work was a critical part of the reformatory ideal. It was to instill within the inmates the values of the Protestant ethic. Hard work, orderliness, discipline, self control, and submission to authority, it was believed, were the qualities for success in America. At first there was a tailor, shoe making, blacksmith. and repair shops just for the internal needs of the institution. But as the number of inmates increased so did the number of jobs to keep them busy. Much of this early work had to be of the hand-labor type. This was because the institution had to put large numbers of people to work, and machinery might rob someone of the opportunity for a job. Besides, machinery was expensive and as yet the reformatory had little capital for such items.

The first outside contract went to Joseph Winterbottom and W. M. Cochrane to teach the young inmates how to make rattan and reed chairs. Soon, seventy-five inmates were employed in this chair-making project. Another key industry was the farm for which the reformatory bought some additional land and succeeded in raising all the vegetables needed for the mess hall. In addition, the agribusiness provided a yield of forty tons of hay, 436 bushels of oats, and forty-two bushels of wheat. Inmates were put to work excavating and building additional buildings as the reformatory grew.[21]

We have already noted that after legislation was passed limiting the distribution of prison-made products, the reformatory placed greater emphasis on military drill as a way to keep inmates occupied. Inmates were given uniforms and assigned ranks according to their behavior. Having been drilled on a daily basis, the units were then judged by the state's National Guard at a twice a year competition. Quickly a regimental band was formed as well. The Board of Managers felt that, "The military feature of our work has been useful in the way of stimulating discipline, as well as affording a means of exercise in connection with our gymnasium."

Another critical area for reform was religion. A "Christian character" along with a work ethic was fundamental to success, it was believed. A chapel was constructed to hold six hundred people. When it was dedicated in December, over one thousand people came. The 193 boys who entered with arms folded, and who then, at the tap of a little bell by McClaughry, quietly and obediently took a seat, impressed the spectators. Soon a choir and a glee club were set up to give concerts,[22] so there was often activity in the chapel besides the required attendance at services. Yet those services were the bedrock of the chapel's events: on two Sundays a month a Catholic priest ministered to the Catholic inmates, and the rest of the time services were nondenominational but evangelical in character. Sabbath school was optional but did offer the opportunity to earn merit points.

As these efforts at reform suggest McClaughry was fully committed—ideologically and operationally when resources allowed—to the reformatory ideals because it called a halt to the young criminal "by placing him where he will be compelled to regain his liberty by fitting himself for the duties of citizenship, where neither wealth, nor power, nor political influence of friends will avail him anything toward securing his release before that work is accomplished."[23]

But forces outside the reformatory complicated McClaughry's work. Gaps between the "ideal" world and the "real" one are often too great to bridge. One of the first problems was financial. Very early critics claimed that the cost of the Huntingdon Reformatory was three times that of the Eastern Penitentiary.[24] Indeed, there had been many start up costs. This was a new institution with no history. As McClaughry said "the law establishing the Reformatory was new and untried. No precedents existed in Pennsylvania for the methods proposed." Furthermore there was that "lack of momentum which attends fully organized institutions and makes government easy."[25] His defense was that the cost to society of a young criminal was far greater than the cost of running the Reformatory.[26] Second, the institution was filling up rapidly with inmates. Though the population of the entire state had grown by 27 percent since 1880, during McClaughry's short tenure of just over a year the number of inmates had gone from fifty to roughly five hundred.[27] Third, the reformatory was distant from large markets at which it could buy its necessities and sell its products, and this increased costs and reduced the possibility of income. Fourth, the famous Johnstown floods of June 1889—in which over 10,000 lives were lost—while not directly hurting Huntingdon, hampered transportation throughout the state. Fifth, consequently costs for things, especially fuel, were very high.[28]

In part due to these uncontrollable problems, and in part to some half-hearted acceptance of the reformatory idea by state politicians, criticisms began to grow. The problem was twofold. On one hand the inmate population did not lend itself to reform. By 1891 the majority of the inmates were gang members from Philadelphia. On March 1st, some 23 inmates instigated an insurrection. After this had been put down the *Philadelphia Inquirer* claimed there had been brutality towards the inmates. Indeed, McClaughry believed in tough love and some of his discipline could be interpreted as brutal. For example, he turned to spanking.

> One day the sharpeyed [sic.] Major, detecting one of the inmates in violation of the rules of the shoe shop, picked up a leather sole at hand and treated the astonished offender to a thorough and impressive spanking.
>
> The effect was so wholesome and touching that it came to the Major as an inspiration that he [had] stumbled across the ideal nineteenth century system of punishment. He adopted the process at once and is charmed with its success.[29]

McClaughry was simply mimicking the Elmira model. Zebulon Brockway was known for his slapping and spanking at the New York Reformatory.[30] Afraid he would be accused of brutality, McClaughry wisely went to the Governor of the state and to the head of the State Board of Charities to get approval. He returned to the reformatory convinced and a weekly "spanking school" resulted. Infraction of the rules immediately decreased because "inmates have a wholesome dread of the shame, disgrace, and stinging pain of the Major's orthodox spanks."[31] Local papers felt the need to defend him in January, 1891:

> We must consider that he has much of the riff raff of the Commonwealth under his care; boys of low instincts who never had the benefit of parental care, or if so, refused to submit to it; boys full of mischief and deviltry who need a kind yet at times a stern man to bring about the reformation such as the law contemplates. If there is a man in the country that can do this, Major McClaughry is that man.[32]

In spite of this tough love, the more hardened inmates (the "riff raff of the Commonwealth") took the more lax regimen of a reformatory as an opportunity to escape. For example, in the first year, three escape attempts occurred. Other inmates quickly followed either escaping the institution or violating their conditions of parole. James McGinnis, in the reformatory for burglary and larceny, had been doing well, even having been given special privileges to drive a team hauling out of the compound dirt left over from continuing construction. Apparently, life at the reformatory got to him and one day he just kept driving. Guards even fired three shots at him but he made good his get-away. After some second thoughts he gave himself up the next day.[33] Monroe Royer had better luck; he escaped and was gone for over a year. Daniel Boyle was out on parole but was rearrested after committing additional crimes. Samuel Geiger after being free for only three weeks was brought back because of going to dens of vice and getting into fights. Laporte escaped for six months before being caught and returned. One young man named Marley could not take it anymore and broke ranks during drills and scaled the high fence only to be easily recaptured.[34] Fred Maher (or Moyer) escaped in April,

1890. He had been working on an island opposite the institution and asked permission to go off and get some nails for the project. He crossed the river and fled. He was caught shortly after in Altoona.[35]

Inmates responded to the reformatory regime in a number of other ways. Striking out at reformatory personnel was one practice, and guards bore the brunt of this behavior. To the outrage of many latter-day puritans like McClaughry there was considerable "gross indecency," code phrases for masturbation and homosexuality. Two inmates were punished in February, 1890, for attempted sodomy. Some were put into solitary for "grossly indecent exposure of person."[36] A few reacted to their confinement with suicide. William Dickerson tried to hang himself in January, 1891. Within a week another inmate, Charles Richter, was found hanging in his cell.[37] As such stories hit the newspapers of the state many lost their enthusiasm for the experiment at Huntingdon.

Such recalcitrant behavior of these young criminals was disheartening to the Major too. McClaughry came to Huntingdon filled with hope (and maybe naiveté).Though he never lost his zeal for the reformatory ideology, there was disillusionment with its transfer to practice. Start up costs for him, both physically and psychologically, took a toll. In April 1891, amidst rumors of his bad health and problems between him and the Board of Managers, McClaughry resigned to take the seven thousand dollar per year post as Chief of Police in Chicago.[38]

Although everyone tried to put a good spin on the move, it was most likely precipitated by some problems between McClaughry and the Board of Managers. In the nineteenth-century tradition of politics in penology he tended to favor old friends and there were rumors of appointments to key positions of pals from Joliet.[39] Even more telling, there was evidently some disappointment over the reformatory ideas because shortly after McClaughry left, the Board of Managers, disgusted with the inmates, abandoned the reformatory ideals and moved to the time-tested Pennsylvania notion of solitary confinement.[40] For all intents and purposes, the reformatory was dead in Pennsylvania. In the meantime, McClaughry headed to one of the greatest challenges of his career.

NOTES

1. First Biennial Report of the Managers of the Pennsylvania Industrial Reformatory, January 1, 1891, p. 6.
2. Robert McClaughry to Rutherford Hayes January 12, 1889. Hayes papers, Rutherford Hayes Presidential Library.
3. *Joliet Press,* November 21, 1888.
4. *Huntingdon Globe*, January 3, 1889.

5. Robert McClaughry to W. Williams, March 26, 1889. Hayes Papers.
6. *Huntingdon Globe,* December 20, 1888.
7. *Ibid.*, February 7, 1889.
8. age/number
   15/1
   16/6
   17/5
   18/9
   19/12
   20/5
   21/4
   22/2
   23/5
   24/1
9. *Huntingdon Globe,* March 5, 1891.
10. *Ibid.*, May 2, 1889.
11. *Managers Report*, January 1, 1891, p. 6.
12. Pennsylvania Industrial Reformatory, First Biennial Report, 1889-1890, p. 15.
13. General Superintendent's Report in the Biennial Report of the Managers of the Pennsylvania Industrial Reformatory at Huntingdon, January 1, 1891, pp.18.
14. *Huntingdon Globe*, December 20, 1888.
15. Report of the Managers, January 1, 1891, p. 6.
16. *Pittsburgh Dispatch,* May 31, 1890.
17. Pennsylvania Industrial Reformatory, Third Biennial Report, 1889-1890, pp.48-49.
18. Huntingdon *Globe* October 17, 1889.
19. *Ibid.*
20. Pennsylvania Industrial Reformatory, First Biennial Report, 1889-1890, p. 21.
21. Report of the Managers, January 1, 1891, pp. 8-10.
22. Huntingdon *Globe* November 14 and December 5, 1889.
23. *Ibid.* p. 21.
24. Huntingdon *Globe* February 6, 1890.
25. General Superintendent's Report in the Biennial Report of the Managers of the Pennsylvania Industrial Reformatory at Huntingdon January 1, 1891, p. 15.
26. General Superintendent's Report, January 1, 1891, p. 22.
27. Huntingdon *Globe* February 26, 1891.
28. McClaughry's Report to the Managers in The Report of the Managers January 1, 1891, p.14.
29. Philadelphia Press, December 17, 1890.
30. Pisciotta, pp. 36-37.
31. *Ibid.*
32. Huntington *Globe* January 30, 1891.
33. Ibid., November 21, 1889.
34. *Ibid.*, June 6, 12 and October 2, 1890.
35. *Ibid.*, April 4, 1890 and Altoona Tribune April 4, 1890.

36. Record of Special Punishments, 1889-1897; Records of the Pennsylvania Industrial Reformatory, pp.6,12,32.
37. *Ibid.*, pp. 27-28, 72, 127-28.
38. *Ibid.*, April 16 and 23 and 30, 1891.
39. Philadelphia *Times* April 15, 1891.
40. *Huntingdon Globe* March 17 1892.

Part Four

POLICING CHICAGO

Chapter Eighteen

Chicago in the 1890s

"... careless of appearances."

The mayoral election in Chicago was particularly important in 1891. The winner would be rewarded with overseeing the Columbian Exposition, a world's fair celebrating the five hundredth anniversary of Christopher Columbus' discovery of America. The spectacular success of the World's Fair in Paris, in 1889 (and the traditional disdain of Chicago by cities like New York, Philadelphia, and Boston) made the Windy City's Fair an important exercise in boosterism.[1] One Chicago reporter, lamenting how the Parisian fair had embarrassed America, cautioned Chicagoans to be careful or "we shall be ranked among nations who have shown themselves careless of appearances."[2]

All kinds of work was necessary to prepare the city for such an event, not least by a newly elected mayor, but equal amounts of glory and power awaited as well. In addition to the prestige of being mayor at this particular time, this election was important also in seeking to break the hold on city politics by the political machine of Carter Harrison and the gambling syndicate of Michael Cassius McDonald. Harrison had already held office four times. In those periods the professional gamblers had tightened their grip on the vice industry. No wonder that "Gamblers Row," the major string of gaming houses in Chicago, was not only in the downtown financial district but actually in the shadow of city hall. Equally important, many felt that the unofficial city hall was The Store, a saloon/gambling house owned by Michael Cassius McDonald. Since the incumbent mayor, DeWitt Cregier, had become engulfed in a series of scandals tainting his administration; his reelection was questionable, and consequently, Carter Harrison came out of retirement and announced his candidacy. The result? Cregier and Harrison, posing as the "regular" democratic candidates, split the vote allowing a Republican reformer, Hempstead Washburne, to squeak by with a 369-vote margin.[3]

The new mayor had impressive credentials. The son of Elihu B. Washburne, the famed politician who had supported Lincoln and Grant in their careers and after fifteen years in Congress (for which he earned the sobriquet "Father of the House") had became minister to France, Hempstead Washburne came to public life with considerable exposure to education, culture, and politics at the highest levels. Furthermore, he had made himself a considerable reputation on his own as a local lawyer, serving two terms as city attorney from 1885 to 1889. Coming to power as a good government reformer, his first concern was however to get the city ready for the Columbian Exposition. Streets, dirty and always littered, needed to be cleaned up. One hundred and seventeen miles of roads begged for pavement. Six hundred and three miles of new sidewalks were needed. The number of tramps, especially with the economic downturns of the 90s, increased to over 30,000 in 1893. One religiously oriented commentator thought the hobos were "like the frogs in the Egyptian plague, you could not escape from the tramps, go where you would." Homeless and penniless men slept at night in police lockups especially the Harrison Street Station.[4] Yet at the top of Washburne's agenda was to rid the city of its greatest evil, the vice fraternity.

" . . . THE HAUNTS OF SIN OF A GREAT CITY."

Vice—gambling, saloons, and prostitution—had existed for a long time in Chicago, as they do in most cities. In fact, in the late 1850s Mayor Wentworth had frequently kept the vicelords in line and the outraged puritans quiet by conducting symbolic crusades against The Sands, the city's pre-Civil War sin district. After the war the vice industry grew rapidly but it was a topsy-turvy development. At no time did the vicelord/machine alliance dominate without challenge. Indeed, it was the constant threat of the good-government reformers that kept the vicelords on guard. The battle began in earnest in the early 1870s.

In 1873, the Republican Party, which dominated everywhere in Illinois, committed a major blunder by insisting on the enforcement of the Sunday closing laws for saloons. Two perceptions prevailed at the time on the nature of the Sabbath in America. The traditional "puritan Sabbath" advocates saw Sunday as a holy day rather than a holiday on which church activities dominated. Social activities should be familial and wholesome. At the very least businesses should be closed. Those favoring the "continental Sabbath" wanted

Sunday as a day of rest and recreation, with or without church, depending on one's preference. America in the last half of the nineteenth century, at least, was caught up in this classic battle between religious fundamentalism and secularism. German voters, a very large voting bloc, considered Sunday closing laws to be an assault on their lifestyle. Under similar circumstances in 1855, a Lager Riot resulted and inspired the creation of the modern police in Chicago. In 1873, however, the Germans abandoned the Republicans. They, with many of the less puritanical Democrats, formed the People's Party. Their candidate, a well-known member of the gambling fraternity named Harvey Colvin, promised a wide-open city. For the first time the gamblers of Chicago became very active in politics. John Corcoran, a major gambler from the north side, became Colvin's campaign manager. Thomas Foley—a billiards champion, baseball promoter, and saloon keeper—sought the position of alderman of the first ward, the heart of the vice district. From his notorious saloon, The Store, Michael McDonald organized the gambling house runners who got out the vote encouraging people not only to vote but to do so numerous times each. Colvin and Foley won and the gamblers took over the city for a season.[5] Lessons were learned and ambitions whetted.

GAMBLING

Yet the gambling syndicate did not remain unchallenged. For example, in 1876 Monroe Heath was elected mayor and a series of raids resulted. The election of Carter Harrison in 1879 brought peace and prosperity to the gamblers and saloon keepers again. In fact, for most of the long reign of Mayor Harrison, with McDonald as vice boss in the background, the gamblers flourished.

Michael McDonald's syndicate of gamblers/machine politicians dominated for much of the remaining nineteenth century. McDonald was credited with creating the parlor (or casino) form of gambling in the city in the early 1870s. Hating the police as a whole, he was once asked to donate a dollar for the police officers' burial fund; he reached into his safe and gave $10. "Here's ten," he was reported to have said, "go bury ten more."[6] When raided in 1880, McDonald went to the newly elected mayor, Carter Harrison, and had the offending Superintendent of Police, Simon O'Donnell, demoted and sent to a high crime area. He then got William McGarigle, a sympathetic officer, appointed superintendent.[7]

Even when the good-government people were in power it was hard to close down the gambling dens. The only police tool was the raid. They could do this in two ways. They could knock and announce their presence and intent, or they could just crash in. Either way, it was most likely that news of the raid would have preceded the police and that the gambling paraphernalia—so essential as evidence—would have disappeared. In fact, the police probably had two forces, one to conduct raids for the public and the press, the other to leak out news of the raid to prepare the gamblers.[8] Caught between the public and the politicians, police policy seemed to be pragmatic: it being impossible to abolish vice, it became important to regulate it, to keep it from erupting into a major issue. Maintaining order, in this case, was more important than enforcing the law.

However, public tastes did have an effect on gambling. Throughout the 1880s the public slowly turned from parlor gambling, which had always been a little seedy given the odds heavily in favor of the professional gamblers, to the more sportsman-like horse racing. After the Civil War numerous influential people began to form jockey clubs, organizations devoted to the improvement of horses in America. To do so they proposed competitive racing and the offering of a winning purse. Horse racing tracks, the most famous being the Garfield Park and the Washington Park tracks, began to dot the urban and suburban landscape.[9] At first this supposed sport of gentlemen was deemed acceptable as long as its seasonal races were in the bucolic suburbs and they were not run on the Sabbath. Of course, in this fast growing era, the city soon caught up with the rural areas and the more secular minded questioned the Puritan Sabbath. More important was the introduction of gambling. On track gambling soon occurred in the pari-mutual system. Under this system the Jockey Club would authorize a select few to take bets at the track. They would keep accounts in a book, establishing a record of bets and bettors, and calculating the odds. This task was too lucrative to be left to the blue bloods and the gambling syndicate soon took it over and a host of "bookies" inundated the tracks. For example, when Washington Park opened in 1884, twenty-four book makers showed up. Within three years they dominated all tracks.[10]

Yet the gambling clientele at that point was only a small segment of all the people at a racing event, but technology soon changed this. Western Union telegraph lines connected the tracks to pool rooms in the city—a place far from the race track in which groups of people, clerks and ordinary workers on break, would form a pool of bettors. The pool room proprietor would then be the bookie, taking in and giving out money based upon the wire-fed information coming from the track. Most of these pool rooms were located in "Gambler's Alley," in the heart of the financial district, but soon they spread everywhere. This "pool room evil" became a major concern of those of a more puritanical mind set. In any "purity crusade" the pool rooms would be the first to be attacked and by 1887 they were outlawed.[11]

SALOON

Closely associated with the gambling enterprise was the saloon. Numerous working-class saloons were scattered throughout the city. Characterized by their swinging shutter doors and wrought-iron windows, these were poor men's clubs. Generally, a counter ran the length of the room where customers would stand with a foot on the brass foot rails and occasionally take aim at spittoons strategically placed around on the saw dust floors. Numerous posters, mostly advertisements or sports figures, were prominently displayed. The sleazier saloons would have a picture of a partially disrobed woman hanging behind the bar. A few tables and chairs, perhaps a billiard table, amounted to the only furnishings. One was expected to stand and drink whiskey straight with only a water chaser. Free food might be provided for the price of a drink. The so-called "free lunch" was most likely invented by Joseph Chesterfield Mackin or "Chesterfield Joe" shortly after the Chicago fire in 1871; in the highly competitive saloon world, he started serving free hot oysters to drinkers in hopes of boosting his customer base. By the 1890s one saloon in the working class 17th Ward served a choice of frankfurters, clams, egg sandwiches, potatoes, vegetables, cheeses, bread, and many varieties of hot and cold meats, often amounting to thirty or forty dollars' worth of food every day[12]—or around $800 in today's dollars.[13] It was hardly a coincidence that there was a "Whiskey Row located in the workingman's space in the "Back of the Yards," the meat packing and processing area of the city, and moreover that, largely as a result of drunken brawls, most Chicago homicides occurred in these very saloons.[14]

Every single building in another "Whiskey Row", on the west side of State Street from Van Buren to Harrison, was either a saloon, a wine room with girls, a gambling house, or a combination of all three. Numerous "dives" or one-room sparsely-furnished joints devoted to little but serious drinking sprung up too. Frequently, these places were owned by a former criminal flirting with going straight. Sometimes the proprietor was still an active crook and the place became a watering hole for the criminal classes. Tom McGinnis, a noted professional gambler, had saloon/gambling place called the Berlin Cafe. Al Connolly, a Democratic Committeeman for years, started a dive in 1891 and it became a favorite place for sneak thieves and pickpockets. Johnny Rafferty, leader of the city's confidence gangs, likewise owned a saloon. Sime Tuckhorn's place—one of the toughest on Whiskey Row—was a hangout for thieves. Bob Duncan, known as the "King of Pickpockets," had two places, one a concert saloon with girls upstairs, the other a craps and faro joint. One student of pickpockets in the United States thought Duncan's places were the best known hangouts for pickpockets in the country. Perhaps the most infamous dive owner lent his name to a common practice in the dives. Mickey Finn and his wife, "Gold Tooth Mary," robbed many of their patrons at the Lone Star dive after putting knock-out drops in their drinks.[15]

Along with such dives, the first so-called "concert saloon" opened in 1873 and shortly dozens were in operation. As long as you drank you were allowed to dance in such places as The Alhambra, Tivoli Gardens, The Garden, The Park, and The Foxhall, in this case "dancing" being double speak for solicitation for sex. One historian, Perry Duis, called the concert saloon a "department store of vice," and indeed the more elaborate ones had many stories. Usually the main floor was a saloon with seductively clad "Grisettes" or waitresses pushing drinks, along with a stage for "theatrical presentations." Upstairs there were cubicles for prostitutes and their customers.[16]

Euphemistically named "The Store," Chicago's preeminent saloon closed in 1888 but Varnells, which catered to a higher-class clientele, took its place. In 1891, Varnells renovated with $40,000 invested in Mexican onyx, Florentine mosaic, mahogany, and silver decorations.[17] Most of such saloons offered gambling and prostitution in addition to drinking. Besides providing entertainment eagerly sought after by the men of Chicago, the success of these places was based upon political influence. Some saloon keepers actually sat on the city council as aldermen. The police were also in on the take, but the chief offender, from the perspective of the good government people, was the judicial system. The justices of peace were particularly easily bribed and often conducted proceedings without a jury. Any success at bringing the saloon down had to be preceded first by attacks on gambling and then prostitution.

PROSTITUTION

There was another vice problem, over which most religious people and good government reformers became morally upset, but about which they had difficulty sustaining a political will and ability to deal. After the Chicago fire of 1871, prostitution became the biggest and most profitable business in vicedom. The town, filled with young bachelors on the make and politicians with a wide open city attitude, provided a ready market for sex workers. Thousands of streetwalkers roamed the entertainment districts.[18] Many prostitutes operated out of saloons and gambling houses, and such parlor prostitution became so prominent and brazen that by 1889 a guide to the Chicago brothels was published, entitled *Sporting and Club House Directory*. Unlike gambling, which was very public and hard to miss in Gambler's Alley, prostitution had found a more discrete way to deliver its services. The "red light district," a small section of the city in which numerous brothels and houses of assignation were allowed to exist, was a unique bit of social policy. Earlier, areas on the North Side—especially on Clark Street—had formed with names like "Bad Lands" and "Little Cheyenne." The latter was named after the notorious railroad town of the 1870s. In retaliation, the people of Cheyenne, Wyoming, named their red light district "Little Chicago."[19] By the 1890s the nineteenth precinct of the first ward, an area of the near South Side called the Levee, had forty-six saloons, thirty-seven brothels and eleven pawnbrokers, and would be the undisputable sin district of Chicago.[20] Respectable Chicagoans had little reason to go into the Levee, tucked away in a seedy "low rent" area of the First Ward. In fact, being there raised questions about one's moral character. Those who desired such services knew where to go; and those who found them morally repugnant knew the places to avoid.

Not that moral crusaders were inactive. In 1886 the Florence Crittenton Anchorage, a shelter for prostitutes, was set up by the Women's Christian Temperance Union with a mission "to care for unfortunate girls who have been led astray and to protect the innocent and friendless from being led into the haunts of sin of a great city."[21] The religious community would occasionally equate the city to Sodom and Gomorrah and demand stronger enforcement of the law. The political machine then might carry out some raids for public relations purposes, but generally it just deflected criticism. Probably the most notable outraged puritan was a visitor from England, William Stead. Eventually, he would write a book asking what would happen *If Christ Came to Chicago (*1894).This self righteous journalist would titillate his readers with the whore house routine.

> In the morning, just before 12, the colored girl served cocktails to each of the women before they get up. After they dressed, they took another refresher, usually absinth. At breakfast they had wine.

Then the work began.

> The girls sat in couples at the windows, each keeping watch in the opposite direction. If a man passed they would rap at the window and beckon him to come in.

All trace of hustling would cease if a suspicious person, perhaps an uncorrupted police officer, appeared. This window advertising went on all afternoon with the women working fifteen-minute shifts.

> At five they dined. and then the evenings business began, with more drinking at intervals, all night through, to the accompaniment of piano playing with occasional step-dancing, and adjournments more or less frequent, as customers were [more] or less plentiful.

It all ended at four or five in the morning only to begin all over again the next day.[22]

Though prostitution was illegal, laws were rarely enforced. The police realized that, in spite of the religious community's insistence, prostitution could not be banished. Keeping a lid on the Levee became policy, particularly in the so-called panel houses that were rife with a specific crime known as the "panel game." This crime was made possible by a sliding partition in the wall of the room. While the customer was disrobed and preoccupied, a friend of the prostitute slipped in to take valuables and money from the pockets of the victim's clothes. Only rarely did an embarrassed victim report the crime, but if he did the police would rush to punish the house. In 1890 there were at least 200 panel houses, most of them on Custom House Place, Clark and State Streets, and Plymouth Place. In the mid 1890s the police estimated an average of $1,500,000 was stolen every year in the panel houses. The police policy was essentially this: as long as no criminal complaints came out of the sin district, it could persist provided owners paid the police "fees" to carry on business uninterrupted.

The ordinary street cop was therefore an important aspect of the business of prostitution. And yet brothels remained wary, creating systems to warn of the arrival of police officers bent on a raid. One officer observed that "all the houses were equipped with electric bells, and a sentinel, whose duty it was to watch for the police and give a signal to the inmates, was stationed at each end of the street between Polk and Harrison."[23] Some officers took advantage of the prostitutes. One Chicago cop, whom the prostitutes dubbed Pat the Terrier, regularly walked into the brothel demanding food and whiskey. Commonly a madam served him the equivalent of $15 in food and drink in a week. Other fees were collected by regular cops for higher placed officers.[24]

Not all officers were like Pat the Terrier. One, who styled himself as "The World's Greatest Detective," was Clifton Wooldridge. A member of the police department from 1888 to 1910 he was a one-man crusader against crime and vice. According to him—and he was a master of self-promotion—he made nearly twenty thousand arrests in a twenty-year career. He was responsible for sending two hundred crooks to prison and three thousand to the House of Correction, and for "rescuing" nearly one hundred girls from the brothels.

If Wooldridge's accounts of his career are to be believed, the Chicago police was not thoroughly corrupt.[25] In a city with over one thousand officers it would be wrong to think the entire department tainted. There were some officers, islands of incorruptibility in an otherwise sea of sharks, looking for leadership to make them proud of their occupation, good news to the newly appointed reform chief, Robert McClaughry.

NOTES

1. Eric Larson, *The Devil in the Windy City: Murder, Magic, and Madness at the Fair That Changed America* (New York: Crown Publishers, 2003), pp. 16, 32, 49, 60, 80-81, 119, 134, 156.

2. Quoted in *Ibid.* p. 15. See also *Chicago Tribune,* May 13, 1889.

3. Virgil W. Peterson, *Barbarians in Our Midst: A History of Chicago Crime and Politics* (Boston: Little, Brown, 1952), p. 57.

4. William T. Stead, *If Christ Came to Chicago* (Chicago: Laird & Lee, 1894), pp. 23-24.

5. David R. Johnson. *Policing the Urban Underworld: The Impact of Crime on the Development of the American Police, 1800-1887. (Philadelphia*: Temple University Press, 1979), p. 175.

6. Richard Lindberg, "The Evolution of an Evil Business," *Chicago History* 22 (July, 1993), p. 43.

7. *Ibid.*, p. 44-45.

8. *Ibid.*, pp. 176-77.

9. *Ibid.* p. 45.

10. *Chicago Tribune*, July 24, 31, 1887.

11. Anthony Comstock, "Bookmakers and Poolsellers," *Independent* 44 (May 5, 1892), pp. 3-5.

12. Jon M Kinsdale, "The 'Poor Man's Club: Social Functions of the Urban Working-Class Saloon," *American Quarterly* 25 (1973), pp. 472-89.

13. John J. McCusker, "Comparing the Purchasing Power of Money in the United States (or Colonies) from 1665 to 2003," Economic History Series, 2004, UCR http: www. eh. net/hmit/ppowerusd/.

14. Jeffrey S. Adler, *First in Violence, Deepest in Dirt: Homicide in Chicago, 1875-1929* (Cambridge, Massachusetts: Harvard University Press, 2006). pp. 6-44.

15. Herbert Asbury, *Gem of the Prairie: An Informal History of the Chicago Underworld* (Dekalb, Illinois: Northern Illinois University, 1986), p. 172.

16. Perry R. Duis , *The Saloon: Public Drinking in Chicago and Boston, 1880-1920* (Urbana and Chicago: University of Illinois Press, 1983), pp. 237-38.

17. *Ibid.*, p. 239.

18. *Chicago Times,* February 20, 1870.

19. Asbury, pp. 106-111.

20. Stead, p. 133.

21. Quoted in Besse Louise Pierce's *A History of Chicago Vo.l III: The Rise of a Modern City, 1871-1893* (New York City: Alfred A Knopf, 1957), p. 460.

22. *Ibid.*, p. 44. For corroboration of this view see also Wooldridge, pp. 367-69.

23. Wooldrige, p. 367.

24. *Ibid.*, p. 43.

25. Asbury, pp.125-27.

Chapter Nineteen

Policing the City

"Now the Chicago police force is divided among all nationalities."

GEOGRAPHY

After some twenty years with a constable/night watch system, in 1855 Chicago created its modern police department. This was largely due to an ethnic riot over beer. The more puritanical and xenophobic politicians of the time had raised liquor licensing fees so high that many taverns closed down. Irish and German minorities rioted (it was called the Lager riots) throwing the city into chaos. Shortly after Chicago's modern police was created.

The police immediately became a patronage pool for a series of political bosses, rather than a neutral force for the general public. Mayor John Wentworth, for example, used the police as a private body guard. He waged a major war against the growing private police industry shortly before the Civil War.[1] After the war, a series of governors, mayors, and machine bosses sought to control the police. Up until the late 1870s control of the city police—like in most major cities in America—was in the hands of the governor. By 1880 police control had returned to the mayor. The main qualities essential to the police occupation was ethnic politics.

By 1890 the population of Chicago was a little over one million (1,099,850). Chicago residents born in foreign countries, amounting to some 450,666 people, remained over 40 percent of the total population. Germans still predominated with 161,039 (or a little over 10 percent of the total) with Irish born folks following at 70,028.[2] The Germans continued to add most to the city population in this period although groups from eastern and southern Europe began to establish a presence. Although the Irish declined in population, they continued to hold strength in the area of government service. For example, of the total number of people employed in public services (government and police), Germans holding jobs declined from 13 percent to 12 percent between 1880 and 1890. On the other hand, the Irish increased from 20 percent to 24 percent.[3]

By the mid 1880s there were 1,091 police officers, a police-population ratio of 1.3 officers per thousand residents. One hundred years later there would be five officers per thousand residents. But such a ratio was not out of line with other large cities in the nineteenth century. For example, at the same time Philadelphia had 1.93 and New York City had 1.36 officers per thousand citizens.

The Chicago police department was divided into five large areas called precincts. City center—in what is roughly the Loop area today—was central district. It was mainly concerned with the overall administration of the department, the detective division, and the daytime guarding of the streets and shops of downtown. It had been known previously simply as the "day squad." Of course, the nefarious "Whiskey Row" and "Gamblers Row" fell under its jurisdiction. Directly south of central district—and moving in a clockwise pattern around the city—the police precincts were laid out beginning with the First Precinct on the South Side, along the lake and down to the southern city limits at 39th Street. Near downtown, the First had the slums and the sin districts to police. Further south were stable residential areas with large concentrations of Irish in the southwest. Due west of the First was the Second Precinct, which encompassed high crime "terror districts" close to center city as well as residential and factory lands further out. North of the Second was the Third Precinct. It was here that the famed DesPlaines police district was located. Its action during the Haymarket disturbances lent the sobriquet "the noble Third" to this precinct. North of the Third was the Forth Precinct, largely residential with a preponderantly mixed German and Polish population. As more and more "new Germans" arrived and were involved in the city's radical movements, this area became known as the "hot bed of anarchism." Finally, making the clockwise movement to the east, along the north shore the Fifth Precinct was characterized by the largest single concentration of middle-class Germans. The Fifth, Fourth. and Third Precincts were subdivided into three police districts each. A few, such as the DesPlaines and West Lake districts, gained notoriety due to the Haymarket riot. It was the West Chicago district in the Fourth that had most of the problems with anarchists. These radicals gave fiery speeches and led demonstrations against working and living conditions in the city. The First and Second Precincts had five police districts each. The Harrison Street and West 12th Street districts were known for their high crime and vice areas.

A short description of the Harrison Street Station, the "nerve center of criminal Chicago," is revealing. A two story building, the main floor was devoted to office administration. Here, under McClaughry's watch, the Bertillon identification bureau would be placed. The time honored "Sweat Box"—a room devoted to rough-house interrogation called The Third Degree—was tucked away in the interior. Upstairs had rooms for officers "on call." Until the 1890s, when McClaughry would change the work schedule, the individual officer was on duty for twelve hours and on call for twelve. Those on call were divided into two groups: those allowed to go home but required to respond immediately if an emergency arose, and those sleeping at the station. When occasion demanded—for example, during a particularly harsh snap of weather—homeless people were allowed to sleep in these quarters. The lock up was in the basement, its cells resembling cages for wild beasts. These cages opened onto corridors on the right and left. Remaining corridors had cells only on one side with the wall forming part of the cage. Each cell had one bench. An open gutter at back provided the sanitary outlet. These cells were always filled to capacity, and frequently, the corridors acted as temporary sleeping arrangements for tramps.[4]

DEMOGRAPHY

In 1890 the median age of the Chicago police department was 34, and the average 35.2. By 1870 big city police departments had become important avenues of upward mobility for various ethnic groups. Reflecting the immigrant character of Chicago, in 1887, 555 members of the police department had been born outside America, at 35 percent the Irish having the highest number, and the Germans making up 8 per cent of the force. About 75 percent of these officers actually lived within the boundaries of the police district in which they worked,[5] and typically the ethnic make up of the police force mirrored the community they policed. For example, 52 per cent of all the German officers worked in the Forth and the Fifth Precincts. By 1877 a reporter could proclaim:

> Now the Chicago police force is divided among all nationalities. And this is well, not so much because every nationality has an individual right to be represented in the force—it has nothing of the sort—but because business can be best expedited in that way, and the ends of justice and the interests of humanity are so best subserved [sic.]. Now the German districts are largely patrolled by German policemen, the Scandinavian by Scandinavians and so on through the whole list. By this means each policeman is his own interpreter and many serious blunders and mistakes avoided.[6]

In reality not all police districts had such a tidy fit. Many downtown districts—such as Harrison Street, West 12th, DesPlaines, and West Lake Street stations,—had changed tremendously causing Chicago officers and their families to suffer in ways similar to those reported by Andrea Kornmann, the wife of a New York City officer. In 1887, Kornmann had complained that people in her residence building did not want anything to do with her when they discovered her husband's occupation.[7] Such tensions were not only a problem for the individual officer (and his family) but for those administrating the beat cops.

Leadership at the Superintendent (Chief) level had rarely been strong, and had always been political. Some had been good officers earlier but never understood their new role. Some had character and vision but were stymied by mayors, aldermen, or machine bosses; a few had been thoroughly corrupt. One superintendent, Elmer Washburn, had been head of the government's Secret Service during the Civil War and warden of the Illinois State Penitentiary at Joliet, but knew nothing of big city policing. His administration had been a disaster and he left when the machine candidate, Harvey Colvin was elected.[8]

Between 1879 and 1897, nine superintendents came and went without finding the time or power to establish control.[9] There were two reasons for this. First, superintendents were often caught up in the higher political battles between the mayor, city council, boss machines, and good government reformers. Second, they had little control over their subordinates. Captains and lieutenants were promoted or demoted by the mayor. Frequently, they ruled their precincts and districts as oriental potentates. They may be called, with very little exaggeration, the "Chicago Shoguns." Cops, out on their beats, as long as they kowtowed to their captains and sergeants, could do what they wanted. They could drink in the saloons, go home for a rest, visit a brothel, or neglect to do their duties. Headquarters was far away and largely ignored. It was into such a situation that Robert McClaughry came in 1891.

NOTES

1. See Frank Morn, *"The Eye That Never Sleeps."*
2. *The People of Chicago: Who We Are and Who We Have Been: Census Data on Foreign Born, Foreign Stock and Race, 1837-1970. (Chicago*: Department of Development and Planning, 1976), pp. 21-22.
3. Bessie Louise Pierce, pp. 22, 24, 516-18.
4. Stead., p. 25.
5. For more detail see Frank Morn's "The Chicago Police in the mid 1880s: an Exercise in Demographic History" A paper read to the Academy of Criminal Justice Sciences conference in Las Vegas, Nevada, March, 1985.

6. Quoted in John Flinn, *History of the Chicago Police* (Chicago: Police Book Fund, 1887), p. 72.

7. A Policeman's Wife [Andrea Masria Kornmann] *Our Police* (New York: J.J. Little and Co., 1887), pp. 79, 81.

8. Flinn, pp. 138-39.

9. Robert M. Fogelson, *Big City Police* (Cambridge, Mass.: Harvard University Press, 1977), p. 23.

Chapter Twenty

McClaughry and the Police

"Everything will be left to Major McClaughry."

PUBLIC RELATIONS

Chiefs of Police, then and now, are ultimately political figures, and this politics plays out on many levels: their appointment and tenure are political acts; local politicians, the press, and powerful social groups are important constituencies. Then, of course, there is politics within the organization itself: high-ranking officers, detectives, and ordinary patrolmen are important political clusters ready to elevate or shoot down the chief. Of all the political challenges McClaughry faced, perhaps the easiest to deal with were those outside the organization. On one level, the lines were clear. The Harrison machine and vicelords were adamant in their opposition. In that case, McClaughry simply stiffened his resolve. Working-class people were a bit more problematic. Their dislike of the status quo was personal. However, the poor and working classes lived in areas of high crime potential and had a vested interest in an honest and efficient police force. The business, religious, and social elites were McClaughry's power base and he made sure throughout his administration to respond to them.

Of course, as chief of police, the Major, as the press liked to refer to him, was a spokesman of the nature and threat of crime. Any chief needs to alert the public to a crime problem to assure financial support. At the same time the public had to be convinced that the police could handle ordinary problems. Chicago had always had a crime problem, but the coming of the World's Fair posed special challenges. McClaughry was concerned about the number of criminals coming to fleece tourists at the Fair. McClaughry and Thomas

Marsh, the deputy superintendent, early on had indiscreetly let their concerns be known. This angered the mayor, and in a series of moves at damage control, McClaughry assured the community that they were safer now then one year ago. But the Fair was going to cause some problems that could be resolved if the city would allow him to hire an additional five hundred officers. Still nonplussed, the mayor suggested that the department perhaps was top heavy, and that getting rid of some of the higher ups would help loosen money to hire at the rank and file levels.[1] This personnel issue would be a constant tension between the Major and the Mayor.

There will always be a delicate (perhaps a teeter-totter) relationship between the mayor and his chief of police. This was exacerbated as McClaughry began to make more public appearances. Throughout his career in criminal justice, be it in corrections or policing, McClaughry took every opportunity to preach reform. In Chicago he had ample opportunities to speak. Very early upon his arrival he was called to make a speech at the Workers' Church before an overflowing audience of four hundred workers on the topic of "Crime as Relating to the Working Class." In that speech he acknowledged that crime was the biggest social and financial burden facing society. For every population increase of 25 percent, he believed, there was a 60 percent increase in crime. Several reasons accounted for this. First, there was the apparent breakdown in family "where the child is reared in an atmosphere of wrong." Second, due to the lack of parental care, children were growing up in the streets where most models of behavior were ruffians. Third, in both the rich and poorer classes, idleness was a cause of crime. Every child should grow up understanding how to make a living, he believed. "If the parent cannot teach this the state should, and such measures are now being undertaken in Illinois." Fourth, while intemperance was another major source of crime, the chief cause was gambling—not just gambling in the great halls and lowly shops but worst of all gambling in the home because "it teaches the youth that it is right to accept values without returning an equivalent . . . ." Then shifting in his speech to areas of his greatest expertise, McClaughry insisted that offenders had to be dealt with firmly but kindly. "All punishments must be dealt out in the spirit of kindness and not revenge, and with punishment must also follow instruction and education."[2]

Shortly after this address to the workers, McClaughry returned to similar themes before the Illinois Conference of Charities when he talked about "The Waifs." According to his statistics there were around ten thousand homeless children throughout the state, most being in Chicago. Since such children generally turned to theft to survive, he believed that homeless children must be supplied with jobs, rather than the state relying on private charity. "Prison officials tell us," he reminded the audience," that the least percentage of criminals comes from the employed."

> We can never successfully cope with this problem until the State takes charge of all dependent children under the age of 14, gives them instruction, and provides homes for them. At present we have no facilities in Chicago for separating children from the adult offenders. It would be well for this conference to throw its influence on the side of a movement that would provide a separate institution for youthful offenders.[3]

In his public relations role McClaughry was always visible at other social and charitable functions. For example, every Thanksgiving the Chicago Waifs' Mission sponsored a free feast for the homeless children of the city. About 1,200 homeless "waifs" devoured a ton and a half of turkey, three hundred and fifty pies, and a quarter ton of grapes at the Calvary Armory. McClaughry was there to give a sermonette. He told the crowd of boys that they had more power to make the future community great and noble than all the police forces and soldiers in the state. He implied, but did not say, that these same boys could bring down the great city as well.[4] Later he would deliver an address to over seven hundred people at a meeting of the Citizen's League of Chicago for the Suppression of the Sale of Liquor to Minors. Pre-empting criticisms of his attending such an event, McClaughry wholeheartedly supported the organization, for as a warden at Joliet and Chief of Police in Chicago he had seen all too often the "product of the saloons."[5]

Indeed, McClaughry had a curious, almost twentieth-century position in the field of criminal justice. He was by inclination and experience most dedicated to corrections, prison reform, and administration. But now he was a chief of police in one of the country's largest cities, giving him one foot in corrections and another in policing. His dual experience was visible for example at the annual convention of the National Prison Association held in Baltimore in 1892. McClaughry was chair of the Committee on Police Forces of the Cities. His annual report was a major address to the conference on the police of America. After outlining the recent major accomplishments—better distribution of police patrol squads, the introduction of the covered patrol wagon, and the adoption of the telegraph and telephone—he focused on the three major obstacles to reform. First, political interference remained the biggest problem. As long as politicians had a voice in the hiring and firing of officers, no crusade against crime could be made. Second, there was no clear classification of differing degrees of criminality, and this left the police in a vast limbo of enforcement. And, third, in most places magistrates continued to collect fees from those who posted bail in court, a practice that tended to corrupt the judges. Then in prophetic ways he saw the future being one in which policing would be even more difficult because of the growing concentration of America's population into the cities. In very modern ways he declared:

> No problems of municipal government can be more important in years to come than those which are connected intimately with the organization and direction of the police systems of our great cities. This being the case, it behooves patriotic Americans to look to it at once that our police departments are not made tools of designing politicians, nor managed in the interests of those whose action is governed by solely mercenary motives. With the additional duties laid upon them almost daily, motives which have to do with their dearest concerns of business and social and family life, no effort should be spared to bring about the day when the police forces of our cities shall be composed of the best material physically, intellectually, and morally that the cities can produce. Drunkards and incompetents must not be permitted to remain in the ranks because of political pull. When this is accomplished good men will seek service. They will give their thought to the study of their duties and their lives to the profession of their pride.[6]

Of course, in a city dominated by the political machine the greatest obstacle to creating a sense of professionalism was politics.

POLITICS OF POLICING

As a new reform mayor, Washburne sought out Robert McClaughry to become Superintendent of Police. This was quite a remarkable decision given that McClaughry had no police experience. Later, McClaughry remembered that call from mayor-elect Washburne. The mayor and other civic leaders—such as John R. Walsh, Joseph Medill, and William Story—"insisted on my accepting the position as chief. They said they expected a large influx of criminals during the holding of the fair, and they thought that I, with my wide acquaintance among the criminals of the country, would be the man for the job."[7]

There was considerable opposition to McClaughry's appointment particularly from the Democratic aldermen who belonged to the machine.[8] McClaughry was not a resident of the city or state, they insisted.[9] Of course, such charges masked real concerns. The new mayor was committed to reform. "Maj. McClaughry will not be hampered in any way," the mayor was quoted as saying:

> I have known several mighty good men in the position of Chief of Police who were handicapped by having worthless men thrust upon them for political reasons. Maj. McClaughry will not be given any such weight to bear. He can pick

> out his own men from Assistant Superintendent to the station janitor. Everything will be left to Maj. McClaughry. I will carry out my pledge to divorce politics from police business by intrusting all appointments to him. And I know merit alone is what will count in his selections.[10]

McClaughry noted that, "Mr. Washburne has given me to understand that the only condition on which I could accept the office was that I shall divorce the police from politics. That condition meets with my own views entirely."[11] And indeed he would have to contend with "brokers," men like "Pap" Edwards, who ran an employment office specializing in using political influence to get people jobs in the police force for a fee.[12] In protest of the announcement of McClaughry's appointment, two of the city's more prominent gambling houses closed for a day of mourning.[13] Corporation Counsel, the chief legal counsel for the city, saw through the hoax and quickly announced that McClaughry was born and raised in Illinois but had just taken employment outside the state. Residency in the city was not required for the position, he noted.[14] Prominent businessmen were so overjoyed that they took up a collection to supplement McClaughry's salary, an offer he quickly declined.[15] Still, many of the political hacks on the force viewed McClaughry's selection with concern. One newspaper crowed:

> Just what the new chief will do is a matter of great anxiety to the members of the department. The patrolman who splinters his locust [night stick] against the telephone poles out in Brighton, the dapper young men whose 'influence' has made detectives at headquarters, the lieutenants, the captains and the inspectors are all crowding each other on the anxious bench when the new chief begins to swing the ax.[16]

On the other hand, McClaughry wanted his good officers to know, that some

> have complained that to carry out the strict letter of the law would sometimes bring an influence to bear to dismiss them. Such a complaint will be no longer possible. The officers may rest assured that so long as they obey instructions they will be retained and no influence will dislodge them.[17]

Even in his new role as police chief, McClaughry remained active in the National Prison Association (NPA), forerunner to the American Correctional Association. He was not ready to compartmentalize himself as either a warden or chief of police. He was one of the earliest figures to straddle both fields. In 1891 he was secretary to the NPA. In addition—along with Charles Felton, Benjamin Murphy, and Joseph Golden—he continued to be on the important committee on police. After some survey research, the committee on policing were able to report that:

> The first and greatest difficulty in endeavoring to build up an efficient police system is its dependence upon politics. The Aldermen of each ward have been expected to name the policemen who should be appointed from that ward and placed on duty at the several precincts. Aldermen naturally promise the places to the men who are instrumental in securing their election.[18]

Even after the tone set by McClaughry had been put in place many found it hard to move out of a political mind set. MClaughry would complain to the governor that, "the money appropriated for police protection is of very little more use than for the maintenance of a uniformed political club."[19] In October, 1891, when an assistant superintendent was to be appointed, political affiliation was brought up again. One promising candidate was frowned upon because he was a Democrat. "The claim is made that in order to preserve the nonpartisan nature of the force the assistant should be a Republican, as a majority of the inspectors are Democrats," the chief wrote the governor.[20] Thus the adherence to McClaughry's anti-partisan policy was already degenerating. Such heavily laden politics from the outside made the administering of the police even more challenging. This tug-of-war between old style machine cops and those who wanted reform played out dramatically up and down the police organization, particularly in the leadership ranks.

MANAGING THE POLICE: LEADERSHIP RANKS

For any police chief, it is essential that the most immediate administrative staff—the deputies and inspectors—be a solid part of the team and not backroom connivers. Because of the political nature of police administration, numerous former chiefs were still in the Chicago hierarchy when McClaughry arrived. One area of concern was that of the inspectors, an office created in 1880 to assist the superintendent. In ten years the number of inspectors increased and they served as a policy and advisory cabinet to the superintendent. Also, that office had become a dumping ground for previous superintendents displaced by the changing political winds. Simon O'Donnell, Frederich Ebersold, and Amos Hathaway—all prominent old-timers, two of whom had been superintendents themselves—were inspectors McClaughry asked to resign. In their place Frederich Marsh, Nicholas Hunt, George Hubbard, and Michael Schaack were appointed to inspectorships. To forestall any accusations of theirs being political appointments, McClaughry had chosen men evenly divided between the political parties.[21]

Even so, considerable dissension existed in the higher ranks. To long-timers, McClaughry was an outsider going against the way things had been done for the past thirty-five years. Several of his immediate subordinates were "fostering the spirit of faction, sowing the seeds of dissensions, and keeping the department in a constant state of turmoil with their personal quarrels, or in promoting their personal ambitions, or trying to satisfy their personal grudges . . . " McClaughry later claimed.[22] Some officers were even defiant. Sometimes the public abetted this by expressing their attachment to a particular officer. For example, in October it was learned that the "grateful" citizens of the Second Precinct wanted to give Lieutenant Max Kipley a gold watch. A delegation of citizens came to the chief to see if he would object. When McClaughry did object they went to the mayor who sided with the chief. Such gratuities were in poor taste and set a bad tone for policing, the mayor and major agreed. Yet the citizens went ahead and made the presentation, thus showing the power of the precincts over headquarters.[23]

Another administrative innovation was the creation of the chief inspector position. The inspector of the First Division, in this case Frederick Marsh, a friend of McClaughry's, who would cause a leadership crisis later on, was to be elevated to chief inspector. In addition to the regular tasks of inspector, a chief inspector would be in charge of the detective bureau and the newly established bureau of identification. This was also an attempt to centralize and systematize the identification process, whereas before all criminal photographs and identification materials were kept in the various divisions.[24]

In addition, for the first time a bureau of information was created. The media is always critical in creating an image of the police. The press outside the city—those of New York City and Boston, for example—could be counted on for negative news when it came to Chicago. Even within Chicago there were several very partisan presses eager to jump all over the mayor and McClaughry. Even the friendlier press—in this case the *Tribune*—needed finessing. That is why such practices as "posing the perp" arose (meaning displaying recently arrested suspects to selected reporters so as to give them a scoop). Having too many police spokesmen in the higher ranks led to confusion and contrary stories. Creating and controlling a media outlet became essential for the reform chief. The Bureau of Information would collect news for the press that related to the work of the police. It was clear that McClaughry wanted to control the image of his force by controlling the information flowing from it to the media.[25]

Not only did he want to control information going out of the department, he wanted to encourage information coming to him from within the organization. To inspire some participatory leadership, McClaughry began a series of conferences with the leadership ranks of each division. The first of these occurred with the First Division in December 1891. They discussed the crime and vagrancy problem and how best to solve it.[26] This was a remarkable thing to do. Leadership styles come in a variety of ways. Influenced by the military, the police was slowly edging its way towards a semi-military model after the Civil War, and thus the common style was authoritarian: what the leader said was the way things were done. Because of the political nature of criminal justice administration—police and prisons—such a style was absent until the twentieth century. Another prevalent style was anarchy, or the lack of leadership. This was quite common in Chicago because of the influence of mayors and other political "machines." As in nature, bureaucracies abhor a vacuum and other ranks, most notably the captains, become a power base. McClaughry's participatory style was an attempt to build support in the higher ranks and sort out his basic ignorance of Chicago police and political problems.

Another way to build support and administrative efficiency was to give the inspectors more responsibility. A Board of Examiners, made up largely of his inspectors, was created to consider all applications for employment submitted to the Superintendent. The *Tribune*, always an enemy to the bosses and gamblers, applauded the idea:

> If the Superintendent carries out his ideas to the letter political influence will have little to do with a man getting on the force. One great trouble has been that men secured their places through Aldermanic influences and on account of their political standing, and not because of merit . . . . Another great trouble has been that a man after placing himself under obligations to politicians to get a place has been assigned to duty in the ward where he had been accustomed to work in the interest of a set of politicians.[27]

Under McClaughry's plan, the Board of Examiners would not see any of the endorsements for a particular applicant or know of any political affiliations of the person. The only qualifications would be the ability to read and write the English language and passing a physical examination.[28] The *Tribune* considered this one to be the most important reforms of the police to date.

> If that plan can be carried out there will be an end to the influences which have dominated in times past in the selection of men to do patrol duty as well as of those who supervise the rank and file of the police force. It is notorious that positions have too often been obtained as a reward for service at the primaries and polls or for the purpose of controlling votes in the future . . . [29]

One way to maintain control over subordinates was by making transfers. By scrambling personnel, particularly those in high command positions, the Major could keep them from establishing a power base. For example, as the November elections drew near, McClaughry began to transfer personnel, particularly the ranking officers, from the First District, that stronghold of the machine and vice lords. They had been too active in the last election and, in order to insure honesty in the upcoming ones, these officers had to go.[30]

The ultimate way to control would to be to put the command structure itself under scrutiny. Consequently, in October 1891 McClaughry transferred the entire headquarters of the First District, which for years had been at the famed Harrison Street Station, to the central headquarters. He claimed it was on the grounds of efficiency but of course issues of control and supervision were equally important.[31] The old First District or Division became a regular station with day and night squads. The Inspector of the First Division would now be in control of the Detective Bureau which had been at the main headquarters for some time. Other division headquarters were shifted to different precincts as well.[32] Such reforms had only superficial impact. The officers who managed the districts—the captains—remained a powerful challenge to the chief.

POLITICS AND THE CAPTAINS

Perhaps the strongest officer of rank in the nineteenth century urban police was the captain. Chiefs came and went rapidly. Such a high turnover left little time for an administrator to really take control or for any sense of reform or professionalism to take hold.[33] The ranks of captains often were filled with demoted chiefs. In Chicago, the various districts were veritable satraps with strong captains, who were the chief administrative officials at this level. For example, Captain Michael Ryan, a corrupt and incompetent officer, enjoyed the patronage of the bosses of the Levee, Bathhouse John Coughlin and Michael Hinky Dink Kenna, and was known as "the police chief of the 1st Ward."[34] Since the logical place to look for a future chief was the captain level, the appointment of outsider McClaughry was particularly galling. The Major was not from the police ranks and he was not even from the city. Numerous captains, either from the immediate McClaughry era or already in place when he arrived, set the tone of the department and its expectations of leadership. Take John Bonfield, for example.

The Chicago police had perhaps never had such a controversial figure as John Bonfield. Born in Canada in 1836, he came to Chicago as a child in 1843. In the 1850s he worked as an engineer on the Chicago & Alton railroad. After that he tried and failed at several businesses before joining the force in 1877. A bit old for policing perhaps, but brothers in well placed political positions got him his job. Although a Republican he became a staunch supporter of the city's most famous political boss, Carter Harrison. Within a year he was a lieutenant in the detective division. In 1881 he set up a call box system in the city from where an officer (and by paying a $25 fee, certain businesses as well) could call the precinct headquarters for assistance. This was quite an innovation since the telephone was of recent invention. Very few Americans had access to telephones. In addition, he created the flying squad, a group of hand-picked officers who sped to emergency calls in a wagon pulled by specially trained horses. Most beat cops strolled their territory. Horses were rarely used in day to day patrol only occasionally brought out for crowd control. He gained the long lasting enmity of the working classes because of his handling of strikes and riots; convinced there was a terrorist plot by the anarchists, he was brutal in his handling of strikers, defending his actions to the mayor after one particularly bloody strike by saying that, "A club today, to make them scatter, may save the use of a pistol tomorrow."[35] In fact we shall see that it didn't because Bonfield was involved in the Haymarket "massacre."

In May, 1886, a peaceful demonstration of workers gathered at Haymarket Square, a large plaza for the numerous wagons bringing produce into the city and a place for speakers to vent their frustration over the capitalist system of Chicago. Over two thousand people were gathered there on May 6th but due to rain the crowd dwindled to a few hundred by the time Bonfield's DesPlaines force arrived. A bomb was thrown at the police killing several of them outright and igniting a city-wide hysteria with Bonfield at the center. To most, he was a hero. In the official history of the police he was called "an advanced member of the new school officers."[36] But a vocal minority, particularly from organized labor and from various radical and liberal groups, called for his resignation. Pressures were so great that he did leave the force to form a private detective agency shortly before McClaughry arrived, but his ghost lingered about the force and when it came to appointing the head of the World's Fair Police, McClaughry named Bonfield.[37]

If Bonfield was a tangential presence to the Major, Michael Schaack certainly was not. Born in Luxembourg in 1843 he was in Chicago by the mid 1850s. After working the Lakes as a merchant seaman, Schaack became a member of Ludwig's detective agency before joining the force in 1869. Inspired by the Pinkerton agency numerous small agencies sprung up in Chicago. Ludwig was one of them offering night time property protection and detective services. After he became a Chicago police officer, Schaak got involved with numerous high profile violent encounters as a patrolman and with murder investigations as a detective. Named a captain in 1885, within two days the Mulkowsky murder took place, a crime that caught national attention. This recent immigrant from Poland brutally murdered another Polish family, the Kledzies. Even though a captain, Schaack could not resist the perplexing nature of the crime and, after some creative sleuthing, he apprehended the killer and became a nationally visible policeman. But his most notorious activity had to do with the anarchist and what had happened at the Haymarket square. Those events in 1886 had such an impact on Schaack that he published a book in 1889, *Anarchy and Anarchists,* a history of anarchism in the world, but most specifically in America and Chicago. It was a remarkably thorough and almost scholarly tome. With this book Schaak became one of the nation's authorities on the terrorist threat of anarchism.

In his book, Schaak praised captains like Bonfield but criticized the high administration. The central detective bureau and the people at headquarters were "notoriously incompetent," he felt.[38] "There was neither order, discipline nor brains at headquarters," he maintained. "Every officer did as he liked, and the department was rent and paralyzed with the feuds and jealousies between chiefs and the subordinates."[39] A strong defender of Bonfield, he believed that they, Schaak and Bonfield, represented a "new police," one that stressed discipline and was "as close to a military system as conditions would allow."[40] On one hand, such views could resonate with the new chief who would arrive a short time later.

On the other hand, Schaak had a monumental ego hungering to be chief himself. Such ambitions had been fueled, in 1891, shortly before McClaughry was appointed. The office of inspector had been reformed. For administrative reasons, the city had been divided in half, a north side and a south side separated by the Chicago River. One inspector was put in charge of each division. These inspectors became deputy chiefs. Shortly before McClaughry arrived Schaack was made the inspector for the north side.[41] He would hold that position until his unexpected death in 1898.[42] Clearly, McClaughry had a potential ally or troublemaker in Captain Schaack.

McClaughry would have an ongoing battle with many of these Chicago Shoguns. Some of the more egregious actors were fired, but others were so entrenched and protected by the machine that success was limited. Take for example the notorious officer, Captain Hayes. He retained an interest in a saloon after his appointment to the force. In addition, he managed the men under his command in the interest of his political friends. Even though Hayes fought to remain, mustering some considerable support from friendly aldermen, he lost his battle and gave up his badge.[43] Or consider another attempt at pruning the ranks that had to do with age qualifications. All officers over fifty years of age—and of course this would hit the upper ranks more dramatically—were to be retired. Many captains, and Schaack was one of them, scurried to prove they still had a few years' eligibility left. Most claimed that the 1871 fire had destroyed any real proof of their birth records and, in an effort to prove his case, Schaack even traveled to Luxembourg to validate his age. He continued to resent how the outsider, McClaughry, was trying to change the way things had been done for decades. So many of these captains, and Schaak was no exception here, had climbed up the ladder of police power after serving as detectives, another area of concern for the Major.

DETECTIVES

Detectives had become a power base within the police by the time McClaughry arrived on the scene. This was remarkable since they were a late arrival to the force. Like many newly created police departments in the years before the Civil War, detectives were noticeably absent from the Chicago police. As the modern police developed in Europe, detectives became equated to spies, something to be avoided in a democratic society. The most prominent American detective business, Pinkertons, was essentially a spy service. Also, in practical terms, the patrolman on the beat was most likely to make arrests. Modern-day clearance rates for crime [that is crimes solved with an arrest]—generally around 20 percent—suggest that even with sophisticated forensic aids detectives are not all that successful, and they were probably far worse in the nineteenth century. After the Civil War, detective bureaus began to be established, Chicago gaining its first in 1865, a full decade after the modern police force was established there.

There are numerous possible reasons for the rise of detective bureaus in city police. There was a model of investigators in the business world. Started in Chicago in 1855, the same year the modern Chicago police was established, a nationwide private detective business was prospering by the late nineteenth century. This was the Pinkerton National Detective Agency. William Pinkerton, son of the founder, was running the Chicago office and referred to popularly as "The Eye." His brother, Robert, was doing much the same in the New York office. They and their father, Allan, had established all of the techniques of surveillance, rogues galleries, a code of ethical standards, and a nationwide organization of intelligence gathering. Before he died in 1874, Allan Pinkerton had written nearly a dozen books, true detective stories or case studies that could act as primers for aspiring detectives.[44] Several Chicago detectives had moved up the ranks quickly having prior experience with Pinkertons or some other private police. Edward Steel, made chief of detectives in 1887, had started his career in Hamblein's Merchant Police. Henry Palmer previously had been head of the detective department of the Milwaukee & St. Paul Railway Company, as had detective Stephen Wood. Another prominent city detective, Michael Granger, had been a Pinkerton.[45]

The Civil War had militarized the mind of most citizens, and so they would have been fairly accustomed to things like intelligence gathering. Even though the patrol—that backbone of the modern police force—was in place to maintain order and prevent crime there appeared to be a spike in crime as hundreds of career criminals flooded the cities. Detectives could send a message to the criminal world about societal intolerance with growing violence and professional criminality. Another reason was bureaucratic. Typical police organizations were pyramidal in shape with ever-decreasing opportunities for promotion upward to encourage and reward work performance. If one could not move up the bureaucratic ladder then a separate function, the investigations area, could offer incentives. Furthermore, like most cities, Chicago was on the horns of a dilemma. The more puritanical oriented wanted laws against vice enforced. But the machine saw the impossibility of ending vice and sought to exploit it through a system of corruption. Uniformed officers could collect bribes but it was more prudent for plain clothes officers to do so. Finally, it was increasingly clear that "justice" from the perspective of the police was not being done. With the creation of the modern police more arrests resulted. For example, in 1875 there were 38.9 arrests per officer. Next year that number jumped to sixty-six and continued to rise to a high of eighty-two in 1883. The proportion per officer decreased thereafter because hiring increased and simply spread out the number of arrests among more officers.[46] But the raw numbers continued to rise. More arrests meant more people coming before local judges and that meant crowded court room dockets. Many judges were corrupt, to be sure, selling off suspended sentences for a bribe, but the sheer number of people appearing in the courtroom both demanded assembly-line justice and resulted in many hardened criminals slipping through the cracks of the system. Those convicted were sent to Joliet only to find prison officials dealing with overcrowding by giving early releases. Understandably the police became frustrated with seeing recently arrested felons out walking the streets. One notorious female footpad or street thief, Minnie Shouse, had been arrested over three hundred times but served very little time.[47] Therefore, it became a standard procedure of beating up felons, a sort of "sidewalk justice." Of course, uniformed officers could do this but it was more discrete for plainclothes personnel to do it.

Consequently, by the late nineteenth century police detectives were a fixture in policing. They had gone from half a dozen after the Civil War to nearly fifty by the time McClaughry arrived. On one hand, these detectives were generalist; they took whatever crime popped up. The bureaucratic structure favored this. There were no specialized divisions—homicide, burglary, arson, or such—in the detective administrative structure. On the other hand, either due to past experience or personal inclination, some specialization occurred. Two black detectives, William Green and William Smith, sought out black thieves. Patrick Tyrrell, formerly with the U.S. Secret Service, focused on counterfeiters. Pawnshops were covered by William Thorpe and Henry Palmer. William Boyd and James Morgan sought horse thieves. Murder investigations were the specialty of Andrew Rohan and Michael Whalein. Stephen Wood, a former railroad cop, continued to search for crooks who worked the trains.[48]

Perhaps the single most famous Chicago police detective, Clifton R. Wooldridge, specialized in street crime and sex offenses. Clearly, he was a man filled with self-importance, but it is also true that numerous others vouched for his good reputation. In 1901, he published a book, *Hands Up! In the World of Crime,* in which mayors, attorneys, former chiefs—including McClaughry—claimed him to be the best detective in Chicago. In twelve years of detection he was responsible for 1,176 arrests (with sadly only 125 convictions), recovering over $75,000 worth of stolen property, rescuing seventy-five underage girls from brothels, and shutting down twenty brothels and forty-five panel houses. While the book was clearly self promoting, it is valuable if read between the lines. For example, if Wooldridge's work style was typical very little real sleuthing seemed to take place. Instead, Wooldridge was a free-wheeling plain-clothed patrolman prowling high crime areas hoping to snag a criminal. Numbers of truly desperate characters waltz through the pages, including, interestingly, a large number of black women. There was Emma Ford, "The Levee Terror," a 200-pound 6-foot thief, robber, and burglar who always fought like a wildcat when arrested. And there was Hattie Briggs, another huge black woman who ran a dive and resisted arrest with violence. In 1892, Wooldridge went after Lizzie Davenport, another black woman who ran a panel house. He claimed that the most "notorious strong-arm women" of the city (Flossie Moore, Pearl Smith, Ida Anderson, and Minnie Shouse, to name a few) were part of the Davenport house. "It was not an unusual thing for ten or fifteen robberies to occur in this house within twenty four hours," he claimed.[49]

If Wooldridge's words are to believed these detectives were difficult to manage. Their clothing and work patterns were nondescript. Given the nature of deployment detectives were hard to pin down. Housed in the Central District they often worked in precincts under the direct supervision of captains; it was an administrative nightmare just determining who was in control of the detective. The most important place to find detectives was at the Harrison Street Station, in the heart of the Levee. This was where Clifton Wooldridge spent most of his time. The most vicious and dangerous crooks were in the Levee and consequently, according to Wooldridge, this was where the best policemen would be. Such statements had to be self serving because the Levee was a central place for police corruption too. The rogues' gallery and the Bertillon identification bureau were located here as well. Most of Wooldridge's exploits occurred within the confines of the Harrison Street Station.

The Harrison Street district may have been central to vice and street crime, but the ethnic nature of Chicago presented a problem for all detectives. More than most American cities Chicago was filled with "enclaves of foreign elements." Many of these recent arrivals came from places where the police were very oppressive. They assumed the Chicago police detective to be the same as those found in the "old country." Some attempts were made to have patrolmen reflect the ethnicity of their beats, but the detectives were often out of sync with the diverse nature of the city. Because of the fear towards the police residents would not cooperate even with detectives who were of the same ethnicity. When crime occurred in their neighborhoods residents resented detectives coming in to take one of their own. In the late 1880s, the official historian for the Chicago police, John Flinn, interviewed officers and reflected their attitudes.

> On every hand the officer is beset with difficulties that would speedily discourage an ordinary detective. Those settlements of foreigners are clannish to a degree. Every effort is made to deceive the police, to throw them off the scent and cover the tracks of the criminal, who, as such, is known to hundreds of his acquaintances. Everywhere the detective is met with protestations of ignorance, and nowhere is he able to find one willing to comprehend a three-word sentence of English.[50]

Many of these detectives would move up the ladder to become captains and perhaps a chief. Their work style and feelings of self importance would shape their relations with McClaughry, a man who had not even been a police officer. The Major knew enough to leave things more or less alone. Yet those detectives who were patently corrupt were fired. And much corruption ran up and down the occupational ladder in all nineteenth century departments. Detectives, particularly those working vice, had the strongest temptations. Shortly, through some organizational reshuffling McClaughry found an extortion racket run by some detectives. A $10 fee had been required from people arrested to drop the charges.[51] Once again McClaughry used the transfer to undermine the power and corruption of his officer, this time it was the detectives. "Not long ago," declared McClaughry,

> I transferred two Central office detectives to outside precincts, where they are not known and where they would not have an opportunity to do anything crooked if they were so disposed. Everybody supposed that the transfer was one of the kind which take place periodically, and only passing attention was given it. But the real reason for shifting the men was suspicion that they were crooked.[52]

Those who might embarrass the department by the misuse of their position were reprimanded. One police practice common in past administrations became an embarrassment to McClaughry. Officers, particularly detectives, used to get books of free passes to ride the city railroad system. McClaughry did not object to the companies donating such pass books but he did not want the department asking for them. Apparently once, when McClaughry was out of town, a subordinate accustomed to the old ways requested the pass books and this caused a stir. McClaughry had to make it clear that such gratuities were not to be solicited by the department.[53]

Relations with the detectives were always tense. McClaughry angered some with the appointment of John Norton as detective. Norton, a big powerful man weighing over 260 pounds, had been a private detective for the Northwestern Railroad when tapped by McClaughry for detective work. Although he was a favorite of the chief, the rest of the detectives resented this man who had never walked a beat—and never would in all his forty-six years as a Chicago police detective.[54] Even Wooldridge disliked McClaughry; the Major's desire to control flew in the face of free-wheeling detectives like Wooldridge. When discussing the history of the Harrison Street Station, after giving paragraph attention to virtually every Chief, Wooldridge scarcely mentioned McClaughry.[55]

Outside the department, the machine hounded the Mayor and the Major and even sustained the old ways of corruption in policing. Inside the organization the captains and detectives, with their ambitions and work rhythms, posed administrative problems as well. Even more important were the vast numbers of patrolmen.

PATROL OFFICERS AND THE SUBCULTURE

The creation of the modern police, first in London, then New York and Boston, placed an emphasis upon patrol and, hence, preventing rioting and crime. Very quickly as the political machine became an urban fixture, the job became politicized. By the time McClaughry assumed his position as chief, a definite police subculture had emerged. Patrolman felt they were a distinct and unique occupation, though none would dare refer to it as a profession as yet. The "us v. them" mentality took many forms. Of course, the "us" was the patrol officers. The "them" side of the couplet was a bit more complicated. The obvious "them" was the criminal class and the growing number of terrorist radicals. But others were more interesting. Another was the public, even though there was greater sympathy after Haymarket. Another was the press and those politicians crying for reform. But also, and most disturbing to leaders like McClaughry, the "them" was police leaders. Any technological innovation, take the call box as an example, was seen as an administrative device to control patrol officer's behavior and discretion. Ostensibly, the call box was for the patrol officer to phone for help. But each officer regularly had to check-in, a means by which managers could keep tabs on the patrolman.

Put in a chief who was an outsider, like McClaughry, and you have a recipe for a disastrous term of office.

There were many reasons for the beginning of this "us v. them" mind set. First, it was probably due to the officer's displacement from his clients. Some attempts earlier were made to link officers to their corresponding ethnic group. Though this policy might still be true in some isolated residential areas, by the 1890s the mix of population was moving faster than the makeup of the police. Consequently, many officers were policing areas of ethnic hostility. Such a disconnect from the people they served could not help but build a sense of isolation and uniqueness for the patrolmen.

Another factor contributing to a police culture was the work schedule. For example, one patrol officer, Ed McCann, fought an attempt to reduce wages in 1894. Though McClaughry was gone by that time, McCann's description of the patrolman's duties was relevant during the Major's tenure, especially after some reforms he instituted. There were two distinctive patrolmen, according to McCann's description. The night patrol worked a nine-hour shift, whereas the day shift worked eleven hours at a stretch. Every second day the officer was on reserve duty, easily accessible for emergency situations. Most working person's schedules in nineteenth century America were long and arduous. Certain other requirements marked the officer as distinct. Patrolmen stood out because of their uniform. They were not allowed to wear civilian clothes, even when off duty. This was a major revolution in thinking, one largely due to the Civil War. When the modern police force was created there were all kinds of resistance to the idea of livery; wearing of uniforms was for the servant classes and decidedly undemocratic. Within twenty-five years the uniform issue had been laid to rest and now the police wore them all the time. Even though the police were increasingly seen as unique, they could not formally organize. Most workers in late nineteenth century had arduous and demanding work environments, witness the growing worker's self consciousness and the rise of labor unions in this period, the police could not formally organize so they did it informally with a sub culture.[56]

Another ingredient making up this subculture was the nature of politics. Most officers owed their positions and futures to the political machine. Patronage in policing went back for over 50 years. There were those who wanted to undo the machine's influence. Although it will not become a tremendous power for another decade, there was the presence of the "goo goo" movement. Good Government reformers wanted to dismantle the machine and searched for all signs of corruption and efficiency. Of course, the police were the most visible attribute of government, so officers believed that certain politicians and hostile press were watching. Those under siege developed a special kind of comradeship.

Although not affiliated with the goos goos as they would be fifteen years later, the purity crusaders also watched the police with a jaundiced eye. Segregated sin districts had the advantage of being largely hidden from public view. But on occasion events occurred to remind the Sunday morning bible thumpers of the Gomorrah-like character of Chicago. Various Societies for the Prevention of Vice sprung up to attack the saloons, gambling dives, brothels, and the machine and police who protected them. Even the most honest officer felt attacked and the need to "circle the wagons" and defend themselves against attack.

Police subculture development was even helped along within the criminal justice system. The courts were a particular problem for the police officer. On numerous occasions the courts dismissed felons. For example, Kitty Adams was a uniquely ruthless female footpad or robber who used a razor as a weapon. She worked with other women, usually Jennie Clark, and would grab a victim and hold him with a razor to his throat while the other went through his pockets. On one occasion they were arrested and brought to court for assaulting an old man. The judge stopped the proceedings and lectured the victim. "It serves you right," the judge declared.

> You ought to have known better. You are an old man and look as though you might be a Sunday-school teacher. Probably you are a Sunday-school teacher, and have been doing like many others when they want to have a good time. What business had you out at that time is what I'd like to know. Let the prisoner be discharged.[57]

Such courtroom decisions were common and so it was not surprising that patrol officers believed they stood alone with little support from the judiciary.

Another marker of a group defining itself as a unique occupation and forming a subculture was a growing body of literature. No other literature in this process is as important as history. When an occupation begins to think of itself in historical terms it proclaims its uniqueness. In 1887, John Flinn, under the auspices of the police book fund, published a *History of the Chicago Police*. Richly detailed, it ran nearly six hundred pages, carrying the history of the police from its creation to 1886. Everyone in the department, from Chief to custodian, found themselves in the book. Of course, the reason for this book was a critical event in Chicago policing.

Critical events are those happenings or tipping points that cause a dramatic change in the way people in general and police officers themselves think about their occupation. Not only for Chicago but for every police department in the country the Haymarket bombing crystallized opinion. This event in 1886, when a platoon of Chicago officers was attacked by a bomb, presumably thrown by a terrorist, caused Chicago to go on a hysterical witch hunt resulting in the execution of several anarchists. The "martyrs" to the police were their fallen comrades. The notion that someone out there was out to get them became very real.

Therefore, for several reasons a police subculture was in place by the time McClaughry arrived. Police administrators like him had to control this culture. One cannot direct the police if they do not listen. Old-timers were the problem. The hope was that the newer officers could be directed away from the subculture.

In late June, 1891, the first "new blood" began to appear to take entrance exams for the police. Fifty candidates appeared before the Board of Examiners. But even such an examination process could easily be corrupted. In October, 1891, for example, McClaughry uncovered a scheme to cheat on the merit examination. Apparently, some officers incapable of passing the written examination sent substitutes to take the test for them. The same was true of those mentally capable of passing the mental test but not the physical. As the *Tribune* reported, "It is quite evident, if reports are true, that someone is doing a brokerage business in getting men on the force."[58] McClaughry called in seventy-five candidates for re-examination as to their physical fitness. Only fifty-eight showed up.[59]

In light of such breaches of ethical conduct, McClaughry had to show some administrative muscle. He initiated a series of demotions and firings of patrol officers. For example, within a week of the new testing of officers, eighteen were disciplined, the variety of their offenses indicating the kind of problems facing the new superintendent. Six were fired for conduct unbecoming to an officer. Three had been absent from work without permission. Two had been drunk, and another four had been found in saloons when they should not have been there. In fact, many thought that it had been in the last twenty years that drinking in the police had become so prevalent. By November 1891 the mayor and superintendent began a policy that automatically dismissed officers for drunkenness. Before, drunkenness was punished by a slight fine and forgiveness, but now it became grounds for dismissal.[60] Another person was disciplined for "maltreatment of a citizen."[61] Some spoke up loudly and often in criticism of Mayor Washburne.[62] Several others were caught supporting gambling and forced to leave the force in August.[63] Officer James Abbey was under investigation for brutality in August.[64] In November, an office named Clarence Barchard was dismissed for wife beating.[65] By the end of 1891, 214 discharges and sixty retirements had occurred.[66] Certainly, as the rise of the subculture demonstrates, individual officers, and groups of officers, might resent taking orders from others, especially from those leaders with little police experience. McClaughry had experience managing resistant populations. Both the prison and police department were filled with willful men. Both created an "us v. them" culture. Unlike his predecessors who were political and less professional, McClaughry wanted to show his grit with a series of procedures to make the police department more efficient and, most of all, to control his men.

PROCEDURE

McClaughry's first day at work was calculated to impress personnel with his energy and waylay concerns by the machine. First, he appointed as Assistant Superintendent the former chief and his old war buddy, Frederick Marsh. Marsh showed him around the city, going to four stations. When McClaughry was asked about any new changes, he responded as usual with a story. "I am something of the Irishman who went out to thrash. The Irishman sat around for a day or two doing nothing until the farmer asked him what he was waiting for. 'I'm waiting to get acquainted with the barn.'" McClaughry's statements to the press most often took the form of folksy stories going back to the influence Lincoln had on many public speakers. When pushed on the issue of politics he assured the reporters that no hiring or firing would be part of any political agenda.[67] That said, however, a crisis awaited calling upon him to let go several hundred officers.

Special funds always exist in bureaucracies to deal with unplanned problems. The Chicago police had a fund to hire "emergency" policemen to supplement the regular force. The previous mayor, DeWitt Cregier, made five hundred appointments on the eve of the election largely to insure votes for his candidacy. No official appropriation had been allocated for their hire. Now the new mayor and Superintendent were faced with a "stuffed" force and no money to pay them. Consequently, just as McClaughry was saying he would fire no one for political reasons, he had to let go five hundred of these emergency officers.[68] A further cost cutting policy, one said to save the department $12,000 a year, was attacking the furlough system. In the past, officers were allowed to take a furlough but McClaughry ended that; any officers wanting time off now did so without pay.[69]

To better control the department one had to control the flow of information. Information is power, and captains—and perhaps their underlings, the sergeants—had dominated information for much of the history of the department. McClaughry, in 1892, started the Daily Police Bulletin, a single sheet printed and given to every officer at roll call each day. It gave the names and descriptions of wanted criminals. Also, it told of changes in personnel, promotions, transfers, citations for bravery, and new rules and regulations. The real importance—besides the obvious one of educating the force—was that it sent a message to the troops about who was in control.[70]

McClaughry soon introduced other procedural elements. For example, he instituted a rule that officers should not arrest without a warrant anyone accused of a crime which the officer had not seen being committed. Of course, this goes contrary to the police power based upon "probable cause." In a sense, everyone has a "common law" privilege to arrest, [that is they can arrest if they see a crime being committed] but the police have additional power based upon probable cause, which is a heightened form of suspicion. The highly politicized city courts challenged officers who cited probable cause for an arrest they had made; this led to releases at the courthouse that angered many officers.[71] One station, the central station, chose to disregard one of McClaughry's orders. The Chief wanted anyone brought into the station to be "booked," or officially charged. In a classic example of defiance the detectives failed to book a notorious confidence man by the name of Van Tripp. They claimed to have brought him in just so that the newer men might get a spot on him [or fix the image of him in their minds]for future reference.[72]

The procedures of the ordinary officer were sloppy. In December 1891, McClaughry began issuing instructions to officers in an attempt to professionalize them. For example, search warrants had been handled improperly and McClaughry wanted to change that. Too many things gathered in a search disappeared. Consequently, a strict inventory of the items taken needed to be written on the back of the warrant. Furthermore, officers needed to be in the court with all of their witnesses on court days. "Officers must be more careful in handling known thieves. It is not uncommon to see officers walking ahead of prisoners charged with crime, and otherwise acting in a careless manner."[73] After some adverse decisions by the local courts, McClaughry began to require his officers to have a sworn complaint against those arrested.[74]

At first, the reforming of ordinary procedures seemed slight.[75] Then on November, 12th, 1891, McClaughry introduced sweeping changes. Along with the mayor, the superintendent agreed that the force would be improved "if certain old-timer members were retired to make way for younger and brighter men; more in accord with the spirit of the times, and the improved method of police management."[76] Of course, this was related to the coming of the World's Fair. In his memo the superintendent told the Mayor that "to the end that the police force of this city during the World's Columbian Exposition of 1893 may be composed of active, intelligent, efficient, and ambitious material and for the present good of the service, I deem it advisable that all police officers, regardless of present rank, who have reached the age of 50 years and upwards, be immediately retired from service" and their place be filled according to civil service testing.[77] Most of these older officers, those over fifty years of age, if they had served the required twenty years would be retired at half pay. When McClaughry was asked about such a policy he was reluctant to criticize. But, jokingly noting that he was already fifty-two himself, he wondered aloud if he should retire as well.[78] Most likely those politicos and vicelords unable to take a joke perked up when they heard that story. Assistant Superintendent Brennan, a holdover from the previous administration of Cregier, was retired as if he were a captain. Inspector George Hubbard, a man who had been superintendent earlier, replaced him. Marsh was to be transferred. McClaughry would allow appeals and affidavits before finalizing the process.[79] In all, thirty five were placed on pension rolls.[80] Apparently, Inspector Schaack's arguments were effective because his name was not on the final roster of retirees and indeed he will remain after McClaughry is gone.[81]

At the end of his first year, 1891, McClaughry reported to the city council what he had done and what was further needed in preparation for the World's Fair, that exhibition for which he had originally been hired. His greatest achievements were administrative. Police districts had been redrawn. Numerous corrupt or inept officers were forced to retire. Others were alerted to change their ways or face termination. Arrests and search procedures had been sharpened. Information outlets, to the press and to the officers themselves, were created and centralized in the office of the chief. But there remained much to do. The power of the captains and the subculture among the patrol officers remained a problem. The rivers and harbors of the city needed patrolling. "Considering the very large portion of our City covered by water frontage, it seems almost like criminal negligence to defer the much needed protection which could be provided at so little expense," he announced to no avail. Also, he wanted to light the alley ways. "Our alleys are constantly used by evil disposed persons and they also provide an easy method of escape for criminals from pursuing officers." Chicago, with two ambulances compared to New York City's 21, needed a better ambulance system. Finally, a mounted patrol was needed. "A mounted force would also be the greatest service in case of tumults or riots or management of large crowds, that we may expect in attendance almost every day of the coming World's Fair."[82] But crowd and criminal control at the World's Fair was only a part of the problem. Perhaps the greatest concern was over the radicals, those un-American anarchists, bent on terrorist acts that might endanger and embarrass the city at the five hundredth anniversary of Columbus' discovery of America.

NOTES

1. *Chicago Tribune*, February 10, 1892.
2. *Ibid.*, October 26, 1891.
3. *Ibid.*, October 28, 1891.
4. *Ibid.*, November 23, 1891.
5. *Ibid.*, January 25, 1892.

6. *Ibid.*, December 7, 1892.
7. *Chicago Record Herald,* May 12, 1913.
8. *Chicago Tribune*, April 7, 1891.
9. *Ibid.*, April 27, 1891.
10. *Ibid.*, May 18, 1891.
11. *Ibid.*, April 27, 1891.
12. *Ibid.*, November 21, 1891.
13. *Ibid.*
14. *Ibid.*, April 29, 1891.
15. *Ibid.*, May 7, 1891.
16. *Chicago Herald,* May 16, 1891.
17. *Chicago Daily News*, May 1, 1891.
18. *Chicago Tribune*, October 14, 1891.
19. *Ibid.*
20. *Ibid.*, October 24, 1891.
21. *Ibid.*, May 27, 1891.
22. *Ibid.*, August 1, 1891.
23. *Ibid.*, October 1, 1891.
24. *Ibid.*, December 7, 1891.
25. *Ibid.*, December 16, 1891.
26. *Ibid.*, December 12, 1891.
27. *Ibid.*, June 5 1891.
28. *Ibid.*
29. *Ibid.*, June 14, 1891.
30. *Ibid.*, October 14, 1891.
31. *Ibid.*, October 18 and 20, 1891.
32. *Ibid.*, October 23, 1891.
33. Fogelson, p. 23.
34. *Ibid.*, p. 25. Also see Lloyd Wendt and Herman Kogan's *Lords of the Levee: The Story of Bathhouse John and Hinky Dink* (Indianapolis & New York: Bobbs-Merrill Company, 1943).
35. Quoted in John J. Flinn, *History of the Chicago Police* (Chicago: Police Book Fund, 1887), p. 246.
36. *Ibid.*, p. 338.
37. *Ibid.*, pp. 338-47, *Chicago Tribune* has his obituary October 20, 1898, and Robert McClaughry and John Bonfield, "Police Protection at the World's Fair," *North American Review,* Vol. 156 (1893), pp. 711-16.
38. Michael J. Schaack, *Anarchy and Anarchists* (Chicago: F.J. Schulte & Company, 1889), p. 183.
39. *Ibid.*
40. Quoted in Schaack's obituary in *Chicago Tribune,* May 18, 1898. Interestingly, both Bonfield, in October, and Schaack in May died quite unexpectedly in the same year.
41. *Chicago Tribune*, April 27, 1891.
42. *Ibid.*

43. *Ibid.*, June 17 and 26, 1891.
44. See Frank Morn's *"The Eye That Never Sleeps."*
45. Flinn, pp. 374, 377, 386, and 389.
46. David Johnson, p. 215.
47. For this and other numerous examples see Clifton Wooldridge's *Hands Up! In the World of Crime* (Chicago: Police Publishing Company, 1901), pp. 233-35.
48. *Ibid.*, pp. 378-81, 386, 389-94.
49. Wooldridge, pp. 29, 43-49, 60, 67.
50. *Ibid.*, p. 373.
51. *Chicago Tribune*, October 26, 1891.
52. Ibid.
53. *Chicago Tribune*, July 30, 1891.
54. Raphael Marrow and Harriet I. Carter, *In Pursuit of Crime: The Police of Chicago, A Chronicle of a Hundred Years, 1833-1933* (Sundbury, Ohio: Flats Publication Company, 1996), p.221.
55. Wooldridge, p. 280.
56. *Chicago Inter Ocean*, February 7, 1894.
57. Wooldridge, pp. 298-99.
58. *Chicago Tribune*, October 23, 1891.
59. *Ibid.*
60. *Ibid.*, November 8, 1891.
61. *Ibid.*, July 7, 1891.
62. *Ibid.*, July 7, 1891.
63. *Ibid.*, August 4, 1891.
64. *Ibid.*, August 2, 1891.
65. *Ibid.*, November 26, 1891.
66. *Ibid.*, September 22, 1891.
67. *Ibid.*, May 19, 1891.
68. *Ibid.*, May 21, 1891.
69. *Ibid.*, May 26 1891.
70. Raphael Marrow and Harriet I Carter, p. 227.
71. *Chicago Tribune,* August 9, 1891.
72. *Ibid.*, September 26, 1891.
73. *Ibid.*, December 27, 1891.
74. *Ibid.*, February 28, 1892.
75. *Ibid.*, November 3, 1891.
76. *Ibid.*, November 12, 1891.
77. *Ibid.*, November 14, 1891.
78. *Ibid.*
79. *Ibid.*, November 17, 1891.
80. *Ibid.,* November 12, 1891.
81. *Ibid.*, November 26, 1891.
82. *Report of the General Superintendent of Police of the City of Chicago for the Fiscal Year Ending December 31, 1891* (at the Chicago Historical Library), pp. 4-6.

Chapter Twenty-One

Crusades against Crime and Disorder

" . . . to preserve the peace of the city."

MCCLAUGHRY AND THE RADICALS

McClaughry had additional problems besides administrative ones. Policing has a mission: minimize crime and maximize public order. On his side or not, citizens presumed McClaughry's police organization would make the city safe. Due to the anarchist movement, dramatically displayed at Haymarket square, Chicago was obsessed with radicals. Eight Anarchists were arrested and convicted in a sensational trial. Four—August Spies, Albert Parsons, Adolph Fischer and George Engel on the barest of evidence—were hanged in 1887. They became martyrs for the working men of Chicago and mass protestations and demonstrations followed for years. Feelings towards anarchism continued to run deep during the administration of McClaughry.

Anarchist meetings occurred with intensity after the executions. The martyrdom just proved the capitalist plot, felt most anarchists. Then, as more and more people advocated the pardoning of the remaining Haymarket radicals, meetings of support increased. Wisely, most of the gatherings occurred outside the city limits in places such as Waldheim. Still, there were calls to the police to suppress such meetings. Hesitant to do so, McClaughry, however, did have his police take down a red flag from Lucy Parson's house, the symbol of the movement. She was the widow of one of the executed Haymarket Four.[1]

Then the Greif Raid occurred. On Thursday November 12th, one hundred police officers raided two anarchist gatherings at the meeting halls of Thomas Greif on the near Westside of Chicago. Twenty three people were arrested. People at the meeting claimed they were members of the Painter's Union and the Socialistic Publishing Society, and yet the speeches told a quite different story, advocating the violent overthrow of the government, and the red flags decorating the hall were emblazoned with mottos such as "Anarchy Forever," and "Onward is our motto."[2] Of course, radical groups were outraged by the raids. But McClaughry, caught between his beliefs in the Constitutional right to peaceful assembly and his fear of radical conspiracy, supported the actions of the police.

> I have no objections to these people holding meetings. What I object to is their utterances. No man has the right to agitate measures contrary to good government as the peace of society. Inspector Lewis was entirely justified. The meeting was being conducted under a red flag, the men were armed, and the speeches were made with the view of inciting an uprising. It is not the intention of the law that we should wait for the throwing of a bomb. A man who is caught in the act of committing a burglary is as guilty as if he had committed it. The red flag is a symbol of revolution and defiance of the law the world over. There is no doubt that those who were participating in the meeting were in accord with the spirit indicated by such an emblem. The Anarchist want revenge on Chicago for the execution of their brethren, and they intend to do it if possible by giving it the reputation of an unsafe place for investment or for visitors to tour exhibits at the World's Fair.[3]

Apparently, Thomas Greif's living rooms were one floor away from the meeting hall. When the police busted in there was a young woman, Mary Greif, dying of consumption upstairs. Later the girl died further inflaming the working classes who claimed that the police actually murdered the woman. McClaughry saw through such accusations and dismissed them. After all, he would claim, there were two meetings going on over her head and a noisy saloon in operation below. To charge that the police "shocked" her to death with their boisterous entrance defies logic. "If noise hastened the death of Mr. Greif's daughter there was more before than after the police arrived," he concluded. If property belonging to the union had been inadvertently destroyed the superintendent promised the city would make good. If it wouldn't then he would do so out of his own pocket.[4] A delegation of labor leaders called upon the mayor who, with McClaughry and the City Council present, supported the police.[5]

Nonetheless, in an already divisive society—sharply divided between labor and capitalism—all kinds of labor unions, both conservative and radical, denounced police oppression.[6] Thomas Greif went to the courts and was granted an injunction against the police. The judge believed it was wrong for the police to break up peaceable meetings.[7] Over fifteen organizations also met, most of them Germanic groups collectively called the Turner Society, to protest the police activities.[8] The Arbeiterbund, the International Working

People's association, began a crusade protesting police raids of radicals.[9] This spilled out to encompass most of organized labor.[10] And even though McClaughry paid for the damages that resulted from the raid, Greif brought civil suit against the police.[11] In addition, the City Council investigated the incident, accusing the police of breaking all kinds of property and entering without a search warrant. When McClaughry showed up at the City Council's [the legislative body for the city] hearing forbidding several key officers from testifying some members of the Council worried that the chief and the police felt they were above the Council. McClaughry assured them that they did not feel that way. He did feel, however, that the labor lawyers were twisting many of his statements to make the police look bad.[12]

The police remained sensitive to the anarchist issue. In January the police raided Greif's Hall again.[13] A raid of some Bahn-Frei Turnverein meetings earlier in December had occurred when they should not have. McClaughry ended up reprimanding his officers and reminding them that they could not simply equate being German with being radical.[14]

For McClaughry the largest concern was May Day, the traditional day of marching and demonstrating for working class people. The International Eight-Hour May Day parade promised to be troublesome to many Chicago elites. The movement, it was claimed, was European in origin, largely made up of Germans and Bohemians. As far as McClaughry was concerned, "They can parade and speak as they like; but if they advocate murder or dynamite or wave a red flag we will interfere. We are prepared for peace or war. They can have which they like."[15] Over fifty officers watched the parade and three flags were confiscated.[16] A delegation of labor called upon McClaughry to recover the flags to no avail.[17] This time the courts upheld the police action.[18] Strikers continued to complain against police treatment and the city was sharply divided over the issue.[19] It would not be until June 1893, during the waning days of McClaughry's career in Chicago that newly elected governor, John Peter Altgeld, would pardon the remaining Haymarket anarchists.[20] These radical groups to many nineteenth century minds were so un-American. In fact, in ten years one of them will kill the President of the United States. These groups would consume much of McClaughry's energy throughout his tenure as chief. But there were other groups who were perhaps very American who would compete for attention. These were the great vice lords of Chicago.

MCCLAUGHRY AND THE SALOONS

Of course, the saloons continued to be frustrating for McClaughry and the latter-day Puritans of Chicago. Washburne was not against drinking; he "was thoroughly German on that issue," he declared. As long as the saloons were orderly and obeyed the law he was ready to tolerate them.[21] However, the law was a little ambiguous on the matter of closing. It said that the saloons should close for business at midnight. Many simply closed their doors, drew blinds over windows, and continued to serve those still in the joint. Mayor Washburne, at first, felt this practice was permissible, since saloons were just catering to those who were still in the place but not admitting new customers. McClaughry disagreed. He felt that the 12:00 o'clock ordinance meant the liquor should stop being served altogether at midnight. He held to that position, in spite of a petition-packing delegation of saloon owners marching on city hall trying to convert the Mayor to their views.[22] Shortly, the city prosecutor found that the courts supported McClaughry's position.[23] Now the mayor saw the light and announced

> For the last two years nearly all of the saloons in the tough districts on the west side have been keeping open all night. The police officers had grown tired of making arrests and seeing the men discharged, or, if fined by the justices, having their fines remitted by the [previous] mayor.[24]

Restaurants serving liquor were another problem. McClaughry felt that they should be regulated just like the saloons. Many of these restaurants were thinly disguised saloons anyway, he maintained.[25] Numerous saloons, in fact, had started serving lunch in an attempt to identify themselves as restaurants and thereby stay open to serve liquor longer. In response, McClaughry made it clear that small lunch counters in a saloon would not redefine it as a restaurant.[26] Many saloon owners claimed that they were being mishandled and persecuted by the police, particularly by the inspectors. McClaughry wanted to continue the saloon closing policy but also remove any potential claims of political prejudice by the officers. Consequently, he instituted a policy in which all prosecutions of the saloons would emanate from headquarters so as "to remove all grounds for such accusations."[27] Then when a series of late night robberies began to plague the streets and street cars of Chicago in the summer of 1892, McClaughry laid the blame squarely on the saloons.[28] Nonetheless, particularly in the Levee, Chicago's notorious sin district in the First Ward, not only did the saloons stay open, police officers could even be seen inside drinking beer.[29] By December, 1892, after all McClaughry's efforts, the saloons were as defiant as ever causing the *Tribune* to comment that "police orders, like new brooms, sweep clean only while they are new." As a result, McClaughry remained convinced of two things: saloons were a shelter for all kinds of crooks, and the politicians were the key in thwarting his policies.[30] Saloons and various drinking violations remained a problem for the teetotaler chief. Often these drinking palaces were also gambling halls. This opened up another challenge in regulating the vice world.

MCCLAUGHRY AND GAMBLING

In the last analysis it was the gambling fraternity who had the most power and were the greatest problem for reformers. In the earliest days of the Washburne administration, before McClaughry came on board, a delegation of gamblers communicated to the mayor through chief Marsh that they would support him for re-election if he allowed the gaming to continue. Their request and deals were denied.[31] McClaughry was a dedicated enemy of the gamblers. But even here he understood the role of the police. Although the social evil had to be confined within certain limits, he did not intend

> to be fanatical in compelling obedience to the laws nor to have it remarked that I should have lived in the days of the blue laws. I shall proceed in a line of common sense, or at least shall try to do so. The police force is not to make men moral, neither is it to assist in running politics. It is, as I have already said, simply to preserve the peace of the city and to see that the laws and ordinances are obeyed.[32]

In this regard McClaughry was not far off pace with other members, correctional or police, on the practical problems of vice policy. Again, the report of the Committee on Police of the National Prison Reform Congress on which McClaughry had considerable influence, was revealing:

> The social evil [meaning here gambling and prostitution], in some communities, can easily be suppressed; but not in all. In mining districts and in cities where the population is heterogeneous and cosmopolitan, the most that should be required from a police force is that it shall keep social moral offenses under such control as to minimize the effect of their presence.[33]

In response, rumors soon circulated that the "gambling trust" had bought off the administration. With characteristic humor, when he was told that a $30,000 bribe had been offered to him, McClaughry said, "the money hadn't appeared, although [I] had sat up nights waiting for it."[34] Mayor Washburne, on vacation, wired McClaughry from Michigan," I hear the gamblers claim we are fixed. Take a fresh hold and shake them like rats."[35]

The Major was not going to give up on the battle with gamblers. The more egregious would have to be put in their place. Numerous raids of policy shops and gambling houses followed McClaughry's ascension to power.[36] "Public gambling must be suppressed in Chicago as long as I am head of the Police Department," he declared in July, 1891. "If any person can prove to me that any officer is derelict in his duty or stands in with the gamblers, that officer will have to go, no matter who is backing him."[37] He and the city prosecutor came up with an idea to suppress gambling. In the past, any raid of a gambling joint led generally to the arrest of the proprietors. Clients were not as culpable as the professionals, went the line of reasoning. Also, they were most likely losing to the professional and any additional monetary loss would be excessive. McClaughry, however, felt that one way to deter customers was to threaten them with heavy fines as well as a deterrent.[38]

In one instance the war on gamblers prompted some police innovations. In one raid, that of a gambler named William Skakel operating at 170 Madison Street, a ticker tape used in pool room activities was confiscated. Skakel, making the case that it was not for gambling, said that it was for news releases. The case was dropped due to a lack of evidence. Shortly after, McClaughry working with the City Prosecutor, created a manual for officers on how to gather evidence, particularly when dealing with gambling paraphernalia.[39]

Perhaps, the greatest presentation of gambling regalia was an entire room called the pool room. Pool rooms were literally places where people came together in the city to form a betting pool on a horse race. What made these places possible was the development of the telegraph wire transmitting results from the more suburban tracts to the pool rooms. And although city and state laws were shortening the race season to thirty days,[40] thanks to the wire, results could be had from tracks far away, thus extending the gambling season year round in spite of local restrictions. In March, 1892, the Mercantile Telegraph Co. was raided under suspicion of being a pool room.[41] Two hundred people were arrested.[42] James Townsend, president of Mercantile Telegraph, took the police to court claiming his was a legitimate business and not involved with the gamblers. That the courts agreed and restrained the police once again shows how difficult the police's job was to stamp out vice in these circumstances.[43]

In spite of periodic raids the gamblers continued to operate, and even after nearly a year of activity under McClaughry, the gambling houses were thriving. Although generally he was not openly criticized it was clear that some were beginning to question the superintendent's policies.[44] One major source of criticism was the newspaper the *Chicago Times*. In 1891, Carter Harrison purchased the *Times* making it the only real "regular" Democratic Party paper. And, of course, Harrison spent considerable energy undermining the administration of Washburne and McClaughry, as in this article with the headline, "How is this, Hempstead!"

> The city administration is not as pure and holy as Mayor Washburne and his lieutenants would have us believe. Chief McClaughry and his lieutenants have an understanding with the gambler's trust. If they were not the order would not have gone forth from Maj. McClaughry's office two months ago that poker and "crap" games would not be interfered with.[45]

Indeed, it was obvious that many of the gambling dens had advance notice of the raids. So McClaughry started to make quiet, solitary excursions into the gambling world, and found large numbers of operations going on. "This experience had been a revelation to me," he said after his first personal raid.[46] McClaughry headed a raid on the House of David crap game arresting sixty-five participants.[47] Four months later he went out again and noted that there must be some police leaking information to the gamblers because three out of the five places were closed when he got there.[48] Eventually McClaughry traced the leak to one of his own trusted subordinates, Frederick H. Marsh.

McClaughry had known Marsh for fifteen years. Marsh had headed the Committee on Prisons and Reformatories in the state legislature when McClaughry was warden of Joliet, and on several occasions Marsh was charged with investigating McClaughry's running of the prison. Later Marsh became a sheriff of a rural Illinois county, and some years after that McClaughry helped him gain an appointment to be a United States Marshal. Then, after Haymarket, Marsh got a job with the Chicago police and skyrocketed in five years to be the superintendent immediately prior to the coming of McClaughry.[49] In the reshuffling of offices, Marsh was made chief inspector, which in effect made him second in command directly under McClaughry. There had been considerable political opposition to Marsh and several attempts to undermine him but McClaughry always deflected them, allegedly saying, "If he goes so do I."[50] In June, 1892, while McClaughry was out of town, some gamblers approached the mayor with a copy of a loan note for $5,000 dated 1890, the time during which Marsh was superintendent. It implied that Marsh had a history of taking money from gamblers. Mayor Washburne asked for his resignation, something Marsh would not do until McClaughry returned.[51] When notified during his trip of the incident, McClaughry declared Marsh to be an honorable man. "He has zealously assisted me in my efforts to suppress gambling and I will not readily believe any amicable relations to exist between him and any gambling fraternity."[52] A clash between the mayor and the major was expected, all the more so when McClaughry returned suggesting that he was going to re-investigate the investigation already done by the mayor.[53] Political pressures and loyalties were brought to bear; McClaughry backed down and Marsh was dismissed.[54] But McClaughry continued to befriend Marsh, for example by writing a letter recommending that Marsh head up the World's Fair police. He withdrew the letter after an angry reaction to it in City Hall.[55] Finally in December of 1892 a new investigation concerning Marsh was opened. Due to pressure from McClaughry and the newly elected governor, John Peter Altgeld, Marsh was temporally reinstated with full rank and pay as Chief

Inspector, a strategic move since there had already been talk that Altgeld wanted to appoint Marsh to be warden of Joliet or Adjutant-General of the state. When in January 1893, Marsh assumed duty totally vindicated, the new governor could with good conscience make his appointment. Indeed, behind the scenes McClaughry had worked hard to restore his friend, a man caught up in the mean battles between the gamblers and City Hall.[56] The Marsh incident shows the power of the gamblers in Chicago to spark corruption and controversy. Though these gamblers dominated the halls they also influenced the more bucolic race tracks.

In the finally analysis it was the great race tracks and the gamblers connected to the jockey clubs that were the most controversial problem. There were two great race tracks in Chicago at this time, and to be fair to the gamblers there did indeed seem to be some favoritism at work. For example, the Hawthorne track went largely uninvestigated, but the Garfield Park was another matter. Throughout McClaughry's administration, the chief was at war with Garfield Park for two reasons. First, the track always tried to extend its racing season. The mayor frequently stepped in and undermined the chief by allowing such extensions, such as the time the Democratic National Convention was held in Chicago. Second, there was the problem of the pool sellers. The tracks being public entertainment, Illinois law disallowed the tracks from making a profit. Therefore, there was no admission charge to attend the races.[57] But the Jockey Clubs charged pool sellers a fee to take bets at the track and this was seen by many as making a profit, something against the law called the Kenny Ordinance.[58] In a reversal for McClaughry the courts struck down the Kenny Ordinance in the summer of 1892.[59] Immediately there was a resurgence of gambling both at the tracks and in the city pool rooms, resurgence that many saw as a deliberate move to defy McClaughry:

> It begins to look as if the gamblers were preparing to measure strength with Chief McClaughry for a final struggle to see if they cannot lay him out and conduct their unlawful games in spite of him. At no time since Major McClaughry was appointed Chief of Police has there been so much open gambling as now.[60]

A subsequent decision reinstated the ordinance. In September, McClaughry ignored any previous injunctions and sent over thirteen officers who raced around the track amidst the catcalls of over seven thousand spectators to round up the horses and close down the track.[61] It was an act that the motion picture industry of a later time would lampoon in Keystone Cop movies. In the melee an outraged horseman, James Brown from Texas, resisted and shot Officer Henry McDowell. Then in a show of outrage and police solidarity the police moved in and shot Brown point blank. With typical Chicago irony, flags were lowered at city hall for McDowell, and the saloons did the same for Brown. The gamblers of the city, headed by political and vice boss Michael MacDonald, wanted the mayor and the chief arrested for murder,[62] and also used the occasion to drive a wedge between the mayor and the chief.

Rumors were rife that the mayor and the Major were torn and that soon McClaughry would be asked to step down. Of course, the gamblers were behind those rumors. Shortly after the Garfield raid there was an investigation in which the major testified in court that in a conversation between the mayor and the chief, McClaughry had said that the Republicans would give $50,000 to the Republican campaign fund if the mayor closed down Garfield Park. On the witness stand, McClaughry denied saying that, and instead related that he had simply been bringing the mayor up to speed with rumors flying around City Hall about such a bribe. McClaughry's performance on the witness stand revealed his puritan fervor. For example, when the lawyer for the gamblers, Alexander Sullivan, questioned his honesty and the possibility of perjury, McClaughry exploded at the lawyer, saying: "I would like you to hold your tongue, sir. I came here to testify, not to submit to insults or outrages at your hand, sir." When the lawyer tried to calm things down by saying he had not intended anything by his remarks, McClaughry again broke in: "Then shut your mouth. You should have enough to care for your own piety."[63]

Clearly there were both jealously and power politics at play between the mayor and the chief, and the Garfield Park rumor was not the only thing to ignite the feud. For example, earlier the mayor had fired McClaughry's private secretary, T. L. Perkins, apparently for no good reason. On the surface they seemed to get along, largely because of McClaughry's habit of being a true and loyal subordinate. But there had been a shift of thought on gambling. When elected, the mayor had been openly against gambling and had brought in McClaughry to get rid of it. Now, the mayor realized that gambling could not be ended and so it would be best if a few legal gambling facilities be allowed to stay open. McClaughry, however, believed that they should either all be left open or all closed.[64] The split and politics seemed so evident to some that rumors began to circulate that McClaughry would even run for mayor, gossip he stoutly denied.[65] As a public show of unanimity the mayor wrote a public letter to McClaughry praising his administration; shortly after McClaughry returned the favor.[66] Public support, especially from the church community, continued to build. Any attempts of the gamblers to take over city council failed. It was widely acknowledged that since McClaughry had come to town the McDonald gambling syndicate had encountered its toughest and most unrelenting opponent.[67] Nevertheless, in a last ditch effort the gamblers tried to test the policy by getting an injunction against police action. It was denied in November: betting on horses was gambling and therefore illegal, said the courts.[68]

In the meantime, the gamblers had another card up their sleeves. In January 1893, the "Pen Fraud" case going back to McClaughry's days at Joliet hit the headlines. Apparently, a one-mile long drain ditch had been constructed across prison grounds by Brainard & Co. McClaughry was accused of allowing that company to do the construction without a competitive bid process.[69] An investigation dragged on and it became clear that this was another attempt by the McDonald syndicate of gamblers, still angry over the Garfield Park closing, to besmirch McClaughry. After several key witnesses were discredited, McClaughry was exonerated.[70] The vice lords would be a persistent enemy to McClaughry all his days in Chicago. But there was much more to Chicago's vice world than alcohol and gambling. Prostitution had an extraordinary presence as well. Often all three were connected.

PROSTITUTION

Remarkably, little was done about prostitution. Those prostitutes connected to the saloon were caught up as casualities of that crusade, but no police policy was directly aimed at the brothel. That might have been a testament to the isolated nature of the red light district; saloons and gambling places were after all much more public, many of them located quite openly in the shadow of the financial districts and city hall. But in some sort of "Victorian compromise," sex, even illicit sex, remained a private matter. The great movement to close the brothels of Chicago was still fifteen years away from becoming a reality. Morality and practicality crossed swords here. Red light districts were tucked away and not in the purview of ordinary citizens. Unless something sensational occurred, these establishments did not make it into the newspapers. Part of the historical reason for this was that after the Civil War concern over public health grew. Clean streets, potable water, sewage systems, public cemeteries, removal of dead animals, and public hospitals were just a small number of city services that arose in the name of public health. Hence, many in the new public health professions, being concerned with venereal disease, thought it better to have the prostitutes easily accessible for medical inspection than scattered across the landscape as individual street walkers. Brothels were sources of information. Of course, saloons were too. The famed William Pinkerton got most of his education about Chicago crooks by visiting The Store. But saloons were controversial; brothels placed a premium on staying out of the limelight. A well cultivated Madam could be an important source of information. Besides, brothel prostitutes were easier to police and control than bar girls and street walkers. A brothel's blatant criminality did open it up to a raid. Panel houses remained a bane, and the part that closing these thieving places played in Wooldridge's career attests to police concerns. Radicals and vice entrepreneurs remained a constant problem for law enforcement. But that concern was not evenly spread and the Madams of the Levee went on their merry way with little interference even during the management of the police by a latter-day puritan. Vice was a public order issue. But the police needed to minimize crime too.

CRIME

Of course, the police—no matter the leadership at the top—were powerless to suppress all crime. Floating gangs of career criminals would come into one city, commit their acts, and then flee to another. As to be expected, many crimes were committed in a fit of passion. Jealous lovers, outraged neighbors, and other crazed individuals did not sit down and contemplate the consequences of their actions. Disorderly conduct was most often the spontaneously result of excessive alcohol consumption and perceived insult. And yet the greatest source of arrests were assaults. From 1878 to 1893 arrests for assault increased thirty times. By 1893, according to one historian, there was one resident arrested for every eleven Chicagoans.[71]

Some criminals, driven by inner demons, would have their way regardless of the police. One such criminal in Chicago during McClaughry's tenure was Herman W. Mudgett a.k.a. H.H. Holmes. Whether or not Mudgett was, as some claim, America's first serial killer, certainly he became a national figure tied to Chicago and its World's Fair. Born in New England in 1860, he picked up a wife (and deserted her) and a modicum of medical knowledge in Michigan before coming to Chicago. He seduced a married female pharmacist on the South Side not far from where the World's Fair was being built.[72] She mysteriously disappeared and Holmes took over the pharmacy, dispensing medicines and medical advice. He was physically attractive and very charming and soon his drug store filled with female customers and employees. Nearby, at 63rd and Wallace, he constructed a residence in 1892, eventually to be called The Castle. It was a three storied structure with rooms to take advantage of "flat fever," the need for apartments by recently arrived young women trying to make their way in Chicago. The Columbian World's Fair was just down the street, adding to The Castle's appeal. By the time McClaughry was in place as Superintendent of Police, Holmes was well established and using his house as a killing machine. Many of the rooms had vents allowing Holmes to pipe in toxic gases. The basement had a dissecting table and another cell-like room that was air tight. Even more bizarre was a crematorium in the basement where he disposed of many bodies. The number of his victims remains unknown. When he was finely arrested in 1895, Holmes confessed to at least twenty-seven. However, it may have been many more. For he had advertised his home as a boarding house for tourists visiting the Fair, and after the Fair closed, over fifty tourists reported missing were traced to The Castle. Yet detectives were unable to clear those cases with Holmes' arrest. Eventually, Holmes left Chicago, but Pinkerton detectives, particularly Frank P. Geyer, hounded him across the country and collected substantial evidence to build a case that led to his arrest, conviction, and execution.

As Holmes' killing house shows, much crime was committed in private places outside the legitimate realm of police patrol. For example, after the Chicago fire of 1871, a flurry of commercial establishments were developed. These businesses were private property quickly filled with large numbers of people. Police patrol stopped at the entrance to such businesses. The rise of the department store, a late nineteenth-century revolution in merchandising, created an atmosphere for respectable housewives to succumb to temptation and shoplift.[73] Other crowd fleecers such as pickpockets likewise took advantage of crowded urban space to steal. Professional pickpocket gangs rode the trolleys and infested most entertainment and sports events.

Crime on the streets, areas open to police patrol and supposed deterrence, could cause considerable embarrassment, as happened when Admiral Paul de Nazimoff, of the Russian navy, was robbed on the streets of Chicago by a female beggar. Exclaiming, "I am not in love with the city where I was robbed," he went on to show just how much work was left to do to prepare for the World's Fair. He continued, "I would not care to return. The city is so dirty I would regret to have to live there, although I suppose it is a good business place."[74] Such statements were disturbing as the city was getting ready for thousands of tourists expected at the World's Fair.

WORLD'S FAIR

Indeed, there was a great deal left to do to prepare for the Fair, and McClaughry's chief responsibility in it was policing the event. Indeed, every one—respectable and not—looked forward to the Fair, and McClaughry was hired specifically to be the chief during this gala celebration. Clearly the thousands of visitors—including the inevitable criminals—needed police services both in the city at Jackson Park and at the fairgrounds. But such added services required more police officers and that meant more money. McClaughry believed that the fair eventually would need three hundred officers but he could only spare thirty.[75] He was able to broker a deal in which the governing board of the fair would compensate the city for additional officers. At first they offered to pay each officer $60 per month but McClaughry got them to raise it to a more respectable $76.

McClaughry took this opportunity to argue before the City's Finance Committee for more money to hire additional officers. New York City, he reminded the city politicians, had thirty-nine square miles of territory to police; they had 3,200 patrolmen to do so. On the other hand, Chicago had 183 square miles to police, a task performed by 2,200 officers.[76] Of course, one way to get more police was to get more out of the existing corps. Most officers worked twelve-hour shifts. Some sergeants in the busier stations however worked eight-hour shifts. Because they were busy they frequently had a number of patrol officers assigned to them to help. Those officers who lucked into an eight-hour shift, depleted the ranks of street cops. McClaughry ended that practice. All desk sergeants were moved from eight to twelve-hour work days.[77] Such moving around of patrolmen was necessary because of the anticipated number of criminals coming to fleece the tourists.

The expectant arrival of thousands of professional criminals called attention to one of McClaughry's favorite programs: the Bertillon system of identification. Anticipating the invasion of professional criminals McClaughry sent requests to the nation's prisons for photographs and Bertillon measurements of prisoners who might be released during the life of the fair. Such a request had more credibility coming from a man well known in the world of prison administration than merely a police chief. Most of the data was turned over to his son, Matthew Wilson McClaughry, who was increasingly regarded as the greatest expert on the Bertillon system outside of France. "Now, when the descriptions of all the crooks in the prisons of this country, who are to be discharged between now and 1894, have been obtained they will think twice before coming here to operate, knowing that we have their description and that if arrested they will be liable to be prosecuted under the Habitual Criminal act," the Major declared.[78] In December, 1891, McClaughry issued an order that all persons charged with a felony be brought to the newly established Bureau of Identification and be photographed and recorded.[79] By March 1892, the Chicago police had three thousand criminals listed in its Bertillon file. The Chief then became prominent in asking for a Bertillon exhibit at the fair to show how progressive his force was.[80]

The potential onslaught of criminals at the Fair gave rise to other problems such as the limits of police jurisdiction. As private businesses have shown, unless called into the property to investigate a crime, police surveillance was limited in private places like department stores and hotels. But the Fair was different. On one hand the Fair seemed to be a private event governed by a consortium of businessmen. On the other hand it belonged to the city. Chicago was the official host. Buildings and land would revert to the city after the events closed. So proper policing of the Fair was fuzzy and McClaughry was key in sorting things out. Of course, such celebratory exhibitions were not new. Going back to New York City's "Crystal Palace" exhibition in 1853 special policing protection was necessary. But this was the first time for Chicago. A World's Fair Police, a nineteenth-century example of a special district police, was to have all jurisdiction within the grounds except in cases of emergency. Although not McClaughry's preferred choice, John Bonfield was chosen to head up that police force, whereas the city police would be in charge outside the fairgrounds.[81] Though the Fair's governing board wanted a police station on the fairgrounds. McClaughry argued effectively that the city should not do this. The City Park Authority would not like such a station after the fair was over, he argued.[82] Instead, a police station would be built in Hyde Park, the residential area closest to the Fair grounds.

The needs for more policing inspired by the Fair forced the city Finance Committee to recommend the hiring of an additional one hundred officers. These police were divided into 1st class officers, 2nd class officers, and substitutes. The one hundred would come from the substitutes, fifty going to the World's Fair area around Hyde Park. The other fifty would be scattered among the other divisions.[83] In December, McClaughry called three hundred substitutes to active duty near the Fair site.[84] It must be remembered that the Fair itself had a special police, frequently referred to as the Columbian Guard or World's Fair Police. There was some concern with the Guard and frequently there were attempts to simply place the city police on the Fair grounds. Of course, such ideas were deeper than the city's purse and went unfounded.[85]

The addition of more official officers and the specials ones on the fairgrounds led to some other problems. During the opening dedication ceremonies there was a "civic parade" watched by a quarter of a million people, and charges were brought against the police for brutality. The Chicago and New York papers played it up but in the final analysis only one officer was brought up for investigation. Immediately, McClaughry and the Police Trial Board were accused of cover-up and whitewash. McClaughry responded:

> If they think I have decided in advance to acquit my officers I will leave the investigation in the hands of a committee of my critics. They claim to have evidence that I cannot get. Let them hear it, and on their certificate that an officer should be discharged I will make that order.[86]

This brought up a discussion over the Billy club, that time honored American police tool of intimidation. Many argued after the civic parade that the police should be disarmed. Thomas Byrnes, the chief in New York City, was seriously contemplating it. McClaughry drew a distinction:

> In New York the officers on post are always within supporting distance of one another. In some parts of the city they are so thick in the streets that they scarcely have room to swing their big clubs. New York has 1,000 more policemen with 100 square miles less territory to cover than Chicago. Were conditions equal I would not say that the removal of the clubs from the police might not be a good idea.[87]

Criticism of the police actions soon died out and letters of support mounted.[88] Eastern newspapers, however, continued to print critical reports about Chicago. On one of his visits, McClaughry was astonished over the misinformation circulating in Boston. The Boston papers claimed that Chicago was overrun with crime and that McClaughry had advised people to arm themselves. It claimed that 75,000 revolvers had been sold in one day. Bostonians then were given a list of crimes allegedly committed in one day that had actually occurred over a three-week period.[89]

Such information, besides showing urban jealousies, indicated that police departments of other cities had dim views of Chicago policing. Much like Chicago's policing system, urban policing elsewhere was characterized by politics. These political machine driven police departments looked aghast at the reform efforts of McClaughry. But the major believed that there were a small number of chiefs tired of boss politics in policing. So he sent out invitations, hundreds of them, to the chiefs of America to come to the Fair as tourists and as founding members of a new organization..Only a small number showed up but McClaughry hosted, helped establish, and became a charter member of the newly formed National Chiefs of police Union, which would change its name to the International Association of Chiefs of Police at the turn of the century. This organization would become critical in the history of police professionalism, particularly in combating the problems of politics in policing. McClaughry, always pushing his notions on criminal identification, took five wagons filled with the chiefs to the Harrison Street station where the Chicago police identification bureau was located. McClaughry boasted that his Bertillon bureau was second only to that found in Paris. Impressed by what they saw, he and his fellow chiefs would begin a crusade to have a federal bureau of identification that would eventually end up in the federal prison at Leavenworth, and later in the FBI.[90] McClaughry made sure that his correctional cronies would hold their annual convention at the Fair, as well. He hosted them, even promising the more timid that they would be safe even if it took the entire Chicago police department to insure it.[91]

The Fair was a heady experience for this man from central Illinois. Making the city a safe place, a showcase for the rest of the country, was drawing to a close. Policing the city during the Fair was what he was picked for and the success of the Chicago World's Fair, in part, was his success. On the other hand the mean streets of Chicago had not been kind. Machine politics chugged along and it increasingly looked like Carter Harrison was going to be elected mayor, for the fifth time. Besides, McClaughry's heart remained in prison administration. As the Fair drew to a close he and many others in Chicago were eager for the Major to move on.

NOTES

1. *Chicago Tribune,* November 10, 1891.
2. *Ibid.*, November 13, 1891.
3. *Ibid.*, November 14, 1891.
4. *Ibid.*, November 16, 1891.
5. *Ibid.,* November 17, 1891.
6. *Ibid.*, November 17, 1891.
7. *Ibid.*, November 19, 1891.
8. *Ibid.*, November 21, 1891.
9. *Ibid.*, December 3 and 7, 1891.
10. *Ibid.*, December 28, 1891.
11. *Ibid.*, December 31, 1891.
12. *City Council Proceedings. February 29, 1892* (Chicago Public Library), pp. 1857-59.
13. *Chicago Tribune,* January 7, 1892.
14. *Ibid.*, January 19, 1892.
15. *Ibid.*, April 17, and May 1, 1892.
16. *Ibid.*, May 2, 1892.
17. *Ibid.*, May 3, 1892.
18. *Ibid.*, May 26, 1892.
19. *Ibid.*, July 4, 1892.
20. *Ibid.*, June 27, 1893.
21. *Chicago News*, April 30, 1891.
22. *Chicago Tribune*, June 24 and 26, 1891.
23. *Ibid.*, July 30, 1891.
24. *Chicago News,* April 30, 1891.
25. *Chicago Tribune,* August 8, 19, and 21, 1891.
26. *Ibid.*, December 11, 1892.
27. *Ibid.,* November 3, 1891.

28. *Ibid.*, August 18, 1892.
29. *Ibid.*, September 29 and 30, 1892.
30. *Ibid.*, December 3, 1892.
31. *Chicago News*, April 3, 1891.
32. *Chicago Daily News*, May 1, 1891.
33. *Chicago Tribune,* October 14, 1891.
34. *Ibid.*, September 1, 1891.
35. *Ibid.*
36. See for example *Ibid.*, July 8, 9, 12 and 14, 1891.
37. *Ibid.*, July 8, 1891.
38. *Ibid.*, July 12, 1891.
39. *Ibid.*, December 4 and 5, 1891.
40. *Ibid.*, April 15, and 16, 1892.
41. *Ibid.*, March, 24 1892.
42. *Ibid.*, April 12, 1892.
43. *Ibid.*, March 24, 1892.
44. *Ibid.*, April 8, 1892.
45. *Chicago Times*, January 4, 1892.
46. *Chicago Tribune*, February 2, 1892.
47. *Ibid.*, February 18, 1892.
48. *Ibid.*, June 30, 1892.
49. *Ibid.*, June 7, 1892.
50. *Ibid.*, June 5, 1892.
51. *Ibid.*
52. *Ibid.*, June 6, 1892.
53. *Ibid.*, June 14, 1892.
54. *Ibid.*, June 14, and 15, 1892.
55. *Ibid.*, July 22 and 23, 1892.
56. *Ibid.*, December 12, 1892.
57. *Ibid.*, July 24, 1892.
58. *Ibid.*, August 9, 1892.
59. *Ibid.*, August 18, 1892.
60. *Ibid.*, August 21, 1892.
61. *Ibid.*, September 3 and 4, 1892.
62. *Ibid.*, September 8, 1892.
63. *Ibid.*, September 7, 1892.
64. *Ibid.*, August 2 and 27, 1892.
65. *Ibid.*, September 29, 30 1892.
66. *Ibid.*, September 9 and 10, 1892.
67. *Ibid.*, September 12, 13, and 18, 1892.
68. *Ibid.*, November 2, 1892.
69. *Ibid.*, January 24, 1893.
70. *Ibid.*, March 16, 17, 18, 19, and May 9, 1893.
71. Bessie Louise Pierce, *A History of Chicago, Vol III* pp. 304-305.

72. For the connection of Holmes and the World's Fair, see the popular book by Erik Larson, *The Devil in the White City: Murder, Magic, and Madness at the Fair That Changed America* (New York: Crown Publishers, 2003).

73. This phenomena was studied by Elaine Abelson in *When Ladies Go A-Thieving: Middle-Class Shoplifters in the Victorian Department Store* (New York: Oxford University Press, 1989).

74. *Chicago Tribune,* January 4, 1892.

75. *Ibid.*, August 1, 1891.

76. *Ibid.*, January 23, 1892.

77. *Ibid.*, May 31, 1892.

78. *Ibid.*, October 12, 1891.

79. *Ibid.*, January 3, 1892.

80. *Ibid.*, March 11, 1892.

81. *Ibid.*, March 20 1892.

82. *Ibid.*, August 23, 1891.

83. *Ibid.*, November 17, 30, 1892.

84. *Ibid.*, December 3, 1892.

85. *Ibid.*, July 2, 1893.

86. *Ibid.*, October 29, 1892.

87. *Ibid.*, October 31, 1892.

88. *Ibid.*, November 3, 1892.

89. *Ibid.*, December 11, 1892.

90. *Ibid.,* May 19, 1893.

91. *Ibid.*, June 8, 1893.

Chapter Twenty-Two

Moving on

" . . . it was a battle from the first day."

Almost from the beginning of his tenure, rumors instigated by opposition politicians and angry police officers flew around that McClaughry would soon be gone. For example, within a few weeks of his appointment, newspapers began suggesting a rift had developed between the mayor and the chief. When the state reformatory law was passed, everyone in Springfield, Pontiac, and Chicago felt the superintendent would be offered the new post.[1] Almost immediately McClaughry saddened the hearts of the machine and syndicate by saying he was not yet ready to resign. He announced:

> I want to say to the public that I do not intend to leave the position of Superintendent of Police when a fight is on. I have undertaken the task of rescuing the department from politics, and no one knows the obstacles that are being encountered. A great many different forces are being used to defeat my purpose. The gamblers are making a strong and bitter fight, and are using money and influence to thwart the plans of the department. I am using all my energy and devoting all my time to accomplishing the desired end. My work keeps me up until 12 o'clock almost every night in the week. Aside from the fight that I am compelled to make against the gamblers and the criminal classes there are other influences at work. It is no small task to separate the police from politics aside from the other factors with which I have to contend. This work of reorganizing the Police Department can and will be accomplished in time. It is a work of several months and all I can say now is to ask the public to be a little patient. While we may be regarded as moving slow, we are going in the right direction and I am confident that the desired result of establishing a police force, the whole duty of which is to preserve the peace and keep down crime, will be accomplished.[2]

The matter of McClaughry's possible resignation was reignited in December 1891, when the Chicago City Railway Company sought a new general manager and McClaughry's name figured prominently. Besides his ability in leading people and handling large institutions he was praised for his ability in dealing with the public. "He seems to know how to harmonize contending elements and factions," the Tribune felt, "and just now that is what is needed by the South Side company."[3] Yet he distanced himself from this position too.

In the first few months of 1893, as McClaughry continued his crusades against the professional gamblers, the "Pen Fraud" case dragged on draining him of much energy and enthusiasm for Chicago. By June, although the final report to the state legislature exonerated him of any wrongdoing, considerable damage had been done.[4] Far more disturbing was the mayoral election of April 1893, which brought Carter Harrison Sr. back to power again, his fifth term as mayor. He had been the boss politician for years and the expectation was that the city would be thrown wide open again. McClaughry immediately turned in his resignation revealing some of his deepest thoughts on criminal justice agencies. Much later as he reminisced:

> I do not like police work. The strain is terrific. I would much rather have the management of a prison. During my term of service as head of the Chicago police department we waged war unremittingly on the gamblers, and it was a battle from the first day.[5]

Harrison stalled and McClaughry lingered on. For a time the crusades against the gamblers continued. For example, five patrol wagons raided and closed "Prince" Harry Varnell's place in April 1893 and arrested sixty-seven persons.[6] Then in May three pool rooms were closed.[7] It was clear that the Mayor did not want McClaughry to leave until the World's Fair was over.[8] Many were pleased that McClaughry was not so easily cast off. The *Tribune* felt he had been an excellent chief:

> . . . at the end of two years' administration by him the force is in excellent discipline. Its efficiency was demonstrated admirably last Monday [May 1st] in handling the great crowds that attended the inauguration. The drunkards and the loafers have been weeded out. The men have confidence in their officers. There is more harmony between the officers and the Chief than there has been at any time in the history of the department. . . . He promised to take the department out of politics. As a police officer Maj. McClaughry has no politics. Fully 90 per cent of the men are Democrats. Only one of the five Inspectors, Ross, is a Republican, and his efficiency is acknowledged so generally that there is no thought of removing him.[9]

But the elections and change in administration had relegated McClaughry to a lower position. When the new mayor came out with a reorganization plan, he did not ask McClaughry to implement it. Instead, an assistant superintendent was to be in charge of the reforms.[10] Soon local papers reported that "Harrison's ax drops" and thirty-five officers were fired or transferred. Most of the "reforms" were aimed at the Harrison Street station, the center of the vice districts of Chicago.[11] The mayor wanted to bring the "Harrison Street Blues" back to pre-McClaughry days. Any raids on gambling houses were aimed at those who had not paid their percentage to city hall.[12] Then Carter Harrison's true colors began to show. In an interview in July, Mayor Harrison claimed that Chicago was cosmopolitan, and not some puritan village, and that he would run the gambling crusades as he saw fit.[13] This led the *Tribune* to ask, "Who is running the police department on the gambling issue?" Harrison was for it and McClaughry was against it.[14] The answer was forthcoming. On July 31st, McClaughry's resignation was finally accepted and Michael Brennan, an assistant superintendent who had been fired when McClaughry came to office but restored with Harrison's reelection, was made the new superintendent.[15]

Within a month Carter Harrison Sr. was dead, a victim to a crazed office seeker. But his permissive policies lingered on and within a year a grand jury investigation of gambling in the city found the houses running full throttle —with the police and the politicians in full accord.[16] Soon, captains and other prominent officers began to be fired for political reasons. Alexander Ross, the only Republican police inspector, was fired with the mayor publically declaring he was getting even for the inspector's political activity against him.[17] McClaughry's policies on politics and gambling had been undone. Although frustrated with Chicago politics, McClaughry had seen the city through the World's Fair. Now he quietly moved on to what seemed to be a more hospitable environment: prison administration. Of course, there new politics would be waiting.

NOTES

1. *Chicago Tribune*, July 29, 1891.
2. *Ibid.*, July 30, 1891.
3. *Ibid.*, December 13, 1891.
4. *Ibid.*, June 16, 1893.
5. *Chicago Record Herald*, May 12, 1913.
6. *Chicago Tribune*, April 25, 1893.
7. *Ibid.*, May 18, 1893.

8. *Ibid.*, April 20, 1893.
9. *Ibid.*, May 7, 1893.
10. *Ibid.*, June 1, 1893.
11. *Ibid.*, June 16, 1893.
12. William T. Stead, pp. 233-35.
13. *Chicago Tribune,* July 9, 1893.
14. *Ibid.*, July 16, 1893.
15. *Ibid.*, August 1, 1893.
16. William Stead, p. 235.
17. *Chicago Evening-Journal*, January 12, 1894.

Part Five

STATE POLITICS AND PENOLOGY: MCCLAUGHRY AT PONTIAC

Chapter Twenty-Three

Youth Crime in Illinois

"... not punishment for past offenses, but training for future usefulness."

After leaving the Chicago police department, McClaughry returned to corrections splitting the next eight years between the new reformatory in Pontiac, Illinois, and a short stint at the state penitentiary at Joliet. Quickly politics caught up with him again. Since his active Democratic days before the Civil War, McClaughry had walked precariously between political parties; both Republican and Democratic politicians appreciated his professionalism. He seemed to exemplify the "disinterested" qualities with no political and personal gain or vendetta in mind.[1] However, the environment of late nineteenth-century America was so politicized that steps toward such professionalization stumbled.

While Chief of Police, he was a target for urban politicians. Now he became the bull's eye for downstate politicians. Though Pontiac, a small town one hundred miles south of Chicago, became a rescue from those horrible days in big city policing, it too presented political challenges. At this time of Republican domination in the rural politics of Illinois, the wrangling became even more intense, as it would also do in more abbreviated form at Joliet. In the end, his employment at the federal prison at Leavenworth would take him out of the bickering arena of state politics and place him on national stages.

The challenges he faced were by no means only political. His work at the Illinois reformatory and adult prison placed him squarely amidst growing and conflicting ideas on the nature of humans. New criminological paradigms emerged to challenge ideas that had prevailed for decades. His attempts to filter reformatory ideals known as the "new penology" into the adult prison are best seen and appreciated against the older ideas of nurture on the one hand and beliefs about the "born criminal" on the other. Whether nurture or nature explained criminality, Chicago became an important show case for ideas on the origin of crime and criminals. Social disorganization, immigrant displacement, economic development, and family dysfunction, though found in all major cities, were displayed particularly vividly in Chicago. By the 1880s Americans were making clearer distinctions between the first offender and the habitual criminal. The word "recidivist," meaning going to prison repeatedly, first entered the common language in 1883.[2] In a sense, this term in itself suggested that prisons were failures. Their only success was as a school for further criminality. Concerns over the vulnerability and malleability of young people led to the Child Saver Movement and eventually the juvenile justice system in Chicago and then elsewhere. These Child Savers–and the workers at the newly opened reformatory at Pontiac at first belonged to this perspective–believed in nurture. At the same time the nature of inmates at Joliet challenged the notion that a criminal could be rehabilitated. In a real sense the intellectual paradigms were being played out in Illinois and McClaughry was center stage. As he had experienced it earlier in Pennsylvania, McClaughry saw crime and disorder increase in Illinois during this period.

YOUTH AND MISBEHAVIOR IN ILLINOIS

By the 1890s Illinois had undergone tremendous change.[3] The transportation revolutions that had begun in the 1850s continued making Chicago the hub of the railroad industry. Population numbers had nearly doubled since the end of the Civil War so that by 1890 more than a million people lived in the city. Many of these residents were immigrants bringing a variety of new lifestyles and expectations. Perceptions of crime and disorder increased as well. By the early 1890s there was one arrest per eleven persons in the city. Disorderly conduct headed the list with a six-fold increase over previous years, though whether there had been a real increase in misbehavior or public tolerances for such activities had decreased was not clear. Whatever the case, the criminal justice system and public perceptions of crime were affected. Moreover, a census of youthful offenders in 1892 found that nearly one half of the 14,816 offenses were against the social order, and by 1898, there were 875 children in the Cook County jail.[4] "Future peril rather than present danger" prompted citizens to call for special institutions for teenage criminals.[5]

Young people, particularly males, were vulnerable to the robust nature of nineteenth-century America. Rebellious and adventurous, they took risks with little concern for long term consequences. Ethnic prejudice and economic conditions disrupted family life and at times destroyed it. Of course Chicago, with its remarkable growth, had a large population of young people, and gangs started to form in the 1860s and increased rapidly in the '80s and

'90s. For example, one group of a dozen boys, seventeen to twenty-two years old, hung around the Bridgeport section of the city playing cards and robbing men as they came home from work with their pay. In the 1880s gangs of Irish and German boys had club houses in basements of saloons along Ashland Avenue. One such group of twelve, the Hickory Street gang, also made up of twelve to eighteen year-olds, met in a basement to read "dime novels", play cards, drink beer, and plan street robberies.[6] On the South side, near where the University of Chicago would be built, other similar gangs created alley sheds as club houses that they called their "Joint." Besides hanging out there and playing draw poker, occasionally, for fun, they would war on each other but also come together for burglary sprees.[7] On one occasion the police shot and seriously wounded Henry Clancey, the head of a youth gang, as he fled arrest. Three others, all in their early teens, were captured with a wagon full of loot.[8]

One street and one public school were so often the scene of such crimes that they became known as "Bloody Maxwell." Maxwell Street, on the near southwest side, was a working-class area known for its street crime and general disorder. By the 1890s the Maxwell Street police station was one of the busiest in the city.[9] At one point the arrest of boys under sixteen averaged nearly sixty a month at the Maxwell Street station.

In 1881 a feud between rival gangs started at the Walsh School, a public school at the southern section of Maxwell Street, which lasted for thirty years. It worsened in the 1890s when the Edwards Law went into effect requiring all children to attend school, including rowdies who otherwise might not have attended. Gang members carried guns and knives to school and took pot shots at each other in the classrooms. Over time numerous boys were killed and even more were shot, stabbed, or beaten with clubs, often in the playgrounds and nearby streets. Two gangs dominated: the Irishers and the Bohemians. The Irishers lived east of a main north-south avenue called Johnson Street, while the Bohemians lived west of it. Johnson Street, one of the main streets to Walsh School, became contested territory.

The life and death of Buff Higgens, leader of the Irishers, may be illustrative. Born in Ireland, his family moved to Chicago and settled on Johnson Street by the 1880s. He went to Walsh School for a few years before heading up the Irish gang, leading them into several battles against the Bohemians. At thirteen he dropped out of school but still hung around to lead a gang that broke windows, robbed fruit stands, stoned peddlers, and tormented merchants. By fifteen he was a noted thief; then in 1893 he broke into a house and was discovered by the owner, whom he murdered in panic. Higgens was quickly caught and hanged, becoming a folk hero among the youth of Chicago.[10]

Numerous other gangs existed as well. Jimmy McGann and his five sons had a thieving gang. By the turn of the century, Jimmy had sons in the reformatory, the House of Corrections, Joliet prison, Cook County jail, and one dead, killed by Jimmy himself in a drunken brawl.[11] Other "thieving families" arose, perhaps most astounding among them that headed by Margaret Weiss, a widow living on Maxwell Street with a large family of ne'er-do-wells, remarried into another equally nefarious large family, so that by 1890 she had a tribe of thieves and pick pockets numbering more than one hundred.[12]

Of course, there is more to Illinois than Chicago, and rural Illinois had its share of disorder.[13] To a certain degree small town living did mitigate blatant disorder, for when everyone knew nearly everyone else that was a considerable deterrent to misbehavior. Americans in this period had a profound trust in rural life and an equally negative view of the city. Orphan trains therefore steamed from the cities to the countryside loaded with young people gathered up from the streets of the city to go to the farming communities of rural America. Illinois received more than its share of these urban urchins.

Even in rural situations dangers existed, to be sure. The arrival of a circus, carnival, or other traveling show was viewed with both excitement and suspicion. Tramps, particularly with the economic downturns in the 1890s, were a problem. But it was boy bandits who caused the most trouble, bandits such as the Maxwell brothers, Ed and Lon, who started with petty crime in the early 1870s. A decade and a half of lawlessness followed with the brothers committing crimes throughout western Illinois, Wisconsin, Minnesota, and Nebraska, interrupted only intermittently by short stints in Joliet prison. After the brothers shot down two sheriffs in southern Wisconsin, the public panicked and made a run on ten-dollar nickel-plated revolvers in Macomb, Illinois, which became known as "Maxwell Terrifiers." Eventually Ed was caught in Nebraska and lynched. Lon got away to Montana but was lynched there in 1889 bringing an end to the career of the boy bandits.[14] This phenomenon of rural criminality many found puzzling. That children of broken families in Chicago and other big cities would be lured to a life of crime through lack of nurture and the corrupting influence of the city was understandable. It was more difficult to explain the boy bandits who came from hard working respectable parents. The increase of crime, particularly among the youth of America, perplexed those who tried to answer the question: why do people commit crime?

CRIMINOLOGY: NURTURE OR NATURE

In response, new ideas on criminality began to arise challenging the foundations of McClaughry's thinking and career,[15] chief among them those of

Cesare Beccaria. His theory implied that nurture, the manipulation of the law, and penal practices could somehow shape human nature—a theory shaped by Evangelical Protestantism that believed in the possible redemption of humanity over the sterner Calvinistic ideas of predestination. Capitalism was competitive, cruel, and demanding; independence and freedom too intoxicating. Such a society, some felt, had failed many who needed an asylum from and preparation for the stormy demands of late nineteenth–century life. Middle-class America felt that instilling their values, along with lower-class working skills, would change vulnerable individuals and help them fit into contemporary society. Punishment needed to be painful with the expectation that it would alter the offender's behavior. To a large degree, the invention of the penitentiary and certainly of the reformatory system reflected this nurturing ideal. Clearly the "child savers" who were increasingly coming on the scene in this period believed in nurturing the delinquent.

Essential to the "new penology" coming out of the Cincinnati meetings and the founding of the National Prison Association in 1873, was the belief that delinquents could be converted into law-abiding citizens. Leaders in the reformatory movement believed that typically in the case of a delinquent his family had failed to teach him necessary life skills and self-restraint, that urban life and poverty had undermined the young boy, and that together these factors had lead to a life of crime. These reformers, anti-city to the core, believed that the rhythms, rigors, and responsibilities of rural life could erase the blemishes of urban life. Nelson McLain, eventual superintendent of the Illinois State Home for Delinquent Boys, believed that misbehaving boys should be "taken away from evil associations and temptations, away from the moral and physical filth and contagion, out of the gaslight and sewer gas; away into the woods and fields free from temptation and contagion; out into the sunlight and the starlight and the pure, sweet air of the meadows."[16] Consequently, reformatories should be placed in a country environment and mimic rural values.

Nurturing cut both ways: one could be taught evil as well as righteousness. Young delinquents therefore needed to be separated from corrupting influences, such as of adult criminals, for their own good. The reformatory was to be a guarded sanctuary. Residents inside as well as society on the outside were to be protected. Assignment to a reformatory should be done with minimal interference from the courts and the practices of "due process" because the reformatories, believed the Illinois State Commissioners of Public Charities, was "not to punish for past offenses, but train for future usefulness."[17] Sentences should be indeterminate, allowing delinquents some control over their own rehabilitation. Inmates need to be protected from idleness and self-indulgence through military drill, physical exercise, and constant supervision.

Although middle-class values were at the core of the nurturing process, only lower-class work skills were taught, and industrial and agricultural training predominated. No education beyond remedial elementary schooling was offered; after all, so the Commissioners reasoned, these children came out of the lower and working classes and that is to where they would return.[18]

Who better could be nurtured than young people? The post-Civil War nation in general became more child conscious, and this extended to care of troubled and abandoned children. Houses of Refuge and Children's Aid Societies of an earlier time were joined rapidly and rigorously. The child saving movement in Illinois was largely in the hands of several key middle- class women, among them, Lucy Flower and the Chicago Women's Club who helped create the Protective Agency for Women and Children in 1887; Louise de Koven Bowen, a woman of property and standing, who was thoroughly dedicated to delinquent and dependent young people; and Jane Addams, Julia Lathrop, and Florence Kelly, to name a few, who brought to Chicago a commitment to the nurturing perspective.[19] These female philanthropists provided food, clothing, education and counsel to slum bound kids. Hull House, a settlement house on the west side of Chicago, became famous for the care it gave to immigrant families. Soon a Juvenile Protective Association was created by these child savers to address child abuse.

By the 1890s another criminological perspective arrived in America, this time through Caesar Lombroso whose study of criminals in Italy emphasized heredity—or nature—as a key factor in deviant behavior. Following upon the heels of Darwinian explanations of human origin and nature, Lombrosoan anthropology became quite a fad by the last decade of the nineteenth century because it suggested the impossibility of reforming criminals and, in so doing, connected with doubts that had already begun to creep into ideas about the value of nurturing twenty years earlier. Many of those working closely with the poor and the lower classes began to think of them as hereditary losers. This belief was reinforced when, in 1874, Richard Dugdale began his study of the Jukes crime family which many saw as proof of evolutionary degeneration. Dugdale's book, which traced the family tree of one family with a remarkable history of crime and dependency, quickly became a best seller. Like many influential books, what you took from it depended upon how you read it. Those of a nurturing persuasion could see society's failings. Others saw genetics at work. In his book, *Prisoners and Paupers* (1893) Henry M. Boies, a member of the Pennsylvania State Board of Public Charities, declared it "established beyond controversy that criminals and paupers, both, are degenerate: the imperfect, knotty, knurly, worm-eaten fruit of the race." Boies, and others, began to advocate castration as a remedy. The medical practice of vasectomy began in Europe in the 1890s and found a following in the United States.[20]

Many prison physicians, such as Dr. Hamilton Wry, the physician at Elmira Reformatory, were impressed by Lombroso's criminal anthropology and urged laboratory study of criminals. Dr. Harry Sharp, a doctor working at the Indiana Reformatory in Jeffersonville, introduced vasectomy to the United States in 1899, and thereafter it became known as the "Indiana Idea." Connecticut, in 1896, became fearful of lower class "misfits" breeding together and began regulating marriage. This eugenics movement became a significant force in America as Kansas, New Jersey and Ohio followed Connecticut's example. Eugenics, grounded in Lombrosoan philosophy, became a particular challenge to the nurture-oriented reformers like the child savers and McClaughry. One can see the tensions between the nurture and nature advocates as they played out in institutional developments.[21]

INSTITUTIONS FOR YOUTHS IN ILLINOIS

Bureaucracies for children, dependent or delinquent, were scarce in Illinois before the Civil War. When Illinois became a state in 1817, a child under seven was not responsible for a crime. Ten years later the age of accountability was raised to ten years, still remarkably young. Four years later, in 1831, most children under eighteen years of age were exempted from serving time in the new penitentiary at Alton, and mostly would go instead to the county jail. But the jail system was notoriously bad. By 1869 there were seventy-eight jails in Illinois, and a total of ninety-eight children under the age of sixteen could be found in forty of these places labeled as "moral plague spots" by inspectors.[22] The Chicago jail was the worst, no matter whether during its period as the "log cabin," as Bridewell, and House of Correction phases. The "log cabin" phase lasted from 1832 to 1851. Built on the public square it became quickly overcrowded and by 1849 most inmates were doing "ball-and-chain" work, meaning that gangs of prisoners, tethered together, went about town doing various projects like repairing the roads.

The Bridewell, a plank jail with fifty-two cells at the corner of Polk and Wells, replaced the old log cabin in 1851. Chicago's City Council was in control of the jail and it soon became a plum for the political machine. A "Keeper" paid the Alderman to get his position as warden, and this keeper in turn got his money from fees for feeding the prisoners. But this he quickly abused, feeding them a diet known as "mush-and molasses," that undernourished the inmates. When citizens complained about the prisoners laboring on the streets, the inmates were put to work in lumber yards making planks for the road system. Wooden planks had become a necessity, especially in rainy seasons, as roads turned to mud. If there was no work to be had, then prisoners simply wandered around carrying a ball and chain. Aldermen reserved the right to pardon and release anyone, and this inevitably led to some political interferences and abuses. Yet the Keeper was glad to get rid of some prisoners because by 1871 there were 250 inmates and jail conditions had become deplorable, as *The Tribune* reported:

> The present City Bridewell is notoriously one of the foulest abominations in this city. It is a den of infamy, moral and physical. The unfortunate inmates are treated like brutes and the institution can be warranted to insure the permanent degradation of every prisoner, male or female, old and young, who enters it.[23]

Within four months the problem was temporally solved when most of the city, including the Bridewell, was burned down in the Chicago Fire. Fortunately, a few months before the fire most prisoners had been removed to the newly constructed House of Correction on the west side.

The period from 1871 to 1920 is characterized as the House of Correction era. Aldermanic control of the Chicago jail ended and instead the mayor appointed three inspectors, along with a superintendent. A prominent reformer, Charles Felton, would be the superintendent from 1871 to 1890. A new brick structure was built with one wing of 288 cells for men and a second wing of two hundred cells for women. Young people were placed with the adults. Later, in the 1920s, a sixteen-year old described his experiences in the jail. They could only have been worse earlier.

> The horrors of that House of "Correction" [sic.] cannot be described. I can only say that when there I lost all respect for myself, felt degenerated and unhuman [sic.]. I shall never fully recover [from] the effects of that old south house. I always felt it was an insult to put me there. In my anguish I planned vengeance and hatred. Hanging, life-imprisonment in Joliet–anything would be better than a year in that vermin-ridden, unsanitary, immoral, God-forsaken pit.[24]

As early as 1855 a reform school was opened in Chicago but it burned down a year later. A new one was constructed, but it too went up in flames, along with much of Chicago in 1871. Another reform school had been built about one hundred miles downstate in Pontiac in 1869, but it was punitive in nature and often described as a "junior prison." In 1876, there were 180 boys in Pontiac; six years later it was overcrowded with 250. In 1888, when its name was changed to reformatory, the law declared that any first offender between sixteen and twenty-one was to go to Pontiac, further overcrowding the place.[25] In reality Pontiac became a junior prison awaiting a superintendent deeply committed to the spirit of the "new penology." In 1893 the child saving movement gained momentum eventually culminating with the juvenile court act of 1899.[26] Of course, reformatory activists like McClaughry were already on the scene by then. But what was perhaps most important for the future of child offenders was the election of a reform minded governor.

NOTES

1. See Svend Ranulf's *Moral Indignation and Middle Class Psychology,* originally published in 1938 but republished in 1964 (New York: Schocken Books, 1964), and his earlier work *The Jealously of the Gods and Criminal Law at Athens* (Copenhagen, 1933).

2. Simon Cole, *Suspect Identities: A History of Fingerprinting and Criminal Identification* (Cambridge, Ma: Harvard University Press, 2001), p. 54.

3. Much that follows I owe to Alexander W. Pisciotta's "A House Divided: Penal Reform at the Illinois State Reformatory, 1891-1915," *Crime and Delinquency* vol. 37 no.2 (April, 1991), pp. 165-85.

4. Ray Ginger, *Altgeld's America: The Lincoln Ideal Versus Changing Realities* (New York: New Viewpoints, 1973), pp. 210, 228.

5. *Chicago Tribune,* September 29, 1892.

6. Frederic M. Thrasher, *The Gang* (Chicago: University of Chicago Press, 1926), p. 17.

7. *Chicago Tribune*, March 20, 1888.

8. *Ibid.*, March 23, 1888.

9. Much later this police station will be in the opening footage and credits for a popular television police series called the Hill Street Blues.

10. Herbert Asbury, *Gem of the Prairie: An Informal History of the Chicago Underworld* (New York: Alfred A. Knopf, 1940), pp. 212, 218-19.

11. *Ibid.*, p. 215.

12. *Ibid.*, p. 216.

13. Catherine McNicol Stock, *Rural Radicals: From Bacon's Rebellion to the Oklahoma City Bombing* (New York: Penguin Books, 1997), pp. 79,134.

14. John E. Hallwas, *Western Illinois Heritage* (Macomb, Illinois: Illinois Heritage Press, 1983), pp. 137-143. Also John E. Hallwas, *Dime Novel Desperados: The Notorious Maxwell Brothers* (Urbana, Illinois: University of Illinois Press, 2008).

15. Robert M. Mennel, *Thorns & Thistles: Juvenile Delinquency in the United States, 1825-1890* (Hanover, New Hampshire: University Press of New England, 1973), pp. 78-101.

16. Quoted in Anthony M. Platt, *The Child Savers: The Invention of Delinquency* (Chicago: University of Chicago Press, 1969), p. 66.

17. Quoted in *Ibid*, p. 106. Original in the *Biennial Reports of the Board of State Commissioners of Public Charities of the State of Illinois* (Springfield: Weber, Magie and Co., 1879), pp. 273-79.

18. Ibid., pp. 54-55. For a fascinating study see James Bennett's *Oral History and Delinquency: the Rhetoric of Criminology* (Chicago: University of Chicago Press, 1981), pp. 89-103.

19. Platt, pp. 75-101.

20. Mark Haller, *Eugenics: Hereditarian Attitudes in American Thought* (New Brunswick, NJ: Rutgers University Press, 1963), pp. 42, 49.

21. *Ibid.*, p. 50.

22. Platt, pp. 118-119.

23. *Chicago Tribune* July 26, 1871.

24. Clifford Shaw, *The Jack Roller: A Delinquent Boy's Own Story* (Chicago: University of Chicago Press, 1930), p. 154.

25. Platt, p. 106.

26. Joan Gittens, *Poor Relations: The Children of the State of Illinois, 1818-1990* (Urbana, Illinois: University of Illinois Press, 1994), pp. 101-104.

Chapter Twenty-Four

John Peter Altgeld

"Our Penal Machinery and Its Victims"

Robert McClaughry's work in Illinois in this period can best be understood against the backdrop of John Peter Altgeld's political and intellectual ideas and ideals. A German immigrant, Altgeld grew up amidst hard times in Ohio. Thanks to his native abilities and hard work he became a prosperous lawyer and prosecutor in Missouri before moving to Chicago. He worked his way up in the legal profession in Chicago and won a judgeship as a Democrat. Eventually he would become chief judge of the Cook County court system before resigning to run for governor. Throughout his career he never forgot his humble origins and became a steadfast defender of the workingman and the union movement.[1]

As a practicing lawyer, Altgeld had became disillusioned with the justice system. He had seen criminal justice up close as an insider and felt it did not really address the crime problem; it was too politicized, more concerned with the economic and political well being of a few hacks than justice for the individual or the elimination of crime. He expressed this discontent and moral outrage in his 1884 book *Our Penal Machinery and Its Victims*. While researching this book Altgeld met McClaughry, and they immediately developed a mutual respect.[2]

Our Penal Machinery is a remarkable manifesto. On the one hand, it attacked the current system and by implication many of its practitioners, along with the police, courts, jails, and prisons. The very word "machinery" was a metaphor for a vast factory exploiting the masses for the "robber barons" of justice. Altgeld was progressive simply for thinking of the connections between crime, police, courts, and corrections as an interlocking system. On the other hand, the book reflected current reformatory ideology. It charged that the contemporary punitive system created criminals rather than reformed them.[3]

A young warden at Joliet at the time, Robert McClaughry, was impressed. As a representative and beneficiary of the system, McClaughry was just as much the target of Altgeld's attacks as other political hacks. Yet, as he was demonstrating at Joliet, McClaughry was also a reformer imprisoned by the system. Later he would break out, so to speak, and go off to Pennsylvania to implement these reform ideals. Forced out of that position through a combination of politics and poor health, he returned to Illinois and his career as head of Chicago's police became entangled with that of Altgeld who ran successfully for governor in 1892, when during the campaign Altgeld sent a private letter to Chief McClaughry condemning the police raids on anarchists' meetings in 1891.[4]

The election of 1892 was a heated one. Altgeld's supporter base, the German-Lutherans, was a sizable group in Illinois. But it extended further than the German community to all recent immigrants and organized labor. An energetic campaigner, the *Chicago Inter-Ocean* noted, "Judge Altlgeld has visited more families, kissed more babies, inspected more dairies and helped set more hens than any man before who wanted to be Governor."[5]

Republicans had fallen on hard times across the nation. Agrarian discontent, growing immigrant populations, dislike of numerous Republican supported school language laws, had put the G.O.P. on weaker footing. On the national level, Grover Cleveland became a Democratic president, the first to be elected since before the Civil War. In Illinois John Peter Altgeld became governor, the first Democrat to hold that office since 1856.[6]

As governor, Altgeld achieved considerable fame, both statewide and nationally. Altgeld railed against many current practices in prisons throughout his governorship. Such criticisms and reforms reflected his commitment to the reformatory. One of those issues had to do with the way prisoners were costumed:

> The effect of putting stripes on convicts has been found to be this: that it does not affect those already hardened except to make them a little more desperate, nor does it affect those who are by nature dull and brutish, except to lower them a little, but it tends to crush whatever spark of self-respect and manhood there may be left in a higher grade of prisoner, and in that way tends to still further unfit them for an honorable struggle in life, and an irreparable injury is thus done to society as well as to the convict, which was not contemplated by the law.[7]

Already in July, 1896, Altgeld had seen to it that the prisoners at Joliet were clothed in plain gray suits rather than stripes, the latter being reserved as a sign of disciplinary action.

Altgeld's reforms included the growing number of female prisoners. At Joliet, women had been segregated from the general population for decades on the third floor of the administration building but did not have a separate facility until November 1896 when a three-storied structure for women opened across the street from the main prison complex. Stretching from the administration building was the cell house. On the first floor was the chapel, a knitting room, ironing rooms, kitchen, and the fan room for heating and ventilating the building. "The air in every department is changed every fifteen minutes," reported one impressed newspaper. Each cell was seven by eight by ten feet, provided with a window, an exhaust flue, hot air duct, water, incandescent light, a shelf for storing trinkets, and hooks for clothing. Entirely built by prison labor from stone mined at the nearby quarry, when open it was claimed to be "the finest female prison in the world."[8] By the time McClaughry got there in the 1890s the demographics of this female prison had shifted considerably. Previously, whether foreign or native born, most of the female prisoners were white. But in the mid 1890s, African American females showed up in greater numbers. Where they were eighteen percent of the women incarcerated in the 80s, they constituted fifty-two percent in the 90s. Two thirds of these were from the mean streets of Chicago.[9]

Chicago had been a power base for Altgeld; Carter Harrison's political machine fully supported the governor. Many conservatives resented this pro-labor democratic governor. His pardoning of the remaining Haymarket anarchists still serving time in prison outraged some, while others were angered by his refusal to send troops to crush the Pullman strike. Over his head, President Grover Cleveland, a close friend and political ally, did send the army, for which Altgeld openly criticized him thereby creating a rift between the leaders of the Democratic Party that will have repercussions in 1896. But as his popularity decreased, and the strength of his opposition increased, Altgeld made a key decision. He appointed McClaughry as superintendent of the reformatory at Pontiac, Illinois.

NOTES

1. For a general treatment see Ray Ginger's *Altgeld's America.* Also, Harry Barnard, *Eagle Forgotten: The Life of John Peter Altgeld* (New York: The Bobbs-Merrill Company, 1938).
2. Harry Bernard, p. 170.
3. David Falcone, John Peter Altgeld: Progressive Apologist For Social Justice (PhD dissertation for the Saint Louis University, Saint Louis, Mo, 1989), pp. 91-137.
4. Bernard, pp. 254-55.

5. Quoted in Horace Samuel Merrill's *Bourbon Democracy of the Middle West, 1865-1896* (Baton Rouge: Louisiana State University Press, 1953), p. 235.

6. Robert D. Marcus, *Grand Old Party: Political Structure in the Gilded Age, 1880-1896* (New York: Oxford University Press, 1971), pp. 187, 194.

7. A biennial message given by the governor, January 6th 1897, as quoted in Waldo R. Brown, *Altgeld of Illinois* (New York: Huibach Publications, 1924), pp.184-85.

8. *Joliet Daily Republican,* November 12, 1896.

9. L. Mara Dodge "'The Most Degraded of Their Sex, If Not of Humanity': Female Prisoners at the Illinois State Penitentiary at Joliet, 1859-1900," *Journal of Illinois History* 2 (1999), p. 224. Also see L. Mara Dodge, "'One Female Prisoner Is of More Trouble Than Twenty Males:' Women Convicts in Illinois Prisons, 1835-1899," *Journal of Social History* 32 (1998-1999), pp. 907-30.

Chapter Twenty-Five

Pontiac Reformatory

"Treachery and difficulty are never lacking in and about public institutions"

BENJAMIN SHEET'S ERA

Over fifteen years after Elmira opened, Illinois created its reformatory, an institution for young first offenders. The logical choice to head up the Pontiac Reformatory was Robert McClaughry. But he was still chief of police in Chicago. So it was Benjamin Sheets who became its first General Superintendent. Yet apparently McClaughry was an original member of its Board of Managers because on January 11th he wrote to the new governor resigning his position.[1]

The new Board of Managers consisted of J. R. Scott, A. D. Cadwallader, Valintine Jobst, and Samuel Fallows, the president of the Board. A month after his resignation McClaughry, still the Superintendent of Police in Chicago, voiced growing concerns over the politics of a majority of the new board and "enemies in the [state] House led by Hon. Ed Merritt." Several things bothered McClaughry: first that the "enemies" wanted to forbid the governor from removing Board members for misconduct and incompetency; second that some wanted to pay the Board a salary. Though McClaughry conceded that the Board might be paid for some of their expenses, he was adamant that the Board should be in office primarily simply for the "love of the cause." He was at root concerned that they not have too much power. For example, rather than allow the Board to appoint underlings, he felt that was a job best left to the Superintendent. Lastly, he was concerned about any policy that allowed the Board to arbitrarily remove the General Superintendent without a thorough investigation. Fuming over the city politics of Chicago, McClaughry knew that

> Treachery and difficulty are never lacking in and about public institutions. Powerful conspiracy may be organized against the best man in the world, and he be disgraced and ruined, unless he be permitted to meet his accusers face to face and be tried upon the charges plainly and properly formulated.[2]

Political concerns continued to mount especially as rumors grew that Altgeld might eventually appoint McClaughry as head of the reformatory. Apparently, Altgeld was slow to officially accept McClaughry's original resignation from the Board. In March, McClaughry, feeling the growing political pressures as chief of police in Chicago and the investigations going on in state capital over his prior administration at Joliet, wrote the governor again.

> I have noticed, from time to time, in the public prints, statements to the effect that certain charges had been filed against me, with the Senate Committee on Penal and Reformatory Institutions touching my official acts as Warden of the Illinois State Penitentiary, and I see by the enemy papers that the Senate has today ordered an investigation into said charges. I cannot consent to hold official relations with any State Institution while this investigation is pending, and therefore beg you to consider my resignation as final and unconditional from and after this date.[3]

Without the administrative skill of McClaughry Sheets was stymied over his new job. First, although the buildings were only twenty years old, the physical plant was in bad condition because the intensive way a correctional facility is used makes it prematurely old. Sheets complained that the buildings were a fire trap, a danger to the inhabitants and workers. The water supply had been bad for years causing a constant problem of inadequate resources and potential disease. The gas lighting and sewage systems were horrible. In any correctional facility a natural breakdown of such services causes a crisis larger than might occur in most other places. Yet officials on the outside tended to assume that any malfunction was inmate inspired rather than the infrastructure itself wearing out. Consequently, Sheets spent most of his time carrying out reconstruction of the place. Existing buildings had to be repaired or replaced. A new 300-bed cell block was built. New industrial shops were started.

A second problem was a political "catch 22." The governor would not allow the facility to begin its new regime until its physical plant was repaired. The repairs could not start until inmates arrived to do the work. Finally, in 1893, two years after the enabling law was passed, the governor gave his go ahead; enough work had been done to make the place habitable.

Third, the inmates had changed in number and kind. By July 1893 there were 480 inmates, a third arriving that year. Most of them were the more troublesome "full grown young men."[4]

The blush was soon off the bloom for Sheets. In September 1893, at just the time the system was to be really up and running, obviously frustrated, he ruminated that: "I regret that I cannot leave behind greater evidence of the work and labor performed during my stay here," He went on to lament that "Coming here at considerable sacrifice, on my part, impelled by a sincere desire to be instrumental in founding this institution, I have labored under great discouragements and disadvantages." Alluding to the parsimonious nature of the state legislature, Sheets wrote, "The problem seemed to be not what is best for the institution or its inmates but how little we can get along with."[5]

MCCLAUGHRY AT PONTIAC

Sheet's departure cleared the way for Robert McClaughry's arrival in 1893. Local papers expressed their pleasure: "The Major is a man of advanced ideas on the subject of the reformation of juvenile offenders and also well versed in the system of government to be used under this new law for the reformation of criminals."[6] He was an immediate hit with the small, central Illinois town ninety miles south of Chicago and with a population of seven thousand. The McClaughrys were glad to be back in small town America. A speech given to the local Free Kindergarten Association gained him praise for a "cultured and entertaining lecture."[7] His family quickly got involved in the local culture, his daughter becoming a mainstay in local choral concerts.[8]

But danger followed even to the sleepy hamlet in central Illinois. Apparently a "murderous crank" was out to get McClaughry. Dr. Peter Langdon came to America from Dublin, Ireland, in the early 1870s. After a stay in Tennessee, he moved to Metropolis, Illinois, got in trouble over larceny, and landed in Joliet prison for three years. Not long into his stay there, his behavior was such that he was deemed insane and shipped off to an asylum from which he escaped. In the 1880s he was arrested again for larceny and sent to Joliet where he blamed McClaughry for all of his problems. In 1893 he turned up in Pontiac armed and acting strangely. He went to the McClaughry residence but was told that the Major was out of town. Conspicuously hanging around town, he was heard to say that he planned to harm the warden. Concerned citizens shunned him, and suggested to him that McClaughry actually lived in Monmouth, Illinois. Langdon went to Monmouth where he was arrested by the sheriff who had been alerted by McClaughry's family. Coming shortly after a deranged man had murdered the Mayor of Chicago, Carter Harrison, this incident resonated with the McClaughry family. McClaughry's was a most ominous entry into the administration of the reformatory.[9]

From the outset, McClaughry saw that "the difficulties to be overcome in making the Reformatory successful [were] many and varied:" the absence of a wall around the place remained a threat to security; the lack of shops and suitable employment for the inmates was demoralizing; the rapidly increasing number of inmates was taxing the facility; and the water supply remained inadequate.[10] But one issue facing McClaughry had to do with religion and it took on political overtones.

The office of chaplain was a critical part of nineteenth-century penology. One of McClaughry's early complaints before he assumed office was that the Board wanted to control the appointment of the chaplaincy. Apparently, the Board had wanted the office to be held only for one year and then rotate among the various protestant denominations. McClaughry saw that this office could very early be a political plum for the Board. He argued for, and got, a more permanent position. But this left a larger question to be resolved. What of Catholicism? Most rural Illinois had considerable prejudice against Catholics. But McClaughry, perhaps prodded by the governor, saw the need for having a priest at the reformatory:

> I am not a Catholic but a *true* Presbyterian, yet I have many friends among the Catholics because I have always treated them fairly. Their influence, in an institution like this, where they are so largely represented is powerful in favor of discipline and obedience if it can be secured.[11] [emphasis added by McClaughry]

In keeping with the political tone of penology at that time he advised the governor to make sure that even a Catholic on the Board be able to work with existing members Felton and John Ela. "A fool Republican (and there are plenty of them) could make lots of trouble," he warned.[12]

Besides blatant politics, there was a certain naiveté connected to the start up of the Illinois reformatory. Actually, when McClaughry took over in 1893 Illinois was to not follow any reformatory model exclusively. "The law establishing the Reformatory was new and unfamiliar to the courts throughout the State," he maintained. "No precedent existed in Illinois for the methods which it proposed. Through the influence of counsel, or friends of offenders, the courts, in many instances, were imposed upon, by being induced to send to the Reformatory incorrigibles, vagrants, feeble-minded, disturbers of the peace, with occasionally an ex-convict."[13] Ideally all inmates were to be age ten to twenty-one and be first offenders, but this did not end up being the case.

Instead, inmates were typically placed into two age groups. Those from ten to fifteen years of age, thought to be young and more impressionably affected by good and bad forces in the institution, were to live in a family/cottage situation. Stronger emphasis on academic instruction characterized this group, with six hours per day of schooling required in the winter and three hours per day in the summer. Also important were chapel attendance, recreation, and play. Labor was very much a secondary concern, and was typically light and generally on the farm.

Those from fifteen to twenty-one years of age were to be treated more sternly and live in a congregate style, more like at Elmira. Academics were de-emphasized with only two hours set aside for schooling per day. In fact, if an inmate had already completed the eighth grade, he was exempted from all academics. Instead, the focus was on labor, with eight hours of work assigned in the various shops such as shoe, broom, and brick making and chair caning. In addition, the young people typically dressed in military uniforms and practiced marching and drills each day.

Much of McClaughry's short term at Pontiac was a replay of his style at Pennsylvania. All incoming inmates were interviewed by the Major, who took their life histories, and recorded their place and date of birth, parentage, personal habits, level of education, mental capacity, immediate personality problems, and peer group associates. Then the physician evaluated their general health and noted any possible hereditary problems. A chaplain then assessed their religious history. All newcomers were informed that release dates were based upon individual behavior. An institutional mark system, similar to that used by Brockway in Elmira and by McClaughry in Huntingdon, rewarded conformity and punished misbehavior.

One case reveals the shrewd, if not cynical, views of the superintendent. William Johnson wanted clemency. He came into the reformatory on January 20th, 1893, for committing larceny. His record in Pontiac was not good. Eight reports for misconduct amounted to the loss of fifteen days of "good time." Currently, he was undergoing punishment for sawing the bars on his cell door in hopes of escaping. "To all my inquires as to what he would be willing to do if released, he returns the stereotyped reply of the thief, that he will do the best he can. The boy seems to have no moral sense whatever."[14] He was denied any parole hearing.

Release decisions were made by the Board of Managers but McClaughry's opinion could not help but be important. All those in the first division who had obtained a string of nine scores and had at least a fifth grade education were eligible. Older inmates had to have a job waiting for them with the expectation of at least six months of employment. If released the parolee was given a new suit of clothes, ten dollars, and transportation to their final destination. As a parolee, there were rules to be followed: to refrain from crime, to lead a good and industrious life, to abstain from alcohol, on the first day of the month to report their economic doings (showing how much they had earned and spent over the month) to the Superintendent of Pontiac, and not to leave their job or change jobs without permission of the Board of Managers.

Sometimes parents went over the head of the superintendent and the Board to plead directly to the governor. In such cases McClaughry gave his opinion and considerable case history of individuals to sway the governor. For example, the mother of Frank Hamilton pressured Governor Altgeld for his early release. Drawing upon institutional records McClaughry stepped in to recount the inmate's history. Hamilton had been in reform school from March 1889 to February 1890. He had gotten out one month late due to bad behavior. By 1894 he was back in the reformatory for burglary and larceny. Most recently he had lost "marks" for "falsehood, destroying clothing and general crookedness." With rare exception his history in Pontiac was filled with bad marks. McClaughry was against any early release.

> I think the inmate needs to earn his parole, because he needs the training and discipline necessary to do so; second, because the effect upon other inmates of releasing him before he has earned his release under the rules, will be very bad. He is known throughout the institution, and an exception made in his case, must have very good reason behind it, or it will result in injury to the discipline.[15]

Hamilton was like many of the inmates coming to Pontiac. There was a dramatic increase in the number of inmates. At the end of 1892 Pontiac had 341 inmates. That number more than doubled by 1894 to 762. Two years later it was at 1,127. Third, the reformatory staff could not effectively separate the juveniles from the young adults. Initially Sheets, then McClaughry, argued for an abandonment of the combination method used at Pontiac. Rather than keeping all boys in the same institution there should be two separate places of confinement, they reasoned. Such pleas fell on deaf ears in the state capital. Fourth, security problems remained, especially with the sixteen to twenty-one age group who often were multiple offenders. The security "wall" was really just a board fence easily compromised. From 1891 to 1895, sixty-three escapes occurred. Finally, some problems with the rehabilitative program itself existed. For example, the workshops could not sustain themselves. The backbone of the work system, the shoe shop, soon was losing money and idleness became chronic. Furthermore, the parole system, a darling of the reformatory advocates, was arbitrary and capricious.

In spite of these problems, McClaughry was able to make some positive contributions. By the end of 1896, shortly before he left, several buildings were finished. The principle edifice was the administration building, an eighty by one-hundred-foot, three-storied structure of red brick with white stone trim. There was a large annex for a bakery, cold storage, and kitchen work. But making room for inmates fell behind the numbers coming to the reformatory. At this time there were 480 cells for 1500 inmates so there would be two, and sometimes three, persons to a cell. The water plant was completed as well. An 18-foot deep reservoir had been cut with a capacity of 5 million gallons of water. The extracted soil was used to smooth out the bumpy prison grounds. Now several industries had been set up with the purpose to provide work and skill development that could be used upon release. By 1894 a trade's school and one wing of the projected cell blocks were built.[16] Stone cutting and polishing was added to the granite shop. Carpentry, masonry, printing, and black smithing were new options, and in addition inmates could work in the kitchen, laundry, or on the farm. Finally, a weekly newspaper, *The Pioneer*, was published by the inmates in which current, but censured, news and literary contributions by the inmates appeared.[17]

Politics continued to be a problem for McClaughry, sometimes with confusing and comical results. For example, less than a year after McClaughry took over as superintendent of Pontiac, the local Democratic County Central Committee became angry with the Democratic governor for appointing a Republican. In a blatant statement reflecting nineteenth-century state politics they

> Resolved, That the Democratic County Central Committee of Livingston County, now in session, condemn the action of said Board of Managers in not placing at the head of the said institution as Superintendent, a Democrat, and that this Committee is opposed to the sentiment that prevails with said Board of Managers.
>
> Resolved, That we are satisfied that Democrats possessing all the requirements and qualifications to fill the position in said institution, can easily be found, and that such men should by all means have charge of said institution during a Democratic State administration.[18]

This proclamation, adopted by the entire Democratic Congressional Committee of the district, compelled McClaughry to respond in a lengthy letter to the governor to each of the politically motivated charges.[19]

Such rural politics would not go away. In December, 1895, a state legislator, M. Clary of Odde, complained it was "impossible for a democrat to get any kind of a position, even as a guard, at the State Reformatory, under the present Superintendent." And that "the Republican leaders in this section have been getting for their heelers and henchmen good places, and are making sport of our unsuccessful efforts." McClaughry denied all of Odde's claims and suggested that his anger was due to his nephew failing to get a job at the Reformatory.[20]

In the meantime, the 1896 election was looming larger and would affect McClaughry, taking him out of Pontiac and back to Joliet. They would also end the political career of Altgeld.

NOTES

1. Robert McClaughry to John P. Altgeld, January 11, 1893, Governor John Peter Algeld Papers January, 1893 folder, Illinois State Archives. Hereafter referred to as Altgeld Papers.

2. Robert McClaughry to John Peter Altgeld, February 18, 1893. Altgeld Papers, February, 1893 folder Illinois State Archives.

3. Robert McClaughry to John P. Altgeld, March 8, 1893, Altgeld Papers. March, 1893 folder. Illinois State Archives.

4. *Pontiac Sentinel,* July 7, 1893.

5. "Report of the General Superintendent, August 31, 1893. Illinois Reports to the General Assembly, 1893.

6. *Pontiac Sentinel*, August 18, 1893.

7. *Ibid.*, October 27, 1893.

8. *Ibid.*, July 5, 1895 for example.

9. *Chicago Tribune*, November 13, 1893.

10. Robert McClaughry to John P. Altgeld, August 11, 1893, Altgeld papers Misc. folder. Illinois State Archives.

11. Robert McClaughry to John P. Altgeld, September 2, 1893, Altgeld Papers September, 1893 folder, Illinois State Archives.

12. Robert McClaughry to John P. Altgeld September 11, 1893. Altgeld Papers, September 1893 folder, Illinois State Archives.

13. Report of General Superintendent, October 1, 1894 in Illinois Reports to General Assembly, p. 25.

14. Robert McClaughry to John P. Altgeld December 20, 1893. Altgeld Papers, December, 1893 folder Illinois State Archives.

15. Robert McClaughry to John P. Altgeld May 7, 1895. Altgeld Papers May 1895 folder Illinois State Archives.

16. *Pontiac Sentinel,* January 5, 1894.

17. *Ibid.*, November 27, 1896.

18. Proclamation of Democratic County Central Committee, March 8, 1894 in Altgeld Papers, March, 1894 folder. Illinois State Archives.

19. Robert McClaughry to John P. Altgeld, May 7, 1894. Altgeld Papers, May, 1894 folder. Illinois State Archives. All emphases were in the original.

20. Robert McClaughry to John P. Altgeld January 7, 1896. Altgeld Papers, January 1896 folder. Illinois State Archives.

Chapter Twenty-Six

State Politics and Prisons

"Politicians are constantly exerting their pulls . . . "

JOLIET, AGAIN; POLITICS, AGAIN

Political battles began heating up as the elections of 1896 neared. A side skirmish of those battles would take McClaughry out of Pontiac and back to Joliet. Much dissatisfaction with Altgeld existed in Illinois. Although a commanding figure in the Democratic Party nationwide, he had not taken care of his back yard, and Illinois had fallen on hard times under Altgeld. The World's Fair had closed throwing many out of work and muffling the boosterism common for the first three years of the 1890s. Carter Harrison Sr., the Democratic political boss of Chicago and main supporter of Altgeld, had been assassinated. A general economic downturn nationwide did not help. Election results in small Illinois mining, railroad, and factory towns (a base of strength for Altgeld) were indicative. In 1892, 52 percent of their population went democratic. Four years later only 48 percent did so. Voters were enraged as well and went to the polls to express their frustrations. For example, in 1892, 874,000 people voted in Illinois. In 1896, 1,091,000 did so.[1]

Perhaps the most critical issue in the politics leading up to the very partisan election for governor had to do with prison labor. Prison industries had been a critical part of prisons going back to the earliest days. Various labor groups, most notably the Knights of Labor and the American Federation of Labor, were gathering popular and political support. The Anti-Convict-Contract Association was formed in Chicago in 1886, its founder, George Schilling, once a staunch pro-Altgeld man, working to end prison industries. Various states began passing laws forbidding convict-made products on the open free market. The high water mark for such legislation came in 1889.[2] When existing contracts ran out in 1890 many prisoners were left idle. The Penitentiary Commissioners entered contracts with businesses that set up a piece-price system which was little different from the old contract operations and open to attack by Altgeld during his race for governor.[3]

Organized labor did not want prisoners to be idle nor to stop profits from being made. Rather, their overriding concern was that prisoner-made goods had an unfair advantage in the open market. It was morally unjust to threaten the livelihood of honest citizens by the labor of those who had violated the laws of the state, pro-labor people felt. Labor advocates, disliking the inhumane treatment of prisoners by private employers and contractors, had a political agenda addressing the convict labor issue. Organized labor wanted to restrict the kinds of occupations introduced into the prison industry, limit the number of prisoners employed on marketable goods, and put in place restrictions on the number of hours prisoners worked in the industries. This would level the playing field for those workers outside the walls. This put reform-minded bureaucrats like McClaughry in a bind. On one hand they could agree with the pro-labor forces. On the other such policy complicated the managing of increasingly idle prisoners. It complicated the politics of the governor as well.

The more partisan Republicans of Illinois thought Altgeld's previous election success had hung on the issue of convict labor; now that same issue, they thought, could be turned against him. Although Illinois ended the concept of contract labor in 1886 it still existed in various ways. By 1896 numerous industries were still going on at Joliet. The cooper, stone, cigar, broom, knitting, harness, saddle, chair and cane seating were industries flourishing under the control of the state. Nine hundred and forty six inmates were employed in these state run industries. Nearly three hundred convicts worked for the shoe and granite contractors. On the one hand, the purpose of the new law was to assure that the state got a fair share of the profits from its captive labor force, the prisoners. Why should a businessman get all the benefit? And indeed, some prison products were advertised and sold on the open market. Republican politicos, hungry to be back in the governor's mansion, claimed this to be hypocrisy. Under the banner of "Convict-Made Merchandise," saddles were sold at $11.75. The *Joliet News* and the *Joliet Sentinel*, both democratic newspapers, advertised and collected money for the sales but, it was claimed, this was a sleight of hand by the governor.[4] Of course that was not really the issue. Under the old system prison goods went to the open market and profited the business classes.

Under the new system those same goods were sold on the open market but the profits went to the state. Any restriction of those goods to just "state use" remained on the horizon. The battle raged on with lines drawn by party and ideology. Basically, the Republicans, catering to the business classes, favored the contract system. They resented state control of prison labor and disparagingly called Joliet "Altgeld's Manufacturing Establishment."[5] Under the old system, they thought, workers were driven. Now, under governor controlled state-managed systems there was no incentive to work and the quality of the work that was done declined.[6]

Altgeld, a pro labor man, and his warden R.L. Allen, defended the current system. In an interview with the Chicago *Times-Herald,* the warden claimed that the "Joliet Penitentiary [was] self-supporting under [the] new plan." Allen declared the old system to be "barbaric." In the old days, he insisted, "the contractors were the real prison authorities. They work the men, not as if they were wards of the state, but as if they were owned by the contractors," he felt. The prison officials were neither more nor less than human thumb screws, paid by the state, to assist the contractors in squeezing the last bit of work out of the unfortunate convicts," claimed the warden.[7]

There were other prison related issues that became politicized as the election neared. One had to do with Altgeld's use of the power to pardon prisoners. The *Chicago Tribune* constantly accused Altgeld of excessive use of the pardon.[8] Of course, the elephant in the living room was the pardoning of the Haymarket anarchists. Many were outraged over these releases. Others got out early as well further infuriating many. Two prisoners awaiting sentencing in Danville, Illinois, were lynched and leaders of the mob defended their actions saying that the governor would have pardoned the crooks too soon.[9] Any objective examination of statistics would have shown that Altgeld pardoned fewer prisoners than previous governors, but the perception, enabled by the Haymarket releases, was used to discredit the administration.[10] He used the pardon issue to advocate for parole. "We frequently receive from three to five applications for pardon a day," Altgeld complained, "and the work this entails is so great that it cannot be properly attended to by one man."[11]

On a couple of occasions his pardons threatened his reform agenda and allies. Two Democratic politicians, McNulty and Chapman, were prosecuted by the Chicago Civic Federation for election fraud. The Federation was the main reform agent in the "good government" movement. McNulty protested his innocence but struck a deal so that he would only be fined. Instead, the judge sentenced him to Joliet and then denied him a new trial. Chapman was being persecuted by a well financed group of lawyers and private detectives, the governor felt. Altgeld simply used his pardon power to redress some miscarriages of justice.[12] In 1899 after his ouster from office, he wrote in his *Live Questions*, that "it is not the common people who destroy the institutions of government. It is the class that clothe robbery with respectability, bribery with pretense, and corruption with patriotism."[13]

Another innovation by Altgeld, with the total agreement and support of McClaughry still sitting at Pontiac, was legislation proposed for an indeterminate sentencing structure. Of course, this had been a key provision of the reformatory movement for nearly fifteen years. Instead of a fixed sentence, as had been so common in adult prisons for two generations, Altgeld wanted the courts to refrain from imposing an exact duration of the prisoner's incarceration. Criminal acts would have a spread, from a minimum to a maximum number of years, and inmate behavior while in prison would determine release. The Penitentiary Commissioners, along with the warden, would hold hearings and determine release. When placed on parole, the prisoner would be given suitable clothing, transportation to his place of employment, and ten dollars in cash. Violation of conditions of parole would lead to a return to prison. Such a system was already used at the Reformatory but now it was extended to Joliet. During the first year of operation 146 inmates were released. As vindication of Altgeld's position, only fifteen of the 146 parolees violated their parole and became fugitives.[14] Such reforms, as progressive as they might be, could not compensate for Altgeld's sinking popularity and the election was a disaster for the democrats.

"Clean Sweep in Will County," declared the very partisan *Joliet Daily Republican*. The entire Republican ticket won in the county and most of the state.[15] John Tanner, the new governor, was born near Booneville, Indiana, in 1844. Shortly thereafter, the family moved to southern Illinois where Tanner grew up on a farm near Carbondale. A grandfather had served in the Revolutionary war and his father died in a Confederate prison camp. He enlisted in 1863 and was with General Sherman's army from Kentucky to Georgia. After the war he farmed, was elected sheriff and Circuit Court Clerk, and eventually became state senator. After this he was U.S. Marshal for southern Illinois. With the help of three former governors–Oglesby, Beveridge, and Fifer–and thanks to the growing animosity towards Altgeld, he won the election of 1896 handily.

Much to his disappointment, McClaughry was immediately replaced at Pontiac by a former state senator, George Torrence. McClaughry did not want to go. For that matter, Torrence did not want the position. But the governor was a close friend and Torrence relented and took over the reformatory in March 1897. In the meantime, the new governor reappointed McClaughry as a warden of Joliet. After working diligently at the reformatory, the place he felt was the situation with the most potential to reform people, McClaughry was once again cast amidst the most hardened offenders at the Illinois State Penitentiary.[16]

In many ways this was not the Joliet prison McClaughry had known ten years earlier. On one hand, thanks to Altgeld and Warden Allen, some of the reformatory ideals had come to Joliet. The indeterminate sentence, new parole procedures, the disappearance of the stripes, and a new women's facility suggest some progressive changes.[17] But numerous problems awaited, some political, some procedural, some personal.

Many inmates from Pontiac followed McClaughry to Joliet, and this emphasized the weaknesses of the nurturing argument. Seventeen to twenty incorrigibles were transferred from the reformatory to the prison, and local newspapers noted:

> They are dare devil rascals and laugh and jeer at the picture of the prison or anything else. Their bravado and utter indifference to the penalties of the law are remarkable. To them prison holds no terror or fears. They are depraved and illiterate, but when Warden McClaughry gets through with them they will probably change their minds a little.[18]

Most of the prisoners at Joliet were in their twenties and were jailed for dangerous but not sensational crimes. However, a few were known throughout the country and were penal celebrities. One such was Adolph Luetgert who had arrived early in McClaughry's second stint at Joliet. Throughout 1897 and 1898, Luetgert achieved considerable notoriety in America. Owner of a sausage factory on the North side of Chicago, he was accused and convicted of murdering his wife. Her body was never found. Luetgert said she had run away in a crazy fit. The jury did not agree and in a sensational trial that was followed throughout the country he was convicted and sentenced to life at the penitentiary. McClaughry was there to greet him but was already gone when Luetgert's health deteriorated and he died in May 1898.[19]

Other politically charged problems confronted McClaughry. The issue of parole would not die. Such conditional release had created new jobs and power centers in criminal justice. A Parole Board, picked by the governor, held hearings with eligible inmates who made their case for early release. The warden would have considerable influence. He sat on the Board, but before that, unless a hearing was mandated because of the time already spent in prison, he determined whether or not the inmate would even appear. This was a logical outcome in an era distressed over the widespread corruption of judges. As a result, specific conditions were affixed to release on parole. Freed inmates needed to work, have a place to live, and adhere to suitable life styles as defined by middle-class bureaucrats. Then parole officers watched over the released prisoner and had the power to revoke parole and send them back to prison. On the surface, inmates felt parole to be a boon, but it was not. Control over their lives was increased not diminished. As we shall see, the true winners were those people working in the prisons of America.[20]

The parole law in Illinois had gone into effect on July 1, 1896. Although it was an important part of McClaughry's reformatory agenda, it would always be associated with Altgeld. In fact, nationwide it was connected to President Grover Cleveland and the Democratic Party. Most Republicans hated it and lay in wait to make it a political issue. Although a creature of state politics–ever aware that the slightest misstep could lead to his dismissal–McClaughry tried to transcend partisan politics in the name of creating a new criminal justice profession within penology and implementing the ideals of the reformatory movement into adult prisons.

Almost immediately after the passage of the parole bill, 238 prisoners were released. Called Altgeld's "pardoning machine," most were let out in the last few weeks of his administration. Kate Ford, a notorious accessory to murder in Ottawa, Illinois, was one of the most controversial.[21] The Chicago police officials blamed the rise in crime on the recently paroled convicts.[22] McClaughry, ever the defender of the concept, felt parole was good. If there was anything wrong, he felt, it was the politics connected to it.

> Politicians are constantly exerting their pulls with the parole board and with me to secure the parole of men that ought not to be released. But their efforts always fail. The worst recommendation a prisoner up for parole can have in my eyes is the unusual interest taken in him by a certain class of politicians.[23]

Of course, McClaughry had to live with decisions made by Altgeld. One such decision involved Harry Schwartz who had murdered a U.S. Express messenger, Kellogg Nicholas, in 1886. He was sent to Joliet for life but Altgeld commuted the sentence to twenty years. McClaughry was faced with Schwartz's early release in 1898. Although he tried to prevent it, he was outvoted by the parole board. So while parole brought power to the warden, still McClaughry was bound and confounded by the system that let Schwartz get out and go on to became a poster boy for those against such early release.[24] One noted female criminal, Carrie Meyers, added fuel to the fire. She was known for running a school that taught children pick pocketing, shoplifting, and till tapping. Breaking the conditions of parole brought her back to Joliet and gave more ammunition to those questioning the idea of early release.[25] In fact, each subsequent generation brought more questions and opposition to the notion of parole.[26]

McClaughry understood the problem of prisoner release. How does one learn to live in ordinary society after spending several years in an extraordinary one like a prison? Recognizing this, McClaughry was an early and persistent advocate of a home for ex-inmates, a kind of half way house.[27] But in this regard, McClaughry was far in advance of nineteenth century reformers.

For many reasons McClaughry's stay at Joliet was short. First, and more persistently bothersome, was politics. Pressures to staff his institution with political hacks continued. On the one hand, McClaughry was a beneficiary of politics. His entire career had been shaped by political appointments. On the other hand, he was trying to create a profession. Speaking to a convention of superintendents of public institutions in Illinois he caught this stance, one foot in politics and the other in professionalism. "I believe in politics," he began.

> I am no Mugwump, but I believe that our political parties will be all the better and our institutions all the safer, when those who have to do with the defective, dependent and helpless classes, which are coming to constitute so large a portion of our population, shall be thoroughly trained for their business.[28]

Other reasons for his early departure had to do with health. McClaughry, and much of his family, had always suffered from poor health going back to the Civil War. Sometimes, of course, they were merely a face-saving device to cover early forced departures due to politics. Other times they were genuinely ill—which is no wonder, given living and working in close proximity to large groups of men who place a low priority on hygiene and health. In the spring of 1899, the state legislature proclaimed Joliet prison to be a "Death Trap" and pondered its removal to another location. Drainage problems and industrial smoke made it an unhealthy environment, it was declared. At first, McClaughry defended the institution, not least because the prison was key to the town's economy. But then he went on to say:

> If I were a citizen of Joliet, I don't think I would object to the removal of the prison. All the trade and population that it brings to Joliet is more than offset by the injury that a prison naturally does to the good name of a town. If a man wishes to leave the farm and go to a town to educate his children he is not apt to go to a prison town.[29]

Of course, most citizens and politicians felt tied to the penitentiary, and so, very quickly, McClaughry proclaimed himself neutral on the subject.[30] But the issue would not disappear. Next month, it was revealed that more people died of tuberculosis in Joliet than in any other state prison. The death rate for that disease was 16.3 per 1000. The next highest in the country was at Sing Sing at 8 per 1000. Rather than hold the prison responsible–with its overcrowding and confined living space–prison officials blamed the incoming inmates who they said brought the disease with them into the institution.[31] Apparently, all of this talk of health hazards spooked McClaughry. Claiming that living and working at the prison—with exposure to prisoners and smoke and gases—undermined his health, McClaughry resigned after a little over a year at Joliet. Family physicians recommended a change of environment, he claimed. In keeping with the politics of prisons, ex-Congressman E.J. Murphy was named in his place. In the meantime, the McClaughry family looked westward to Leavenworth, Kansas.[32]

Although McClaughry remained an important figure in the reformatory movement his experiences at Joliet proved the problems of adult rehabilitation. To reach young first offenders and rehabilitate them held some promise. First at Huntingdon then at Pontiac, his experiences pointed both to the promise and pitfalls of this new penology. Committed to the reformatory ideology, he continued to act as a bridge for those ideas to the world of adult offenders. Joliet proved just how difficult it was to reform those not eager to reform. Pontiac and Joliet were only thirty miles apart, but in terms of penal experiences they were worlds apart. The nurture/nature paradigms, dramatically displayed at the Pontiac reformatory and the Joliet prison, would not dismay him. More than most he continued to struggle with the difficulty of merging a reform ideal into the world of real punishment.

But other forces were at work as well. State politics—with friendly governors and mayors finding places for him to work his idealistic notions, and unfriendly ones giving him the boot—were critical to McClaughry's career. For this man, who appeared almost angelic in appearance and attitude, such a seamy career environment seemed like a big mistake in central casting. In spite of his attempts at professionalism McClaughry remained a captive of politics. Shortly after he left Pontiac and Joliet he was to be able to transfer his idealistic notions and practical skills to a new level, that of the newly developing federal corrections system. He will be confounded by politics there too. But in the meantime—overlapping his stay in Chicago, Pontiac, and Joliet—he was taking his ideas to another level.

Politics would play out there too, only this time it would be the politics of professionalism.

NOTES

1. Richard Jensen, *The Winning of the Midwest: Social and Political Conflict, 1888-1896* (Chicago: University of Chicago Press, 1971), pp. 43, 257.

2. See E.T. Hiller, "Development of the Systems of Control of Convict Labor in the United States," *Journal of the American Institute of Criminal Law and Criminology* 5 (1914), pp. 241-69; and "Labor Unionism and Convict Labor," *Ibid.*, 5 (1915), pp. 851-79.

3. Harvey Wish, The Administration of Governor John Peter Altgeld of Illinois, 1892-1897 (Unpublished doctoral dissertation at Northwestern University, 1936), p. 310.

4. *Joliet Daily Republican* October 29, 1896.

5. *Ibid.*, October 28, 1896.

6. *Ibid.*, October 27, 1896.

7. *Ibid.* And *Chicago Times Herald* December 9, 1895.

8. *Chicago Tribune*, October 27, 1894 and July 1, 2, 3, 1893.

9. *Ibid.*, May 30, 1895. For an analysis of lynching as a response to the perceived weaknesses of the criminal justice system see Michael J. Peifer's *Rough Justice: Lynching and American Society, 1874-1947* (Urbana and Chicago: University of Illinois Press, 2004).

10. Harvey Wish, pp. 135-36.

11. Quoted in *Ibid.*, pp. 136-37.

12. *Ibid.*, p. 138.

13. Quoted in *Ibid.*, p. 139.

14. Ibid., pp. 313-14.

15. *Joliet Daily Republican,* November 4, 1896.

16. *Pontiac Sentinel,* February 19 and March 5, 1897.

17. *Joliet Weekly Republican,* (not to be mixed up with the totally different *Daily Republican)* May 29th, 1896.

18. *Ibid.*, January 7, 1897.

19. Robert Loerzel, *Alchemy of Bones: Chicago's Luetgert Murder Case of 1897* (Urbana and Chicago: University of Illinois Press, 2003), pp. 258-60.

20. David J. Rothman, *Conscience and Convenience: The Asylum and its Alternatives in Progressive America* (New York: Aldine de Gruyter, 1980, 2002), pp. 159-201.

21. *Joliet Daily Republican,* December 11, 1896.

22. *Joliet Weekly Republican,* January 21, 1898.

23. *Ibid.*

24. *Ibid.*, September 3, 1898.

25. *Ibid.*, January 18, 1899.
26. Rothman, pp. 159-201.
27. *Joliet Weekly Republican,* November 9, 1898.
28. *Ibid.*, February 4, 1898.
29. *Ibid.*, April 14, 1899.
30. *Ibid.*
31. *Ibid.*, May 26, 1899.
32. *Ibid.*, June 16, 30, 1899.

Warden Robert McClaughry.

Rock Quarry.

Bathtubs.

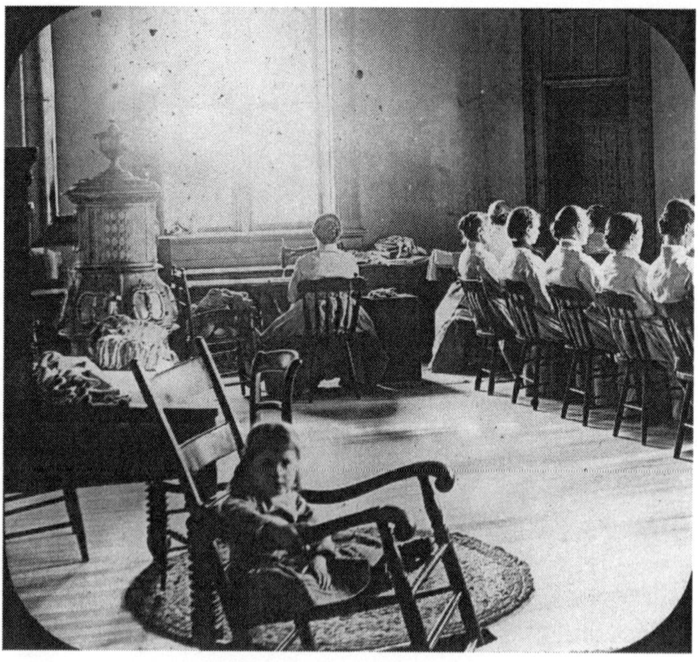

Women prisoners sewing.

Hauling.

Women's ward.

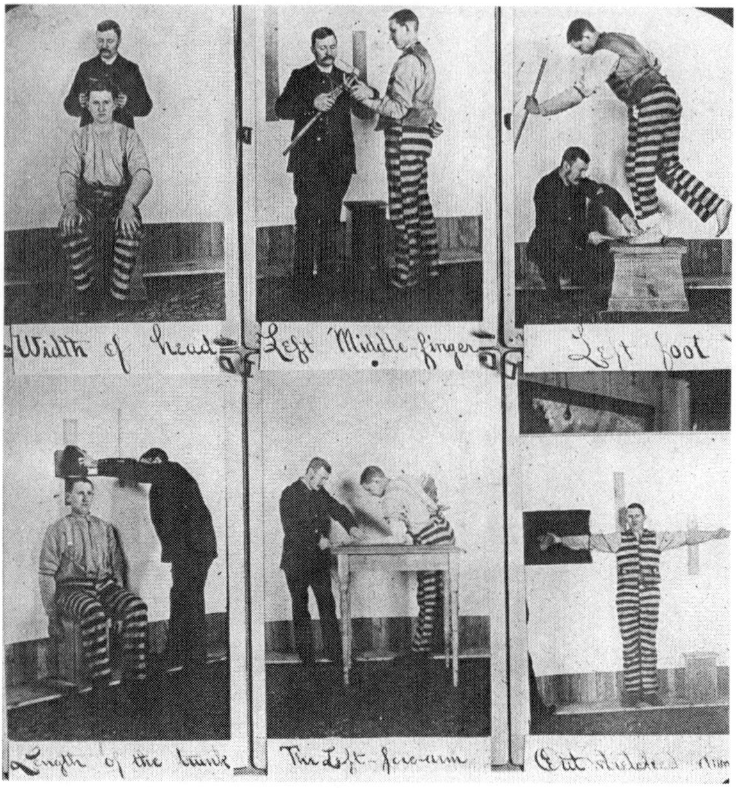

Bertillon system of measurement.

The Lock step.

Solitary.

Church service.

"Up the Hill" prisoner burial grounds.

Mug shots.

Part Six

GROWING A PRISON PROFESSION

Chapter Twenty-Seven

Rise of Professionalism in Penology

"The Citizens at large know little about prisoners."

PROFESSIONALISM

Some occupations–such as those of a doctor and a lawyer–were attempting to achieve professional status in the last third of the nineteenth century. Many others laid claim to that designation but only a few trudged through the professionalization process. At any time, those wanting to have their occupation recognized as a profession need to monopolize skills and knowledge not readily available to the public, and to have a socially worthy mission to benefit the wider community. While maintaining their occupational credibility as practitioners, such leaders need to step forth to take on new roles in shaping societal views of their particular occupation.[1] In the late nineteenth century, prison keepers were way ahead of most other criminal justice personnel in this process. Many in charge of the prisons and asylums of America wanted to be separated out from those political hacks who had predominated for a generation,[2] and who had given the field a reputation for being "afflicted with crankery."[3]

Important to such a professionalization process is the political and sales task of convincing both the general public and politicians of the uniqueness of the occupation and the acquired wisdom of its practitioners. Curiously, another group that often needs convincing is active workers in the occupation. This might be particularly difficult for penologists in America where politics continued to so strongly affect their work and how it was perceived. Furthermore, because federalism prevailed over centralization and wardens were literally all over the map, communication and regional rivalries became unusually important. The appropriate and perhaps necessary battleground would be an organization or association of like-minded people among whom issues could be discussed and relationships established.

Throughout his years as a warden, reformatory superintendent, and chief of police, Robert McClaughry significantly influenced the professionalization of penology. As an active member of the National Prison Association and later the National Association of Chiefs of Police, politics played out in many ways but consistently McClaughry acted as a bridge between differing mindsets. This is especially true in the National Prison Association. The National Prison Association started in 1870 after the so-called Declaration of Principles set forth in Cincinnati in which several reformers dissatisfied with existing penal institutions and philosophies came up with a blueprint for reform. After some promising starts in the 1820s and 1830s, the penitentiaries and prisons of America had fallen on hard times and reformers wanted to change the penal system. One of those reformers was Enoch Cobb Wines.[4]

Born and raised on a New England farm, Wines studied at Middlebury College. After graduation he taught at a variety of boys schools before taking on ministerial duties at a Congregational Church in Vermont and a Presbyterian one on Long Island. There was a short stint as a lecturer at Washington College in Pennsylvania and an editorship of the Monthly Advocate of Education. He took on several social causes and essentially became a pulpit reformer. Shortly before the Civil War, he was teaching in St Louis but the conflict closed that school down. He then obtained a job as the secretary of the New York Prison Association in 1862, and there came into contact with reformers and philanthropists like Francis Lieber, John Griscom, Abraham Beal and Theodore Dwight.

Wines understood that any successful reformation of prisoners needed the help of the wardens. So it was that with the wardens' permission and along with Theodore Dwight he undertook an extensive tour of prisons in the late 1860s resulting in a 570-page *Report on the Prisons and Reformatories of the United States and Canada*. Such a scholarly achievement was monumental in and of itself: after a forty-five-year history the "American invention" of the penitentiary was being evaluated. Wines met and admired several individual wardens but on the whole felt that prisons by the end of the 1860s had failed; they simply did not try to reform the prisoner. Indeed, prison officials' "skepticism as to the possibilities of reformation indisposed them to exert themselves to bring it about," reminisced his son some twenty years later.[5] Politicians and prison managers were more interested in prison profits than prisoner reform and thus societal safekeeping. As his son would say later, "He regarded the subordination of this end in prison discipline to the financial aspect of prison management [to be] itself a crime."[6]

While he was secretary of the New York Prison Association, Wines wanted to establish an international conference. To do so—he was told by European penologists—he had to create a national prison association in America. To this end, at a Cincinnati meeting of like-minded reformers, the National Prison Association, known today as the American Correctional Association, was formed. The Governor of Ohio, Rutherford Hayes, presided over this meeting starting a career with the NPA that would last the rest of his life. When Wines died in 1879 the organization died as well for a few years until 1883 when it was revived, largely through the work of Hayes, Sanbourn, Brockway, and Rounds. Hayes brought considerable political capital to the professionalization of penology in these formative days. Throughout the late nineteenth century he helped to reestablish the defunct organization and mollify the tensions between the various political groupings. He was a reformer too but unlike most "churchy" ones he was a politician—and a former president of the United States.

"Rud" Hayes had grown up in Ohio. Eventually he went to law school at Harvard but returned to Ohio to establish a career in law. During the Civil War he served with distinction and received numerous promotions mustering out as a major general. Like so many veterans of the war, a critical reference point for the rest of his life would be the battles and comrades he encountered during the conflict. In addition, numerous combat wounds plagued him for most of his life. After Appomattox, Hayes served twice as a Congressman from Ohio and three terms as governor. During one of his terms as governor, in 1870, he hosted the first meeting the National Prison Association. Elevated to the presidency of the United States in 1876 he went down in history as a single term president [by his choice] who won with fewer votes than his opponent. Unfortunately for him, Hayes' election would always seem a shady backroom affair with critics referring to him as "His Fraudulency." This is unfair, though his presidency was fairly undistinguished. Most of his effort went toward civil service reform but it would take the assassination of his successor and dear friend, James Garfield, to make any headway there. In a historical irony another of his dear friends and protégées, William McKinley, will be shot down as president as well. One notable presidential accomplishment, in regards to criminal justice, was Hayes' signing an order allowing women to argue before the Supreme Court.

After his presidency Hayes busied himself with social issues. For example, he helped establish and develop Ohio State University. Much of his later life would be devoted to making it a nationally important university. Particularly interested in the plight of southern freed slaves he worked tirelessly to bring the freedman more educational opportunities. He served on the boards of both the Slater and Peabody Funds to upgrade educational opportunities for African-Americans.

His concerns about criminality and criminal justice grew as well. This was a vitally important issue because at the time there were, according to Franklin Osborn, 45,000 convicts in 130 prisons in the United States.[7] As governor, Hayes had been criticized for his too generous use of pardons; though ultimately criminals were responsible for their acts, Hayes believed, there were repressive forces in society that spawned crime. "Whoever interferes with equal rights and equal opportunities," he felt, "is in some real degree, responsible for the crimes committed in the community."[8] In a remarkably progressive way, Hayes placed much blame for crime on the greed and extravagances of the wealthy that deprived the poor of a decent income. Convinced criminals could be reformed, he insisted, and crime was due to poverty and could be reduced with more equitable distribution of wealth. So he became active in prison reform.[9]

The National Prison Association, having lapsed into inactivity after Wines' death, was revived by Hayes and five others in Saratoga, New York in 1883. William Rounds was made secretary. Theodore Roosevelt, on his way to be a cowboy in the Badlands of the Dakota Territory, was named treasurer.[10] Hayes became president and it was in this capacity that he presided for a decade lending his prestige and political skills to help the growth of the organization and trying to mediate between the various contentious groups.[11]

General Roeliff Brinkerhoff, another member of the Saratoga group, became a political force representing the more theoretical and academic crowd. He was named vice president of the newly established organization, a position he held for ten years as loyal assistant to Hayes. Born in New York to Dutch lineage going back to colonial times (his grandfather had fought in the Revolutionary War and his father in the War of 1812) he enjoyed social privilege and position. He taught school for a while, then studied law. When relatives moved to Ohio, he followed to practice law in Mansfield. When the Civil War broke out he enlisted, receiving numerous promotions before being mustered out as a major general.

After the war, Brinkerhoff became interested in a variety of social issues. His first outlet came in the founding of the National Conference of Charities and Corrections, an organization largely made up of reform-minded philanthropists and religious leaders. It had held its first annual meeting in Chicago in 1879. The organization's interests were widespread but focused on the problems of the insane, the feeble-minded, orphans, the blind, and prison inmates. In 1880 he wrote a report for the NCCC on prisons in the United States. In trying to collect his data, he found that no one in Washington, D.C. could help, so he took it upon himself to write to the prison wardens of

America. Good relationships resulted and thereafter his interest increasingly focused on the problems of prisons. In 1883 he gave a talk at a charities' convention on "The Post Penitentiary Treatment of Criminals," commenting that, "It was the first time, so far as I know, in this country, that the workings of the parole system as applied to high-grade prisons were fully presented."[12] He felt that,

> The citizens at large know little about prisoners. The newspapers never say anything about them; the pulpit never names them; political platforms are oblivious to their existence; even the labor unions, and kindred associations which clamor so fiercely against the competition of prison labor, never talk about the United States [sic.] prisons. Surely, their existence must be a myth.[13]

In March, 1884, Ohio–the home state of both Hayes and Brinkerhoff–became one of the first states to pass an indeterminate sentencing and parole law. This was the first such law in the nation and it was Brinkerhoff who pushed it through the state legislature. A month later in April, the Ohio State Reformatory was created. There was considerable opposition to this new institution and Brinkerhoff recalled that some: "Thought it sentimentalism, and called it a 'dude factory', where as an adverse senator expressed it, 'convicts would be furnished with 'quail on toast and Brussels carpets.'"[14] Thereafter Brinkerhoff split his time between the National Conference on Charities and Corrections and the National Prison Association. Like Hayes, though a Democratic politically, he represented those reformers who had a more abstract and idealistic rather than a practical approach to the prison issues of the late nineteenth century.

THE POLITICS OF PROFESSIONALISM

The politics of penology in the last third of the nineteenth century became critical as new ideologies emerged. These political battles illustrate both McClaughry's views and those quite different ones of thinkers and practitioners of penology. On a more fundamental level, there was the politics facing every warden locally. Even McClaughry–in spite of his growing national reputation–was subject to the local and state politicos, as seen in previous chapters. Fortunately for him, he generally had friends in high places ready to bail him out or support his cause.

Then there were the politics regarding the mass citizenry. The public needed to be educated about the prisons and prisoners instead of remaining mired in "out-of-sight, out-of mind" attitudes. The best access to the public was through speeches and media interviews. Local constituencies of citizens and politicians alike could be reached within the confines of the state, in

McClaughry's case Illinois, but yet greater numbers of people could be persuaded more effectively from a national pulpit.

On another level there was the politics within the profession. Political groupings among penologists were threefold. There were those purely academic and religious individuals who had no direct experience with crime, criminals, or criminal justice agencies. These pulpit penologists came from an ancient strain of puritanical do-gooderism with wide concerns earlier manifested in creating the penitentiaries, founding orphanages, and reforming insane asylums. Now, first through the National Conference of Charities and Corrections, they became increasingly interested in the plight of the prisoner. More interested in the "kept" than the "keepers," they felt they had a stewardship: God had blessed them with many advantages, and in return they needed to give something back to the less fortunate. Beliefs in perfectibility, that these individuals wasting away in prison could be saved, gave them motivation. Such evangelicals were the "elect" with a *noblesse oblige,* a responsibility to uplift society and assure that the "city on the hill" remained a beacon to the world.

Second, there were the wardens themselves. On one level these practical penologists were united. These hard-nosed custodians' day-to-day contact with the criminal element blunted much optimism on reform; generally they cared less for the souls of the inmates and more for controlling their bodies. Increasingly pressured and preoccupied with turning a profit and making the institution self–sufficient, they were more interested in the mundane and practical elements of management. Furthermore, as political appointees, in microcosm they reflected public feelings in their locations.

But there was another group of wardens who wanted to take a new direction in penology, wardens who had either been converted by the reasoning of such luminaries as Zebulon Brockway or who had themselves a predisposition for reform. It was among this latter group that Robert McClaughry moved. The politics of this group may be put into two categories. McClaughry, and those who agreed with him, needed to convince conservative wardens of the importance of the reformatory philosophy. Though it had already been tried on younger first offenders, McClaughry was now pushing on adult prisons this philosophy with its emphasis upon the indeterminate sentence, parole, and institutional regime conducive to reform.[15] Those battles will be waged among the practitioners. But on another level, McClaughry sought to convince the academic/charitable types, those who were largely responsible for setting up the organization, of the importance of insights coming from practical experience, that one could indeed be an "enlightened bureaucrat."

NOTES

1. For some examples of this literature see William R. Johnson, "Education and Professional Life Styles: Law and Medicine in the Nineteenth Century," *History of Education Quarterly 14* (1974), pp. 185-207. Gerald E Markowitz and David Karl Rosner, "Doctors in Crisis: A Study of the Use of Medical Education Reform to Establish Modern Professional Elitism in Medicine," *American Quarterly* 25 (1973), pp. 83-107. Jerold S. Auerbach, *Unequal Justice: Lawyers and Social Change in Modern America* (London: Oxford University Press, 1976. Roy Lubove, *The Professional Alturist: The Emergence of Social Work as a Career, 1889-1930* (New York: Atheneum, 1971).

2. See Frank Morn's *Academic Politics and the History of Criminal Justice Education* (Westport, Connecticut: Greenwood Press, 1995), pp.1-21.

3. *National Prison Association*, 1887, p. 100.

4. The Committee of 12 was filled with prominent politicians and philanthropists. Rutherford Hayes, governor of Ohio at the time; James G. Blaine of Maine; former governor of New Jersey Daniel Haines; Horatio Seymour governor of New York; Theodore Dwight; Amos Pilsbury from Albany penitentiary; F Sanbourn of Mass; E. W. Hatch of the Conn. Reform School; Charles Coffin of Indiana; Zebulon Brockway of the Detroit House of Corrections and William Welker made up the group. *National Prison Association*, 1886, p.8.

5. *Ibid.*, 1890, p. 80.

6. *Ibid.*, p. 81.

7. *Ibid.*

8. Ari Hoogenboom, *Rutherford B. Hayes: Warrior & President* (Lawrence, Kansas, University of Kansas Press, 1995), p. 523.

9. *Ibid.*, p. 539.

10. *Ibid.*, p.486.

11. A listing of NPA convention sites for this period is:

1884 Saratoga, NY 9/6-10
1885 Detroit 10/17-21
1886 Atlanta 11/6-12
1887 Toronto 9/10-15
1888 Boston 7/14-19
1889 Nashville 11/16-20
1890 Cincinnati 9/25-30
1891 Pittsburgh 10/10-14
1892 Baltimore 6/7-12
1893 Chicago 6/7-10
1894 St. Paul 6/16-20
1895 Denver 9/14/18
1896 Milwaukee 9/26-30
1897 Austin, Texas, 12/2-6
1898 Indianapolis, 10/15-20
1899 New Orleans 1/21-24 [adjourned]

1899 Hartford, Conn. 9/23-27
1900 Cleveland, 9/22-26
1901 Kansas City Mo. 11/9-13
1902 Philadelphia, 9/13-17
1903 Louisville 11/3-8
1904 Quincey, Ill., 11/15-19
1905 Lincoln, Neb., 10/21-25

12. General Roeliff Brinkerhoff, *Recollections of a Lifetime* (Cincinnati: The Robert Clarke Company, 1900), p. 255.

13. *Ibid.*, p. 264.

14. *Ibid.*, p. 275.

15. For a masterly discussion of this body v. soul issue see Michel Foucault, *Discipline & Punish: The Birth of the Prison* (New York: Pantheon, 1978).

Chapter Twenty-Eight

Academics v. Practitioners

"Those who had . . . a theory and those who understood the facts"

Tensions soon arose in the National Prison Association between these more academically religious and philanthropist reformers and the more practically-minded wardens. Within a couple of years after the organization was reinstated in 1883, McClaughry was there taking an active role. Like many of his colleagues who administered prisons, he quickly tired of the formal and theoretical speeches given by the dominant latter-day puritan and evangelical do-gooders and instead suggested that the wardens meet by themselves to discuss questions of practical prison administration.[1]

First steps were taken in December 1886, when Joseph Nicholson, superintendent of the Detroit House of Correction, Charles Felton of the Chicago House of Corrections and McClaughry met and drew up a petition for founding the Wardens' Association. In March 1887, at an organizational meeting in Detroit, the charter members besides Joseph Nicholson, Charles Felton, and McClaughry were Hiram Hatch of the Michigan prison, E.C. Watkins of the Ohio prison, G.W. Mitchell of the Chester, Illinois prison, and James Massie of the Ontario prison in Toronto.[2] These were practical men trying to establish their voice in a predominantly elite organization. But some, like McClaughry, had larger visions. Unlike the religious and philanthropic crowd who focused solely on the inmate, these managerial reformers were intent on changing the law and penal institutions.

The Wardens' Association had three self-proclaimed purposes: 1) prevention of crime by arrest, conviction, and incarceration of the criminal class; 2) reformation of the criminal in prison; 3) prevention of the renewal of criminal life after release from prison. One key practical device to carry out these three goals would be the adoption of the Bertillon System of criminal identification.[3] This meant that these wardens had to convert both the "academics" in the larger organization and those other wardens not ready to abandon older belief systems.

At the Toronto conference in 1887, Hayes had to leave early and Brinkerhoff presided. From his unique vantage point Brinkerhoff felt he saw something that needed to be addressed:

> To the cursory visitor coming in from time to time to listen to the discussions upon this floor, it may have seemed that there is little unity of faith among the members of the congress; and hearing them refuse to pass any resolutions indorsing any special propositions pertaining to penology, he may have concluded that the congress has no convictions upon which we are agreed.[4]

Brinkerhoff quickly tried to dispel this apparent chaos: "They may differ as to the ways and means of bringing those precepts to bear upon prisoners, but as to its necessity there is no question."[5]

In 1888, the Association met in Boston. Earlier that year a letter from Zebulon Brockway to Brinkerhoff signaled a new approach and posed a greater crisis within the organization especially for the wardens. Brinkerhoff recalled that Brockway felt "it was time for the congress [NPA] to get beyond the discussion of buckets and brooms and consider principles rather than methods."[6] Of course, many wardens wanted to discuss the bucket and broom issues and the movement toward a separate and free-standing wardens' association took on momentum, with an organizing meeting held in Chicago in 1888.

Apparently, fearing that the "revolution" of the wardens would emasculate the National Prison Association, the secretary of the national organization, Frederick Wines, rushed "in hot haste" to the wardens to bring them back into the fold. Wines acknowledged the sharp distinctions between the newly formed wardens' association and the national body. "The Wardens' Association is a purely official body, in which all outsiders are spectators. The National Prison Association is voluntary, not official, in its character; and its discussions are open to all who are present," he maintained.[7] Yet Wines recalled that in the early years the wardens gave the organization the "cold shoulder," for he saw them

> at the meetings of this congress, sitting in a corner and discussing matters by themselves, in a whisper, refusing to take any part in the public proceedings, and intimating that the gentlemen who were speaking were ignorant of the subject which they were discussing, and seemed to them to be afflicted with crankery. They said that it was not their place as wardens, to attempt to enlighten them, or to take part in the deliberations.[8]

McClaughry could not let such a statement go unanswered. "I am a little in favor of letting bygones be bygones," he said,

> But as Brother Wines are [sic.] confessing for our side, I want to confess a little for his side. He said that, in the beginning, the wardens gave the Prison Association the cold shoulder, and that he had seen sessions of the association with the wardens in one corner looking rather askance at the persons who were reading papers. That is true, to a certain extent. Yet the wardens, when they went to these early Prison Association meetings, were made to feel, whether intentionally or otherwise, that they were to sit at the feet of the Gamaliels who were running the machine, and learn, without much to say. At last they came to the conclusion that they would organize an association of their own, and they took the steps to do so, and called a meeting at Chicago.[9]

McClaughry continued to vent the deep feelings of the wardens and thus assured his position as leader of the practitioners. At first:

> We did not understand each other. But there grew up a better understanding between those in practical charge of the prisons of the country and those valuable men, (I do not call them cranks), those able men who study and write and publish papers upon the subject, from which we can all get benefit, if we study them carefully. They are not practical prison men, and some of their ideas we cannot put into practical operation; but I do [not] know of one from whom a practical prison man who is honestly seeking help cannot get it. Whatever may have been the faults of the past, I rejoice that they are past, and that we are cooperating now, since we understand each other better.[10]

Rutherford Hayes, reminiscing in 1890, recalled some of the early tension in the organization over which he presided for so many years. Earlier, he believed, the association had had two classes:

> [t]hose who had . . . a theory, and those who understood the facts. Those who had the facts . . . therefore had no theory, and those who knew very little as to theories were the men best acquainted with the facts. Then we had the leaders of the greatest prisons and the managers and superintendents and those in charge of reformatories, and they knew the facts; and we had scholarly men, philanthropists, those who had read and studied, and the classes were, perhaps, quite separate, but today, after having met for twenty years somewhat frequently in different ways, those who were practical men have become thoroughly informed on that which was supposed to be chiefly understood by the theorists, and those who were theorists and speculators and general philanthropists have become, by frequent visits to prisons, to reformatories, and by constant contact with the practical men of prison life, to some extent practical men in the matter.[11]

The wardens, due to pressure from the national organization and some politicking from McClaughry, decided to remain affiliated with the national group, but tensions remained.

"At any rate," McClaughry declared, "we shook hands across the bloody chasm and made our association an adjunct of the Prison Association and the two have run in perfect harmony ever since." McClaughry and his fellow wardens simply wanted to be understood and appreciated by the "theorists." Wines quickly jumped in and said "not theorists but amateurs."[12]

In spite of McClaughry's efforts, many wardens continued advocating breaking away. The national association wanted the wardens just to blend in and not be a distinctive section. Yet R. H. Dawson, from Ohio, pushed the wardens to have a distinct identity. "I think it would be a good thing just to get the wardens together, if they did no more than talk and get acquainted," he believed.[13] Nicholson, the president of the wardens' association in 1889, felt their independence was good because it allowed "free intercourse of views and experiences, free from the influence of over-zealous philanthropists."[14] Next year the debate went on. A.W. Berggren, from Joliet prison in Illinois, thought the wardens were just a "side show" for the national organization. This time with the total agreement of McClaughry, he requested that the wardens meet at another time of the year. It was permissible to belong to the national too, but the wardens should have their own distinct identity, he believed.[15]

Indeed, a look at the membership rolls of 1892 suggests both the wardens' marginalization and their importance to the organization if it were to survive. Twenty-eight members that year were clearly practical prison administrators. Philanthropists and reform minded people made up thirty-six of the membership. Twenty-six others were either members of the criminal justice system, such as police chiefs and judges, or academics. Eighteen politicians such as members of Boards of Managers for a states correctional system were represented too.[16] These latter two groups were fluid, coming and going depending on the location of the host city for the conference meetings that year, and were largely passive spectators. But the main battles continued between the philanthropists and practitioners.

On the one hand, the national organization continued to pressure the wardens' association to disband. On the other, the wardens still felt they were not given enough opportunity at the national meetings. As late as 1890 one feels the tone of resentment in President Nicholson's comments. Criticizing the national organization for such a "limited space of time" to discuss "live topics from a practical stand point" he called the warden association members to make up their minds and exert more practitioner autonomy. [17]

Two years later another effort arose to disband the wardens' association. In part this was due to continued pressures from the national group, but it was because of some unresolved political conflicts within the wardens' association itself. Ultimately, one of the key reasons for the establishment of the association—to get the Bertillon system of criminal identification accepted universally—had failed.

Frustrated, President Nicholson resigned in 1892. Before doing so he moved that the wardens" association dissolve. "The organization had practically failed in the object for which it was intended and that the members felt that they could do more good to the cause by their disintegration."[18] There was much objection and a lively discussion followed. G.E. Chamberlain, warden of the Connecticut State Penitentiary at Wetherford, wanted to continue. "We wardens meet as strangers from year to year, we do not get acquainted. We listen to some professor who gives us a theory on prison matters. Our time is always limited at these conventions. We seem to be barred out from them."[19] James Massie, warden from the Central Prison in Toronto, Canada, agreed. "We felt at its very beginning almost, that we did not receive that support that we thought we had a right to expect. There are many subjects that can only be discussed among ourselves . . . and experience is gained that the older can impart to the younger."[20]A committee was set up to make a recommendation on Nicholson's motion to dissolve. Mark Crawford, superintendent of Chicago's House of Correction, James Massie of Toronto, E. C. McMillin warden of Iowa's prison, and McClaughry were on that committee. In a short time they reported back recommending that the wardens continue as a section of the national organization and that they be given one day at every year's conference for practical discussions of prison management.[21]

The same story could be related to other more practical and specialized components of the National Prison Association. Chaplains quickly followed the wardens and organized. Very few "treatment" people were in the prisons in the late nineteenth century beyond chaplains and doctors. If reformatory ideals were to come into the adult prisons the numbers of treatment people would increase. The support (or lack of it) for chaplains was a gauge indicating the real reforming nature of the wardens. In terms of support, many wardens—and McClaughry was one of them—attended the chaplains' sessions. In 1887, the chaplains unexpectedly asked him to speak, largely because he was known as a "crowd pleaser." As a "reformatory person," McClaughry supported the chaplain, especially in the role of heading up the prison school. Joliet had two chaplains by this time, a Catholic and Protestant. He warned that, "A warden may entirely nullify and destroy his chaplain's influence in the prison."[22] George H. Hickox, a prison chaplain speaking to the newly formed chaplains section, reiterated that, "The prison authorities have not been very careful or very anxious for the chaplain's success."[23] Just like the wardens, the chaplains were trying to be recognized as a profession.

Indeed, the National Prison Association was "professionalizing." At first it was just a general assembly dominated by reformers. The breakaway of wardens was a quest for autonomy and professionalism. Throughout the last five years of the 1880s the meetings and the organization became more structured. By 1890 an overall meeting format was in place. There would be a general session on the opening day with welcoming remarks by some high dignitary from the host city. Then a call to order would follow with opening remarks from the president, generally Rutherford Hayes. On the second day there would be a general meeting in the morning with various papers read. In the afternoon, by 1890, the wardens' association would have its own special meeting. That evening a dinner with some general but formal speeches being made was held. Day three had a general session again in the morning, and that evening was turned over to the chaplains' association. On the fourth day the general session in the morning composed of reports from the standing committees and special committees; standing committees for Criminal Law Reform, Prevention and Reformatory Work, Prison Discipline, Discharged Prisoners, Police Forces in Cities, and Work of Prison Physicians, to name a few, became a permanent fixture. McClaughry served on most of these committees. That general session was followed by tours of the host city in the afternoon and speeches in the evening. Day five allowed for another general session in the morning and the wardens' association again in the afternoon. That evening more general speeches were on the agenda. The next day was taken up with general sessions, committee reports, official thanks to the host city, and closing remarks.

Such formal and structured conference programs disguised the strained relations between the more academic and the more practical members of the organization. McClaughry would spend much of his career in the organization building bridges between these two groups. One would be wrong to assume, however, that all wardens were on the same page. McClaughry's work as facilitator and educator in the larger meetings was important, but his positions and politics were greater among the warden themselves.

NOTES

1. *National Prison Association,* 1886, pp. 9-10.
2. *Ibid*, 1887, p.8.
3. *Ibid.*, 1889, p. 47.
4. *Brinkerhoff*, p. 300.
5. *Ibid.*, p. 301.
6. *Ibid.*, p. 308.
7. *National Prison Association*, 1887, p.18.

8. *Ibid.*, p. 100.
9. *Ibid.*, pp. 102-103.
10. *Ibid.*
11. *Ibid.*, 1890, p. 10.
12. *Ibid.*, 1889, p.102.
13. *Ibid.*, p. 92.
14. *Ibid.*, p. 9.
15. *Ibid.*, 1890, p. 78.
16. *Ibid.*, 1892, pp. 284-93.
17. *Ibid.*, 1890, pp.34-35.
18. *Ibid.*, 1892, p. 107.
19. *Ibid.*, p. 107.
20. *Ibid.*, pp. 107-108.
21. *Ibid.*, pp. 109, 174.
22. *Ibid.*, 1887, p. 75.
23. *Ibid.*, 1890, p 111.

Chapter Twenty-Nine

"Buckets and Brooms"

> "As usual with me, I do not agree with any of the gentlemen who have preceded me."

POLITICS IN THE WARDENS' SECTION

Nicholson's resignation and motion for dissolution had been read by Edward Wright, warden of the Western State Penitentiary in Pennsylvania. Wright represented one of the clusters of political tensions within the warden's association. Little unanimity existed among the wardens and major political jockeying occurred among these penal practitioners. Such infighting threatened their place in the larger organization and their professionalizing process. The wardens might be in some agreement on their place in the larger organization, but numerous disagreements existed amongst them on the nature of the penitentiary, the place of the reformatory ideology in adult prisons, and most of all the role of prison administrators in advocating the Bertillon system of identification.

The political shakeout was deceptively simple. A small group, with McClaughry as leader, had an expansive view. They saw themselves in the vanguard of the reformatory movement. But even more so, they viewed criminal justice in a total systems perspective. Prisons and penology (the word "corrections" had not been coined yet) could not be divorced from the police and courts. What happened in one area affected the others. Reform had two purposes: to make the "accidental" criminals fit to go back into society and keep the career crook from doing so, and to make the running of the prison more efficient. A more conservative group—and they were the majority who had joined up and constituted those who had wanted to focus on the "buckets and brooms"—they did not want to go too far beyond the walls of the prison management. It was up to McClaughry and his like-minded colleagues to bring these conservatives into a profession with a loftier agenda than just management. One of the first things to do, as professionals, was to make sure everyone spoke the same language, to forge an agreement on key words. Word usage over the years got sloppy.

PENITENTIARIES

On one level divisions were historic along the lines of the original two models of the penitentiary movement. By the late nineteenth century some semantic confusion or sloppiness surfaced. For those aspiring to be a profession there was little agreement on vocabulary. Houses of Corrections had become standard usage designating an urban jail. The difference between a prison and a penitentiary was less clear. Increasingly, people–including many penal workers–slipped into using the words interchangeably, a clear sign of some significant historical forgetfulness. As in all amnesia there must have been some sort of trauma. That blow was that the penitentiaries had failed! Invented as a New Nation solution to crime, crime rates and prison populations continued to soar. In spite of the failure, these institutions were kept. Alexis de Tocqueville, in his travels and writings in Jacksonian America, commented that as early as the 1840s, seventy-five of the inmates in those institutions he visited were black or recent immigrants. From 1850 to 1858, "foreigners" out-numbered natives in New York's inmate population by four to one.[1] In short, for many the penitentiary/prison became a place for disposable people. McClaughry tried to clear the air but seemed as confused as others on the issue:

> In the west we understand by penitentiaries what New York people mean by state prisons. The three state prisons there are Dannemora, Clinton, and Auburn and the penitentiaries are the jails or county prisons.[2]

Penitentiary people took umbrage at such a definition. The number of Pennsylvania model penitentiaries had diminished by the last third of the nineteenth century but a few, particularly in Pennsylvania, still existed. Elsewhere the old Auburn model spread but changed substantially. Overcrowding did away with solitary living and silent working situations even in Pennsylvania. Wardens from these Pennsylvania penitentiaries remained to take on any new reforms but still favored their silent/solitary system. Perhaps their influence was declining so rapidly in America—at a time it was steady or increasing in Europe—these wardens sang the swan song; they became shrill and obstructionist in the wardens' association. In part this was due to the frustrations over the lack of progress of the Pennsylvania model in America. But also it was due to some arrogance over the fact that they were succeeding elsewhere in the world.[3]

Clearly the greatest spokesman for this Pennsylvania group was Michael Cassidy, warden of the Eastern Penitentiary of Pennsylvania for twenty years. Born in Philadelphia, in 1829, Cassidy became a carpenter at Eastern Penitentiary in 1861, worked as a guard, overseer, and in 1881 as warden. Thereafter he became a regular gadfly at the wardens' association meetings. He liked to preface his numerous remarks by saying, "As usual with me, I do not agree with any of the gentlemen who have preceded me."[4] A lot of this was a quirk of personality; it took him a long time to even join the organization. Instead, he liked to attend and pose as an "interested observer." He constantly "wished it understood that he was present as an interested but independent spectator of the proceedings of the association."[5] But a lot had to do with genuine disagreement over the nature of punishment and its administration. McClaughry and Cassidy crossed swords on numerous occasions, their philosophies and personalities were diametrically opposite. Cassidy was confrontational and obstructive; McClaughry, on the other hand, was a compromiser and facilitator.

Arguing fifty-year-old arguments in 1886, Cassidy felt "the severest punishment is to take labor away from an individual, and leave him alone." And again "when you ignore the individual, and treat him as a mass, in the shop, altogether, big and little, good and bad, you cannot expect to produce results."[6] When other wardens, particularly McClaughry, complained over certain governance issues Cassidy responded,

> My friend from the west has gone off entirely into the regions of gush. [laughter] The philanthropist and evangelist may go around singing; but a prison warden, to be successful in his business, must understand the whole of it; and that part which pertains to maudlin sentiment is not a part of the warden's business. A prison government, to be a good government, must be a one man government; and their [sic.] must be no interference with that one man.[7]

McClaughry lashed back:

> I differ from my friend. It may be that it is sentiment, and that it is gush and nonsense; but I tell you that there is a good deal of power in a little kindness, and you can, by indulging it a little, acquire a power that you can't get by enforcing the power of the law merely. I know my friend speaks from more experience than I do; but I think we can show as good results as he can in this respect.[8]

As late as 1898, the Major tried to mend the differences of the Pennsylvania and Auburn models and pitch the reformatory ideology at the same time:

> The two systems should be combined in one general prison plan, so that even the working hours may mean, not the mixing of the good and bad elements of a prison population, but a quarantine of the bad and the mutual helpfulness of the good. If you have three grades, why not have three prisons in one and adopt rooms without grated doors for the highest class of prisons?[9]

These may have been small battles, side skirmishes over semantics, but they did indicate fundamental differences of opinion existing among the wardens. There were a host of other issues dividing the wardens, the largest being the rise and spread of the reformatory ideology. McClaughry was at the center of it all.

THE REFORMATORY

Even among the non-Pennsylvania wardens there were divisions. By the 1880s the reformatory model of penology had become fashionable. McClaughry had left Joliet in 1888 to head a reformatory in Pennsylvania. Later he would be the superintendent of one in Illinois. Zebulon Brockway, one of the earliest founders of the NPA, was chief exponent of reform. Of course, Brockway had the luxury of running an actual reformatory in Elmira, New York. These institutions, and the ideology behind them, were for young first offenders. In his career McClaughry would run a reformatory too but much of the time he was a warden of prisons for adult repeat serious offenders. Nonetheless, McClaughry was pushing the reformatory principles—the indeterminate sentence, parole, and emphasis of procedures to reform the inmates—on to the adult prisons. Opposition, especially coming from Cassidy, immediately arose.

Cassidy was against any use of the word reformation. As is often the case of any early stages of a movement, considerable energy went into the choice of words. Wines suggested the substitution of the word "treatment" but Brockway and McClaughry forged ahead with the word reformatory.[10]

McClaughry was no idealist. His reformatory views were based upon a reasoned expectation. In 1889, when asked about his perceptions of the reformatory ideal, McClaughry reflected:

> What I understand by it is, not that we are to make a saint of every sinner; not that we are expected to send out a first-class citizen in every criminal discharged by us; but that we are to put into practical operation such measures as will tend

> to make them better, rather than worse men. We are expected by all practical means to put our men in a position to be self-sustaining, and at least as good citizens as they are capable of being, after they are discharged.[11]

McClaughry was concerned, however, over the popular suspicion and dislike of the reformatory/indeterminate ideology. Too many "graduates of Elmira" were released only to go on and commit more crimes, he noted. Reformers needed to take care in who they let out or else the wider citizenry would lose faith in the idea. Furthermore, he added, people needed to be able to distinguish between those let out because they deserved to be and those who wardens were forced to let out because of the expiration of the sentence.[12] McClaughry was in the minority as many wardens clung to incapacitating their inmates rather than reforming them. Cassidy remained a strong opponent gaining considerable support, among others from warden A. A. Brush of Sing Sing:

> When Brother Cassady said yesterday that he begun to hate the word "reform," I wondered what kind of a man he could be; but I have almost come to that position myself through hearing the nonsensical and foolish talk of men who ought to be wise. Gentlemen, you cannot make angels all at once out of prisoners; when you talk about making them so much better than the outside world, you are talking foolishness.[13]

In a heated discussion on the value of Prisoners' Aid Societies, Cassidy was adamant. Showing his innate anti-intellectualism, a strain running throughout the warden's section, he did " not agree with any one of the philanthropists who are rated as authority on the treatment of the average criminal, whether in or out of prison."[14]

Again, after Brockway gave a long speech defending the indeterminate sentence, Cassidy came out strongly against it.[15] It seemed to him that the reformatory people were stressing ideology over practice. The older officials, the penitentiary adherents, tended to emphasize practice over ideology. McClaughry was in the middle trying to reconcile both camps. Dipping into his religious background he was "satisfied that the difference between us is no greater than between the Old and New Presbyterians; one sect says, "In Adam all die," and the other, "all die in Adam."[16] What he neglected to mention at the time was that both persuasions in Presbyterianism were still divided.

But even trivial matters separated the reformers from the old school people. For example, McClaughry announced in 1886 that in the name of reform he was allowing visitors to bring in some small delicacies for the inmates. Cassidy bridled at such practices. "You know that no man can be a prison warden unless he holds all the lines. If he lets go of any of them he is liable at any moment to have trouble. The plan advocated of admitting delicacies is all very well for sentiment, or to please the poor wife or sister who comes to see the prisoner, but we can't supervise those things; and if you let in one thing, another comes in; and it opens the door for mischief that you cannot control."[17] Discussions on prison architecture, personnel, work and federal prisons were all cast against the backdrop of the tensions between those favoring the reformatory ideology and those opposed.[18]

By 1890, even though there was not unanimity, the reformers could take pride in some advances. Frederick Wines, an old scion of the reformatory movement, gave a long talk on "Twenty Years Growth of the American Prison System." He pointed out that in two decades, thirty-one penal and reformatory institutions had been created. Sixteen prisoner aid societies to help discharged prisoner had been formed. In other words, the political battles of the previous years had shown a measure of success. Of course, much remained to be done but this twentieth year anniversary of the association was a landmark.[19] Yet one component of the reformatory ideology remained very controversial.

Parole had been an important part of rehabilitating young first offenders. McClaughry thought it appropriate for adult prisoners as well and continued to argue for reformatory principles and their extension into adult prisons. Parole for multiple offending adults had been increasingly adopted by many states. In 1895, Illinois extended its parole law to include Joliet and Chester. By 1898, twenty-five states had parole laws.[20]

As parole spread, criticism—particularly from the bench and bar—increased. Court personnel, especially the judge, resented their sentencing being compromised by wardens. The police thought the increase in crime was due to early release of felons. Philip Deitsch, Superintendent of Police in Cincinnati, reflected this opposition in a speech to the assembled wardens. "I do not approve of parole and I will give you my reason why, "he began.

> You say a man is a good fellow and deserves to be let out on parole. Why, the laws of the prison compel him to be a good man to start with. If he doesn't obey he is punished and he knows that. Second he is cunning. He says, If I behave myself and am right good I will be paroled; I need not serve my term; I will go out among the boys again.[21]

Of course, Cassidy was against parole. In 1897, speaking out in opposition he made a relevant point:

> Any contrivance, mechanical or legal, that can go behind the action of the properly constituted courts is a dangerous proceeding. Nearly all parole laws are of that character. In discharging men in that way there is a reversal of the decisions

> of the court. It is narrowed down to the opinion of a prison keeper and he is liable to be influenced in one way or another. Men are fallible and prison keepers especially. The individual [inmate] himself must accomplish every reformation. [22]

At the next year's conference in 1898, Cassidy repeated his concerns:

> Compromise with crime is pernicious. The parole law, setting aside the decision of the court, is a pernicious proceeding. Any contrivance that will interfere with the properly constituted court is a dangerous proceeding.
>
> In this system of parole the whole matter of the trial of the court, the decision of the court and jury is set aside entirely without question by a prison keeper. The revision of the decisions of the properly constituted court is narrowed down to the opinion of a prison keeper. Such a condition of things will not exist in a popular government. The whole thing will fall to pieces before a great while.[23]

McClaughry remained adamantly in favor of parole but against any political interference in the paroling process. It should be done by experts and not politicians or "cranky reformers and unpractical people with fads," he contended.[24] For parole to work more effectively, he noted, the past life of the prisoner needed to be considered. He advocated the use of a grading system with different buildings, clothes, food, privileges, and treatments. He did understand there to be a potential problem in releasing men sooner than they ought to be because of overcrowding. So the question comes up, he maintained, "which is the least of evils—to retain the prisoners under training in the overcrowded institution, or send them out on a small margin of probability that they might get on in free society?"[25] But society outside the walls was not necessarily friendly to ex offenders.

McClaughry—in one of those moments showing his tendency to see problems as transcending just the prisons—expressed concern over the way police treated parolees. Speaking from real experience, he said that he felt that,

> The police of Chicago as a rule feel kindly toward paroled men, and are disposed to help them along. The trouble in Chicago is that certain detectives, discharged policemen, who run so-called detective agencies, really run blackmail establishments, and they worry and badger a fellow after he comes out until they get what little money he has left.[26]

In spite of the opposition, McClaughry felt that for true reformation, parole had to be the wave of the future. Defective as it may be, he maintained, it was far better than the old system "where the jury fixed the length of sentence, and where almost every sentence which did not reflect the prejudice of the locality that furnished the jury, was a compromise reached after a scheme of "marking" and "averaging," or sometimes of gambling or casting lots in the jury room, that tended to destroy in the minds of both prisoners and people all respect for courts of justice, and presented in the prison such a hotch potch of sentences for the same crime, as to effectually destroy in the prisoner's mind all notion of justice."[27]

In the final analysis, McClaughry felt four things were needed to implement a successful parole system. First, those who most benefitted from an early release had to be identified. Second, facilities and procedures to reach those who were most reformable needed to be in place. Third, those who could be reformed had to be taught job skills and self discipline. Finally, the hopeless criminal had to be discovered and kept from getting out early. By this he was once again advocating one of his favorite measures, the acceptance of the Bertillon system of identification.

THE BERTILLON SYSTEM

The biggest issue facing the wardens' section was the Bertillon system of criminal identification. Its place on the agenda was always prominent, thanks to McClaughry. In fact, the creation of the warden's association was primarily due to McClaughry's desire to get the Bertillon system accepted in American criminal justice. It became a personal crusade for him (and his sons) for much of the last two decades of the nineteenth century. Significantly, it caused barely a ripple in the larger organization, probably because it seemed too "hands on" for the more academic and reformer types. So this became something of a tempest in the warden's teapot.

For several reasons the Bertillon system of criminal identification was important beyond the warden's association. First, it showed clearly the impact of developing science, specifically forensic science, in the nineteenth century and the struggles going on in the criminal justice system over adopting it. Second, it indicated McClaughry's pan-professionalism. He saw the necessity of this device for police in criminal apprehension, for the courts in appropriate sentencing especially since the "habitual offender laws" were sprouting up across the country, and for prison keepers when it came to making the best decisions on who should or should not be released from prison early. For example, in Illinois if a person committed a second offense—no matter the crime—they would not get less than 15 years for a sentence. A third offense would assure a sentence of at least 20 years. Criminals therefore had a vested interest in hiding their criminal identity. And people in criminal justice—in the name of justice—had a vested interest in finding these hidden hardened criminals, McClaughry thought. The objective of professional criminals—and here McClaughry was generous in thinking of a true criminal being a repeat offender—was to avoid long terms. The objective of the Bertillon system was to foil them.[28] Third, such an identification system was for McClaughry an important part of the reformatory ideology. Critical to parole decisions was determining those prisoners indeed ready to be released and those merely playing the "pious dodge"—posing as reformed in order to get out sooner to carry on with a life of crime.

For McClaughry, Felton, and Nicholson—the instigators of the wardens' association in the first place—the Bertillon system of identification was the primary issue to be pursued. Nicholson remembered that it was after the Atlanta conference in 1886 that the idea came up. Traveling together the three discussed the latest revelations on the Bertillon identification system. They created a circular letter to all prison and reformatory wardens calling for a meeting to be held in Detroit on March 8th, 1887. It was there that the wardens' organization was formed and the Bertillon system became its banner cause.

There was to be a president, (Joseph Nicholson was selected) a vice president, secretary (the position held by McClaughry for several years), and a treasurer. It was pretty exclusive; one had to be a warden to be a member. Though the first meeting of the Warden's Association was filled with items of practical concern to prison wardens (prison construction, prison diets, prison doctors, and prison sanitation, it was the Bertillon system that became the reason for the organization. Much of the 1887 meeting was taken up with discussions on the Bertillon system. In fact, at first, the official name of the organization was the Wardens' Association for the Identification of Criminals.[29] McClaughry invited charter delegates to visit him at Joliet and establish a Bertillon bureau. He wanted "a complete register of all criminals serving time, and a sure means of identification, if caught in criminal acts after liberation from prison."[30] Thereafter McClaughry personally took on the Bertillon cause.

Therein lay a problem. Many prospective members were confused thinking the association was a single-issue organization.[31] Others had numerous questions—often sincere, but sometimes nonetheless silly—about the system. Among them:

- Can pulling one's ear over and over again make it longer and therefore throw off the measurements?
- No, McClaughry assured them.
- Would such a central file hurt the ex-offender?
- Not unless the ex-offender recommits a crime, McClaughry retorted.
- Is the Bertillon system a deterrent?
- Yes, once crooks knew about its effectiveness they tend either to stop their criminality or move to those areas that do not use the Bertillon system, McClaughry answered.

- Would it be of help to the wardens?
- Yes, it would allow wardens to know better their prison population and tailor treatments.[32]

Since the system had been developed in France, its measurements were in the metric system. Most wardens did not understand such numbers and wanted conversion to American measurement increments. McClaughry advised against this because it restricted its utility just to America and many criminals were transcontinental in their predatory patterns.[33]

Several wardens continued to worry that too much personal information was collected and given out on the ex-offender. McClaughry constantly reminded them that first offenders were safe as long as they did not commit more crimes. The collected information would not be used unless needed due to a second offense. Only habitual offenders had to worry, he contended.[34] Some were concerned that mistakes would occur; they did not have faith in the statistics of it all. McClaughry countered using France as an example. The system had been used there in over 100,000 cases, he claimed, with no mistakes. Although many people had similar measurements along some indicators, if enough measurements were taken the uniqueness of the individual would emerge by twenty years of age, he assured the assembled wardens.[35] Even in discussions on parole he made it clear that the Bertillon system would help to identify habitual crooks so as not to grant them early release.[36] Perhaps a bit too enthusiastically, McClaughry even suggested a broader use of the system. For example, he noted, a businessman traveling abroad might want to have his measurements taken and recorded as a safeguard for identification.[37]

More direct opposition soon manifested itself. For example, A. A. Brush, warden of Sing Sing, was reluctant:

> I have not yet joined this association. When written to, last year, on the subject, I fully intended to do so; but I am either very stupid, or else I have got into the wrong crowd. I cannot see what on earth prison officials have to do with this matter. It belongs to the courts. Then it is a matter of the police dept., and not us.[38]

General Chamberlain, warden of the Connecticut State prison for 16 years, joined the group for the first time at their 1887 meeting, and with his fresh eyes identified some of the political problems. "I am a strictly practical man," he offered. "I have come here for practical information. Some of the theoretical ideas that I have heard to-day would not apply [to] the men I have to deal with." He was against the parole system. Though he approved of the Bertillon system as a new useful technology, he felt it was something with which the prison people should not get involved.[39] Prisons were places to punish and hopefully reform criminals. Identification, thought the more conservative wardens, should be done by the police officials not prison ones.

Cassidy saw some value in the Bertillon system too, but thought the wardens' association was the wrong instrument for it. Although attending the meetings, Cassidy still refused to join because he thought it to be a single issue organization (to get the Bertillon system accepted), and he could not support such an organization. So he continued to be a gadfly.[40] When McClaughry invited Bertillon expert, George Porteus, to illustrate the system in 1889, Cassidy objected vehemently "to introducing any police surveillance into a prison. I object to Mr. Porteus coming here, for the reason that [he] is engaged in police business," declared the warden from Pennsylvania. Cassidy was voted down.[41]

McClaughry continued to press on. Representing a new breed of pan-professionals, McClaughry asked for a resolution allowing the prison-based Bertillon data bank to be used by police and court personnel. This addressed one of the persistent objections over why the prisons should be doing this. Many felt that the police and courts would never come to the wardens for Bertillon information. McClaughry's resolution was voted down.[42]

Apathy, if not out-and-out opposition, toward the Bertillon system continued and stymied the growth of the wardens' section of NPA. Two years after its founding, Nicholson was perplexed and wondered why so many wardens stayed aloof from the association.[43] Only 14 prisons leaders were represented in the wardens' association by 1889. Felton admitted that "its organizers are beginning to think that it should never have had a being, as but few prison wardens have become members of it; hence its usefulness has not been made apparent."[44] Consequently, President Nicholson in his opening speech to the wardens in 1889 recommended that they expand their mission beyond solely advocating for the Bertillon system. McClaughry responded by setting forth a new mission statement which also showed the divide between practitioners and "theorists":

> The object of the Wardens' Association, besides the registration of criminals, is to have meeting, in connection with the National Prison Association, for the discussion of questions and difficulties that arise in our experience—such discussions as may be beneficial to us.[45]

Nonetheless the Bertillon system remained a flash point. In 1890, Warden Tufts again attacked it. The system was based upon the wrong assumption, he felt. The measuring of all prisoners labels them as criminals:

> My own observation is that the great proportion of prisoners are not criminals, and that the right thing to do is to have them taken out of their temporary con-

> dition and passed out of sight, not to have them perpetuated by any system of registration in a central bureau.[46]

Of course, this forced McClaughry once again to assure the assembled wardens that

> The only possible way in which they can appear again is by their committing crime again. Their record is more secure than by any other system ever devised. The proposed statistical collection does not give the name of any prisoner. We only want the number, not the name. There is no inquiry into heredity. The Bertillon system puts no mark on anyone. No man can be pursued by the police or by any detective by means of this system. The man is absolutely protected unless he shall commit crime again. The system furnishes no means for pursuing a man who has ever been a criminal, who proposes to lead an honest life.[47]

Nonetheless, in 1890 President Nicholson remained depressed over the indifference in the wardens' association.[48] Two years later, in 1892, his depression and frustration over the association's failures since 1887 found public expression. "For some time I have been haunted with the query 'whither are you drifting?' To which I can only answer, 'Into the Quick Sands of Sentimentalism.'" Perplexed over the indifference of prison managers to anything non political, he continued to push for the Bertillon system but remained disheartened. "And now, after nearly six years of faithful effort to bring all the wardens of the United States into our association in furthering its work I must confess that we have failed."[49] With all the zealousness of a Biblical prophet, McClaughry did not lose heart. In fact he was given complete credit for introducing the Bertillon system to America. Felton acknowledged that McClaughry "has furnished time, brains, and money towards its adoption in prisons."[50]

In 1897 McClaughry went on a prison tour in Europe. He came back even more committed to the Bertillon system. The translation and publication of Alphonse Bertillon's writings on the subject was sponsored by the Major. McClaughry's reputation was increasingly identified with the Bertillon system; and he understood this. For example, in 1898, as discussions once again focused on parole, McClaughry pointed out how adoption of the Bertillon system would help:

> To this end there should be an immediate adoption in every prison, penitentiary, reformatory, workhouse, house of correction, and police department in the United States, of the most efficient system of identification in existence—I know you are ready to hear me add—"The Bertillon System."[51]

That same year, his son, C. C. McClaughry, who was a deputy warden of the Indiana State prison, joined his father:

> I recently examined the Bertillon case containing about fifteen thousand cards, I think, at Joliet, to get some idea of the migratory habits of criminals, and I discovered three hundred and sixty faces which I quite easily recognized. Most of them were men who had passed through the Chicago house of correction while I was assistant superintendent. I have been at Michigan City only about thirteen months, yet I found twenty men who had been or are now at Michigan City prison, and of these six are now before our Board as first offenders. In looking through this case I selected only such faces as I could readily recognize. With a little more time to study the features and names I have no doubt I could have discovered a great many more.[52]

Movement and acceptance of the Bertillon system remained slow. And the president of the wardens association believed it "strange and inexplicable that so important a measure should make progress so slowly." McClaughry, the assembled wardens were told, was willing to take on a central bureau headquartered at Joliet. "All he asks is proper cooperation and support, which has not been accorded him in the past."[53]

Although progress on adoption of the NPA by the wardens and the Bertillon system by those in the organization stalled, clearly McClaughry's tireless efforts and political skills were recognized. A paradigm shift was occurring. The academic/ philanthropist wing of the general organization was being slowly displaced. The warden, in number and influence, was increasing. McClaughry's elevation to the presidency of the NPA in 1899 marked that shift.

NOTES

1. Robert Ernst *Immigrant Life in New York City, 1825-1863* (New York: King's Crown Press, 1949), 202.
2. *National Prison Association, 1898*, p. 103.
3. See Michael Cassidy, *Warden Cassidy on Prisons and Convicts* (Philadelphia: Patterson & White, 1897).
4. *National Prison Association*, 1886, p. 319.
5. *Ibid.*, p. 14.
6. *Ibid.*, pp. 56, 57.
7. *Ibid.*, p. 76.
8. *Ibid.*, p. 73.
9. *Ibid.*, 1898, p. 87.
10. *Ibid.*, 1889, p. 95.
11. *Ibid.*, p. 103.

12. *Ibid.*, 1890, pp. 210-11.
13. *Ibid.*, 1886, pp. 142-43.
14. *Ibid.*, 1889, p. 314.
15. *Ibid.*, 1888, p. 138.
16. *Ibid.*, 1889, p. 106.
17. *Ibid.*, 1886, p. 73.
18. *Ibid.*, 1898, pp. 88-89, 99, 91.
19. *Ibid.*, 1890, pp. 85, 100-101.
20. *Ibid.*, 1897, pp. 268; 1898, p. 181.
21. *Ibid.*, 1894, p. 185.
22. *Ibid.*, 1897, pp. 270, 271.
23. *Ibid.*, 1898, pp. 198-99.
24. *Ibid.*, p. 90.
25. *Ibid.*, p. 93.
26. *Ibid.*, p. 314.
27. *Ibid.*, p. 96.
28. *Ibid.*, 1887, p. 122.
29. *Ibid.*, 1887, p. 110.
30. *Ibid.*, 1889, p. 8.
31. *Ibid.*
32. *Ibid.*, pp. 26-30.
33. *Ibid.*, p. 25.
34. *Ibid.*, p. 97.
35. *Ibid.*, pp. 78-79.
36. *Ibid.*, p. 159.
37. *Ibid.*, p. 80.
38. *Ibid.*, pp. 98-99.
39. *Ibid.*, 1898, pp. 62, 67.
40. *Ibid.*, 1887, pp. 105, 106-107.
41. *Ibid.*, 1889, pp. 75, 93-94.
42. *Ibid.*, 1887, pp. 108-109.
43. *Ibid.*, 1889, p. 9.
44. *Ibid.*, pp. 46, 47.
45. *Ibid.*, pp. 89, 90, 92.
46. *Ibid.*, 1890, p. 70.
47. *Ibid.*, p. 71.
48. *Ibid.*, p. 34.
49. *Ibid.*, 1892, pp. 104, 106.
50. *Ibid.*, 1889, p. 57.
51. *Ibid.*, 1898, p. 95.
52. *Ibid.*, p. 79.
53. *Ibid.*, pp. 84, 85.

Chapter Thirty

Ascendancy of the Wardens

"... that my life and services had not been given in vain."

Until McClaughry's appointment, Rutherford Hayes had held the presidency of the association. His status as a former governor of Ohio and ex-President of the United States plus his very aggressive work for various social causes bestowed upon him the mantle of presidency. After Hayes died in 1893, Roelliff Brinkerhoff, a man admitting to no practical or academic experience in penology, became president. He had been the superintendent of the Board of State Charities in Ohio.[1] His service as vice-president for ten years was the extent of his knowledge of penology.

Brinkerhoff felt the prestige of Rutherford Hayes was what secured the larger audiences at the meetings and more influence with the public and other politicians. At first he set out to find another former president, Benjamin Harrison, to follow Hayes, but to no avail. Forced to become president himself, Brinkerhoff held the position for four years.[2] The first meeting under his presidency, the one held in St. Paul, Minnesota, was poorly attended and he felt it was because of the lack of a prestigious person heading the organization.[3] The following years were no better.

At this point, hoping to revitalize the organization with the promise of more opportunities for leadership positions, the organization resolved to elect a president every year.[4] Brinkerhoff was followed by a legend in prison history, Zebulon Brockway, the chief proponent and earliest practitioner of the reformatory movement. His selection showed the success of the reformatory movement throughout the world of penology.

The fact that McClaughry was next, the first real warden of an adult prison to get that job, speaks volumes as to his political acumen and the shift in the organization's demographics. His presidency became a benchmark; thereafter, practicing wardens rather than academics would dominate the leadership positions of the NPA. McClaughry embodied that particularly valuable combination of successful practitioner who was at the same time an ideological reformer. But he was not a pure ideologue; he was a compromiser. Perhaps even more importantly, he was a public speaker.

Words—their eloquence or lack of eloquence, their arrangement, their references—are a glimpse into the soul of a person. McClaughry, intellectually or intuitively, understood this and took great care in his spoken and written language. His words and his Word were sacrosanct. He had always been a man of words going back to his college days when he had studied and taught classics. As a local celebrity in the prison towns in which he resided and in public forums such as the National Prison Association, he was in demand as a speaker. McClaughry found himself in a remarkable place when it came to language. He was an educated man (well schooled in old fashioned patrician ways) operating among people–prison wardens, guards and prisoners—who spoke a different English. Even the lowest of the low crafted their own language, in this case criminal slang. Like all occupations, the guards likewise had their own lingo, a mixture of the criminal cant, bureaucratese, and working-class references. The prison became a veritable tower of Babel.

With this background, it becomes easier to understand how much McClaughry's language contributed to his long and illustrious career. By the post-Civil War era it was believed that words were a reflection of one's character. It was easy to respect McClaughry in this "Gilded Era" as a good man because his language was that of a gentleman. Second, he bridged a growing chasm between religion and science. No one in the NPA was so ready to champion scientific theories and technologies as Robert McClaughry, but at every turn he sprinkled his speeches with religious references and rhetoric. More important, McClaughry represented a new linguistic development in America. Earlier, there had been two rhetorical styles: patrician and plebeian. Patrician language was educated and filled with philosophical and religious ideas and cadences. It identified its speakers as natural leaders. "Plebeian" described the language of the lower classes and increased with the flood of immigrants, particularly from Ireland, that occurred in the antebellum period. After the Civil War, a new style of speech emerged, called the middling rhetoric. It was a marriage between the erudite and the folksy. McClaughry, either by character or calculation, captured that ground. He astonished politicians, wardens, and prisoners by, on the one hand, seeming other-worldly and on the other hand, calculatingly blunt. No wonder he captured the leadership of the NPA.[5]

These elements could be seen in his presidential address. In keeping with his public character and speaking style, the speech was filled with Biblical allusions. The theme of his talk was "No man liveth to himself." The purpose of the National Prison Association was the improvement of the penal institutions and their management, he announced. He called for prison reform, but as a nod to his wardens he cautioned about too much sentimentality. Here was a message sent to those academic/philanthropic members who still remained, that the wardens had taken over the organization. Though the "kept" were important, McClaughry wanted to refocus the emphasis upon the "keepers." The penal system in general should be humane, giving inmates the opportunity for mental and moral improvement, he exhorted. "The right to punish crime does not involve the right to reduce prisoners to mental and moral imbecility," he warned the assembled members.[6]

> But prison reform also insists that you secure the protection of society and the promotion of virtue by the punishment of the criminal, only when you so administer his punishment that he is uplifted and reformed, instead of being degraded and brutalized by it.[7]

Standing before his audience, assuming the role of an Old Testament prophet, he called for society to fight vice and corruption in large and small cities alike. Better and more expansive laws were needed but were useless unless there was more rigorous law enforcement.[8]

Such utterances were not new; for years the more academic/charity members had urged such things—and were typically sloughed off as "soft hearted" by the wardens. But now, truly one of their own, a time-tested warden, had assumed the podium of leadership. What he had to say carried greater weight in the growing of a profession of practitioners than anyone's voice before him.

Certainly, when it came to issues relating to crime and punishment, McClaughry was a leading person in the reform movements of the late nineteenth and early twentieth century's. Though his major concern was prison management, the Major did use his presidency to speak out on policing, criminal law, and criminal investigation as well. There was one area on which he was strangely quiet, and that was capital punishment. Perhaps that silence points up some significant aspects of the death penalty in the nineteenth century and also the character of Robert McClaughry.

Some remarkable things were going on with the death penalty in the generation after the Civil War. A few spectacular executions marked the era. The Sioux uprising in Minnesota in 1862 led to the execution of thirty-eight Native Americans at the same time from the same gallows, the largest mass hanging in America. Five conspirators in the assassination of President Lincoln were hung together in July, 1865. A so-called war criminal, Henry Wirz, the warden of the Confederate POW prison in Georgia, was executed at the

Washington DC penitentiary. Of course, the assassins of Presidents Garfield and McKinley would be executed by the federal government. In 1890, in what might be called "the battle of the currents," Edison and Westinghouse used the newly invented electric chair as a means to push forward their notions of the appropriate current (AC or DC) for American households.[9] Westinghouse won the battle but the big loser was William Kemmler, the first person in America to die in the electric chair.

One reason for McClaughry's reticence about capital punishment was that it did not directly impact him. The national average of executions throughout the 1880s and 90s was 120 per year. Illinois executed only two people in 1890-1891.[10] Though commonplace to think that executions occurred in the state prison, this was not so in Illinois. From 1859 to 1928 all executions (all of them hangings) were done at the jail in the county in which the crime was committed.[11] This relieved McClaughry from any direct participation in the practice. Much was the same for federal executions as he moved into federal prison administration in the first decades of the twentieth century.

Yet federal executions jumped after the Civil War. After averaging eight per decade from 1790 to 1870, the numbers swelled to thirty-five in the 1870s, fifty-three in the 1880s, and forty-three in the 1890s. They dropped to three in the first decade of the twentieth century and two in the second.[12] These federal executions were generally done in the state in which the crime was committed and by the methods unique to that state. As the executions of the Lincoln assassins and Wirz indicate, sometimes the District of Columbus was used for federal executions. Even when he was warden of the federal prison in Leavenworth, Kansas, any executions would have been done in other states or in Kansas if the crime had been committed there. But even here the issue was off McClaughry's desk as Kansas abolished the death penalty in 1907.[13]

But there is a more subtle reason for McClaughry's silence, a reason that goes to the heart of one of this book's themes. Clearly, McClaughry was a very religious man. So were most of his fellow wardens in the NPA. Like the Puritans 250 years before, these profoundly religious men were "typologists," meaning that they looked to the Bible for guidance. Of the two scriptural resources one was clear and documented the other less so. The Old Testament with its ideological commitment to "an eye for an eye, and a tooth for a tooth" was filled with references to capital punishment. Genesis 9:6, Exodus 21:12-14, Leviticus 24:15-22, Numbers 35:29-33 and Deuteronomy 13:6-11, are just a few verses justifying capital punishment. By contrast, Matthew 5:38-45 and John 8:1-11 in the New Testament suggested an anti-capital punishment viewpoint. Like their puritan ancestors these late nineteenth-century pious punishers found justification for their positions in the Old rather than the New Testament.[14]

After 1899, when he took on a new position at the Leavenworth federal prison, McClaughry's activity with the National Prison Association decreased. On several occasions, due to the "press of work" or ill health, McClaughry failed to attend the annual meetings.[15] When there, he was acknowledged as "one of the old brethren," but made very few speeches.

In 1900, McClaughry faced some sad news. Both his longtime colleague, Joseph Nicholson, and his political opponent Michael J. Cassidy, died.[16] Even in Cassidy's memorial the political differences between the two men remained highlighted. Cassidy was a practical man demanding practical results, the eulogy stated:

> He recognized that the bottom fact, i.e. that a prison should be neither a school or asylum or church or club, but a place of punishment to be dreaded, while yet affording inducements for refection and repentance. His life and labors, though absolutely free from the sickly sentimentality which is a besetting evil of our times, have so effectively exhibited to the world the striking advantages of what is known as the "Separate System" of penal confinement, that he lived to see it adopted during his life time by substantially all civilized nations except portions of his native country.[17]

While old political allies and enemies were moving off stage, McClaughry tried to remain active on a variety of committees. For example, when he responded favorably to a report on prison laboratories in 1900, he was enthusiastically asked to serve on a committee with Zebulon Brockway and Professor C. R. Henderson of the University of Chicago.[18]

In some ways McClaughry could sit back and glory in his accomplishments. This was all the easier because of his son Charles C. McClaughry, who was by 1901 the warden of the Wisconsin State Prison at Waupun. After Charles read a report on prison discipline, one commentator noted that, "Perhaps the best thing to do now is to congratulate the father on the son and the son on the father. Mr. C. C. McClaughry is a chip off the old block."[19]

On occasion McClaughry senior was still called upon to talk. In 1903, because he was heading up a federal prison he spoke on the history of the "United States Penitentiaries."[20] The next year he slowly began to realize that his cherished crusade—acceptance of the Bertillon system—might have been misplaced. Fingerprints were challenging the Bertillon system, and McClaughry thought that fingerprinting should complement the Bertillon measurements. He liked to call the Bertillon system "mental photography," thus connecting it to police work. In other words, a study of the Bertillon card would fix in the mind of the officer the identity of a felon so that they could go to a group of people and pick out the person. And so, while he started fingerprinting at Leavenworth hoping it would become a central office for fingerprint data, he could not easily give up the Bertillon system, for so much of his practical and political career was invested in it. He wanted the Bertillon identification system in place and widely used so "that my life and services had not been given in vain."[21]

The presidency of the National Prison Association was a crowning achievement for McClaughry. It validated all the work he had done bringing the wardens and academics together. Reminiscing in 1905 about the "old days," he remembered the NPA in 1888 "to be very insignificant, or at least a very unimportant organization." More important to the theme of this chapter, it seemed that "those who attended were counted as cranks and fanatics by most of those present who had personal charge of prisons."[22] Largely due to the work of McClaughry, bridges between ideologues and practitioners had been built, and in the politics of penal professionalism the practitioners had captured the National Prison Association. He would not completely leave the NPA but the move to a federal prison consumed his energies. Not only was it a new level of politics, now he was a member of a federal bureaucracy, but it was in those heady days of reform called the Progressive Era.

NOTES

1. Brinkeroff said in 1892, "I am not a warden. I am not a prison chaplain. I have never been a prison officer, and I have no special qualifications as to what they ought to do, if to have such qualifications I am expected to have experience, because I have no experience." National Prisons Association, 1892, p. 48.

2. Brinkerhoff, pp. 325-26, 328.

3. *Ibid.*, p. 350.

4. National Prison Association, 1897, p. 16.

5. I am greatly indebted to Kenneth Cmiel's *Democratic Eloquence: The Fight Over Popular Speech in Nineteenth-Century America* (New York: William Morrow and Company, 1990).

6. *National Prison Association*, 1899, pp. 362, 363, 364.

7. *Ibid.*, p. 363.

8. *Ibid.*

9. See Richard Moran's *Executioner's Current: Thomas Edison, George Westinghouse, and the Invention of the Electric Chair* (New York: Random House, 2002).

10. *Chicago Tribune* January 1, 1892.

11. In 1928 the method of execution in Illinois went from hanging to electrocution, and the place from jails to prisons. Because of its size, Cook County (Chicago) still executed people up to 1961. See Jess Maghan, "Capital Punishment," *Encyclopedia*

of Chicago [eds. Janice Reife, Ann Durkin Keating, James Grossmen] Chicago: Historical Society, 2005. On line at http://www. Encyclopedia. Chicagohistory. org.

12. Information comes from the Death Penalty Information Center but was published in the *Chicago Tribune* June 11, 2001.

13. Paul W. Keve, *Prisons and the American Conscience: A History of U.S. Federal Corrections* (Carbondale, Illinois: Southern Illinois University Press, 1991), pp. 102, 188.

14. Scott L. Johnson, "The Bible and the Death Penalty: Implications for Criminal Justice Education," *Journal of Criminal Justice Education* Vol. 11, No 1, Spring 2000, pp. 15-33.

15. *National Prison Association*, 1902, p. 87.

16. *Ibid.*, 1900, p. 54.

17. *Ibid*, 1901, pp. 263-64.

18. *Ibid.*, 1900, p. 236.

19. *Ibid.*, 1901, pp. 173-82, 183.

20. *Ibid.*, 1903, pp. 78-84.

21. *Ibid.*, 1904, pp. 75, 77-78.

22. *Ibid.*, 1905, pp. 48.

Part Seven

MCCLAUGHRY AT LEAVENWORTH

Chapter Thirty-One

Rise of Federal Corrections

" . . . the national government should enact and control a penitentiary."

BEGINNINGS

Up until the late nineteenth century, America had little need for a federal penal system since most crimes were the responsibility of the state criminal justice agencies. Of course, there had been federal criminals before and in the previous one hundred years the response to them varied. During the Revolutionary War, George Washington petitioned the Continental Congress for means to dispose of loyalists suspected of treasonous activities. At first they were put in an abandoned copper mine at Simsbury, Connecticut. Some local jails were used too, as in the case of William Franklin, former governor of New Jersey colony (son of Benjamin Franklin) and noted loyalist, who was placed in an old jail at Litchfield, Connecticut.[1]

After the Revolution some federal prisoners were held in the Walnut Street Jail in Philadelphia. In fact, for a short time Congress took over the jail and appointed Robert Jewell—who signed his documents as "Keeper, United States Prison"—to administer it until 1781. In 1789, when the Constitution replaced the Articles of Confederation and the national government was reorganized, it became the duty of U.S. Marshals to find places for the small number of federal criminals. Because the Walnut Street Jail in Philadelphia accepted federal prisoners as long as the national government paid them to do so, twenty conspirators in the Whiskey Rebellion were placed in the Walnut Street lockup. When the Eastern State Penitentiary was opened in Philadelphia in 1829, it accommodated two "desperate villains" who had been arrested by federal marshals.[2]

During the pre-Civil War period the number of federal prisoners remained small. In 1846 the government asked its thirty U.S. Marshals to report on how many federal convicts there actually were. Fifteen marshals reported they had no federal criminals under their care, and the remainder listed forty eight inmates distributed among the Auburn State prison in New York, the Albany County Penitentiary in New York, Eastern State Penitentiary in Philadelphia, and the Georgia State Penitentiary in Milledgeville.[3]

After the Civil War the number of federal inmates increased sharply. Most were put into state prisons. When California became a state and built its major prison at San Quentin, it took many western outlaws under federal conviction from California, Alaska, Washington, Oregon, and Arizona. In the years between 1865 and 1889, 162 federal prisoners resided in San Quentin. District of Columbia prisoners found themselves in the West Virginia Penitentiary at Moundsville. For a fee, other states accepted federal prisoners too; Joliet under the regime of McClaughry did so, for example.[4]

One of the earliest voices for a federal prison system was Enoch Cobb Wines, founder of the National Prison Association. In his 1867 classic, *The State of Prisons and Child Saving Institutions in the Civilized World,* Wines complained about the difficulty of enforcing decent standards for federal prisoners. The federal government, he wrote, "has no control, no voice, no influence over the discipline of the prisons to which they [federal prisoners] have been committed."[5]

By the 1880s large numbers of governmental officials and private citizens began to advocate for a separate federal prison system. In the South, George Washington Cable started to investigate and report on the horrid conditions of the Louisiana labor camps. A speech to the National Prison Association, in 1883, was so convincing that Cable was immediately elected vice president of that organization. Cable's revelations convinced the national government not to use southern prisons any more thus adding to the burden of northern lockups.[6]

This problem soon became a theme of a popular book. John Reynolds, a businessman convicted of mail fraud, served sixteen months in the Kansas State Penitentiary in Lansing, Kansas.[7] He was a federal prisoner in that state prison, one of nearly a dozen ranging from businessmen to horse stealing Indians. He was treated as if he were an ordinary prisoner. In some instances he was even treated worse, he felt. Upon arrival Reynolds was given second-hand clothes, the striped uniform of a recently deceased black man. Given the social outlook of those days, this was considered a supreme insult. For the first six months he dug coal in trenches and caverns eight hundred feet below the surface of the ground in unspeakable conditions. The largest number of patients in the prison hospital came out of the coal mines. Most of inmates "down in the valley," the name given to the prison cemetery on Peckerwood Hill, were fatalities from coal mining accidents. Eventually, he was put to work as a clerk in the institution. With access to writing materials he began secretly transcribing in short hand an account of his experiences. Also, while in prison he ran and was elected to the state senate, quite a statement on nineteenth-century politics. When he left the prison he visited the Missouri State Penitentiary and the result was a modestly successfully book called *The Twin Hells.* Aside from the description of ordinary prison life one could not help but see that the state was in complete control of this federal prisoner. Although *The Twin Hells* was meant to describe the penitentiaries of Kansas and Missouri, Reynolds was in his own twin hell, a federal prisoner being treated as a state inmate.[8]

Roeliff Brinkerhoff–banker, philanthropist, and long time activist in the National Prison Association throughout the 1880s and 1890s–was also a proponent of a federal prison system. As the right-hand man of the association's long-term president, former U.S. President Rutherford Hayes, in 1885 Brinkerhoff pressured the government to reveal the number of federal prisoners incarcerated in American state prisons. After a lot of probing and fighting bureaucratic resistance in Washington, he discovered there were 1,027 federal criminals incarcerated in state prisons and another 10,000 in county jails. Ten years later there were 2,516 in state prisons and 15,000 in jails.[9] Of course, there were some territorial prisons controlled by Federal Marshals until those areas became states. Utah's territorial prison was filled with many polygamist leaders of the Mormon Church, for example. Montana, Wyoming, Idaho, Oklahoma, Arizona, and New Mexico had small and inadequate lock-ups for some prisoners but most were simply sent east.[10] In 1887 Brinkerhoff gave the closing address to the National Prison Association meetings and called for greater attention to be given to federal prisoners. "There is now substantial unanimity of conviction that they should be cared for in federal prisons, in the charge of federal officials," he claimed. "For a government like ours to convict its citizens of violations of its laws, and then turn them over to the tender mercies of officials over whom it has no control and in whose appointment it has no voice, is a shame and a disgrace which ought to be corrected, and that most speedily." When Hayes died in 1893, Brinkerhoff assumed the presidency and put the federal prison system high on his agenda.[11]

Very early and with McClaughry's help, the National Prison Association, advocated the establishment of a federal prison system.[12] They had a vested interest. Though housing a few federal prisoners brought in some money, it was administratively more trouble than it was worth. Besides, these penologists in the last fifth of the nineteenth century were empire builders filled with self importance. They had created a reformatory movement, brought new administrative changes to the adult prisons, introduced a scientific means to identify criminals, established a viable professional organization in the NPA, and maintained considerable influence in Washington. In short, they were seeking to extend their predominance over the criminal justice system. The penologists were way ahead of the police and even the legal professions when it came to carving out a place in what today is called criminal justice. High on the agenda of the NPA was the establishment of a federal prison system.

President Grover Cleveland appointed A.H. Garland, a politician from Arkansas, to the position of Attorney General in 1885. Garland set out to educate Congress about the problems of federal prisoners in state prison systems. Costs in transportation and housing of prisoners had tripled in the past twenty-five years, he declared. Garland's first approach was to economize. He began to limit expenditures and require greater accountability by federal marshals. Local officials retaliated–especially in those states (Ohio, Michigan, and New York) with the largest number of federal inmates–declaring that they would receive federal inmates only on their terms. Garland then went to Congress and declared that "the national government should enact and control a penitentiary in which to confine its own prisoners. It would be better both for society and the prisoners themselves."[13] As the federal government dithered, several state legislatures passed laws saying that federal criminals who committed their crimes outside of their states would not be allowed in their state prisons.[14] Pressures from the states and the National Prison Association compelled the Congress to take action. Even though Cleveland was defeated in 1888, the new Republican administration continued to press for a law establishing a federal prison system.

With the help of Congressman Samuel Barrows a law finally passed in 1891 allowing for the purchase of three sites for federal prisons. Since no funds were allocated, things moved slowly until 1894 when a military lockup at Fort Leavenworth, Kansas, was converted into a civil prison. Two others, one in Atlanta in the South and the other at McNeil Island in the Northwest, were established as well. Administratively, Leavenworth was transferred from the War Department to the Justice Department, and this also meant that the 517 military inmates had to be relocated. News spread throughout the prison population of widespread commutations. In the first week of June 1895, forty prisoners were pardoned. Shortly after that another one hundred—mostly convicted of desertion—were released. Each man was given a cheap suit and five dollars and sent on his way exhorting support for the Secretary of War's run for president.[15] By June 28th, 1884 for the first time since 1873, no prisoners were held in confinement at Leavenworth. Of course, the stockade would not remain empty long. Of the 2,500 federal inmates housed in state prisons five hundred were quickly transferred. The rest would be moved to the new facility in the near future.

Recently re-elected president, Grover Cleveland, appointed J. W. French from the Michigan City prison in Indiana to be warden at Leavenworth and in charge of its five hundred prisoners. Apparently, there was talk of simply converting the old military stockade into the federal prison. French was adamant that making a model prison out of the old facility was impossible.[16] For example, after the switch, inmates quickly became idle because when Fort Leavenworth had been vacated as a military prison, all of the industries—the boot, furniture, broom, tin ware, and wagon shops—were closed. In addition, state laws emerged abolishing contract labor. The educational program was cancelled due to the lack of guards to watch over the school. By 1896, French announced to the NPA that his prison was "one of the weakest and poorest in the country."[17] That same year Congress caved and authorized the construction of a new federal prison not far from the old stockade.

LEAVENWORTH: THE FRENCH ERA

James W. French, a native of Indiana, graduated in 1874 from the Indiana State Normal School in Terra Haute and taught for a short time before studying law. After being prosecutor of Posey County, Indiana, he moved to the Indiana House of Representatives in 1885. Three years later he was elected to the state senate. Like many wardens he had established a political career and influence upon which to draw. From 1889 to 1891 he was the director of the Indiana State Prison at Michigan City, and then President Grover Cleveland tapped him to be the first warden of Leavenworth. Actually, given the state of the prison, he was more of a construction boss than warden.

Although mandated in 1895, Congress failed to allocate money for the necessary construction and it was put off for two years. Construction began in March 1897. To save money all work was done by prisoners housed in the "old military prison" turned over to the Department of Justice in 1895. With the construction site three miles away, prisoner-workers had to leave the old stockade every morning at 6 am and march to the work zone. The first construction team consisted of three hundred workers. The construction site was surrounded by twelve foot high boarded stockade nearly one mile in length with guards posted at short intervals. Within the wooden walled enclosure, prisoners made brick, broke rock, dug trenches, and built the prison up around themselves. A trench 35 feet deep was excavated and the outer wall was the entire depth to prevent escapes. The wall then was constructed 35 feet high and 4 feet thick. Former soldiers armed with high-powered rifles manned towers that were located at regular intervals along this wall. Guards down on the construction site were only allowed clubs in fear that inmates might overpower the guard and take their guns. After twelve to fourteen hours of labor the prison workers marched three miles back to the old facility exhausted and worn.[18]

Food was scanty and of poor quality. This was largely due to parsimonious Congresses and the corruption of local officials. Illness became epidemic. Cold winters brought meningitis and pneumonia, and with summer came malaria. In 1899, smallpox stopped construction for weeks. Indians from the west and blacks from the south were hit particularly hard.[19]

In spite of long, hard hours of work, French almost immediately fell behind construction schedules. For the delays he blamed the long march to the work site, the large number of unskilled workers, and the half hour daily compulsory close order drills mandated from Washington.

French, a member of the reformatory movement that had taken over the National Prison Association, knew and came under the influence of McClaughry on numerous occasions. Reform of prisoners through special rehabilitative programs was particularly attractive to the new warden. But the intense construction phase stalled any rehabilitative programs. When plans for Leavenworth were unveiled, French declared that, "The reformatory idea in prison management will be given free scope." Later to local newspapers he would continue that, "A man may do in this prison what, as boy and man, he failed to do outside—acquire the rudiments of an education, gain willpower and courage to do right, learn a trade, and leave the prison a reformed and useful citizen."[20] The prison should be only for first time offenders, he argued, and an emphasis placed upon the moral, physical, and educational development of the prisoners.[21] Implementing his own reward system for good behavior, French allowed the inmates to grow mustaches. In addition, he gave each prisoner a muslin pillow stuffed with straw and a quarter-pound plug of chewing tobacco. Orders for lights out were loosened and moved from 8 to 9pm.[22] Special training in brick making and other construction skills were given before construction began. Not only would this expedite the building process but inmates would get skills they could be use when freed, French felt.

In spite of all these provisions, French—as McClaughry after him—seriously miscalculated the type of prisoners coming to Leavenworth. French understood that most would come out of the west but he wrongly considered that these frontier men would be easier to reclaim. Easterners make a choice to be criminals, he thought, but frontier men were victims of the lax social conditions of frontier environments.[23] Almost immediately the prisoners proved French wrong.

Most of the five hundred prisoners were from the Indian Territory and were not accustomed to the regimented life style of prison. Take, for example, the very first prisoner: John Grindstone. Grindstone represented the group of more recalcitrant prisoners that would plague prison officials throughout its early history. An Eastern Shawnee, he had already served a ten- year sentence for murder in the Indian Territory. However, upon his release he murdered again and was incarcerated once more. He would spend the rest of his life in Leavenworth causing all kinds of behavioral problems. He would die of tuberculosis in the institution. Or take George East, a cowboy who had stolen a horse and gotten a three-year sentence. Time weighed heavily on this open range cowboy and he became troublesome. One day he simply walked away from the construction site. When ordered to stop he began to run. Guards shot him down with shotguns.[24] This was the first, but not the last, case of prisoner "suicide by guard" at Leavenworth.

With such rebellious recidivists discipline became a critical issue. Disciplinary actions were constantly necessary and French was forced to answer often to federal officials in Washington. At the close of each day guards turned in slips of paper to the warden "writing up" or citing individual prisoners for misbehavior. Minor infractions led to the prisoner being admonished by the warden. If the misdemeanor were more serious, the prisoner was ordered to "carry the baby" a 25 to 30-pound cannonball chained to his leg. It had to be lifted and carried in order for the prisoner to move about. Later, as the structure of punishment began to take final form, the more rebellious were put in the "dark cell" or solitary confinement.

Then in June 1898, seventeen prisoners led by a Badlands outlaw, William Pierce, broke out causing an administrative crisis. Of course, escapes had been common in prison circles since their invention. As early as 1815 Massachusetts prison personnel were told to "think of the prison as a volcano filled with burning lava, which, if not restrained, would destroy both friends and foes."[25] Individual escapes could be expected and were accepted as not being a threat to the ideology of reform. Reformers had to believe in the innate goodness of humanity; these prisoners—with the manipulation of their physical and social environment—could be redeemed. One or two who fell between the cracks could be written off as irredeemable. But a massive breakout/riot was more ominous for it signified a breakdown of the entire ideology and the system implementing it. And very shortly after the invention of the penitentiary, riots did occur. Major riots happened in January 1859, in the Auburn penitentiary, and at the Ludlow Street jail in April 1895.[26] Such activity was perplexing to the reformatory ideologues. Now the newly developing federal system was confronted with its first prison riot.

In the process of the Pierce-led breakout, a guard named James Musgrove was killed. All prisoners were recaptured shortly, except for Pierce who was not apprehended until a 1903 Wyoming post office robbery. French not only had to answer for the disciplinary problems but now this escape blemished his short-lived administration. The besieged warden claimed he had to watch over as many prisoners as had been there under the old military rule but with less than half the personnel to do so. Furthermore, whereas earlier all offenders were confined to one place, now they were scattered over three miles marching and doing construction, he lamented. Also, before the prisoners were being punished for minor offenses, French claimed. Now, apparently reversing earlier views of the basic innocence of the westerner, the more vicious characters from the Wild West were placed under his care.[27] A federal investigation found that the problems were great and would even get worse. "We could not avoid feeling," read the report, "that the confidence apparently reposed in the convicts by the warden might someday result in disaster."[28]

Perhaps the gravest problem facing French in these formative days of the federal prison was his own personnel. Obviously their numbers had decreased causing considerable stress on the system. For example, the number of guards slipped from 125 during the military garrison days to forty-eight. More important, the morale of the guards had plummeted, and for good reasons. Guards wore a dark blue uniform, probably reminiscent of the old military costume so common in the fort earlier, and each had to pay for his garb out of the $70 monthly salary. In addition, a report by the Justice Department revealed that many of the older guards felt that their reports of prisoner misconduct went unheeded by the warden. "The word of the prisoner [was] as good as theirs, and sometimes better," they felt.[29] In fact, French had blamed two guards for the successful prisoner escape, so it was small wonder guards felt the warden was so busy protecting himself that he did not have the best interests of the personnel at heart.

Guards furthermore resented some of their assignments. Guard duty was arranged around a rotation system of the day watch, night watch, box guard, and line men. Line men marched prisoners to the new construction site. They would rotate such duties every four months causing much readjustment time and familial difficulties. But most complaints came about the "special duty" detail. These personnel guarded the store rooms, laundry, armory, the yard, farm, and the gate. Special duty people had permanent schedules; the regular guards understandably felt those special guards should be part of the rotation system too. Living arrangements caused considerable dissatisfaction as well. Some received free quarters while others were forced to provide their own. Finally, all the guards hated the dreaded "Saturday Afternoon Inspection" at which attendance was required. For those who lived off the grounds or had worked the previous night duty this was particularly loathsome.[30] Taken as a whole, such problems in Kansas and doubts in Washington led to French's leaving in 1899; the replacement made by a Republican President, William McKinley, was Robert McClaughry.

NOTES

1. Paul W. Keve, "At the Mercy of the States," in *Escaping Prison Myths: Selected Topics in the History of Federal Corrections*, John W. Roberts [ed.] (Washington DC: The American University Press, 1994) p. 25.
2. *Ibid.*, p. 26.
3. *Ibid.*, p. 27.
4. *Ibid.*
5. *Ibid.*
6. *Ibid.*, p. 29.
7. Apparently this was a particularly bad place and was written up later by one of its inmates, Carl Arnold, in *One Kansas Inferno* and can be found at the Center for Historical Research, Kansas History Center, Topeka, Kansas.
8. John N. Reynolds, *The Twin Hells, A Thrilling Narrative of Life in the Kansas and Missouri Penitentiaries* (Chicago: Donohue Brothers, 1890), pp. 13, 25, 44-89.
9. Blake McKelvey, *American Prisons: A History of Good Intentions* (Patterson NJ: Patterson Smith, 1977) pp. 194.
10. *Ibid.*, pp. 228-33.
11. Keve, pp. 29-30.
12. For example see *National Prison Associations Proceedings,* 1886 pp. 96, 110; and 1889, p. 70, 74.
13. Homer Cummings and Carl McFarland, *Federal Justice* (New York: MacMillan Company, 1937), pp. 353, 355-56. Also see National Prison Association Proceedings, 1895, p. 184.
14. *Ibid.*, pp. 356-58.
15. *New York Times,* June 6 and 7, 1895.
16. *National Prison Associations Proceedings*, 1895, p. 185.
17. *Ibid.*, 1896, p. 81.
18. Joe Jackson, *Leavenworth Train: A Fugitive's Search for Justice in the Vanishing West* (Carroll & Graf Publishers: New York, 2001), p. 7.
19. *Ibid.*, pp. 6-7.
20. *Leavenworth Times,* March 21, 1897.
21. *New York Times*, February 4, 1897.
22. Jackson, p. 5.
23. *Ibid.*
24. *Ibid.*, p. 7.
25. Robert Adams, *Prison Riots in Britain and the USA* (MacMillan: London, 1994), p. 55.
26. *Ibid.*

27. *Kansas City Times,* June 2, 1898.

28. General Agent of the Department of Justice to Attorney General, August 18, 1898, in the Department of Justice Central Files 1891+ Box 552 National Archives, Washington D.C.

29. *Ibid.*

30. *Ibid.* Also letter from James W. French to Attorney General John Griggs June 5, 1898, Department of Justice Central Files, Box 553, National Archives, Washington D.C.

McClaughry and prison staff at Leavenworth.

United States Penitentiary, Leavenworth, Kansas.

Warden's Residence.

Cells.

Record Clerk's Office.

Shoe factory.

Tailor shop.

Dining Hall.

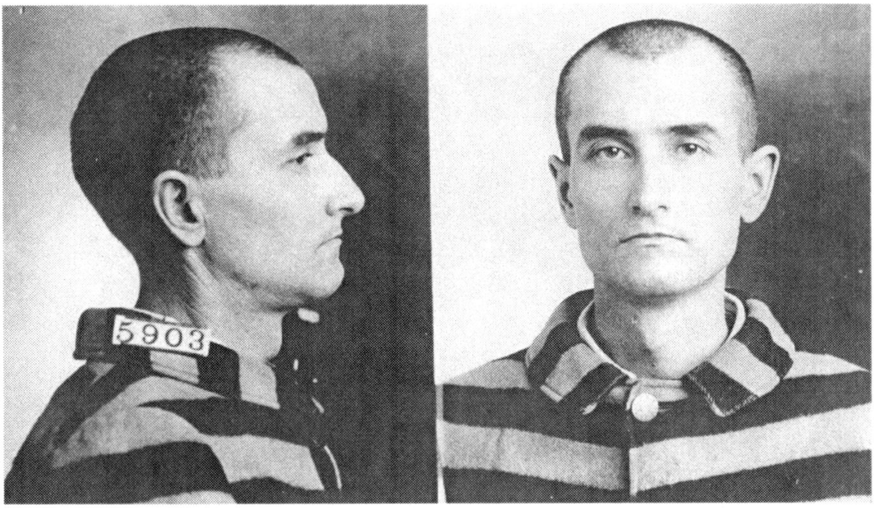

Tom Kating.

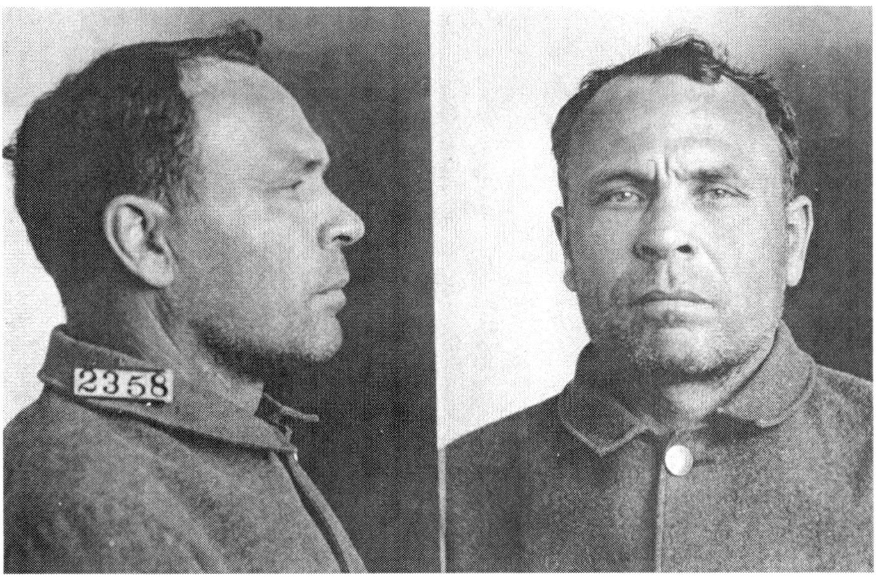

Julius McDonough.

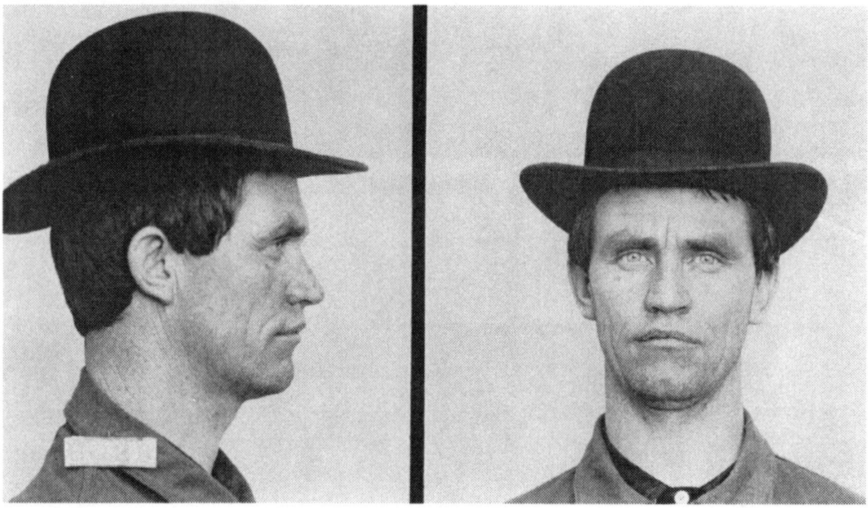

Allison Poe.

Chapter Thirty-Two

McClaughry Comes to Leavenworth

" . . . beneath the grim exterior . . . beats one of the warmest and kindest of hearts."

McClaughry assumed the Leavenworth wardenship in August 1899 and would hold it until June 1913. Many of the formative developments in the federal prison system–for good and ill–came while McClaughry was warden. Immediately, he was confronted with several challenges. First, there was the building up of the institution and the procedures that would make it work. Besides basic construction this also meant implementing some of his reformatory ideas, chief of which was the Bertillon system of identification.

Second, the inmate population presented all kinds of problems testing his administrative skills and reformist zeal. Not only were there some "mutinies"—the word used for massive breakouts—but individual testy inmates required special attention. In addition, McClaughry's career cause, the Bertillon system of identification was challenged with the Will/William West incident.

Third, the guards themselves needed to be courted and controlled. Immediate administrative personnel continued to be a problem. Being intensely loyal to his people frequently got McClaughry in trouble when assistants and guards betrayed his trust. In so many ways McClaughry and guards were from different worlds, and so this latter-day puritan struggled in the various Babylons to which his career took him.

Fourth, society in general and social critics in particular–working as investigative reporters and called "muckrakers"— took aim at McClaughry and Leavenworth and pressured for his resignation. This nineteenth century progressive all of a sudden seemed out of place in the Progressive Era.

Fifth, bureaucrats in Washington and the military just down the road in the stockade constantly tested McClaughry's resolve. The Progressive era ushered in a more "regulatory" society and layers of federal bureaucrats checked and rechecked the activities on the plains of Kansas.

Last, McClaughry's physical strength deteriorated badly as he aged. While revered and respected as a pioneer, in the fast-paced times of the early twentieth century he seemed less relevant. This was all the more ironic since he had laid the foundation for so much future policy in criminal justice. All the battles he fought seemed to have been won. But there was a toll. Never in the most robust health, all of these years in prison environments would have worn an even younger man, and now, well into his 60s, McClaughry's energy and health began to lag. This, at a time, when the taxing activity of construction continued.

BUILDING THE PRISON

At Leavenworth, McClaughry arrived at a work in progress. Immediately, he was immersed in the details of building and furnishing the place. This was not new to him. His activities in the Pennsylvania reformatory had been much the same. Being one of the earliest wardens at the Illinois Reformatory at Pontiac put him in that position as well. One of his great skills was the marshaling of men and material in building up new institutions. To be sure, the building of the physical plant at Leavenworth was still under way and would continue for several more years, but administrative procedures, relationships with personnel, appropriate discipline with the inmates, and politics with the local media were also still being forged. Against the backdrop of a recalcitrant inmate population and a suspicious guard culture, this challenged McClaughry more than any other previous post with the possible exception of being head of the Chicago police.

The architecture of Leavenworth—both its outside appearance and inside layout—belies any rehabilitative rhetoric by reformers like French and McClaughry. The prison stood out on the prairies of Kansas as a medieval fortification. Before the walls were completed, the site was surrounded by a fifteen foot wire fence. Signs were posted all around warning "Halt! Do not trespass upon this reservation. You may be shot for an escaping convict."[1] By January 1901, the foundations of two small cell houses were finished. These were called C and D houses. Under the D house there would eventually be a basement known as the E cell house. As punishment those who did not make their beds or sweep their floors would occupy E. The size of the cells was 4 feet 8 inches wide by 9 feet 6 inches deep. On the lower tiers, the cells were 8 feet

9 inches high. On the upper tiers the cells were 7 feet 5 inches high.[2] Another block of cells, called I house, was to be up over the deputy wardens office and it would be for the growing number of bankers.[3] Separated from the regular prison population, these prisoners were pointed to as a form of favoritism by the administration. Such accusations were probably true. But these bankers were not violent men and this was some form of early "protective custody."

As head of construction, McClaughry was held strictly accountable for the purchase and choice of materials, and also voiced his opinion on building plans based on his prison experience. That process went like this: a superintendent of construction would make a request to McClaughry as goods were needed. McClaughry would confer with the architect then circulate an advertisement for bids. After the bids came in McClaughry–with the advice of the architect–would select the provider.[4] Considerable discussion was, for example, generated over water closets, or interior toilets,[5] as well as about what types of flooring and lighting should be used and where. McClaughry could be adamant on certain aspects of construction and layout, but was so because of his practical knowledge of the inmate population. For example, he changed the dining room plans, advocating for many aisles because "with such a large body of men, it is desirable to reach a man quickly in cases of trouble. This can be done where four sit at a table; the disturber can be yanked out of his seat without disturbing so many men." He went on to say:

> One of the dangerous points in a prison is the dining room, where men can quarrel and knife each other with less danger of detection, when it is difficult to get at the men from the aisles as is the case when the seats are long.[6]

It was 1906 before construction was finally completed, and the long arduous march to and from the military stockade ended. The finished prison was a monument to penology at the turn of the century, as were the other thirty-one prisons and seven reformatories built between 1900 and 1925. These prisons were the crowning achievement of reformers like French and McClaughry. Though to some extent their architecture reflected the new thinking in adult incarceration, the basic look of these new prisons flew in the face of reform. Alfred Hopkins, a New York City architect, told the American Prison Association (the old National Prison Association had changed its name) in 1916 that good architecture had buildings looking like their purpose. "If our penology demands that the spirit of the offender be crushed beneath ponderous walls and prison barred windows, then the old system of design should prevail. On the other hand, if we want to reform them then the old design should go."[7]

The look of a prison, both the exterior for ordinary citizens and the interior for the inmates, was a crucial matter. The completing of Leavenworth coincided with the boom in popularity of the picture postcard. Towns with prisons peppered the nation with these souvenir images. And only a casual examination of the countless images being produced suggested the importance of architecture.[8] The outsides, looking like medieval fortresses in pastoral settings, were all the more ominous because of the apparent tranquility of the countryside. These prisons were to send messages to potential criminals that a horrible place awaited them; the prisons themselves were to be physical deterrents. Inside, however, the place was less concerned with messages and more concerned with custodial convenience. Even McClaughry bemoaned this as early as 1886. Speaking of Joliet he lamented that "our prison was built on the old plan of ornamenting the outside and leaving the inside rather inconvenient."[9] But what did he mean by "inconvenient?" Another model of the prison reflected the mind set of those in power in the Progressive Era: the factory model. So it was not long before images of factories or shops combined with the internal images of cage-like cells and group marches. Now not only were the inmates to be inconvenienced and intimidated: they were also to be exploited in a capitalist system, as economic slaves.[10]

By 1909 a giant domed rotunda dominated the landscape of Leavenworth. Two small cell houses radiated from the back of the rotunda. The main cell houses—the east and west houses—were near completion by 1909. The power plant, school, shops, kitchen, bakery, laundry, and hospital were completed or nearly so. Soon there would be an electrical shop, an ice-making plant, steel and tin shops, a brick plant, a stone shop, a broom factory, and a shoe making shop. Leavenworth began to look like a "company town." That "town" included a chapel that could seat twelve hundred men, decorated with a large mural of Jesus, along with the houses of the warden, deputy warden, and chief clerk on the grounds just a short walk from the administrative offices.

Supplies and inmates arrived by train. Track had been laid from the main line right to the prison through the west gate. Factories inside the prison wall were on each side of the tracks so that raw supplies and materials could be easily unloaded. When new inmates, the "fresh fish," arrived the tracks were lined with two groups. Prison personnel were there to escort and introduce the new arrivals to the prison bureaucracy. But also inmates rushed to intimidate and initiate the new people into their prison culture. Such comings and goings would continue for years until the trains were deemed a security breech no longer to be tolerated.[11]

Besides the main prison and the factory facilities, Leavenworth boasted a prison farm. This extended three hundred yards to the north, east, and west sides of the prison, and had a farm house, green house, hog barn, chicken ranch, and cow barn. Apples, beets, beans, cherries, cabbages, cucumbers, corn, lettuce, onions, peas, potatoes, pumpkins, peaches, radishes, squash, tomatoes, turnips, and watermelons were grown by and fed to the inmates.

The farm produced 15,340 pounds of beef, 19,000 pounds of pork, 8000 gallons of milk and 6000 eggs in most years. In fiscal year 1909-10, McClaughry spent $1,760 on running a farm that produced $15, 897 of food, and this way he was able to keep the daily food costs to an astonishingly low 11.2 cents per man. That pleased the politicians in Washington because Leavenworth had cost $1.5 million to build with another $700,000 needed to finish the job. For a parsimonious Congress that was a considerable sum, one roughly equivalent to $43 million in contemporary dollars.[12]

With so much of the food coming from the prison farm, there were inevitably periods of abundance and scarcity depending upon the season and yield. During roasting-ear time the prisoners' tables were piled high with corn. One prisoner joked over dinner that, "If they don't stop that corn racket, we will all soon be braying like mules." Guards heard the joke and laughter and after chuckling themselves wrote-up the prisoner.[13] However, some prisoners felt the food to be inadequate. One inmate wrote to the President of the United States in 1913 and complained:

> The food was something awful for any human being to try to live on, there was not enough in quanity [sic.] but a big waste, but the quality was such that many of us forced just enough to keep alive. The dried fruit and vegatables [sic.] and cereals were often wormy and rotten, the meat when served was prepared in such away that very little of it was fit to eat. Some of the meals were composed of scraps that had been saved so long that it was nothing less than filth, two or three times a week beans were served for dinner seasoned with chunks of hog gowls [sic.], this meat was so rotten as to have a peculiarly offensive odor besides being only partially cleaned tufts of hair still adhering to the meat which became loosened while cooking and stirring and here you might behold the spectacle of 1,000 men stirring their beans and picking out the hair before eating, the noon meal served at [the] new prison site was prepared at and hauled in wagons from the old prison. The appropriation I believe was all used, and the books I understand show that a good grade of foodstuffs was purchased but as so much of it was rotten I presume they were practicing the same system that Warden McClaughry was practicing at Joliet Ill. i.e. the rebate system, they paid for good foodstuffs, received the worst on the market, and quietly pocketed the difference.[14]

If such inmate complaints are correct, this could be part of the reason that inmate health became a major issue.

Illness in the prison (and there was a lot of it) impacted the pace of construction. In the name of construction and humanity the need for hospitals, better sanitation and ventilation, nutritious food supplies, and more adequate water sources became crucial. Almost immediately upon McClaughry's assumption of duties, a measles epidemic hit the institution. Fifty prisoners became infected. For a man had who left his previous post at Joliet because of his suspected part in poor prisoner health, this must have been unsettling. Disease had always been a problem in state prisons. By the 1890s the death rate of 28 northern prisons was 14.9 per thousand. Southern prisons were worse off with a rate of 41.3 per thousand.[15] In spite of being in such a bucolic environment of eastern Kansas, disease and death plagued McClaughry and his prisons. Of course, prisoners used "health problems" as part of the "con game." For example, of the 15,107 sick calls at Leavenworth in 1907, 351 were true and serious enough to warrant excuse from other prison duties for an extended period of time. Another 1,696 requests resulted in a prisoner being relieved just for the day. However, 12,987 received no treatment at all and were sent back to work.[16]

It was tuberculosis that would continually attack the prison, particularly among the Native American and black populations.[17] In fact, health and sanitation became a major challenge facing the new warden. In 1902, eighteen prisoners died in the facility, most of them of TB. Two years later, 49 died of that disease and McClaughry asked Washington permission to build a hospital.[18] Even eight years later this scourge still persisted, with forty prisoners dying in 1912 near the end of McClaughry's tenure.[19]

In part, disease was due to the lack of sanitary conditions; even though this was a new facility initially there was no toilet; each cell had a "night bucket" and a cuspidor. Prisoners were not much better off than their keepers in this regard. As early as 1875, while he was still warden at Joliet, the dean of the Illinois Medical Association diagnosed McClaughry with tuberculosis and gave him five years to live[20]—though in fact he lived for forty-five more. In 1910 there were five cases of typhoid fever, two people dying from the disease. McClaughry believed the source of the prison's health problems was the impure river water the prison used because the city of Leavenworth charged too much for water. Yet sewage from Atchison and St Joseph was dumped in this river causing all kinds of pollutants, so McClaughry pressured Washington unsuccessfully to construct a water filter plant.[21] As an experiment McClaughry sunk a well on the farm portion of the prison grounds in response. "The wise acres around this place insisted that we would get no water," he maintained. The well went down sixty feet and water did come in and rose to the thirty-four foot mark. It would not be used for humans but for livestock and irrigation. He crowed that it did not cost the government anything and wanted to sink several more.[22] Though Washington was slow on the well project, McClaughry finally won appropriations for a hospital in 1910. He wanted a three storied structure so that the consumptive patients could be on the third floor, look out at the countryside, and catch a breath good air.[23] By fall of 1911 the building was completed and it quickly housed thirty inmates as patients in its eighty rooms.[24]

McClaughry was at his best as a manager of construction. The physical plant—the home of prisoners and prison workers alike—needed to be effective and efficient. Going back to his days as a Civil War officer and post war businessman McClaughry was a master at marshalling resources and men on construction projects. Besides being a progressive builder he still sought to reform the inmate.

REFORMS

In keeping with his personal and professional ethos McClaughry arrived at Leavenworth a reformer. Admittedly reforms came very slowly; McClaughry now was part of a large and distant bureaucracy. Other forces were at work stymieing reform efforts. Besides resistance from the federal bureaucracy, the guard's culture, and the inmates, the public had different views on the possibility of inmate reform. Many simply tilted towards "nature" as opposed to "nurture" as the explanation for criminality in America. Nonetheless, McClaughry began his tenure with reform idealism. As a founding member of the reformatory forces in penology he was an ideologue but years as a warden in the toughest environments in the United States made him practical too. His reforms were always a mix: some were prisoner oriented—how to make the inmate reform— and others were custodial in nature—how to make the prisoner compliant and the prison organization more effective. These were not necessarily mutually exclusive. For the inmate to be a productive citizen in a capitalist wage-earning society, McClaughry felt the inmate must also be cooperative, work hard, be thrifty and self-controlled. The more radical socialist reformers, as we shall see, would think of McClaughry as a lackey of capitalism. They were right. McClaughry was a bureaucrat, a politician, and a capitalist. But these qualities did not mean he was not a reformer, as well. He was a latter day Puritan.

One reform had to do with visitors. Going back to the earliest days of the penitentiary movement, prisons were tourist attractions. Watch dog groups of charity workers hounded prisons to ensure humane treatment. Ordinary folks came as well. "Nine-tenths of the visiting is done out of mere curiosity by persons on vacation, automobile excursions, and similar excursions," he announced. Leavenworth had become a "horrible example" for many local mothers and ladies' groups who brought their children to scare them straight. On June 24, 1910, for example, over one hundred people visited the prison breaking all previous records for a single day's tourism. On most occasions fees were charged to help defray costs and fill the coffers kept deliberately low by thrifty legislatures. The hot Kansas summers, when most tourists came, put an extra burden on custodial staff. McClaughry had always felt it politic to have the public come into those institutions he led. Now things had to change. He announced that "commencing the 1st of July we are going to quit showing ordinary visitors through the institution until further notice."[25] Custodial necessity simple trumped public relations.

Another reform had to do with providing meals. Earlier prisoners had gathered in a mess hall to pick up food and take it back to their cells. Traffic jams in the yard resulted. Under such a situation no extra servings were provided. The next phase came with one inmate assigned to go around to the cells carrying extra bread to be given out upon request. "That bread trip was the beginning of the prison dining room of today," claimed McClaughry in a newspaper interview in 1913. Later still, the prisoners were allowed to pick up their food but eat it outside on the benches rather than in their cells. Finally, in 1913 a large dining hall was finished and the inmates started communal dining.[26] On the one hand such a dining hall allowed prisoners to socialize. On the other hand, this situation created a custodial crisis for the prisoners had to be always under the eye and gun sights of guards. In addition to the regular dining hall, a smaller facility for diners with digestive problems was set up. "They receive what the others get, only in a little more palatable shape, suited to their sensitive stomachs," McClaughry told reporters.

Despite the improvements, prisoners continued to send complaints about dining arrangements to Washington, and in 1908 these were chiefly about the quality of the food itself. According to inmate grumbles, the "meat is never fit to eat; that the milk is always watered, sometimes it is not fresh, and sometimes thickened with chalk; that eggs, canned peaches, or other fruit which used to be furnished, especially to those prisoners on special diet, are no longer issued to them." When confronted with these allegations McClaughry had to confess "that abundance–as in the past–has suffered due to less supplies and higher prices," and that therefore he had been forced to cut back some. Smitten with charges of favoritism—allegations which were probably true—he contended there was no special influence connected to the special men's table.[27]

These prisoner complaints leaking out of the prison made McClaughry more sensitive to newspapers and journalists. This came to a head in 1909 when interviews of two prisoners named C.R. Griggs and Homer Morris appeared in the local media. Washington heard of these interviews (in which some derogatory things were said about the prison and its warden) and chastised McClaughry, who in response claimed not to have granted these interviews and insisted that only on occasion, especially when inmates were to be released and needed help finding work, did he give newspapers any information.

> . . . but you are aware that newspaper men are not to be daunted by mere refusals. They very frequently make up, out of their fertile imaginations, the interviews they desire and publish the same as if they had received them from proper authority. It is a source of great annoyance, and considerable anxiety, to keep such matters regulated so as to protect the prisoners and at the same time not make unnecessary enemies of the newspapers. You are aware that the principal newspaper in this city is owned by the Congressman from this district.

Shrewdly, he went on to claim that being too dictatorial and keeping reporters out entirely would increase the recklessness of their stories.[28]

Next he was charged with denying newspapers to the prisoners. Some inmates filed complaints over being deprived of the *Chicago Journal*. Again, in 1909, the warden defended his policies:

> It is only recently that daily papers have been admitted. Were they admitted indiscriminately they would become a nuisance, because some of the prisoners desire to take them, but for the purpose of trafficking through them with other prisoners.

Some of his more puritanical beliefs seeped through when it came to decisions of which papers to allow in the prison:

> I have prohibited the circulation of the *Chicago Dispatch*, because it contained advertisements of lewd persons and immoral places. I have also prohibited the circulation of the *Chicago American* and the *Chicago Examiner*, for the reason that they are so highly sensational that their circulation produces bad effect upon certain classes of prisoners; but I have no desire to prohibit the circulation of any respectable journal."[29]

Another way to control the inmates was to give them more educational opportunities. McClaughry established a superintendent of education and developed classes for the large number of illiterates in 1912. Classes were one and a half hours long on Mondays, Wednesdays, and Fridays. The two teachers were inmates themselves.

However, it was team sports that seemed most beneficial. Such sports taught valuable lessons. Physical activity spent the energies of sedentary populations, deterring misbehavior. This became more important as the prison construction came to an end and the numbers of idle prisoners increased. Athletics also taught inmates to work together towards a common goal. More importantly, team sports taught people to win gracefully, to accept defeat, to lose without recourse to violence. What better lesson could be could be given to a group of men in a highly competitive society that society regarded as "losers?"

Guards started playing baseball very early at Leavenworth. By 1911 trustees were allowed to play the game as well, and in 1912 McClaughry expanded it to all inmates and established three teams. The "Brown Sox" was made up of the white population. The "Red Skins" acknowledged the large number of Indians in the prison. The "Booker T. Washingtons" was for the black prisoners. Games were short, lasting only five innings; any longer and fan enthusiasm (or boredom) might get out of hand. The diamond was placed in such a way that there was no danger of the ball being hit over the fence.[30] After a game in which the Black Sox defeated the Red Skins, the local newspapers declared the future of baseball assured. "The discipline of the prisoners could not have been better and not a complaint was heard on any side." Someone was heard to say after one ball game that, "I am glad to know that beneath the grim exterior of Warden McClaughry beats one of the warmest and kindest of hearts and to recognize in this worthy action evidence of your Christian kindness."[31]

McClaughry continued to push for other reformatory ideals to be implemented in the federal system. Of course, some of these were benevolent aspirations of his puritanical mind, but others were clearly "empire building" ploys to consolidate more power in the hands of the progressive prison officials. For example, he continued to advocate parole: "What is needed is a penitentiary commission with power under certain circumstances to parole men who have been sentenced to prison by [the] courts," he contended. Of course, this was usurpation of the courts' sentencing power. By the nature of parole, the ultimate determination of release comes from a body of people disconnected from the courts. In June, 1910, news spread throughout the prison that finally a federal parole bill had passed. A new board–with a section for each of the federal prisons at Leavenworth, Atlanta, and McNeal Island–would be set up with three people on each. A federal judge from the particular district near the prison, a private citizen appointed by the President, and the United States Superintendent of Prisons would make up the pardoning authority. Each of the federal wardens would draw up a list of eligible prisoners. McClaughry was overjoyed and felt it would be a boon to improving discipline in the institutions. What he did not acknowledge was that it gave considerable power to the wardens and other prison personnel.[32] By drawing up the lists, parole decisions were ultimately in the hands of the warden.

By releasing prisoners early, as parole was a key reformatory ideal, prison officials gambled that they were turning loose on society reformed people. Of course many unreformed criminals got out of prison early by duping parole and prison officials. Parole officers would be one form of controlling ex-offenders outside the prison. Parole conditions, a set of behavioral requirements such as curfews, were another means of control. But if you were going to risk the possibility of harden criminals being released upon society other tracking mechanisms were needed to extend that control. For McClaughry, going back a decade, it was the Bertillon system of criminal identification.

THE IDENTIFICATION BUREAU

McClaughry's interest in criminal identification went back nearly twenty years. We have seen that while at the Joliet prison he created a bureau of identification, and that at the Chicago police department he established another identification bureau that was eventually taken over by the International Association of Chiefs of Police. He was happy to point out that many chiefs of police–most notably New York City's department–were against the system. It was good to have these less progressive departments against you, he thought. Their incompetence and corruption distinguished them from the more progressive departments with which McClaughry wanted to be identified. Perhaps the difference arose from a conflict over the very nature of criminal investigation: was it an art or a science? Clearly, McClaughry considered it to be the latter. Many detectives, and the life and legacy of Thomas Byrnes at New York would bolster this contention, wanted to think of it as an art. These departments were slow to accept any form of forensic science and criminal identification.

McClaughry wanted to make Leavenworth the national center for the identification of criminals in America. Both the Bertillon and fingerprinting systems would be the foundations of that center which would later, in the 1930s, be the initial data taken over by the Federal Bureau of Investigation as it built its national identification system. Already Leavenworth, due to McClaughry's passion for criminal identification, had a considerable collection. There were 1,860 Bertillon records of military prisoners prior to July 1895. To this he added 5,390 cards from Joliet and Chicago. In addition, McClaughry had accumulated another 5,500 cards from other prisons and police departments.[33] Constantly "empire building" McClaughry continued to press Washington to establish a national bureau initially at Leavenworth. Such a central bureau, he added, would eventually have contributions from all police departments and state prisons. Again with a swipe at the private police and reflecting larger trends going on in the era of Theodore Roosevelt, McClaughry insisted that a bureau would place crime fighting where it belonged: in the hands of government. Then in a prophetic way he went on to say that "as a general proposition, this country will, ere long, be compelled to look after inter-state crime, as we now look after inter-state commerce, and correct the abuses and outrages of the former on the same general principles that we are trying to correct the abuses of the latter. Then we will realize, in full, the uses and benefits of our U. S. Penitentiaries, and their kindred appliances for law-breakers."[34]

Disliking the fractured approaches going on across the country he pushed for one central bureau. Even the one at Leavenworth, the best in the country, should reside in Washington, he concluded:

> Of course, it is entirely possible to have the central bureau at the U.S.P., Leavenworth, but, in order to avoid jealousies, prejudice, or misunderstandings; I think the Department will find it to its advantage to establish this bureau in connection with its headquarters in Washington. Everybody will be inclined to send information to Washington than to Leavenworth, and that is what the Government needs and wants.[35]

By 1907 a central bureau was indeed set up in Washington D.C., and Matthew McClaughry, who already headed up the bureau at Leavenworth, was sent to the capital to take over. It would last only one year there before coming back to Leavenworth. Robert McClaughry remained paranoid; such a criminal identification system aroused the greatest animosity among the career criminals and McClaughry testified that, "they will leave no stone unturned to destroy a Bureau containing such accurate and indisputable evidence as is there stored concerning their records." At Leavenworth the bureau would be in a fire-proof room guarded day and night.[36] Consequently, by fall of 1907 all federal prisons were required to send their Bertillon records to Leavenworth.[37] Three years later, when the operation was again transferred to Washington D.C. there were over 40,000.[38]

Describing the Leavenworth operation– it being a model for the eventual Washington set up–allows an idea of the earliest days of criminal identification. Several case file cabinets were housed at Leavenworth. Over seven feet tall, six feet wide, and two feet deep, these cabinets held thousands of cards. In the beginning one case had over 5,000 Bertillon cards of international criminals. Another held over 5,000 cards of American career criminals. As dactyloscopy became more important, a separate cabinet held 3600 sheets of fingerprints. To give an example of the activity of the identification bureau, in 1910, 490 Bertillon cards and 570 finger print cards were received at Leavenworth, and there were 34 Bertillon identifications and 51 finger print matches made. All of this identification work came in handy in apprehending criminals and prison escapees. For example, fingerprinting would be important in bringing to justice a fugitive who had avoided capture for decades. He was part of the great train escape of 1910.[39] That escape was only one of a growing number of challenges to McClaughry at Leavenworth.

NOTES

1. Allison Poe, *Poe Brothers or the Sequel to a Conspiracy* (np. 1911), p. 17.

2. Superintendent of Prisons and Prisoners [LaDow] to Senator Simon Guggenheim January 25, 1910. LaDow Papers National Archives.

3. Allison Poe, p. 20.

4. Robert McClaughry to Superintendent of Prisons La Dow, October 21, 1907. LaDow papers in National Archives.

5. W.S. Eames (architect) to Robert McClaughry, July 27, 1904. Bureau of Prison papers, Book one: Construction Correspondence, National Archives, Kansas City.

6. Robert McClaughry to W.S. Eames, August 8, 1904. Bureau of Prison papers, Book one: Construction Correspondence, National Archives, Kansas City.

7. *American Prison Association Proceedings*, 1916, p. 450.

8. See Frank T. Morn, "Postcards from the Past: Pictures, Prisons and Popular Culture," in *Material Culture,* vol. 31 (Fall 1999), pp. 53-70.

9. *National Prison Association*, 1886, p. 88.

10. Christopher R. Adamson, "Toward a Marxian Penology: Captive Criminal Populations as Economic Threats and Resources," *Social Problems* 31 (April 1984). pp. 435-58.

11. *Ibid.*, p. 164.

12. Jackson, pp. 162-63.

13. Allison Poe, p. 28.

14. T.A. Kating to the President of the United States, April 20, 1913. Leavenworth papers, National Archives, Kansas City.

15. Blake McKelvey, *American Prisons: A History of Good Intentions,* p. 210.

16. Report of the Prison Physician to the Warden, 1907, LaDow Papers National Archives.

17. *Ibid.*, p. 22.

18. Annual Report of the U.S. Penitentiary, Leavenworth, Kansas, for the fiscal year ending June 30, 1904, U.S. Penitentiary Papers, National Archives, Washington D.C.

19. Jack Cope, *1300 Metropolitan Ave,* p. 38.

20. Robert McClaughry to the General Agent for the Superintendent of Prisons September 2, 1907. LaDow Papers National Archives.

21. Robert McClaughry to LaDow February 9, 1910. LaDow Papers National Archives.

22. Robert McClaughry to LaDow July 20, 1910. LaDow papers National Archives.

23. Robert McClaughry to W.S. Eames, August 4, 1904. Bureau of Prison papers, Book one: Construction Correspondence, National Archives, Kansas City.

24. *Leavenworth Times,* June 21, 1911.

25. *Ibid.,* June 24 and 26, 1910.

26. *Kansas City Star,* June 8, 1913.

27. Robert McClaughry to the U.S. Attorney General, January 21, 1908. Department of Justice Papers, Administration Files, National Archives Washington D.C.

28. Robert McClaughry to the Attorney General, June 12, 1909, Department of Justice Files, Administrative Files, National Archives, Washington D.C.

29. Robert McClaughry to R. V. LaDow [Superintendent Prisons and Prisoners in the Department of Justice] July 1, 1909, Department of Justice Files, Administration Files, National Archives.

30. *Leavenworth Times,* June 6, 1911.

31. *Ibid.,* date unavailable but probably the summer of 1912.

32. *Ibid.,* June 25, 1910.

33. Robert McClaughry to Cecil Clay, November 19, 1906. LaDow papers, National Archives.

34. Robert McClaughry to Cecil Clay November 20, 1906 LaDow papers, [box 3] National Archives.

35. Robert McClaughry to Cecil Clay, December 11, 1906 LaDow papers [box 3] National Archives.

36. Robert McClaughry to Cecil Clay, February 19, 1907. LaDow papers, [box 3] National Archives, Washington D.C.

37. Charles Bonaparte [Attorney General] to Superintendents, Wardens of State Penal Institutions, October 22, 1907. Superintendent of Prisons, Department of Justice papers, National Archives.

38. Matthew McClaughry to LaDow, May 31, 1910, LaDow papers, [box 4] National Archives.

39. R.V. LaDow to Cecil Clay, March 18, 1907. LaDow papers, [box 3] in National Archives.

Chapter Thirty-Three

Crises at Leavenworth

"Then I knew it was up to Warden Tomilson to feel sorry for me."

PRISONERS

Leavenworth's inmate population grew rapidly in the first decade of the twentieth century. Superintendent R.V. LaDow observed to McClaughry in 1910 that his institution was becoming rapidly filled with prisoners largely because of those transferred from state institutions. "With the transfer of prisoners from the Detroit House of Correction, lately received by you, there are practically no other prisoners left in State institutions eligible for transfer to any United States penitentiaries," he noted.[1] And the numbers increased rapidly. In 1902 there were nine hundred prisoners in Leavenworth. Two years later the number had grown to 1,130. As the other federal prisons opened, Leavenworth's population settled at around 1,000.

Until 1906, three hundred prisoners still got up at 6am and marched the three miles to the construction site. Another one hundred marched two miles the opposite direction to work the farms.[2] Of course, such activities stretched the custodial personnel, making security increasingly a problem. By 1904 enough of the facility was completed that six hundred inmates resided there thus ending the time-consuming march every day. Another 503 remained at the old facility in spite of complaints from the military. Army officials did not want the expense of watching prisoners with a prison down the street.

In 1907 Leavenworth's prison demographics looked like this. There were 554 white prisoners, plus

Indian 97
Blacks 293
Mexican 8
Japanese 2

Of these, those under the age of 20 numbered seventy-eight;

20 to 30=484
30 to 40=259
40 to 50=96
50 to 65=70
65+=5

Most of the prisoners were under sentence of one year and a day. Nineteen were there for life. Eight hundred and eighteen were first timers while 146 were recidivists. Most, 496 of them, came out of the Indian territories.[3] By 1909 the overall federal prison population was this:

Atlanta . . . 783
McNeil Island . . . 101
Leavenworth . . . 912
Federal Hospital for the Insane [D.C.] . . . 126
National Training School for Boys [D.C.] . . . 86

Those federal prisoners still in state institutions:[4]

Juvenile . . . 214
Prisons . . . 353
Jails . . . 1600[5]

In this period, seventy-two percent were in the prison for murder, and presumably—since murder is not a federal crime—these crimes were committed in federal territories. A further 3.5 percent were convicted of manslaughter, 9.5 percent for rape, and fifteen percent for other crimes such as mail robbery or fraud.[6] Yet there was a noticeable change in Leavenworth beginning in 1911. Before this date prisoners had been mostly under thirty years of age. Thereafter, McClaughry noted, most of them were over thirty. As an aside–and as a reflection of the changing nature of the West–the number of cowboys declined from twenty-four before 1911 to two.[7]

One of McClaughry's earliest problems had to do with the Indian population and how best to put them to work. McClaughry shared the attitude common to most Americans at the turn of the century that the Indian population was ill-equipped for farming. Later he recalled in an interview that, "As you know the Indian is, by training from childhood, lazy. He belongs to that class of 'never worked and never will.' The squaw has always done the work for him and to suggest that he do some sort of manual labor is an insult to his dignity." Knowing that the American Indians were descendents of Central American cultures such as the Aztecs, Mayans, and Incas who were great workers of stone, he placed the Indian population in the quarries.[8]

McClaughry's relationships with his prisoners were quickly tested. The reputation of the prison among the inmate culture had already begun to form. Shortly after completion of construction the inmates began referring to the penitentiary as the "hard joint." Others called it the "Hot House" referring to the lack of ventilation and the oppressive Kansas summers.[9] Frank Grigware, one of the more notorious escapees, called it the "Big House," an increasingly popular name used by inmates to refer to the prisons built in the first two decades of the twentieth century.[10] Such a phrase might have gone back to the Southern plantation society. Slaves commonly called the owners' mansion the big house. As the names suggest, inmates viewed Leavenworth as an oppressive place, which it was. They reacted accordingly causing discipline problems.

DISCIPLINE

As soon as he got there, in 1899, McClaughry issued a rule book spelling out the restrictions and obligations of the inmates. Among these was that prisoners were forbidden to talk to each other. Of course, as the inmate population increased, this policy died naturally. Further, in deference to authority, prisoners had to take off their hats when talking to a guard, and if visitors were present, inmates had to keep their eyes to the ground. Based upon his reformatory ideology and experiences McClaughry believed privileges to based upon good behavior. As time went by McClaughry put in place some ideas he got from his reformatory experiences. Upon his arrival, McClaughry saw too much discretion and arbitrary action in discipline, and so began to formalize procedures. A first offense severe enough to warrant some time in solitary resulted in two days' loss of good time. A second offense equaled a four-day loss of good time. A third offense took away eight more days. And a fourth breech of the rules resulted in a sixteen-day reduction of accumulated good time. "Discipline is made up of little things more largely than great things," he maintained, "and [if] the prisoners are shown that they do not escape the eye of the vigilant officer, you will not likely have many large offenses to deal with."[11]

A classification system, like that used in the reformatories, created three grades of prisoners. Those in the "third grade" wore stripes and received no tobacco or mail privileges. Second and first grade inmates got a ration of chewing tobacco.[12] McClaughry expanded upon this crude classification system. Those that were safe and not a security risk had their names printed on their uniform in black. These were assigned to the various construction projects. The unsafe ones—and in 1907 there were over one hundred of these—had their names in red and were put in the laundry and other shops. Finally, those who were sickly had their names in green.[13] Of course, such labeling was complemented with the Bertillon measurement system. Locked into such grades was too much for the rebellious. Eager to get out on their own terms some plotted to break out.

THE BIG MUTINY

In November, 1901, McClaughry's worst nightmare came true: a massive escape occurred, the kind that had brought down his predecessor. It was such a big deal and so new from his perspective that he did not really know what to call it. So he reverted to his military background and used the word mutiny. Mutiny is an interesting word. Escape suggests running away to freedom from an oppressive force. In subtle ways it puts a negative connotation on the institution and those who run it. Mutiny seems to suggest attacking and taking over the authority, and is a treasonous act. It puts the onus on the people who fled. The "Big Mutiny" was masterminded by Gilbert Mullins. On his way back from a professional meeting in Kansas City, McClaughry heard that there had been a break out. At first, self assuredly, he thought it had happened at the state prison and immediately felt sorry for its warden. However, it became increasingly clear that the mutiny was at the federal prison. "Then I knew it was up to Warden Tomilson to feel sorry for me," he remembered.

This was a big mutiny with twenty-six men breaking out. Of course, prison escapes had happened before. Even some mass escapes, as under Warden French, had occurred. But this was the first time in McClaughry's career that such a massive breakout had blotted his record. Apparently, a recently-released prisoner named Charles Ennis, who had climbed over the stockade at the construction site by night, had placed guns under a machine at which a buddy worked. Then Ennis tied white strings on telephone poles along the marching trail signaling that guns were in place. At 4 p.m. the next day the break out started. The superintendent of construction and the guards were quickly unarmed and taken hostage to act as shields. Under these circumstances, other guards could not shoot and were easily forced to give up their weapons. One guard, John Walrupe, was killed defending the south wall, though so many shots had been fired that no one could determine who shot the fatal bullet.[14] After Walrupe's death, twenty-six prisoners fled the construction site. The next day two of the prisoners were killed and another pair wounded.[15] Apparently conditions in the prison were so bad and the prisoners so desperate that, according to one prisoner's account, "most of us I am sure preferred death to being brought back alive." At one point, a large posse surrounded five escapees near Nartonville. When they attempted to run through the posse's lines, these escapees were shot down, two of them killed.[16]

Since McClaughry had that very year introduced his favorite identification system, the Bertillon measurement process, immediately after the escape identification cards were sent out to all nearby police departments. Shortly, twenty-three escapees were recaptured. Three were never apprehended. Later it was determined that one of those died from other causes some years later. Another made good his flight to Mexico. The third joined the navy and disappeared.[17] Three of the recaptured felons–Kating, Clark, and Hewitt–were sentenced to life terms for the killing of the guard. Actually, Kating had avoided recapture for three years by wandering around the South and Indian territories doing odd jobs until apprehended in Colorado. Kating in particular would be a thorn in McClaughry's side for the next twelve years.

Kating's perspective and narration of the escape is interesting, though self serving. Writing to the President of the United States for consideration of clemency first in 1911 and then again in 1913, Kating told his side of the story. In 1900 Kating had begun a sentence of five years for grand larceny. Immediately he was put on one of the construction crews. The conditions were horrible. "The long march too [sic] and from the old prison each day of 5 1/2 miles, the nature of the work, the exposure to inclement weather, the quality of the food made it impossible for me to stand this for any length of time without serious injury to my health.," he wrote. Officials were deaf to his several requests to work at the old prison. Each time he was "subjected to a severe reprimand, merely for making the request, a reprimand that was a great punishment in of itself, and a revelation to me for until then I had no idea that it was in the power of the human voice to convey so much brutality, the last time I saw him he threatened to put me in solitary if I bothered him again."[18]

According to Kating, "the plan to escape was general, and was much talked of and discussed among the prisoners." And because

> these matters were so freely talked of among the prisoners that more than once the officials got wind of these plans, and the new prison site was searched

> without finding any guns however, but Captain Trelaford warned the warden and asked for a guard out there at night, the warden refused, said "there was no danger, that were only a lot of Territory bums and if we started anything to shoot us down."[19]

The fact that the prisoners spoke so freely and that there were leaks in the inmate culture gives us some idea about that convict culture. To speak so boldly of such plans suggests some naiveté on the part of the instigators. The fact that so many officials, including McClaughry, did not pick up on it suggests their arrogance.

Kating felt that deadly force would not be necessary. "While willing to take a desperate chance to escape, I did not want to injure anyone," he noted, "and both myself and Hewitt had earnestly cautioned the other prisoners against using any violence, but we did not foresee the consequences, and, during the excitement of the moment, the augmentation of numbers, the guard was killed."[20]

Within a few years McClaughry had to institute procedures to safeguard against future breakouts, which he wrote up in a pamphlet for the guards. A reward of $60 for each returned escapee, dead or alive, was offered. An alarm system was introduced and soon adopted by all the federal prisons. Five blasts, each for fifteen seconds with a five second interval, would announce a crisis in the prison. A recall signal, three plain straight blasts fifteen seconds each in length with ten second intervals, signified that the prisoner had been recaptured. McClaughry was convinced that the Bertillon system was instrumental in the rapid capture of most of the fleeing felons. However, that faith and system was soon to be tested too.

THE WILL WEST INCIDENT

As this major escape attempt suggests many of these prisoners were desperate. Yet few resorted to such grand gestures, and most resisted their incarceration in smaller ways. Take William West for instance. William West [#2626] came to Leavenworth on September 7th 1901 from McAlester, Indian Territory, with a life sentence for murder. His disciplinary record reveals the "rebellion" of the prisoner and the nature of rule breaking in Leavenworth. Every day there was the "2-O'clock court call." This is when those charged with violating prison rules were tried and most likely punished. The deputy warden was the sole attorney, judge and jury.[21] In February 1902, West was punished with two days' solitary confinement for fighting in his cell. In March, he was punished with four days in solitary for grabbing salt in the dining room and nearly causing a fight. In May, 1903, he was written up for talking in shop. The next month he was disciplined for "breaking wind loud in a shameful manner." A week later he was in another fight. In 1904 there was quarreling in his cell, using vile language, and loud talking and laughing at night. In January, 1905, he was accused of "uncleanly habits in his cell and having a lot of dirty wet papers at his cell door every morning." Much of his prison career would be sprinkled with such violations of prison rules and guard impatience. Apparently such activity was not out of the ordinary because he was able to become a trustee in 1916 at which time he did escape for a day. Then in 1919 he was paroled and then given an unconditional pardon by the President of the United States in 1927. Of course, William West was important for another reason besides his disciplinary record.[22]

In May 1903, Will West [#3426] came to Leavenworth from Okomulgee, Indian Territory, on a sentence of ten years for manslaughter. He was not new to the system, however, having served a term in Leavenworth earlier as Johnson Williams [#927]. William and Will West unwittingly caused a challenge to McClaughry's cherished Bertillon system.

When William West entered Leavenworth extensive measurements were taken as a matter of record. The same was true for Will West/Johnson Williams. There measurements were remarkably close as shown in table 33.1.

Immediately Bertillon officers claimed the two men to be the same.[23] "Why are you being measured for a second time?" Will West was asked. Will lied and adamantly said he had never been in prison before. Card #2626 was pulled and placed with Card #3426; they were declared a match. Even the pictures looked identical. The guards assigned to this duty thought that West was trying to get out of work by posing as a new prisoner. Thinking that they would catch him lying, they asked the work supervisor the whereabouts of

Table 33.1. Measurements for William and Will West

	William West	*Will West*	
	[#2626]	*[as #927]*	*[as #3426]*
Height	77.5	73.5	78.5
Outstretched arms	88	87.0	87.0
Trunk	91.3	91.3	91.3
Head Length	19.8	19.6	19.7
Head Width	15.9	15.8	15.8
Cheek width	14.8	14.8	14.8
Right ear	6.5	6.3	6.6
Left foot	27.5	28.6	28.2
Left mid. Finger	12.2	12.9	12.3
Left little finger	9.6	10.1	9.7
Left forearm	50.3	51.8	50.2

prisoner #2626. To their surprise they learned that prisoner #2626 was actually at his work station. McClaughry was immediately called in to examine the two men who looked like twins. He checked the measurements and though there were small differences, well with the margin of error allowed in anthropometry, many jumped to the conclusion that the Bertillon system had been proven wrong.

Such measurement similarities of the Wests suggested several things. First, by comparing the two measurement records of Will West/ Johnson Williams it was clear that some measurements do stay the same over time while others change in minuscule ways. For example, of the 11 measurements taken 2 were identical, 4 differed by one centimeter, and 5 were off by 1 millimeter. This was well within the theoretical paradigm of Alphonso Bertillon. Second, that since measured distinctions could be so close the measuring technician had added burdens of accuracy.

In any analysis of science, in this case forensic science, it is useful to think of the three T's. Theory, technology, and technicians are critical components in any evaluation. Was the theory wrong? Or was the technological apparatus being used at fault? Or was it the skill of the people measuring and recording the numbers? Even though McClaughry had been advocating this system for over ten years, the number of certified technicians remained small. The problem may have lain not in the theory but the technicians. In other words, in these earliest days of identification the technicians had not achieved sufficient technique. Clearly, identical twins–which some prison rumor suggested the Wests to be–could have identical measurements. But the Wests, according to McClaughry, though they acknowledged that they were distantly related, denied being members of the same family.[24] Certainly such a statistical anomaly could not discredit the whole theory; there had to be a certain margin of error. More ominously, however, was the concern that the entire system was wrong.

That was not a position McClaughry could take lightly. He had invested so much of his professional career in the Bertillon system of identification. Six months earlier McClaughry had read Henry's book on fingerprinting. Now he brought in the crude devices to fingerprint the Wests and discovered marked difference in their prints. Baffled he simply introduced the new system of fingerprinting as a supplement to Bertillonage. McClaughry recognized that there was a "national rivalry" between France, with its interest in the Bertillon system, and England with its national pride connected to Dactyloscopy.[25] In some sort of "diplomatic penology" he simply adopted both. Already, McClaughry had assigned his son, Matthew W. McClaughry, to study finger prints. At the 1904 World's Fair, in St Louis, McClaughry hosted an expert on the procedures of fingerprinting. By October, 1905, Matthew began fingerprinting all the prisoners,[26] and the following summer he traveled to

Europe to study fingerprinting more systematically. He used every opportunity to take leadership in the use of fingerprinting. For example, on a trip to retrieve a prisoner in Michigan he stopped at various police departments and prisons to instruct officials in the proper techniques to be used.[27] In 1905, Warden McClaughry would write to the War Department that,

> While the Bertillon system is accurate, I believe that the fingerprint system, which is not less accurate, will supersede it and is of greater advantage to the Army, for several reasons, one of the most important being that the finger print can be taken without any expensive apparatus and by any person of ordinary skill and if properly classified in a central bureau, will prove to be just what is needed for identification.[28]

Bertillon procedures, however, would last at Leavenworth until 1924. These criminal identification tools will be helpful in finding a famous escapee, a man who got away in another mutiny.

THE GREAT MUTINY OF 1910

Three prisoners–Kating, Clark and Hewett–serving life sentences for their killing of a guard during the 1901 escape, conspired with other prisoners nine years later to try it again. On April 21, 1910, at 8:30 in the morning the Union Pacific steam locomotive gave a short toot from its whistle as a signal for the West Gate guard to open up for the engine to enter the prison with a load of lumber. Captain Zerbst–later to be a warden at Leavenworth–gave the okay, then he and a guard, Harry Reed,[29] rode the train to the scales near the power house. Reed stood by the engine while Zerbst busied himself with the scales. All of a sudden Reed was attacked by prisoners Gideon and Grigware. One had an axe; the other blandished a realistically carved wooden pistol. Reed was forced into the locomotive cab quickly followed by Clark, Hewitt, Keating, and Murdock. The engineer was ordered to open up the throttle and blast through the gate making good their escape.

Immediately McClaughry had to explain to the authorities how such a disaster could happen. He shifted the blame.

> The fact is that the engine ought not to be permitted to deliver cars inside the prison yard, and we wanted long ago to build a switch outside for cars, and they could be brought in at our convenience, but Congress did not give us an appropriation to enable us to do it. I can't say that the guards were negligent, but circumstances gave these fellows a chance they were looking for, and they took advantage of it and broke through the gate before anyone could stop them. We have 124 life men, and have to work them in all parts of the yard.[30]

Such breakouts stretched McClaughry's tolerances and prompted to request new procedures. For example, he wanted to construct a side track so that the trains would not come through the gate. This would, he felt, guard against "rushes and dashes which so many of them are so ready to make." As for the "mutineers," as they were called, some were put into solitary; others had to wear restraints. Immediately, McClaughry was attacked for being too severe to the point of injustice. Kating quickly petitioned the Attorney General and complained that his civil rights had been violated. McClaughry had to answer to the charges. "This boot does not hurt him so long as he walks as he should and behaves himself, but he considers it a great infringement upon his rights, hence this statement to the Attorney General," the Major noted.[31] Compelled to justify his actions once again, McClaughry even began to question some long-held reformatory ideals given such an intractable crowd. For example, when a great Montana train robber named Frankhouser escaped using a saw that had been smuggled in, McClaughry wondered if this showed that "our 'Reformatory' ideas of permitting magazines and literature to be sent in by friends need careful revision and radical change."[32] As another instance of desired reform, McClaughry advocated they purchased a vehicle, one of the first in the history of prisons, because it was too difficult to capture these runaways just with horses or on foot.[33] Three months after the escape, a derailing switch was installed outside the prison wall preventing the "Leavenworth train" coming into the prison yard in the future.[34]

Four of the group of escapees was captured within hours, but Murdock and Grigware got away. Murdock was caught two years later in Texas where he was sentenced to the state prison for a new offense. The Bertillon system was instrumental in that identification. At the expiration of the Texas sentence he was sent back to Leavenworth where he spent much of the rest of his life. Grigware, however, dropped out of sight completely.

Frank Grigware was an interesting character. Raised in the Pacific Northwest, he got mixed up with a few bad people and was involved in one of the last great train robberies, called the Mud Cut robbery. Most of the gang members were hardened criminals but, back then, Grigware seemed to have been an innocent boy caught up with bad influences. He, along with the others, was given a life sentence, a punishment some both then and now considered unjust.[35] After his escape he made his way to Canada, married, had a family and lived a law-abiding life. Of course, such an escape and failure to recapture Grigware remained a thorn in McClaughry's side until twenty-five years later in 1937, when McClaughry was vindicated posthumously. Grigware was arrested for a minor infraction of Canadian game laws and a small town finger print clerk discovered his past record. McClaughry's obsession with identification tools had once again paid off. However, efforts to extradite

Grigware were unsuccessful and he was eventually placed on a "not wanted" status due to his age.[36] As the mutinies and inmate criticism suggest, these federal inmates were a hard case. They would be a challenge to any warden who wanted to reform them. McClaughry's principles ran head on with the reality of prisoners who had no desire to conform and reform.

RELATIONS WITH PRISONERS

McClaughry's relations with prisoners and views of them was generally condescending and along class lines. For example, he considered about 10 percent of all prisoners to be moonshiners. They in turn felt persecuted, considering making booze a god-given right that should warrant no government interference. These country folk were religious and therefore not too much of a custodial problem, but still, McClaughry's puritanical tea-totaling ideas biased him against what he termed these "hill billies."[37]

Since Leavenworth was a federal prison McClaughry also frequently came into contact with people of property and standing. In fact one prisoner had been McClaughry's friend from his days as a chief of police in Chicago. John Walsh, a noted Chicago businessman and one-time president of the Chicago National Bank, was doing time for some shady business deals. Such men were McClaughry's "hardest work," he claimed:

> Personally, it gives me great pain to receive him, because I have known him many years; quite intimately as a business man and in a social way. [I] have been recipient of his hospitality in Europe and in this country, and it makes the case a sad one. I anticipate no trouble, except with the swarms of newspaper men and curiosity seekers who will afflict me for a time.[38]

He was correct in that last supposition, for immediately the press began to make connections and accusations. Both the *Washington Herald* and *Chicago Examiner* claimed that Walsh had it easy.

> Even behind the bars in the federal prison at Fort Leavenworth the powerful influences that kept John R. Walsh out of a cell for two years after he was proven a felon have prevailed. John R. Walsh, convict no. 6861, to-night is enjoying practically every luxury that was enjoyed by Walsh the possessor of $25,000,000 and an income that ought to satisfy the wishes of any human being.

Accounts went on to say that he did not have to pose for the rogues' gallery or be Bertillonized. His job, the papers claimed, would be cutting out articles in newspapers. Responding, McClaughry claimed that the newspaper reports were "as near to a complete tissue of absolute falsehoods as the skill and malignity of the writer could make them."[39]

The arrival of bankers like Walsh prompted McClaughry to study and reevaluate the current sentencing laws. Too many non-dangerous men were coming into the prison system, he felt.

> There have been scores, even hundreds, of men who have been dressed in and out by me in prisons in this country who never should have seen the insides of a prison. The punishment of a term in prison is too great for them, and in many cases instead of correcting the difficulty only inflames it and makes bad men out of indifferent men and even men whose impulses are good.[40]

In fact, at one time it could be said that bartenders were more honest than bankers. In 1911 there were 16 bankers in Leavenworth but only one bartender. Of course, bankers rather than bartenders were more likely to break federal laws.[41] One former inmate, a crooked banker out of prison due to parole, declared,

> I have nothing but praise for the warden and the deputy warden. I have been treated well ever since I came here [Leavenworth], and no complaint of any sort to make about the prison. The only disagreeable thing is that there are so many of the worst and lowest of men there. They have it in for the bankers, and will do us a bad turn every chance they get.

Another prisoner, G. A. Corzman, had been a cell mate of John Walsh. Their cell was in the "banker's colony," a place housing nearly thirty bankers in 1911. The "colony" was in the building housing the deputy warden's office, the so-called isolation building. It was the place for the most recalcitrant—the solitary confinement cells—and also the "banker's colony."[42] Nonetheless, these white collar criminals were perplexing to a warden who for so long had been forced to equate criminality with the lower illiterate classes.

Other prisoners were not so easy to get along with. McClaughry tried to remain open to the inmates. He believed that all prisoners had a right to see him. He claimed, probably with some exaggeration, to have interviewed between one hundred and two hundred of them a week. Every day, as part of his administrative routine, he would pass through the prison and all had an opportunity to get his attention, he claimed.[43]

Still there were numerous inmate dissatisfactions toward the warden. Over the years he claimed to have been threatened over fifty times through the mail and one hundred times personally. He was convinced that in prison at least he was safe, protected largely by those prisoners who liked him.[44] There were several "thrilling moments" at Leavenworth. One unruly black inmate after being punished vowed to get revenge. Shortly after, there was a fire in one of the wooden buildings; climbing up to better examine the problem, McClaughry fell ten feet and was trapped. As the fire approached him the same black offender who vowed revenge rushed in for the rescue. Later, as a reward, McClaughry helped the inmate to secure an early release.[45] Other inmates were less forgiving and waged an ongoing war with McClaughry and the prison environment.

T.A. Kating was one of those constant security problems. The Great Mutiny of 1910 had been his second major attempt at escape. The "Oregon Boot," a weighted device that prevented rapid movements, was put on him. Although painful and inconvenient, the Boot was better than some of the other punishments with which Kating was familiar: There was the Hole, a coffin-like cell with steel doors. An inmate consigned to the Hole was given one-half blanket and an oak board for a bed. Three times a day he would be given a quart of water and one ounce of bread. Each morning, at 7 am, the resident of the Hole would be chained to the door as high as he could reach where he would stay until noon. After an hour break for lunch, the inmate was similarly chained once again until 5 pm. Then there was the Isolation Chamber. Inmates there were not allowed to see anyone except one guard. Some prisoners were required to crack a certain number of rocks a day to "earn" their meals. One famous inmate, Julius McDonough, according to prison legend spent five years in isolation.[46]

THE MCDONOUGH PROBLEM

Julius P. McDonough, a military prisoner, was sentenced for assault in 1901. Immediately he was rebellious, unsuccessfully refusing to be fingerprinted and measured for the identification file. It was suspected that he was English and background investigations found he was actually Martin McMahon sentenced for murder in England in 1884. He was forced to be fingerprinted and became the first prisoner in the United States to be identified by the finger print system as an escaped foreign convict.[47] In October 1906, he tried to kill a guard and a fellow prisoner. McDonough had long held a grudge against a prisoner named Jones who had not been punished for activities in the stone shop. McDonough first attacked the fellow inmate with a hammer. Then he turned on the guard. Both narrowly escaped with their lives.[48] McClaughry was outraged and took away any good time McDonough had earned. But he went further, withholding any future good time accumulation. McDonough challenged the warden claiming that this was too severe and unjust. He then used threatening and abusive language in an attempt to stir up the general prison population. McClaughry defended his actions to Washington hoping to get the man deported.

> He has given more trouble to the institution than any fifty prisoners who could be selected from the worst that we have had to deal with, in fact, I might safely say that he has given more trouble than all the remaining prisoners that we have had during his stay here, and has done more to break up discipline, foment trouble, get other prisoners into trouble, demoralize guards, and, in general cause more disorder and misrule than all the rest of the prisoners put together.

McClaughry was convinced McDonough was an unAmerican radical:

> If he is turned loose in this country, the Government will have a vast amount of trouble with him.
>
> As an organizer and leader, he will be one of the worst men yet found in the ranks of anarchy and disorder, and the fact is well known that the leaders of that class of 'undesirable citizens' are already looking to him to head them when he comes out and to furnish plans for their movement.[49]

There was some evidence to bolster McClaughry's claims. Charles Demolli, a former prisoner now working for the radical Western Federation of Miners in Colorado, wrote McDonough offering his help "to crush any haughtiness of the cossacks and nepotism family ruling a governmental institution." That family was to be understood to be the McClaughry family.[50]

Two years later McDonough gained the ear of the Secretary of War and an inspector came to Leavenworth. McDonough's main claim was that McClaughry could not take away from him good time he had not yet earned. Once again McClaughry found himself answering to Washington. Writing to the Superintendent of Prisons, the Major claimed that McDonough's

> influence among the prisoners is pestiferous, and yet, if I lock him up in the isolation cells, (although he may not be required to do a thing, and be fed the best we have,) he will make such a roar about it to the Department as to create false impressions of the attitude of the prison authorities toward him.
>
> The Guards are all afraid of him, and in that way he takes advantage of all conditions in which he can be placed, unless he is locked up isolated from all the others. And I think it is the manifest duty of myself as guardian of the peace here, to treat him in this manner.[51]

No more is heard of this matter but it is safe to assume that McClaughry won this minor skirmish but lost some good will among those in Washington. For the federal bureaucrats, success was not so much winning a battle but a warden who minimized complaints coming to them. Some of this controversy will be used against him later as his career crisis set in. McDonough, released in 1911 after serving his entire sentence, had never regained any of his good time allowance. Before his release, however, he was a witness to a crime that would bring a crisis to the prison. After his discharge McDonough advertised himself as a former prisoner who would give lectures on the "Federal Hell", "and of its responsible officers and employees as tyrants, villains and scoundrels far worse than himself."[52] McDonough's release coincided with a related publication by Allison Poe.

POE BROTHERS

In 1908, Allison Poe and his two brothers were arrested for conspiracy to rob a mail car on a train. Allison had been born in 1879 in Illinois but the family had moved to Kansas when he was five. By the time he was ten he had run away and roamed the Midwest. Eventually, he married and settled down, opening a barber shop. It was at that time he got involved in a plot. Of course, he claimed to be innocent, a victim of a conspiracy to rid his town of his growing political influence. By 1911 he was out of Leavenworth and wrote a small pamphlet describing prison life from the inmate's perspective. Specifically, he criticizes "Old Bob McClaughry," a man who has served as warden "so long that he thinks he owns the U.S. Government."[53] Although McClaughry was famous, Poe believed that "this great reformer is a wolf in sheep's clothes, and, instead of being a reformer, he is a cruel and inhuman ruler."[54] This "pious old saint," as Poe disparagingly calls the warden, was one of the biggest hypocrites in the penal system. For example, "for years McClaughry stubbornly [sic.] fought against the federal parole law and yielded only when he was it [sic.] was useless to resist any longer."[55] Of course, Poe was wrong here but the issue was what the inmate culture felt to be true rather than what was really correct. Poe went on with his accusations, insisting that even though he made $4,000 per year, McClaughry defrauded the government out of thousands more.

> No wonder McCloughy [sic.] finds plenty of time to talk reform, teach Sunday-school classes and deliver patriotic addresses at old soldiers' reunions and make Y.M.C.A. speeches. With a salary of $4000 a year, and with the interest derived from lending the bankers' money and what he has defrauded the government out of in the way of contracts and supplies, he has plenty of time and money to travel over the country, pose as a great reformer and exhibit himself.[56]

Other inmates were quick to join the Poe brothers in their criticism.

KATING LETTER

Thomas Kating, whom we met earlier, was the cowboy sentenced to five years for horse theft. He immediately got into trouble by being a part of both the 1901 and 1910 mutinies. In 1906, Kating wanted to hold a conference of all the 1901 conspirators with their lawyer to get a presidential pardon. McClaughry's reaction shows that he understood the workings of his prison subculture. He wrote the Attorney General to protest:

> These men are considered by the rest of the prisoners as leaders in mutiny and their movements are closely watched by all who desire to engage in that kind of business. If it were known throughout the Prison that their cases were being considered for pardon, that an outside attorney was presenting them to the Department and receiving authority to confer with them in the matter that he desires, it would not be long until the effect of such permission would be seen in further mutiny and rebellion.[57]

In 1913, Kating penned a letter to the President of the United States. He had done so in 1911 as well. The veracity of its contents was debatable but his perceptions were his realities. Clearly his feelings toward McClaughry were very different from those written up in the newspapers. "As to the morale of the institution," Kating wrote,

> reports were that Warden McClaughry had been fired out of all his former positions for cruelty and grafting—that he had been investigated and forced to resign while Warden at Joliet Ill. that he went from there to the Boys Reformatory at Hunnington [sic.] Penn. that following an investigation by the state legislature, and exposure by the press he left Hunnington on a special train for fear of being lynched by indignant citizens for killing young boys in that institution. That he was involved in graft charges and cruelty to prisoners in jail and forced to resign while Chief of Police of Chicago. That he was twice investigated for graft and cruelty and forced to resign while head of the Boys Reform School at Pontiac, and afterward went through a like experience with the same result at Joliet Prison just before coming here, that he held all these positions not because he was a worthy man for the place, but by virtue of the fact that he had a "Political pull" with such men as J.G. Cannon and Senator Cullom behind him.[58]

Although Kating acknowledged his complicity in the two mutinies, his defense was that the system—meaning the institution, guards, and above all the warden—compelled him to attempt escape. He acknowledged that there were some good guards, those pro-prisoner in their orientation, but they were soon filtered out and their place taken by those currying favor from the warden. All the cruelty in the prison, Kating felt, filtered down from the warden's office.

Some of those dismissed guards–according to Kating–had been witnesses to torture and killing of prisoners.

> . . . there was reserved methods of torture for those who violated one of the many petty rules, for instance prisoners were kept for long periods of time handcuffed up to doors in dark cells, on one thin slice of bread a day, a board to sleep on at night, and not an unusual occurrence for a prisoner to be clubbed and beaten or shocked with an electric battery, by this method the prisoners [sic.] hands were chained to top of cell door, his feet to the bottom and the electric battery run up and down his spine and around his stomach.[59]

He not only felt the food was terrible but noticed that the warden favored a small number of prisoners.

> That much of the food was so rotten my stomach rebelled I could not eat it, and when a prisoner was in bad health and really in need of a change of diet, he could not get it although at the very time there was a "banker's table" set apart in the dining room where about sixty of the wealthy class of prisoners dined on milk toast, beefsteak, eggs, pork chops, pie and etc. thereby causing a lot of hard feelings in the prison, and spending the appropriation for the benefit of the few that all of us were justly entitled to share in.[60]

Although the Kating incriminations were not the sole cause, McClaughry's administration increasingly came under scrutiny. Criticisms mounted that would culminate in his retirement. This was aided with increased revelations about his subordinates.

NOTES

1. LaDow to Robert McClaughry February 2, 1910. LaDow papers, National Archives.
2. *Proceedings of the National Prison Association,* 1900, p. 345.
3. Annual Report of the U.S. Penitentiary, Leavenworth, Kansas, for the fiscal year ending June 30, 1907, at the National Archives, Washington D. C.
4. This number would change next year as all federal prisoners went into federal prisons.
5. Superintendent of Prisons LaDow to Ruth Eaton April 30, 1910. LaDow Papers, National Archives.
6. For these figures see *Report of the United States Penitentiary, Leavenworth, Kansas, for the fiscal year ending June 30, 1906.* Bureau of Prisons papers, National Archives, Kansas City.
7. Jack Cope [#72485], p. 38.
8. *Kansas City Star,* January 13, 1909.

9. Pete Earley, *The Hot House: Life Inside Leavenworth Prison* (New York: Bantam Books, 1992), pp. 25-26.

10. Jackson, p. 2.

11. R.W. McClaughry to Major Frank Strong, General Agent for the Department of Justice, July 18, 1903. McClaughry file, Bureau of Prisons Archives, National Archives.

12. Cope #72485, p. 18.

13. Memo written by C.C. McClaughry [deputy warden] dated 1907, Bureau of Prison Archives, McClaughry folder, National Archives, Washington D.C.

14. T.A. Kating to the President of the United States, August 21, 1911. Leavenworth papers at the National Archives in Kansas City.

15. Report of the Warden of the U.S. Penitentiary at Fort Leavenworth to the Department of Justice, June 30, 1902 in the U. S. Penitentiary Papers in the National Archives, Washington D.C.

16. T.A. Kating to the President of the United States, April 20, 1913. Leavenworth papers at the National Archives in Kansas City.

17. *Topeka Daily Capital*, November 20, 1905.

18. T.A. Kating to the President of the United States, April 20, 1913. Leavenworth papers, National Archives in Kansas City.

19. *Ibid.*

20. T.A. Kating to President of the United States, August 21, 1911. Leavenworth Papers in National Archives in Kansas City.

21. Allison Poe, p. 25.

22. Notorious Offender Files, Will West File, Bureau of Prison Papers, National Archives, Washington D.C.

23. Notorious Offender File, Will West File, Bureau of Prison Papers.

24. Warden Robert McClaughry to the Attorney General, June 15, 1907, Notorious Offender File, William West File, Bureau of Prison Papers, National Archives.

25. *National Prison Association Proceedings,* 1904, pp. 73-75.

26. Jack Cope [#72485], p. 22.

27. Matthew W. McClaughry to R.V. LaDow Superintendent of Prisons for the Department of Justice, May 10, 1909. Department of Justice Central Files Box 553, National Archives, Washington D.C.

28. Robert McClaughry to J. L. Camberlain, Inspector General of the War Department October 16, 1905. Bureau of Prison papers, the LaDow papers National Archives.

29. Harry Reed must not be confused with Stephen Reed of the Joliet investigation of brutality.

30. *Topeka Daily Capitol*, April 22, 1910.

31. Robert McClaughry to James Finch [Pardon Attorney] July 2, 1910, LaDow Papers.

32. Robert McClaughry to LaDow, April 21, 1910, LaDow Papers National Archives.

33. Robert McClaughry to LaDow, April 22, 1910, LaDow Papers.

34. Jackson, p. 266.

35. For the most forthright but flawed argument of this position see Joe Jackson's *Leavenworth Train.*

36. Jack Cope, pp. 26-31.

37. See Stephen Creswell's *Mormons & Cowboys, Moonshiners & Klansmen: Federal Law Enforcement in the South and West, 1870-1893* (Tuscaloosa: University of Alabama Press, 1991) and Wilbur Miller's *Revenuers and Moonshiners: Enforcing Federal; Liquor Laws in the Mountain South, 1865-1900* (Chapel Hill: University of North Carolina Press, 1991).

38. Robert McClaughry to La Dow, January 18, 1910, LaDow papers.

39. *Washington Hearld* and *Chicago Examiner* January 21, 1910. And Robert McClaughry to LaDow January 25, 1910, LaDow Papers.

40. *Kansas City Star*, May 18, 1913.

41. Jack Cope, p. 38.

42. *Leavenworth Times,* June 25, 1911.

43. Robert McClaughry to the U.S. Attorney General, January 21, 1908, Department of Justice, Administration Files, National Archives, Washington D.C.

44. *Kansas City Star*, May 15, 1913.

45. *Ibid.*

46. Allison Poe, p. 26.

47. *Kansas City Journal,* February 9, 1911.

48. "Notes of Examination made in the case of McDonough #2358 for attempting to assault guard Agli in the stone shop, and Prisoner Jones #4125 on October 26, 1906. Julius McDonough Prisoner File, Bureau of Prisons papers, National Archives, Kansas City.

49. Robert McClaughry to Superintendent LaDow, October 9 and 21 and November 27, 1907, LaDow Papers, National Archives.

50. Charles Demolli to Julius McDonough, June 23, 1906. Julius McDonough Prisoner Files. Bureau of Prisons papers. National Archives, Kansas City.

51. Robert McClaughry to Superintendent LaDow, August 13, October 8, 1909 LaDow papers [box 11] La Dow papers. National archives.

52. Robert McClaughry to the Attorney General of the United States, June 21, 1913. Julius McDonough Prisoner File, Bureau of prisons papers, National Archives, Kansas City.

53. Allison Poe, p. 20.

54. *Ibid.*

55. *Ibid.* pp. 42-43.

56. *Ibid.* p. 52.

57. *Ibid.* February 17, 1906.

58. T. A. Kating to the President of the United States, April 20, 1913. Leavenworth papers. National Archives, Kansas City.

59. *Ibid.*

60. *Ibid.*

Chapter Thirty-Four

Prison Workers at Leavenworth

". . . good feeling . . . ought to prevail among officers so closely associated . . ."

ADMINISTRATIVE STAFF

McClaughry's relations with his personnel had always been good. He was particularly close to his immediate administrative staff. Prison administration, in the first decade of the twentieth century, was simple. First, there was the deputy warden who at a minimum had a twelve-hour work day. McClaughry wrote to the Superintendent of Prisons that the weight of the day-to-day operations fell to his deputy. "If any danger arises, he is expected to face it first," the Major noted. Judging the fitness of both Guards and prisoners for particular parts of the work and making work assignments was his responsibility. "He must be on hand when the prison is unlocked in the morning, to arrange the work of the day and must remain until after it is locked up at night . . . ." After seeing that the night force is in shape, the deputy frequently returned to the prison during the night, unannounced and unexpected, to see that the night officers were doing their work properly.[1] Such an officer was more than a right-hand man for the warden.

For much of McClaughry's tenure this deputy warden was Frank A. Lemon. He began his position in 1899 and remained McClaughry's key man until some scandals broke over him in 1913 and he was dismissed. He had always been married to his job but, after the escapes of 1901, Lemon became a tyrant. In fact, he had predicted the escapes, even confronting the suspected plotters and warning them of severe reprisals, but McClaughry refused to believe the accusations. After Lemon was proven prophetic, McClaughry turned over more and more power to his deputy warden, whose office, deep in the prison far from the general administrative buildings, was located in the so-called "isolation building" where he ruled like a potentate. It is significant that "The Hole," the name given to the solitary confinement cells, was located in the same building as his office far from the general administrative offices. He knew the names of all the guards and inmates and made surprise inspections of both populations. Discipline of guards and prisoners alike were his responsibility. An army of convict informants kept him current on all inmate discontent. Late-night visits to the local saloons uncovered inappropriate drinking by off-duty guards. With the power to hire and fire any guard or discipline any inmate, he was hated and feared by all, except McClaughry.

Particularly after the 1901 escapes, Lemon became increasingly brutal and McClaughry, still stunned over the escapes, simply overlooked his deputy's practices. Prisoners reported extraordinary punishments personally administered by Lemon—though, of course, one must be cautious and consider the source of these accusations. After all, there was an ongoing battle of wits between the inmates and custodial staff. Still, in light of later revelations and resignations, there must have been considerable truth to many of these stories. Those who took part in the 1901 mutiny, and later the 1910 one too, were singled out for punishment for the slightest reasons. It was virtually impossible for them even to breathe without coming into Lemon's domain of punishment. Prisoners reported being shackled to cell doors in a medieval fashion; hands and legs spread and cuffed for prolonged hours. Cables were strung along the spine and belly of the prisoner and electrical shocks administered. Another troublesome prisoner had broken his arm; not given medical attention, gangrene occurred resulting in death. One prisoner was beaten and kicked by Lemon then transferred to another place where he soon died. Clarence Maitland, a young and rebellious prisoner, was thrown into solitary and beaten for sixteen days, given only bread and water, and chained to the door. Ammonia was sprayed in his face on a couple of occasions. On the seventeenth day his stomach ruptured and death followed shortly in May, 1907. When Lemon heard of his death he said, "If he don't last any longer in hell than he lasted here, they will make damned short work of him."[2] But that was not the end of it. Lemon had a relationship with a local lawyer, William Bond, and ran a kickback scheme. Illiterate inmates wanting legal advice Lemon referred to Bond, and Lemon got some money back from the lawyer. Rumors and exposures became so great that by 1913 Lemon was finally forced to leave his post.[3] Sadly, these administrative personnel became hardened and uncompromising in their views towards the inmates. Rarely one came along who shared McClaughry's reformatory views. W.H. Mackey took Lemon's place and started the baseball league and a vaudeville show put on by the inmates. Mackey, along with McClaughry, may be seen as a bridge between the more custodial-minded and the reform-oriented treatment people.

TREATMENT

Strictly speaking, the treatment staff did not have line administrative or custodial jobs. They were to offer treatment or inspiring activities. At first blush, these people seemed to be of great importance especially to the rehabilitative types among whom McClaughry counted himself to be. Of course, reformatory people like McClaughry thought of these treatment personnel as additional to the system which in and of itself was supposed to be reformatory. Though McClaughry and the reformatory crowd spoke glowingly of rehabilitation, they acted more and more as custodians. Consequently, the real treatment people became a separate tier in the prison staff culture.

The most important treatment person was the chaplain, F. J. Leavitt. Ironically, though he had the greatest potential to have a positive impact upon the prisoners he also had the least power. Besides conducting weekly religious services he did a "character reading" or "word portrait of the inner man" of each new inmate. In spite of being a devout Christian himself, McClaughry paid little attention to his Chaplain. Many prisoners were not endeared to Leavitt either. Known to the inmates as "Holy Joe", one prisoner claimed that Leavitt "delights in seeing his fellow man suffer."[4]

Another treatment person was Dr. A. F. Yohen, the prison doctor, kept busy treating the sick and eliminating the slackers from "sick call." He was the prison's chief advocate for a hospital until it was finally accomplished. Other possible treatment people later would be educators but the prison school in this period was slow in developing, and for now had educated prisoners teaching the classes.

Not only at Leavenworth but throughout all the prisons, worlds were clashing. Of course, tensions between the keepers and the kept were to be expected. But we also have these spokesmen for reform and rehabilitation presiding over a system that was increasingly punitive. In spite of McClaughry's efforts important in this punitory posture was the guard.

GUARDS

Since he had been in the Civil War with a history of battlefield promotions, McClaughry could always expect some respect from his guards. In the last third of the nineteenth century most guards had some military experience.

These men brought with them a sense of military order and discipline. By the turn of the century, this formative experience as a soldier had diminished. As important as the Spanish American War was it did not produce a large number of guards who had been soldiers. Furthermore, by 1905, civil service (rather than political cronyism) became a way to get a job as a federal guard. Civil service requirements demanded an examination and this gave rise to an interesting question: just what requirements were necessary to being a guard?

On the surface of it test questions for the exam might not seem important, just another bureaucratic intrusion. But questions can indicate what it took to be a successful guard. Naturally, McClaughry was asked to help construct the test. Perplexed, McClaughry refused the orders from Washington. The only thing he knew for sure was the necessity of abstinence from alcohol.

> Besides, selecting a guard through examination papers, it strikes me a good deal like selecting a wife in the same way. It is difficult for me, at least, to determine through reading examination papers, a man's capability as a guard. Poets are said to be born, not made; soldiers may understand all the West Point theories concerning the art of war, yet never make soldiers; and guards may, *theoretically*, [emphasis in the original] understand all the mysteries and all the knowledge required to handle their criminal fellowmen [sic.], and yet utterly fail to develop the qualities necessary to success. I am, therefore, very distrustful of my ability to discover qualifications for success by any questions that I can frame.[5]

The progressives in Washington would not countenance such dithering and without McClaughry's help civil service soon appeared at Leavenworth.

In spite of his progressive outlook for prisoners and his professionalization of wardens, he remained a nineteenth century man benevolently caring for his men. When quizzed by Washington about his relations to the guards he admitted

> to some 'softness' in relation to guards, caused chiefly by the fact that most of them have families that are plunged into absolute want the minute the guard is separated from the Government Service, and they wear me out with their importunities and work on my sympathies beyond what should be permitted.[6]

Soft hearted as he might be those who chose to spend their careers watching prisoners were a special group. Maybe war had not hardened them but they brought a personality as rough and tough as those they guarded. There seemed a disconnect between the Major and his workers. In a group photograph taken around 1910 all personnel, 38 of them at this taking, were lined up, grimy face, determined, heavily armed, staring over the heads and surrounding four distinguished administrators. The only one without his hat on, looking out with a softened almost angelic look sharply in contrast to the gloomy "professionalism" surrounding him was Robert McClaughry. In spite of his personal history he seemed strangely out of place, almost other-worldly.

Angelic or not his demeanor could be interpreted by some as weakness. As discussed elsewhere McClaughry always had some troublesome guards with whom to contend. One such person, actually the captain of the guards, was Arthur Trelford. Of all the guards Trelford was the most feared and most hated. On numerous occasions he had to be warned by higher ups to stop beating workers. With so many head injuries to prisoners being reported it was feared work would have to stop. Most inmates believed Trelford had murdered three prisoners. He was the killer of that lonesome cowboy who just got up and walked away from the construction site earlier. Some claimed he let the guards shoot and wound another man, then strolled up to the pleading inmate and shot him again. He was in charge of the work site where the 1901 mutiny started. He had warned the administration for the need of night-time guards at the site but was ignored. When the mutiny started he was taken hostage and was immediately put in harm's way. During the mutiny Trelford knew that the inmates would kill him so he broke away and fled. Prisoners did shoot and wound him but failed to pursue and Trelford survived to take out his anger on the mutineers.[7] Eventually Trelford, upon the recommendation of McClaughry, became Superintendent of the Territorial Prison at Santa Fe, New Mexico. According to the prisoner grapevine, within a few months he was fired from that position for excessive cruelty.[8]

Another guard, Andy Leonard, was so frightened during the 1901 mutiny that he jumped over a wall to avoid being involved. In the process he broke both his legs. Some prisoners saw him and came to his aid. As a reward he sent them to the "hole" every chance he got. As one prisoner observed, "Leonard has a dislike for the man that wears a number."[9]

After civil service provided some protection for complaining guards, critical reports of Major's administration flowed to Washington. For example, when the first Superintendent of Prisons died and R.V. LaDow assumed his duties, there was some attempt to use the guards to get rid of the warden. Jessie Parthon–first representing herself as a newspaper reporter then as an investigator for the Department of Justice—interviewed a guard named L.P. Stephenson, and was told "that crooked work was going on by the warden." She tried unsuccessfully to interview several others. Finally, as LaDow became more comfortable in his job the investigation was called off.[10]

Though Washington was far away, the regulatory atmosphere of the Progressive Era made it more responsive to inmate and guard complaints. In March, 1910, several recently-dismissed guards attacked the warden and the Superintendent of Prisons carried out a secret investigation of the administration at Leavenworth. Though this investigation cleared McClaughry, criticism continued to mount and the federal bureaucracy in Washington became more vigilant.

NOTES

1. Robert McClaughry to R. V. LaDow, January 28, 1908 LaDow papers.
2. Much of this information was reported by a disgruntled prisoner and accepted fully by Jackson, pp. 168-69.
3. *Ibid.*
4. Allison Poe, p. 26.
5. Robert McClaughry to R. V. LaDow, June 4, 1910, LaDow papers, National Archives.
6. Robert McClaughry to R. V. LaDow May 7, 1910. LaDow papers, National Archives.
7. T.A. Kating to the President of the United States April 20, 1913. Leavenworth papers, National Archives, Kansas City.
8. *Ibid.*
9. Allison Poe, p. 54.
10. Robert McClaughry to LaDow, October 18, 1907. LaDow papers.

Chapter Thirty-Five

To All Purposes Futile

" . . . the present warden is too old and too inactive to perform the functions of his office."

FEDERAL BUREAUCRACY

McClaughry had long been familiar with the problems of politics on the local level. His tenure at Joliet and Pontiac made him aware of state politicos and their shenanigans. On the whole he weathered most of those storms. This was less true for Chicago particularly after Carter Harrison's machine came back into play. The political environment, especially during the tenure of Altgeld, was also troublesome. So the call to Leavenworth seemed godsend. At first, being a warden of the federal prison was comfortable. The federal penal system was new and McClaughry was left to build his prison with few restraints, besides economic ones, from Washington. But in 1907 the Attorney General placed the responsibilities for all federal prison matters under a Superintendent of Prisons and Prisoners. A series of superintendents came on the scene and on the whole they were willing to defer to the expertise of Warden McClaughry. And the Major, as a good soldier, followed the rules diligently.

By 1910 the federal government structure was still small but, reflecting the times, growing more bureaucratic. There was a Superintendent of Prisons, at his time R.V. LaDow, directly under the Attorney General. An assistant superintendent, C.H. McGasson, helped LaDow. Besides him, there was R.J.W. Brewster, the Inspector of Prisons who was in charge of investigating prisoners' complaints, of which there were always a large number. Matthew McClaughry had become a Special Agent in charge of the Identification Bureau. With the exception of two secretarial clerks, that rounded out the federal prison staff.[1] However, as winds of change occurred in Washington, there was always the chance that they would be felt with greater force on the plains of Kansas. McClaughry's cautious bureaucratic attitude can be seen in his response to one reformer who asked him to be on a committee on prison labor. He wrote:

> I would like to know how they would feel about it at the department. I have made it a practice not to go off on any side issues since I have been in charge here, and I don't want to do anything that would be considered out of place by my superiors.[2]

Always the good soldier, McClaughry seemed to fit comfortably in the federal bureaucracy. But there were those ready to criticize every aspect of capitalism and government. As these social critics looked around they found Leavenworth a likely target.

MUCKRAKERS

Beginning in the late-nineteenth, but accelerating in the early-twentieth century, a group of writers–some investigative reporters, others socialist critics of capitalism–made their appearance. In books and magazines such as the *Cosmopolitan*, *McClures,* and *The Independent* these writers took aim at corporations, Congresses, and social conditions.[3] In 1911 a radical newspaper in Kansas called the *Appeal to Reason* began a series of muckraking articles against Leavenworth and McClaughry. Although published in the bucolic backwaters of Gerard, Kansas, the *Appeal to Reason* had already attained considerable notoriety in the previous five years as a disseminator of socialist information. Upton Sinclair used the paper to serialize his exposure of the meat-packing industry of Chicago which eventually became the seminal novel, *The Jungle.* In fact, the editor of the *Appeal to Reason* gave Sinclair five hundred dollars for living expenses while he wrote that book.

This time, the *Appeal to Reason* exposed and criticized McClaughry, both a nineteenth-century reformer and member of the establishment.[4] It began with attacks on McClaughry's staff. Frank H. Lemon, Leavenworth's deputy warden, was depicted as a veritable Caligula. According to the investigative reporting, he preyed upon innocent women, tortured prisoners, encouraged sodomy, corrupted young men, and beat to death Clarence Maitland, a sixteen-year old British sailor. One inmate, our old friend Julius P. McDonough, related that in May 1907 he had been in an isolation cell at Leavenworth when Frank Lemon and some of his men took Maitland into a dungeon-like area, hanged him half-naked and beat him to death. The federal government sent in agents to investigate. One secret service agent, an undercover spy, was found out, however, when he vehemently objected to being vaccinated as part of the entry process; to him, that went beyond the call of duty.[5]

The *Appeal to Reason* felt there would be a federal cover-up and continued to push for an impartial investigation and the firing of personnel. "The penitentiary rests like a white marble slab, beautiful and secure. Beneath the slab, however . . . corruption festers and death abounds . . . It is the mission of the *Appeal* to lift the cover and let people see what lies beneath."[6] With so many sons in key positions in the prison, McClaughry justifiably was accused of nepotism. More important, he was accused of knowing of the atrocities existing under him and allowing them to go on.[7]

There had been other charges as well. For example, some critics in 1909 had claimed McClaughry to be incompetent and perhaps corrupt. They cited a 1906 incident in which he gave a load of white enameled face brick (intended for use in some new cell houses) to the People's Theatre of the city. Also, he was accused of being responsible for the escape of William Fay in September 1909. Apparently, he had reassigned Fay to act as a cook in the warden's house, which allowed Fay's escape. Then there were charges of nepotism for hiring his son Matthew, a "habitual drunkard."[8] On July 29, 1911, after a ten-week long series of feature exposées, the *Appeal to Reason* announced that Frank Lemon and five others had been fired and that due to his age and poor health, McClaughry had been allowed to retire.[9] Actually, that announcement was premature because McClaughry was exonerated. But such muckraking smoke suggested there might be some fire.

With the coming of the administration of Woodrow Wilson, Democrats who had been out of national office for two decades wanted key appointments. Also, there was some impatience in Washington with the rehabilitation model of prisons. Already the Atlanta prison had abandoned most of its reforms. Then in 1913, a former marine, Major Henry Leonard, was sent to investigate Leavenworth, presumably "to rid the prison of the foolish plan of trying to make men out of criminals. He was sent there to make criminals realize they really were criminals."[10] His report to the Attorney General claimed that morale of the personnel and the discipline of the inmates were bad. In a severe blow to McClaughry the report suggested that "the present warden is too old and too inactive to perform the functions of his office" and recommended his termination. There needed to be appointed, the report concluded, "an active and virile man."[11] When McClaughry heard of the report he retired declaring, "I beat Washington to it." When told of the changing philosophy, McClaughry had to " . . . confess it does make me feel bad to think that all the years I spent in making a prison a scouring mill to whiten men's souls and fit them for a new coming out into the world, instead of damning them entirely, are to all purposes futile."[12]

"I FEEL RECONCILED IN SAYING 'FAIR WELL, VAIN WORLD'"

McClaughry's last years at Leavenworth had been personally as well as professionally troublesome. Family had always been an essential part of the Major's life. Lineage was so important that one son, Charles, would write a family history in 1913 taking great pride connecting the family to historical characters from Scotland. Names of children acknowledged and honored that past. But it was the immediate family that was most important. McClaughry's family constellation might be seen in two ways: relations between husband and wife, and father and children.[13]

Despite the silence of his wife, Elizabeth was a cornerstone in the Major's personal life. Much of his professional success must be attributed to her support in his private life. Uncharacteristically, Elizabeth was an educated woman, attending the same college in the 1860s as her husband-to-be. Her father, an attorney, had high expectations for his daughters. She was remembered in Leavenworth as "a refined, well educated woman, who aided much in establishing her husband's enviable position in this city." Active in numerous literary clubs and the Presbyterian Church, Elizabeth, following a common nineteenth-century middle-class family pattern, was as prominent in the social life of the cities they resided in as her husband was in the professional sphere.[14]

In many ways the McClaughrys had been a typical nineteenth-century family. In most cases wives of public figures said little and the lines between public and private life were clearly drawn. Interviewed on his seventy fifth birthday, the Major showed where he was when it came to the "new woman" emerging in the twentieth century. "When I recall the women of my day—also the women of this day; and think of what the woman of the coming day are to be," he revealed, "I feel reconciled in saying 'fair well, vain world!' as soon as the call comes."[15]

Elizabeth's position, a wife of a prison warden, brought additional benefits unavailable to most women. Of course, the Major's salary and position made her a solidly middle-class person. But unique to this middle-class woman was the warden's residence. In every prison town the McClaughrys lived on prison property, in a home provided by the state or federal government. These residences were large and spacious, typically built by prison labor as the institution was being constructed. In addition, the prison provided housekeeping and gardening. Certain gifted inmates, commonly called "house boys," were assigned as cooks, cleaners, landscapers, and child care providers. Such state-provided labor made the warden's family life style appear even more upper middle-class than it really was. Elizabeth, and the entire family, was part of the prison environment. Although secure and safe, Elizabeth and the children were surrounded by both the keepers and the kept. Besides the blatant and unapologetic nepotism, many of the children grew up with prison surroundings and service in their blood. While no letters, diaries, or memoirs exist to adequately place Elizabeth's voice in the narrative, the family genealogy speaks volumes.

Robert and Elizabeth's relations with their children were marked by tragedy and triumph. Many births and deaths were strewn across their lives. In a twenty-year period from 1863 to 1883, Elizabeth conceived about every two years for a total of nine children. As in so many nineteenth-century families, many of those children died. The first-born did survive to follow in his father's footsteps. Charles Chase, born in Carthage in 1863, lived to 1926 and became a prominent warden himself, holding positions in prisons and reformatories all over the United States. Not only did he write a family genealogy but also several things relating to criminals. Much of his success, and also that of his brother Matt, can be attributed to the Major. McClaughry, a child of the nineteenth century, practiced considerable nepotism with all his sons getting their starts at his institutions. Apparently, on the cusp of civil service reform, few thought this bad or unusual.

Yet after Charles and Matthew came Frank Bridgeman, who was born in Carthage in 1865 and died six years later while the family temporally lived in St. Louis. Little is known through this research about the next son, named Arthur Cooper (also born in Carthage in 1869), who lived to be 101, but he did not go into the criminal justice system, instead choosing business and becoming a "prominent broker" in Chicago.[16] Always the entrepreneur, he tried to push a new invention in 1915, a foot-peddled flying bicycle.[17] Matt Wilson followed his father and brother into prison work becoming a Bertillon expert. Born in St Louis in 1871, the year six-year old Frank died, Matt lived to 1922, his name forever associated with criminal identification.[18] The next son, James Glenn, was born in Monmouth in 1873 but died two-and-a-half years later. Robert Hume McClaughry was born in Joliet in 1875 but died six months after. John Glenn, born in Joliet in 1878, served in the military during the Spanish American War as a First Lieutenant. In July 1899, he came to Leavenworth and was connected to the construction of the federal prison. In 1908, "Glenn—as he was familiarly known—moved to Indiana to head up identification work at the Indiana State Reformatory. Illness compelled him to resign and return to Kansas. He died in Leavenworth in 1912—leaving a wife and two children—due to illnesses attributed to his duty in Puerto Rico.[19] Mary Catherine, the twin sister to John born in Joliet on March 29th 1878, died over seventy years later in Tucson, Arizona. Finally, Thomas Alexander was born in Monmouth, Illinois, in 1883 but "died in infancy."

So within the space of fifteen months, three life-changing events occurred to the Major. In May 1912, McClaughry's son John Glenn died; then there was his own forced resignation from the prison the following year. But the real life crisis was when his wife passed away in 1914. The death of Elizabeth was very unsettling to this tightly grouped family constellation. No sign of her impending death was evident and it took everyone by surprise. In fact, it was the Major, with a long history of health related problems, who everyone expected to precede his wife in death. So what happened? She and the Major had spent the summer of 1913 traveling in the East visiting friends and family. In December and early January they traveled to Kansas City with no health complaints. After breakfast on January 29th Elizabeth went into the bathroom to freshen up and collapsed with a stroke. She was dead within the hour surrounded by family. Glenn's widow, still in mourning and raising her two children with them, was there. Elizabeth's sister, Emma, the matron of the Wm. Small Memorial Home (a nursing home for "aged women"—upon whose board of directors Elizabeth served)—was living with the family as well. Of course, as he had been for so many years, Robert was at his wife's bedside. After her death, no matter where the extended family traveled Central Illinois remained home and Elizabeth's remains were taken back to Monmouth.[20]

Then McClaughry did something that had been common practice among the puritan families of colonial America: he quickly remarried.[21] Apparently, widowhood was not prized highly in these early families and in 1915, at 75-years old, McClaughry found another wife. In honor of and in devotion to his family he married his wife's sister, Emma Madden, and moved to Chicago. The Major's family was scattered. Matt was at Joliet, Charles in Iowa, and his daughter in Texas. Arthur, the only son not going into prison work, lived in Chicago. With his new wife, McClaughry settled down in Chicago where Emma cared for him until 1920 when a stroke ended the life of what his obituaries called one of the pioneer "humane wardens" in American history.[22]

NOTES

1. Report on the Presidential Inquiry in regards to Economy and Efficiency, November 9, 1910, [box 3] of the LaDow papers.

2. Robert McClaughry to Mrs. J. Ellen Foster, February 12, 1910 Records of the Bureau of Prisons, Correspondence of the Superintendent of Prisons, 1907-1910 [box 2].

3. Louis Feller, *Crusades for American Liberalism* (Yellow Springs, Ohio: Antioch Press, 1950) and Donald DeNevi, Helen Friend and John Bookout, *Muckrakers and Robber Barons; the Classic Era, 1902-1915* (Danville, California: Replea Books, 1973).

4. Louis Filler, *Crusaders For American Liberalism* (Yellow Springs, Ohio: The Antioch Press, 1959), pp. 125, 162, 163, 164, 224.

5. *Kansas City Star*, February 15, 1913.

6. *Appeal to Reason*, April 15, 1911.

7. *Ibid.*, May 27 and July 1, 1911.

8. H. Sullivan to George Wickersham [Attorney General] November 8, 1909. Department of Justice Files, Bureau of Prisons, Administration files, National Archives, Washington D.C.

9. David L. Sterling, "The Federal Government v. The Appeal to Reason", *Kansas History* 9 (1986), pp. 31-42.

10. *Kansas City Star*, May 7, 1913.

11. Henry Leonard to Attorney General, February 26, 1913, Report #10, Fort Leavenworth Papers, National Archives, Washington D.C.

12. *Kansas City Star*, May 7, 1913.

13. A very useful place to start on such a topic is Steven Mintiz's *A Prison of Expectations: The Family in Victorian Culture* (New York: New York University Press, 1983).

14. *Leavenworth Times*, January 30, 1914.

15. *Ibid.*, July 22, 1914.

16. *Chicago Tribune*, November 10, 1920.

17. [Chicago] *Saturday Blade*, December 18, 1915.

18. See *Finger Print Magazine* Volume 2 (April, 1922), pp. 3-5: Also Volume 3 (May, 1922), pp. 1-3.

19. *Leavenworth Times,* November 3, 1912.

20. *Ibid.*, January 30, 1914.

21. Nathaniel Philbrick, *Mayflower: A Story of Courage, Community and War* (New York: Viking, 2006), p. 104.

22. *Chicago Tribune*, November 10, 1920. Pontiac *Daily Leader*, November 11, 1920.

Afterword: Forlorn Hope

"What wish can bless . . . "

McClaughry's dismissal from Leavenworth ended a forty-year career in America's criminal justice system. After his death he slipped into anonymity; he became the forgotten reformer whose reform ideology was long remembered. Why was such an important man forgotten? Well, of course, history does such things. But Robert McClaughry was a unique figure, a historic outlier. In the history of prisons and punishments in America there were two threads: reformers who wanted to protect society by changing the attitudes and behaviors of criminals, and practitioners who wanted to protect society by removing the criminal from society. McClaughry wove these two threads together. Such reformers were hard to find in his generation. It has been rare ever since.

This reformist impulse went back to the creation of the penitentiaries in the 1820s, and even before that. In 1800, the first prison newspaper, *Forlorn Hope*, recognized that

> What wish can bless, or supplicating pray'r
> Prosper the wretch who joys t' inflict despair?
> These bars—these bolts—where mis'ry lies confin'd,
> Can furnish food to feast the poison'd mind.
> Here each endures, while yet he draws his breath,
> A stroke more fatal than the scythe of death.[1]

For McClaughry, most likely this concern went back further to Scotch-Irish antecedents and even to a puritan mindset forged in the pulpits of Geneva, Switzerland, in Glasgow, Scotland, and in Boston, Massachusetts. Whether it was through the New York or Pennsylvania penitentiary models, in the New

Nation there remained a faith in changing criminal character through institutional means. Such intoxication is easily understood. This mood led to the "invention" of several asylums around the mid-nineteenth century.[2]

By the Civil War many wardens, hardened by the difficulty of instilling the ideals of a free capitalist society in those without freedom and little desire to work, had given up on reform and become custodians. Besides, prisons in the east were filled with what were considered by many to be disposable people: Irish and freed African slaves. Though a bureaucrat himself, McClaughry tried to blend earlier faith in redemption through rehabilitation with institutional reform. Like his forbears, he was caught between his desires to reform individuals and the necessity of controlling them, and he looked to both the inmate and the penal system to achieve this. On balance, however, he did not see them mutually exclusive, but rather might be seen as singularly personifying what one scholar called "conscience and convenience."[3]

Embarrassed by his firing (or forced retirement), McClaughry could take comfort in the progress made nationwide thanks to his reformatory campaigns. Going against prevailing practices took considerable courage, energy, and fortitude. Be it in prison administration, or new ideas about the treatment of men and boys, or fighting political bossism in Chicago, or forging new professionalism in police and prison management, or advocating new sentencing laws, or negotiating federal bureaucracy, in all these situations McClaughry was a progressive penologist before progressivism arrived on the scene. Of course he was a captive of his times, too, being both benefited and harmed by the politics of the era. Nonetheless, he seemed to be a Jeremiah crying in the wilderness of the late-nineteenth and early-twentieth centuries. Then the political progressivism of the first two decades of the twentieth century finally caught up with him and his likeminded reformers and drowned them out. His "reformatory ideology" now became the Progressive Design.

PROGRESSIVE PENOLOGY: THE TIDE CRESTS

By the early decades of the twentieth century, McClaughry and other progressive penologists had been able to implement many of the reformatory ideals and practices in adult prisons. Besides the work of McClaughry in the two previous decades, by the early twentieth century a new political/social ideology appeared that validated and facilitated the work of the reformatory people. One aspect of it was political, the other intellectual.

Political progressives–on the national level led by Theodore Roosevelt and later Woodrow Wilson, and on the state level by Hiram Johnson of California, Robert LaFollette of Wisconsin, and Charles Evan Hughes of New

York– reshaped America's political, economic, and social scene. Modern political liberalism in America was born in the Progressive era. Government at all levels became more involved in everyday affairs of the citizenry. In many ways this progressivism was a new Puritanism. Red light districts were closed, gambling activities outlawed, most narcotics criminalized, and alcohol prohibited thanks to the great "purity crusade" led by the progressives (or neo-Puritans) in the first twenty years of the new century.[4] These same progressives sought to protect America's natural and human resources. The conservation movement took off and numerous national parks were protected from the greed of capitalism. New legislation regulated the exploitation of workers, especially women and children. Political bossism was attacked as tainting democracy. Women were allowed to vote with the hope of bringing a new purity to the process. Experts and efficiency were extolled as a means to get at political and social problems. Government, especially the federal one, took on new police powers in regulating the economic and social world.[5]

New intellectual paradigms emerged as well. The modern university grew and began to departmentalize knowledge.[6] Areas of study became departments on the university campuses. As in most organizational environments, politics soon characterized the academic world as various disciplines tried to carve out special places for themselves.[7] Humanities—arts, history, modern languages, music, literature and philosophy—found a place on the new campuses to create the "educated" person. More germane, the social sciences—anthropology, economics, political science, sociology and psychology—began to grow and compete for national attention as fields creating the "professional" person. Psychology was one of the earliest to emerge and define itself as a science. In 1904 there were four departments of psychology in American universities; 35 existed by 1912.[8] Part of the reason for that growth was the visit to America of Sigmund Freud. In 1909, Freud (along with Carl Jung and Sandor Ferenczi) came to Clark University and delivered five lectures on psychoanalysis.[9] The treatment model for deviant and delinquent classes, an outgrowth of this psychology emphasis, began in earnest in the second decade of the century. It would dominate the intellectual field of criminology until challenged in the 1920s.

People like Jane Addams at the Hull House in Chicago, caring for the immigrant and tenement dwellers of Chicago's Southside, prepared the way for the development of social work in university settings.[10] But it was at the University of Chicago, thanks to President William Rainey Harper's commitment to doing research useful to society, that sociology would emerge and affect criminology for decades. The "Chicago School of Criminology" researched and published numerous books such as *The Gang* by Frederick Thrasher, *The Jack Roller* by Clifford Shaw, and *Delinquency Areas* by Shaw, Henry

McKay, and Leonard S. Cottrell. Edwin Sutherland's theories on differential association and his textbook entitled *Criminology* would have policy and intellectual implications for generations.[11]

McClaughry would not have felt comfortable in either psychology or sociology. He battled their nineteenth-century equivalents earlier. But he would have felt completely comfortable at the University of California. The chief of police of Berkeley, California—August Vollmer—convinced the political science professors to start a course in police administration. Along with his various disciples who eventually created a School of Criminology at Berkeley and started the Criminal Justice educational movement, Vollmer emphasized management and organizational skills. This applied sociology placed less emphasis upon the offender, as in psychology and sociology, and more on the agencies dealing with the criminals. McClaughry's concerns and principles had moved into higher education.[12]

Though the reformatory movement of the late-nineteenth century found an ally in the progressivism of the early twentieth, as these ideals were put into practice, some contradictions emerged.[13] Certainly, the old notion of reformer (philanthropist and academic) and practitioners existed. But new dilemmas arose; the ideals of reform and the growing realities of prisoners in institutional settings did not mesh. The worlds of the ideal and the real clashed.

As the juvenile justice movement took off after the turn of the century–itself a manifestation of progressivism–probation remained a darling. Young first offenders were more likely to reform, "child savers" felt. Special laws, courts, and punitive institutions were created to deal with young offenders.[14] Apparently, no one thought there was a conflict between due process rights of young offenders and the emerging juvenile justice movement.

There seemed to be a nice fit between probation and progressivism for adults too. Probation was "scientific" with its pre-sentence report, a biographical sketch helping judges make the most appropriate sentence. It was inexpensive for budget balancing bureaucrats. In 1910, it cost approximately $220 per year to jail a person whereas it cost $22 per year for that same individual to be on probation. Conditions were affixed for successful living on probation. These requirements reflected the neo-puritan's notions of appropriate life style and included curfews, gainful employment, abstinence from alcohol, and casting off of detrimental personal relationships. Most importantly it kept people out of prison in the first place. By the Progressive Era it was assumed that one came out of a prison experience worse off than when one went on. McClaughry's home state, Illinois, enacted its Probation Officer Act in 1911.[15]

Before the end of the progressive era, about the time of McClaughry's forced retirement, doubts arose about probation. For example, the pre-sentence investigation/report ended up being short and unscientific. People were ill-trained for such activity. The logical profession to do it, social work, was in its embryonic state.[16] Probation staffs, connected to trial judges, were politicized. Work loads of probation officers watching over probationers presented a problem as well. From the progressive perspective the ideal number of probationers per probation officer was 50 to 1. In most places, it became 150 to 1. Many probation conditions were childish. Though probably appropriate for young people they seemed outlandish and insulting to adult offenders, and just begged to be violated.[17]

If probation seemed problematic, parole was even more controversial. A panel of experts, a parole board, was to study a detailed summary of the inmate's progress and determine his or her date of release. As in probation, a set of conditions was imposed to shape the life style of the parolee. Parole officers were to check and supervise the former inmate. If the parolee violated parole, either by committing a new crime or transgressing the conditions of parole, he could be revoked and sent back to prison. Frequently, the court system–which was viewed with suspicion by most progressives–could be passed over altogether. But problems similar to those of probation soon were evident. Parole boards had no expertise but instead were filled with political appointments by the governor. Evaluations of the prisoner came from two questionable sources. Prison officials had considerable input. But not all wardens shared McClaughry's vision, and they used the evaluation as a means to threaten compliance to prison rules or to put people out to make room for new ones. Prisoners were required to participate in the process by presenting a "plan" showing rehabilitative progress in prison and post-release prospects. Eager for release, inmates played elaborate games to con prison officials as to their readiness for parole. Understanding such games, prison workers turned a jaundiced eye to the prisoner and parole process. Once the prisoners were paroled, parole officers were soon overburdened and less attentive, and parolees frequently slipped into old ways. Always eager to print sensational stories, the press highlighted crimes committed by those on parole. As a result, by 1915 many questioned this reformatory principle for adult criminals.[18]

The third area of accomplishment for the reformatory/progressives was in the adult institutions. Reformers had to address an important question: how do you prepare people to live in the ordinary world when they have lived in such an extraordinary one? On one level women were emerging as a "girl problem."[19] The neo-puritans were very paternal and patriarchal. More and more girls were going to prison, "for their own good." Some marginal development occurred earlier but the real "sister's keepers" movement took off in the early-twentieth century. Thirteen prisons devoted exclusively to women arose in the Progressive Era. Based upon the cottage plan, these new institutions resembled college campuses more than penal institutions. With the advent of the so-called "flapper era" in the 1920s and 30s, sixteen more institutions for women were constructed. Just as they were gaining new freedoms to vote, more places to incarcerate women were built. But most attention continued to be given to the adult male institutions.[20]

Virtually all of the reformatory ideals spread to the nation's prisons in the Progressive Era. Notwithstanding arguments for probation and parole, which were basically anti-prison, many felt that prisons were necessary to and capable of rehabilitating wayward citizens. Most common old practices–such as the lock step and striped uniforms (long abandoned in Joliet)–were disappearing nationwide. More sports and music programs were becoming part of the progressive prison. Visiting privileges were extended though puritanical America was not ready for conjugal stays. More mail and inmate run newspapers were permitted behind the walls, but with considerable censorship by authorities. Work release programs allowing trusted prisoners to leave the institution for daytime employment started to appear in 1913. At Sing Sing in New York, Thomas Mott Osborne set up the Mutual Welfare League allowing a measure of prisoner self government.[21] Almost in a self congratulatory mood, the first two decades of the twentieth were a boon to the prison postcard, images of exterior and interior of prisons floated across the nation as items of vicarious tourism. Such cultural artifacts suggest an optimistic pride shared by small town citizens (where most prisons were located), progressive penologists, and growing numbers of tourists.[22]

Given McClaughry's legacy, it is no wonder that Illinois' penal policies became progressive in the first two decades of the twentieth century. An indeterminate sentencing law and the juvenile court act ushered in the new century. Patronage practices were attacked with the passage of the Civil Service Law in 1905. Commitment to reformatory/progressive ideals can be seen with the creation of the Illinois Division of the State Criminologist. The first criminologist appointed was Herman Adler, professor of psychiatry at Harvard Medical School, indicating a medical/treatment model was in the minds of Illinois progressives. Adler did in a scientific way what McClaughry had done for years: a diagnostic evaluation of the felon upon entry in to the prison. In 1920, a Progressive Merit System tied "good time" deductions from the prisoner's sentence to conformity to prison programs.[23]

More so than in probation and parole, this prison progressivism ran smack up against the prison walls. Reform seemed to be more a "forlorn hope" than a reality.[24] This might be vividly seen in McClaughry's home state, Illinois. The old prison at Joliet was condemned as brutal and inhumane early in the first decade of the century. As if to validate such views, in 1915 Warden Edmund Allen's wife, Odette, was murdered by an inmate in her bedroom on prison grounds. Echoing McClaughry's concerns of ten years earlier, Illinois progressives advocated a new "reform era prison." Land six miles northwest of the old prison at Joliet was purchased in 1907. State delegates, traveling to Europe in search of new ideas on prison architecture, came back impressed with the panopticon plan. According to this model, laid out by the nineteenth century utilitarian philosopher Jeremy Bentham, circular cell houses would cluster around a massive dining hall. These cell circles would be connected to the dining hall, like spokes on a wheel, by a series of tunnels. Each cell complex would have a guard station in the middle. From such a tower officials could look into every cell; in the name of official efficiency surveillance was maximized and prisoner privacy minimized. Construction of this new progressive prison, named Stateville, would begin in 1917, but because of World War I, it would not open until 1925.

THE EARLY SIGNS OF DECLINE OF PROGRESSIVE PENOLOGY

As did probation, parole, and prisons elsewhere, Stateville fell from its progressive pedestal. Its very architecture was not inmate-friendly; it sent a message of repression and not rehabilitation. Its omnipresent surveillance was a reform for the keepers not the kept. In spite of civil service, prison personnel were caught up in the spoils system. Guards were poorly paid and overworked. A succession of incompetent politicians filled the warden's offices. Ethnic gangs–largely Irish against Italians, but at least eight other smaller groupings too–quickly formed and challenged the administration as to who really governed the "big house." Violence increased between inmates (the famous boy killer Richard Loeb was murdered in the shower, itself a progressive amenity) and against prison workers. A deputy warden was stabbed to death in 1926 and a series of riots marked the remaining decade. In March 1931, a massive riot shook Stateville forcing the militia to be brought in. Dubbed the "Wild West Days" of Stateville, this preeminent progressive prison illustrated the gap between ideals and realities in the reformatory/progressive programs.[25] It took a special warden to address the fall of the progressive prison, and he was Joseph Ragen.

Like McClaughry before him, Ragen had little to show that he would become the nation's foremost warden. Unlike the Major, however, this small town sheriff had little concern with reform. Ragen was foremost a custodian. Professional reformers had no place at Stateville during Ragen's quarter century reign. He ruled the prison like a paramilitary institution. Intense supervision, numerous rules, and oppressive regimens dictated the life of prisoners and guards alike. Charismatic and authoritarian, everything in the prison had to please the warden and his sense of order. Aside from some basic rights (decent food, clean clothing, and safe housing) everything else Ragen considered a privilege. Visitors, mail, recreation, and other amenities were all gifts to be given or withheld by the warden. An elaborate informant system was created, and whenever two inmates were together one of them belonged to the warden. Gang structures were undermined as powerful inmates were co-opted by the warden with good prison jobs. Guards, largely recruited from southern Illinois, had few ties to the community and were therefore dependent upon a guard culture encouraged and directed by Ragen. Reformers and academics had only limited access to the prison. As the prison settled down to become one of the most orderly and "workable" prisons in America, Ragen carefully courted the media. Throughout his tenure the *Chicago Tribune* praised the prison and its warden. Perhaps reflecting public impatience with the progressive penal design, the *Tribune* as late as 1955 approvingly saw that "discipline at Joliet-Stateville is not merely strict: like security it is absolute." Reform was not mentioned.

There was another sign that the reformatory/progressive ideals could not live up to their promise in the extraordinary world of prisons. This harbinger came from Illinois as well. Donald Clemmer, a sociologist working in the Division of Criminologist at the Southern Illinois Penitentiary at Menard for much of the 1930s, revealed that prisoners were creating a culture within a larger one, a subculture. This was an unintended creation of the life of inmates. Eager to assimilate, to find some meaning and sense of belonging in a hostile environment, prisoners created their own society (language, body markings, group affiliations, rules, relationships, friends, and enemies) independent of the prison administration and reformers. Such a cultural development, called "prisonization" by Clemmer in his book, *The Prison Community,* worked against any rehabilitation effort. Prisoners looked to other prisoners, and not prison workers, for behavioral cues. Two cultures developed and they worked at cross purposes. If this had always been true it would explain the historic Achilles weakness in the reformatory plan. If it were a new development, it would bode ill for the future.

THE FALL OF THE PROGRESSIVE DESIGN

Public and political enthusiasm for reform began to dim in the 1920s when one progressive/puritan principle, abolition of alcohol, gave rise to gang warfare on the city streets of America. Names like Torrio and Capone in Chicago, Schultz and Luciano in New York, and the Purple Gang of Detroit made headlines. Chicago's Saint Valentine's Day massacre in 1927 shocked America. Public support for Prohibition declined and repeal went into effect in 1932. But crime did not go away.

A series of modern day desperadoes—armed with machine guns and riding in "Tin Lizzies" to rob small town banks—electrified the nation. Bonnie and

Clyde, Machine Gun Kelley, Pretty Boy Floyd, and Baby Face Nelson (an escapee from Joliet prison) became celebrities. John Dillinger, himself a man put on parole, stymied law enforcement until gunned down at the Biograph Theatre in Chicago.[26]

As these crime menaces increased, so did the federal government's law enforcement establishment. J. Edgar Hoover took over an ailing Bureau of Investigation (originally created by a progressive, President Theodore Roosevelt) and began empire building. Cut out of the same cloth as Ragen at Stateville, Hoover created a training Academy, a crime lab, an identification bureau—virtually taking over McClaughry's old Leavenworth identification system—introduced the Uniform Crime Report, obtained police power for his agents, and created a "most wanted" list, thus making the agency the nation's foremost federal police. Similar things were being done by Harry Anslinger in the Federal Bureau of Narcotics and by Stanford Bates in the Bureau of Federal Prisons. Bates even created a "Super Max" prison in the middle of San Francisco Bay; it is hard to imagine much reform effort at Alcatraz.

In spite of the crime picture the progressives did not lose hope. Crime became a national issue when the National Commission on Law Observance and Enforcement (commonly called the Wickersham Commission) came out with fourteen reports on various aspects of crime and criminal justice. Its ninth report, appearing in 1931, was on *Penal Institutions, Probation and Parole*. The Commission recognized that the prisons of America were in terrible condition (old, overcrowded and unsanitary, filled with idle and hostile inmates) and in dire need of change. Admittedly "the function of the penal institutions is protection of society" the Commission felt, but this, they suggested, could best be done "by reforming the criminal." They examined parole, indeterminate sentencing, and probation with the same critical but hopeful eye.[27] Echoing statements and beliefs of a previous era, the Wichersham reports were not ready for what was to come.[28]

After World War II crime steadily increased, peaking in the 1960s and 1970s, and prompting yet another national commission—the Commission on Law Enforcement and Administration of Justice or the Katzenbach Commission—that published a summary report *The Challenge of Crime in a Free Society* in 1967. As the Wichersham before it, the Katzenbach reports were caught between the hope of reform and the realities of crime and criminal justice in America. An Omnibus Crime Control and Safe Streets Act soon followed declaring a financial war on crime. One federal agency, the Law Enforcement Assistance Administration or LEAA, gave millions of dollars ($40 million in 1973, for example) to make criminal justice more efficient. The presumption behind these studies, laws, and policies, was that rehabilitation remained the main goal in corrections. Even the newly-minted words for prisons and prison workers (Correctional institutions and Correctional officers) semantically carried forth the hope of rehabilitation. The reformatory/rehabilitation philosophy would be sorely tested in the following decades.

Earl Warren's Supreme Court connected itself to the rehabilitation ideals by increasing prisoner's rights and putting stricter controls on the agencies of criminal justice. A host of developments in community-based programs led one scholar to claim the 1960s as the "hey day" of rehabilitation.[29] Though highly criticized, parole continued to expand. In 1931, twenty-one states had no parole board. Thirty years later every state had one. Prison administration finally caught up to McClaughry too. In 1965 every warden in Illinois came up through the system; none had a college degree. Nine years later not one warden started as a guard, and six of the eight had master's degrees.[30] Most institutions, however, developed gangs (and gang wars), committed riots of protest (Soledad, 1970; Folsom, 1970; Attica, 1971), and riots of self-destruction (New Mexico, 1980), much to the horror of Americans and the chagrin of reformers. Besides institutional conditions, one prime concern of the rebelling Attica prisoners was over parole procedures.

Strident reaction throughout the two next decades showed that progressive penology, those reforms for which McClaughry had fought so ardently, was virtually dead. Shortly after the Attica incident, a Committee for the Study of Incarceration, led by Andrew von Hirsh, issued a report, *Doing Justice,* rejecting indeterminate sentencing and advocating "just deserts". Punishment should be tied to the seriousness of the crime and not to possibilities of reform, went their argument. Numerous academic studies followed showing that rehabilitation and treatment strategies did not work.[31] James Q. Wilson's popular book, *Thinking About Crime*, in 1975 announced that rehabilitation had failed. That same year David Fogel's *". . . We Are Living Proof. . . "* argued for a "justice model" in which much of the progressive penology would be abolished.[32] A more conservative "get tough on crime" policy characterized the rest of the twentieth century. Even a Presidential election (Bush v Dukakis) turned on progressive penal policies.[33] Persistent high crime rates led to more people in prison. Even in those places experiencing declining crime (like New York City) credit was given to tough crime control procedures—though one scholar would claim it was due to abortion![34] The war on drugs led to more incarcerations. Inmate numbers went from 240,593 in 1975 to one million by 1996. A flood of prison building occurred. In 1993 there were 113 prisons being built. Cries from conservatives called for the abolition of parole and the indeterminate sentence. Finally, with what was called a "bloated prison system" political pressure began to build in Washington to study once again and reform the entire system.

As the twentieth century wore down and a new one began, rehabilitation rhetoric and hope remained a glimmer. But popular and political tolerance waned. Wars on drugs and terrorism were tiring. Senators introduced legislation to study and reform criminal justice anew. Prisons were a favorite target. "America imprisoned 756 inmates per 100,000 residents, a rate nearly five times the world's average," went the popular press. "Either we are the most evil people on earth or we are doing something very wrong," announced Senator Jim Webb (D. Va.) in 2009. As the century mark of McClaughry's leaving the criminal justice scene neared, it seemed his vision (as well as those with him and since him) had become a forlorn hope.[35]

NOTES

1. From the masthead of *Forlorn Hope,* the first prison newspaper in 1800. The original is at the New York Historical Society, New York City. Quoted in Larry E. Sullivan's The Prison Reform Movement: Forlorn Hope (Boston: Twayne Publishers, 1990), facing p. 76.

2. See David J. Rothman's *The Discovery of Asylum: Social Order and Disorder in the New Republic* (Boston: Little, Brown and Company, 1971). Hereafter referred to as Rothman I.

3. See David J. Rothman's *Conscience and Convenience: The Asylum and its Alternatives in Progressive America* (New York: Aldine de Gruyter, 1980, 2002). Hereafter referred to as Rothman II.

4. For the start-up of this movement see David J. Pivar's *Purity Crusade: Sexual Morality and Social Control, 1868-1900* (Westport, Conn.: Greenwood Press, 1973).

5. George E. Mowery's *The Era of Theodore Roosevelt and the Birth of Modern America, 1900-1912* (New York: Harper Torchbooks, 1958) and Arthur Link's *Woodrow Wilson and the Progressive Era, 1890-1920* (New York: Harper Torchbooks, 1954) are older but useful overviews.

6. Laurence R. Veysey, *The Emergence of the American University* (Chicago: University of Chicago Press, 1965), pp. 22-56.

7. See Frank Morn's *Academic Politics and the History of Criminal Justice* Education (Westport, Connecticut: Greenwood Press, 1995).

8. Thomas M. Camfield, "The Professionalization of American Psychology, 1870-1917," *Journal of the History of the Behavioral Sciences* 9 (January 1973), pp. 66-67.

9. See Nathan G. Hale Jr. *Freud and the Americas: The Beginning of Psychoanalysis in the United States, 1876-1917* (New York: Oxford University Press, 1971).

10. Roy Lubove, *The Professional Altruist: The Emergence of Social Work as a Career, 1889-1930* (New York: Atheneum, 1971), pp. 140-41.

11. James Carey, *Sociology and Public Affairs: The Chicago School* (Beverly Hills, California: Sage Publications, 1975), p. 83, and Steven J. Diner, *A City and Its Universities: Public Policy in Chicago* (Chapel Hill: University of North Carolina Press, 1980), pp. 121-23.

12. Morn, *Academic Politics*, pp. 41-55.

13. Rothman II, pp.43-81.

14. See Anthony Platt's *The Child Savers* (Chicago: University of Chicago Press, 1977), and Rothman, pp. 205-35.

15. Rothman, II, pp. 61-68, 70, 82-92.

16. Roy Lubove, *The Professional Altruist: The Emergence of Social Work as a Career, 1880-1930* (New York: Atheneum, 1971), pp.118-56.

17. Rothman, II, pp. 92-103.

18. *Ibid.*, pp. 69-72, 162-76, 176-77.

19. Ruth M. Alexander, *The "Girl Problem": Female Sexual Delinquency in New York, 1900-1930* (Ithaca, New York: Cornell University Press, 1995); Kyle Emily Ciani, ""Problem Girls": Gendering Criminal Acts and Delinquent Behavior," *Journal of Women's History* Vol. 3 (1997), pp. 203-214; Laura S. Abrams "Guardians of Virtue: The Social Reformers and the 'Girl Problem,' 1890-1920," *Social Science Review* Vol 74 (2000), pp. 436-52.

20. See Estelle Freedman, *Their Sisters Keepers: Women's Prison Reform in America, 1830-1930* (Ann Arbor: University of Michigan Press, 1981), pp. 144-45.

21. Rothman, II, pp. 128-32, 144-45, 427-32.

22. Frank Morn, "Postcards From the Past: Pictures, Prisons and Popular Culture," in *Material Culture* 31 (1999), pp. 53-70.

23. James B. Jacobs, *Stateville: The Penitentiary in Mass Society* (Chicago: University of Chicago Press, 1977), pp. 15-27.

24. See Larry E. Sullivan's, *The Prison Reform Movement: Forlorn Hope* (Boston: Twayne Publishing, 1990).

25. *Ibid.*

26. See Bryan Burrough's *Public Enemies: America's Greatest Crime Wave and the Birth of the FBI, 1933-34* (New York: the Penguin Press, 2004).

27. Sullivan, pp. 137, 141, 167, 194-95.

28. Wickersham Commission Reports, No.9 *Report on Penal Institutions, Probation and Parole* (Montclair, NJ: Patterson Smith, 1968; originally published by US Government Printing Office, 1931), pp. 66-7.

29. Samuel Walker, *Popular Justice: A History of American Criminal Justice* (New York and Oxford: Oxford University Press, 1998), pp. 205-206.

30. Jacobs, p. 8.

31. For example, see American Friends Service Committee's *Struggle for Justice* (New York: Hill and Wang, 1971), and Robert Martinson's *The Effectiveness of Correctional Treatment* (New York: Praeger, 1975).

32. David Fogel, *". . . We Are The Living Proof . . . ": The Justice Model for Corrections* (Cincinnati, Ohio: W.H. Anderson Company, 1975).

33. Willy Horton raped and killed while out on work furlough. Politically charged TV ads helped turn the election to George Bush.

34. Steven D. Levitt and Stephen J. Dubner, *Freakonomics: a Rogue Economist Explores The Hidden Side of Everything* (New York: HarperCollins, 2005,2006), pp. 152-94.

35. See Senator Jim Webb, "Why We Must Fix Our Prisons," *Parade* news supplement, March 29, 2009, pp. 4-5.

Bibliography

PRIMARY SOURCES

Personal Papers

Governor Albert Beveridge Papers in the Illinois State Archives
Governor John Peter Altgeld Papers in Illinois State Archives
Governor John McAuley Palmer Papers in Illinois State Archives
Rutherford Hayes Papers at Rutherford Hayes Presidential Library

Department of Justice Papers in the National Archives

Administration Files
Bureau of Prisons Papers
Construction Correspondence File
Notorious Offender File
Julius McDonough File
LaDow Papers
Records of the Superintendent of Prisons and Prisoners
U.S. Penitentiary Papers in the National Archives in Kansas City, Missouri
Leavenworth Prison Papers
Chicago City Council Proceedings, 1891, 1892, 1893 at Chicago Public Library
Illinois Reports to the General Assembly 1889
Reports of the Commissioners of the Penitentiary, 1875-1885
National Prison Association Proceedings 1886-1905
Pennsylvania Industrial Reformatory, biennial reports of the managers, 1888, 1889, 1891
Records of Special Punishments, 1889-1897, Records of the Pennsylvania Industrial Reformatory
Report of the General Superintendent of Police of the City of Chicago, 1891, 1892, 1893 at the Chicago Historical Library

Newspapers

Appeal to Reason, 1911
Bloomington Daily Pantagraph, 1879
Boston *Globe*, 1932
Carthage *Republican*, 1861
Chicago *Daily News*, 1891
Chicago *Evening-journal*, 1894
Chicago *Examiner*, 1910
Chicago *Inter Ocean,* 1894
Chicago News, 1891
Chicago *Record Herald,* 1891, 1913
[Chicago] *Saturday Blade*, 1915
Chicago Tribune, 1870, 1871, 1876, 1877, 1887, 1891, 1892, 1893, 1920
Chicago Times, 1870, 1892
Huntingdon [Pa.] *Globe,* 1888, 1889, 1890, 1891, 1892
Joliet Illustrated, 1897
Joliet Press, 1888
Joliet *[Daily] Republican,* 1876, 1879
Joliet *[Weekly] Republican*, 1896, 1897, 1898, 1899
Joliet Signal, 1873, 1874, 1879
Joliet Sun, 1875, 1876
Kansas City Journal, 1913
Kansas City Star, 1913
Leavenworth Times, 1910, 1911, 1912
New York Times, 1929
Philadelphia Press, 1890
Philadelphia *Times,* 1891
Pittsburgh *Dispatch*, 1890
[Pontiac] *Daily Leader,* 1920
Pontiac Sentinel, 1893, 1894, 1895
Reformatory Record, 1891
Topeka Daily Capital, 1905

Magazines

Finger Print Magazine, April and May 1922

Speeches

Robert McClaughry, "The Boys of 1861–and Their Boys," a speech read in June 10, 1897 and reproduced in Military Essays and Recollections

City Directories

Joliet, Illinois, 1873, 1874, 1875
Chicago, Illinois, 1886, 1887, 1890, 1891, 1892

SECONDARY SOURCES

Older Books and Articles

Arnold, Carl. *One Kansas Inferno* (np. nd) At Center for Historical Research, Kansas History Center, Topeka, Kansas.

Batman, Newton, Paul Selby and J. Seymour Currey. *Historical Encyclopedia of Illinois and History of Hancock County* [ed] Charles Scofield Vol 2 (Chicago: Munsell Publishing Co., 1921).

Berkman, Alexander. Prison Memoirs of an Anarchist.

Bernard, Harry. Eagle Forgotten: *The Life of John Peter Altgeld* (New York: The Bobbs-Merrill Company, 1938).

Brinkerhoff, Roeliff, *Recollections of a Lifetime* (Cincinnati: The Robert Clarke Company, 1900).

Brockway, Zebulon R. *Fifty Years of Prison Service.* (New York: Charities Publications, 1912).

Cassidy, Michael. *Warden Cassidy on Prisons and Convicts.* (Philadelphia: Patterson & White, 1897).

Comstock, Anthony. "Bookmakers and Poolsellers," *Independent* 44 (1892).

Cummings, Homer and Carl McFarland, *Federal Justice* (New York: MacMillan Company, 1937).

De Beaumont, Gustave and Alexis de Tocqueville. *On the Penitentiary System in the United States and Its Application to France.* (Carbondale and Edwardsville, Il: Southern Illinois University Press, 1964).

Farrow, Edward S. *Farrow's Military Encyclopedia: A Dictionary of Military Knowledge* (New York: By the Author, 1885).

Flinn, John. *History of the Chicago Police* (Chicago: Police Book Fund, 1887).

Gregg, T.H. *History of Hancock County, Illinois* (Chicago: Chas Chapman & Co. 1880).

Hiller, E.T. "Development of the System of Control of Convict Labor in the United States," *Journal of the American Institute of Criminal Law and Criminology* 5 (1914).

Hiller, E. T. "Labor Unionism and Convict Labor," *Journal of the American Institute of Criminal Law and Criminology* 5 (1914).

[Kornmann, Andrea Marisa] A Policeman's Wife. *Our Police* (New York: J.J. Little and Co., 1887).

Lathrop, S.G. *Crime and Its Punishment and Life in the Penitentiary* (Joliet, Illinois: S. Lathrop, 1866).

McClaughry, Robert. "The Soldier," In Memoria of Madison Reece M.D. [a booklet of remembrance at his dying] (Abingdon, Illinois: Enterprise Press, 1894).

McClaughry, Robert and John Bonfield. "Police Protection at the World's Fair," *North American Review* 156 (1893).

Poe, Allison, *Poe Brothers or the Sequel to a Conspiracy* (1911) at Center for Historical Research, Kansas History Center, Topeka, Kansas.

Price, Philip M. *America After Sixty Years: The Travel Diaries of Two Generations of Englishmen* (London: George Allen, 1936).

Reynolds, John N. *The Twin Hells, A Thrilling Narrative of Life in the Kansas and Missouri Penitentiaries* (Chicago: Donohue Brothers, 1890).

"Robert Wilson McClaughry, 1839-1920," *Journal of the Illinois State Historical Society* 13 (1920).

Schaack, Michael J. *Anarchy and Anarchists* (Chicago: F. J. Schulte & Company, 1889).

Shaw, Clifford. *The Jack Roller: A Delinquent Boy's Own Story* (Chicago: University of Chicago Press, 1930).

Stead, William T. *If Christ Came to Chicago* (Chicago: Laird& Lee, 1894).

Thrasher, Frederic. M. *The Gang* (Chicago: University of Chicago Press, 1926).

United States *Biographical Dictionary and Portrait Gallery of Eminent and Self-Made Men: Illinois Volume* (Chicago: American Biographical Publication Co. 1876).

Wetmore, Sidney W. *Behind the Bars at Joliet* (np. 1892).

Williams, Charles Richard [ed.] *Diary and Letters of Rutherford Birchard Hayes* (Columbus, Ohio: Ohio State Archaeological and Historical Society, 1924.

Wooldridge, Clifton. *Hands Up! In the World of Crime* (Chicago: Police Publishing Company, 1901).

Newer Books

Abelson, Elaine. *When Ladies Go A-Thieving: Middle-class Shoplifters in the Victorian Department Store* (New York: Oxford University Press, 1989).

Adler, Jeffrey S. *First in Violence, Deepest in Dirt: Homicide in Chicago, 1875-1929* (Cambridge, Ma.: Harvard University Press, 2006).

Ahlstrom, Sydney E. *A Religious History of the American People* (New Haven, Conn.: Yale University Press, 1972).

Alexander, Ruth M. *The "Girl Problem": Female Sexual Delinquency in New York, 1900-1930* (Ithaca, New York: Cornell University Press, 1995).

Angle, Paul M. *Bloody Williamson: A Chapter in American Lawlessness* (Urbana, Ill.: University of Illinois Press, 1992).

Asbury, Herbert. *Gem of the Prairie: An Informal History of the Chicago Underworld* (Dekalb, Ill.: Northern Illinois University Press, 1986).

Auerbach, Jerold S. *Unequal Justice: Lawyers and Social Change in America* (London: Oxford University Press, 1976).

Ayers, Edward. *Vengeance and Justice: Crime and Punishment in the 19th Century American South* (New York: Oxford University Press, 1984).

Bearss, Edwin Cole. *The Campaign for Vicksburg, Vol 1, Vicksburg is the Key* (Dayton, Ohio: Morningside House, nd.).

Bennett, James. *Oral history and Delinquency: the Rhetoric of Criminology* (Chicago: University of Chicago Press, 1981).

Biggers, Jeff. *The United States of Appalachia: How Southern Mountaineers Brought Independence, Culture and Enlightenment to America* (Np: Shoemaker Hoard, 2006).

Billington, Ray Allen. *The Far Western Frontier, 1830-1860* (New York: Harper & Brothers, 1956).

Bookspan, Shelley. *A Gem of Goodness: The California State Prison System, 1851-1944* (Lincoln: University of Nebraska Press, 1991).

Brian, Denis. *Sing Sing: The Inside Story of a Notorious Prison.* (Amherst, NY: Prometheus Books, 2005).

Brumberg, Joan Jacobs. "*Kansas Charley": The Boy Murderer* (New York: Penguin Books, 2003.

Burrough, Bryan. *Public Enemies: America's Greatest Crime Wave and the Birth of the FBI, 1933-34* (New York: Penguin Press, 2004).

Carey, James. *Sociology and Public Affairs: The Chicago School* (Beverly Hills, California: Sage Publications, 1975.

Cmiel, Kenneth. *Democratic Eloquence: the Fight Over Popular Speech in Nineteenth- Century America* (New York: William Morrow and Company, 1990).

Cohen, Patricia Cline. *The Murder of Helen Jewett.* (New York: Vintage Books, 1999).

Cole, Simon A. *Suspect Identities: A History of Fingerprinting and Criminal Identification.* (Cambridge, Ma.: Harvard University Press, 2001).

Colvin, Mark. *Penitentiaries, Reformatories and Chain Gangs: Social Theory and the History of Punishment in Nineteenth Century America* (New York: St. Martins Press, 1997).

Cordingly, David. *Under the Black Flag: The Romance and the Reality of Life Among the Pirates.* (Orlando, Florida: The Harvest Book, a subdivision of Harcourt Brace, 1995).

Craughwell, Thomas J. *Stealing Lincoln's Body* (Cambridge Ma.: Harvard University Press, 2007).

Creswell, Stephen. *Mormons & Cowboys, Moonshiners & Klansmen: Federal Law Enforcement in the South and West, 1870-1893* (Tuscaloosa, Alabama: University of Alabama Press, 1991).

Diner, Steven J. *A City and Its Universities: Public Policy in Chicago* (Chapel Hill: University of North Carolina Press, 1980).

Dodge, Mara. *Whores and Thieves of the Worst Kind: A Study of Women, Crime and Prisons, 1835-2000* (DeKalb, Illinois: Northern Illinois University Press, 2002).

Dolan, Jay. *The Immigrant Church: New York's Irish and German Catholics, 1815-1867* (Baltimore: Johns Hopkins University Press, 1975).

Duis, Perry R. *The Saloon: Public Drinking in Chicago and Boston, 1880-1920* (Urbana and Chicago: University of Illinois Press, 1983).

Early, Pete. *The Hot house: Life Inside Leavenworth Prison* (New York: Bantam Books, 1992).

Erikson, Kai. *Wayward Puritans: A Study of the Sociology of Deviance* (New York: Wiley & Son, 1966).

Ernst, Robert. *Immigrant Life in New York City, 1825-1863.* (New York: King's Crown Press, 1949).

Faust, Drew Gilpin. *This Republic of Suffering: Death and the American Civil War* (New York: Alfred A. Knopf, 2008).

Filler, Louis, *Crusaders For American Liberalism.* (Yellow Springs, Ohio: The Antioch Press, 1959).

Flanders, Robert Bruce. *Nauvoo: Kingdom on the Mississippi* (Urbana: University of Illinois Press, 1965).

Fogelson, Robert M. *Big City Police* (Cambridge, Ma.: Harvard University Press, 1977).

Foucault, Michel. *Discipline and Punish: The Birth of the Prison* (New York: Pantheon Press, 1978).

Freedman, Estelle. *Their Sisters Keepers: Women's Prison Reform in America, 1830-1930* (Ann Arbor, Mich. University of Michigan Press, 1981).

Gildemeister, Glen. *Prison Labor and Convict Competition With Free Workers in Industrializing America, 1840-1890* (New York: Garland Publishers, 1987).

Gilfoyle, Timothy J. *A Pickpocket's Tale: the Underworld of Nineteenth-Century New York* (New York: W.W. Norton, 2006).

Ginger, Ray. *Altgeld's America: The Lincoln Ideal Versus Changing Realities* (New York: New Viewpoints, 1973).

Gittens, Joan. *Poor Relations: The Children of the State of Illinois, 1818-1990* (Urbana: University of Illinois Press, 1994).

Goodwin, Doris Kerns. *Team of Rivals: The Political Genius of Abraham Lincoln* (New York: Simon & Schuster, 2005).

Goss, Thomas J. *The War Within The Union High Command: Politics and Generalship During the Civil War* (Lawrence, Kansas: University Press of Kansas, 2003).

Greenberg, Douglas. *Crime and Law Enforcement in the Colony of New York, 1691-1776* (Ithaca, New York: Cornell University Press, 1974).

Hale, Nathan G. Jr. *Freud and the Americas: The Beginning of Psychoanalysis in the United States, 1876-1917* (New York: Oxford University Press, 1971.

Haller, Mark. Eugenics: *Hereditarian Attitudes in American Thought* (New Brunswick, NJ.: Rutgers University Press, 1963).

Hallwas, John E. *Dime Novel Desperados: The Notorious Maxwell Brothers* (Urbana: University of Illinois Press, 2008).

Handlin, Oscar. *Boston's Immigrants: A Study in Acculturation* (Cambridge, Mass.: Harvard University Press, 1959.

Harrison, Fred. *Hell Holes and Hangings: The West's Territorial Prisons, 1861-1912* (Clarendon, Texas: Clarendon Press, 1968).

Hicken, Victor. *Illinois Camps, Posts, and Prisons, Illinois Civil War Sketches,* No. 9 (Springfield: Illinois State Historical Library for the Civil War Centennial Commission of Illinois [1965]).

Hirsch, Adam. *The Rise of the Penitentiary: Prisons and Punishment in Early America* (New Haven: Yale University Press, 1992).

Hoggenbloom, Ari. *Rutherford B. Hayes: Warrior & President* (Lawrence, Ka.: Kansas University Press, 1995).

Holt, Marilyn Irvin. *The Orphan Trains: Placing Out in America* (Lincoln, Ne. University of Nebraska Press, 1992).

Howard, Robert P. *Mostly Good and Competent Men: Illinois Governors, 1818-1988.* (Springfield, Ill.: Illinois Issues, Sangamon State University and Illinois State Historical Society, 1988.)

Ignatieff, M. A Just *Measure of Pain: The Penitentiary in the Industrial Revolution, 1750-1850* (New York: Pantheon Books, 1978).

Jacobs, James B. *Stateville: The Penitentiary in Mass Society* (Chicago: University of Chicago Press, 1977).

Jensen, Richard J. *The Winning of the West: Social and Political Conflict, 1888-1896.* (Chicago: University of Chicago Press, 1971).

Johnson, David R. *Policing the Urban Underworld: The Impact of Crime on the Development of the American police, 1800-1887* (Philadelphia: Temple University Press, 1979).

Johnston, Norman. *Forms of Constraint: A History of Prison Architecture* (Urbana: University of Illinois Press, 2000).

Kammerer, Judith L. *Hancock County, Illinois in the Civil War, "Reflections"* (Carthage, Illinois: Journal Printing Company, 1988).

Kann, Mark E. *Punishment, Prisons and Patriarchy: Liberty and Power in the Early American Republic* (New York: New York University Press, 2005).

Keve, Paul W. *Prisons and the American Conscience: A History of U.S. Federal Corrections* (Carbondale, Ill.: Southern Illinois University Press, 1991).

Knobel, Dale T. *Paddy and the Republic: Ethnicity and Nationality in Antebellum America* (Middletown, Conn. Wesleyan University Press, 1986).

Knobel, Dale T. *"America For Americans": The Nativist Movement in the United States* (New York: Twayne Publishers, 1996).

Langsam, Miriam. *Children West: A History of the Placing Out System of the New York Children's Aid Society, 1853-1890* (Madison, Wisc.: University of Wisconsin Press, 1964).

LaPlante, Eve. *Salem Witch Judge: The Life and Repentance of Samuel Sewall* (New York: Harper One, 2007).

Larson, Eric. *The Devil in the Windy City: Murder, Magic, and Madness at the Fair That Changed America* (New York: Crown Publishers, 2003).

Leyburn, James G. *The Scotch Irish: A Social History* (Chapel Hill, North Carolina: University of North Carolina Press, 1962).

Link, Arthur. *Woodrow Wilson and the Progressive Era, 1890-1920* (New York: Harper Torchbooks, 1954).

Lubove, Roy. *The Professional Altruist: The Emergence of Social Work as a Career, 1880-1930* (New York: Atheneum, 1971).

McKelvey, Blake. *American Prisons: A History of Good Intentions* (Patterson NJ: Patterson Smith, 1977).

Marcus, Robert D. *Grand Old Party: Political Structure in the Gilded Age, 1880-1896* (New York: Oxford University Press, 1971).

Marrow, Raphael and Harriet I. Carter. *In Pursuit of Crime: The Police of Chicago, A Chronicle of a Hundred Years, 1833-1933* (Sundbury, Ohio: Flats Publication Company, 1996).

Marty, Martin E. *Righteous Empire: The Protestant Experience in America* (New York: Dial Press, 1970).

Marty, Martin E. *Protestantism* (New York: Holt, Reinhart and Winston, 1972).

Mennel, Robert M. *Thorns & Thistles: Juvenile Delinquency in the United States, 1825-1890* (Hanover NH.: University Press of New England, 1973).

Merrill, Horace Samuel. *Bourbon Democracy of the Middle West, 1865-1896* (Baton Rouge, La.: Louisiana State University, 1953).

Miller, Wilbur. *Revenuers and Moonshiners: Enforcing Federal Liquor Laws in the Mountain South, 1865-1900* (Chapel Hill: University of North Carolina Press, 1991).

Mintz, Steven. *A Prison of Expectations: The Family in Victorian Culture New York* (New York University Press, 1983).

Morn, Frank. *The Eye That Never Sleeps: A History of the Pinkerton Private Detective Agency* (Bloomington, Indiana: Indiana University Press, 1982).

Morn, Frank. *Academic Politics and the History of Criminal Justice Education* (Westport, Conn.: Greenwood Press, 1995).

Moran, Richard. *Executioner's Current: Thomas Edison, George Westinghouse and the Invention of the Electric Chair* (New York: Random House, 2002).

Morris, Roy Jr. *Fraud of the Century: Rutherford B. Hayes, Samuel Tilden and the Stolen Election of 1876* (New York: Simon & Schuster, 2003).

Mowery, George E. *The Era of Theodore Roosevelt and the Birth of Modern America, 1900-1912* (New York: Harper Torchbooks, 1958).

[no author] *The People of Chicago: Who We Are and Who We Have Been: Census Data on Foreign Born, Foreign Stock and Race, 1837-1970* (Chicago: Department of Development and Planning, 1976).

O'Connor, Thomas H. *Bibles, Brahmins and Bibles: A Short History of Boston* (Boston: Trustees of the Public Library of the City of Boston, 1984.

Oaks, Dallin H. and Marvin Hill. *Carthage Conspiracy: The Trial of the Accused Assassins of Joseph Smith* (Urbana: University of Illinois Press, 1975).

Parenti, Christian. *The Soft Cage: Surveillance in America from Slave Passes to the War on Terror* (New York: Basic Books, 2003).

Peifer, Michael J. *Rough Justice: Lynching and American Society, 1874-1947* (Urbana: University of Illinois Press, 2004).

Pestrillo, Ronald J. *Founding the Criminal Law: Punishment and Political Thought in the Origins of America* (DeKalb, Illinois: Northern Illinois University Press, 2000).

Peterson, Virgil W. *Barbarians in Our Midst: A History of Chicago Crime and Politics* (Boston: Little, Brown, 1952).

Philbrick, Nathaniel. *Mayflower: A Story of Courage, Community and War* (New York: Viking, 2006).

Pickett, Robert. *House of Refuge: Origins of Juvenile Reform in New York State, 1815-1857* (Syracuse, NY: Syracuse University Press, 1969).

Pierce, Bessie Louise. *History of Chicago, Vol. III, 1871-1893: The Rise of a Modern City* (New York: Alfred A Knopf, 1957).

Pisciotta, Alexander W. *Benevolent Repression: Social Control and the American Reformatory Movement* (New York: New York University Press, 1994).

Pivar, David J. *Purity Crusade: Sexual Morality and Social Control, 1868-1900* (Westport, Conn. Greenwood Press, 1973).

Platt, Anthony. *The Child Savers: The Invention of Delinquency* (Chicago: University of Chicago Press, 1969).

Randall, J.G. and David Donald. *The Civil War and Reconstruction* (Boston: D.C. Heath and Company, 1961).

Ranulf, Svend. *Moral Indignation and Middle Class Psychology* [originally published in 1938] (New York: Schocken Books, 1964).

Rehnquest, William H. *Centennial Crisis: The Disputed Election of 1876* (New York: Alfred A. Knoph, 2004).

Riegal, Robert and Robert C. Atherton. *America Moves West* (New York: Holt and Winston, 1964).

Rothman, David J. *The Discovery of the Asylum: Social Order and Disorder in the New Republic* (Boston: Little, Brown and Company, 1971

Rothman, David. *Conscience and Convenience: The Asylum and its Alternatives in Progressive America* (New York: Aldine de Gruyter, 2002)

Rugh, Susan S. *Our Common Country: Family Farming, Culture and Community in Nineteenth-Century Midwest* (Bloomington, Indiana: Indiana University Press, 2001).

Rusche, G. and O. Kirchheimer. *Punishment and the Social Structure* (New York: Russell & Russell, 1968 [1939]).

Simon, Jonathan. *Poor Discipline: Parole and the Social Control of the Underclass, 1890-1990* (Chicago: University of Chicago Press, 1993).

Skotniciki, Andrew. *Religion and the Development of the American Penal System* (Lanham, Maryland: University Press of America, 2000).

Speer, Bonnie Stahlman. *The Great Abraham Lincoln Hijack* (Norman, Ok.: Reliance Press, 1990).

Stengers, Jean and Anna Van Neck. *Masturbation: The History of a Great Terror* trans. by Kathryn A. Hoffman (New York: Palgrave Press, 2001).

Stock, Catherine McNicol. *Rural Radicals: From Bacon's Rebellion to the Oklahoma City Bombing* (New York: Penguin Books, 1997)

Streib, Victor L. *Death Penalty For Juveniles* (Bloomington, Ind.: Indiana University Press, 1987).

Sullivan, Larry E. *The Prison Reform Movement: Forlorn Hope* (Boston: Twayne Publishing, 1990).

Veysey, Laurence R. *The Emergence of the American University* (Chicago: University of Chicago Press, 1965).

Walker, Samuel. *Popular Justice: A History of American Criminal Justice* (New York: Oxford University Press, 1998).

Wendt, Lloyd and Herman Kogan. *Lords of the Levee: The Story of Bathhouse John and Hinky Dink* (Indianapolis & New York: Bobbs-Merrill Company, 1943).

Wheeler, Richard. *The Siege of Vicksburg* (New York: Thomas Y. Crowell, Co. 1978).

Wiley, Bill Irvin. *The Life of Billy Yank: The Common Soldier of the Union* (Garden City, New York: Doubleday, 1952).

Zenderland, Leila. *Measuring Minds: Henry Herbert Goddard and the Origins of American Intelligence Testing* (Cambridge: Cambridge University Press, 1998).

Web Sites

McClusker, John J. "Comparing the Purchasing Power of Money in the United States (or Colonies) from 1665 to 2003," Economic History Series, 2004, URC http: www. eh.net/hmit/ppowerusd/.

Maghan, Jess. "Capital Punishment," Encyclopedia of Chicago [eds. Janice Reife, Ann Durkin Keating, James Grossman] URC http://www. Encyclopedia. Chicagohistory .Org.

Articles

Abrams, Laura S. "Guardians of Virtue: The Social Reformers and the 'Girl Problem,' 1890-1920" *Social Science Review* 74 (2000).

Adamson, Christopher R. "Toward a Marxian Penology: Captive Criminal Populations as Economic Threats and Resources," *Social Problems* 31 (1984).

Adamson, Christopher R. "Hard Labor and Solitary Confinement: Effects of the Business Cycle and Labor Supply on Prison Discipline in the United States, 1790-1835," *Research in Law,* Deviance *and Social Control* 6 (1984).

Adamson, Christopher R. "Wrath and Redemption: Protestant Theology and Penal Practice in the Earl American Republic," *Criminal Justice History: An International Annual* 13 (1992).

Adler, Jeffrey S. "'Mother-in-law is to Blame, But I'll Walk On Her Neck Yet': Homicide in Late Nineteenth Century Chicago," *Journal of Social History* 31 (1970).

Adler, Jeffrey S. "'If We Can't Live in Peace, We Might As Well Die,': Homicide-Suicide in Chicago, 1875-1910," *Journal of Urban History* 26 (1999).

Adler, Jeffrey S. "'On the Border of Snakeland': Evolutionary Psychology and Plebeian Violence in Industrial Chicago, 1875-1920," *Journal of Social History* 36 (2003).

Adler, Jeffrey S. "'We've Got a Right to Fight; We're Married': Domestic Homicide in Chicago, 1875-1920," *Journal of Interdisciplinary History* 34 (2003).

Allamen, John Lee, "The Crime, Trial, and Execution of William W. Lee of East Burlington, Illinois," *Western Illinois Regional Studies* 6 (1983).

Barry, Louise. "Legal Hangings in Kansas," Kansas Historical Quarterly (1950)

Beck, E. M. and James Massey and Stewart Tolnay. "The Gallows, the Mob, and the Vote: Lethal Sanctioning of Blacks in North Carolina and Georgia, 1882-1930," *Law and Society* 23 (1989).

Boesche, Roger. "The Prison: Tocqueville's Model for Despotism," *Western Political Quarterly* 33 (1980).

Bergen, John V. "College Towns and Campus Sites in Western Illinois," *Western Illinois Regional Studies* 134 (1990).

Calahan, Margaret. "Trends in Incarceration in the United States Since 1880," *Crime and Delinquency* 25 (1979)

Camfield, Thomas M. "The Professionalization of American Psychology, 1870-1917," *Journal of the History of the Behavioral Sciences* 9 (January 1973)

Chapin, Bradly. "Felony Law Reform in the Early Republic," *The Pennsylvania Magazine of History and Biography* 113 (1989).

Cheatwood, Derral. "Capital Punishment for the Crime of Homicide in Chicago, 1870-1930," *The Journal of Criminal Law & Criminology* 92 (2002).

Ciani, Kyle Emily. "'Problem Girls': Gendering Criminal Acts and Delinquent Behavior," *Journal of Women's History* 3 (1997).

Conely, John. "Prisons, Production, and Profit: Reconsidering the Importance of Prison Industries," *Journal of Social History,* 14 (1980).

Davenport, F. Garvin. "The Pioneers of Monmouth College," *Journal of the Illinois State Historical Society* 46 (1953).

Davis, David. "The Movement to Abolish Capitol Punishment," *American Historical Review* 63 (1957).

DePuy, LeRoy B. "The Walnut Street Prison: Pennsylvania's First Penitentiary," *Pennsylvania History* 18 (April).

Dodge, L. Mara. "'One Female Prisoner Is More Trouble Than Twenty Males:' Women Convicts in Illinois Prisons, 1835-1899," *Journal of Social History* 32 (1998-1999).

Dodge, L. Mara. "'The Most Degraded of Their Sex, If Not Humanity': Female Prisoners at the Illinois State Penitentiary at Joliet, 1859-1900," *Journal of Illinois History* 2 (1999).

Freer, Robert A. "Imprisonment for Debt in Massachusetts Before 1800," *Mississippi Valley Historical Review* (1961).

Frey, Cecile P. "The House of Refuge for Colored Children," *Journal of Negro History* 66 (1981).

Hougen, Harvey. "Kate Benard and the Kansas Penitentiary Scandal, 1908-1909," *Journal of the West* 17 (1978.)

Johnson, Robert S. "Early Crime and Punishment in Illinois," *Illinois State Genealogical Society Quarterly* 18 (1986).

Johnson, Robert S. "List of Convicts in the Illinois State Prison Who Have Been Pardoned, Died or Escaped: 1 January to 31 December 1856," *Illinois State Genealogical Society Quarterly* 18 (1986).

Johnson Robert S. "Convicts in the Illinois State Penitentiary, Alton, Illinois 1 January 1857," *Illinois State Genealogical Society Quarterly* 18 (1987).

Johnson, Robert S. "Inmates in the Illinois State Penitentiary, Joliet, 1860," *Illinois State Genealogical Society Quarterly* 18 (1987).

Johnson, Scott L. "The Bible and the Death Penalty: Implications for Criminal Justice Education," *Journal of Criminal Justice Education* 11 (2000).

Johnson, William R. "Education and Professional Life Styles: Law and Medicine in the Nineteenth Century," *History of Education Quarterly* 14 (1974).

Keller, Charles. "Prison Reform and Indians," *Indian History* 9 (1976).

Keve, Paul W. "At the Mercy of the State," in *Escaping Prison Myths: Selected Topics in the History of Federal Corrections*, John W. Roberts [ed.] Washington D.C. The American University Press, 1994.

Kinsdale, Jon M. "The 'Poor Man's' Club: Social functions of the Urban Working-Class Saloon," *American Quarterly* 25 (1973).

Kitt, Joseph F. "Adolescence and Youth in Nineteenth Century America," *Journal of Interdisciplinary History* 2 (1971).

Lane, Harold E. "The State Use System of Prison Labor in Massachusetts," *Social Forces* 19 (1940).

Langbein, John. "The Historical Origins of the Sanction of Imprisonment for Serious Crimes," *Journal of Legal Studies* 5 (1976).

Launtis, Roger D. and F. Mark McKiernen, "Joseph Smith Jr.'s Red Brick Store (Macomb, Illinois: *Western Illinois Monograph Series* n. 5. Western Illinois University Press, 1985).

Lewis, David. "The Female Criminal and the Prisons of New York, 1825-1845," *New York History* 42 (1961).

Lindberg, Richard. "The Evolution of an Evil Business," *Chicago History* 22 (1993).

Lindsey, Edward. "Historical Sketch of the Indeterminate Sentence and Parole System," *Journal of Criminal Law and Criminology* 16 (1925).

Long, E.B. "Camp Douglas: 'A Hellish Den?'" *Chicago History* 1 [a new series] (1970).

McCarthy, Bernard J. "The Social Functions of Correctional Policy: A Case Study of the Alabama Convict Lease System, 1845-1928," *American Journal of Criminal Justice* 9 (1985).

McKanna, Clare V. Jr. "Crime and Punishment: The Hispanic Experience in San Quentin, 1851-1880," *Southern California Quarterly* 72 (1990).

Mancini, Matthew J. "Race, Economics and the Abandonment of Convict Leasing," The *Journal of Negro History* 63 (1978).

Markkowitz, Gerald E. and David Karl Rosner. "Doctors in Crisis: A Study of the Use of Medical Education Reform to Establish Modern Professional Elitism in Medicine," *American Quarterly* 25 (1973).

Marsh, Eudocia Baldwin. "Mormons in Hancock County: A Reminiscence," *Journal of the Illinois State Historical Society* 64 (1971).

Marty, Martin, "American Presbyterians: Bicentennial Reflections," *American Presbyterian: Journal of Presbyterian History* 66 (1988).

Morn, Frank. "Postcards from the Past: Pictures, Prisons and Popular Culture," *Material Culture* 3 (1999).

Nelson, William. "Emerging Notions of Modern Criminal Law in the Revolutionary Era: An Historical Perspective," *New York University Law Review* 42 (1967).

Nickell, Joe. "The Two 'Will Wests': A New Verdict," *Journal of Police Science and Administration* 8 (1980).

Norton, W.T. "An Old Time Tragedy in the State Penitentiary at Alton," *Journal of the Illinois State Historical Society* 6 (1913).

Neuman, R. P. "Masturbation, Madness, and the Concepts of Childhood and Adolescence," *Journal of Social History* 8 (1975).

Peterson, William. "A History of Camp Butler, 1861-1866," *Illinois Historical Journal* 82 (1989).

Pheyer, Kathryn. "Penal Measures in the American Colonies: An Overview," *The American Journal of Legal History* 26 (1982).

Pisciotta, Alexander W. "A House Divided: Penal Reform at the Illinois State Reformatory, 1891-1915," *Crime and Delinquency* 37 (1991).

Preyer, Kathryn. "Crime, the Criminal Law and Reform in Post Revolutionary Virginia," *Law and History Review*, 1 (1983)

Rafter, Nicole. "Gender, Prisons, and Prison History," *Social Sciences History* 9 (1985).

Resch, John Phillips. "Ohio Adult Penal System, 1850-1900: A Study in the Failure of Institutional Reform," *Ohio History* 81 (1972).

Rosenberg, Charles. "Sexuality, Class, and Role in Nineteenth Century America," *American Quarterly* 25 (1973).

Rothman, David. "Sentencing Reform in Historical Perspective," *Crime and Delinquency* (1983).

Rugh, Susan S. "Creating a Farm Community: Fountain Green Township, 1825-1840," *Western Illinois Regional Studies* 13 (1990).

Rugh, Susan S. "'Awful Calamities Now Upon Us': The Civil War in Fountain Green, Illinois," *Journal of the Illinois State Historical Society* 93 (2000).

Rugh, Susan S. "Civilizing the Countryside: Class, Gender, and Crime in Nineteenth Century Rural Illinois," *Agricultural History* 76 (2002).

Schultz, Marvin E. "'Running the Risks of Experiment': The Politics of Penal Reform in Tennessee, 1807-1829," *Tennessee Historical Quarterly* 52 (1993).

Schwartz, Joel. "The Penitentiary and Perfectibility in Tocqueville," *Western Political Quarterly* 38 (1985).

Smith, Beverly A. "Military Training at New York's Elmira Reformatory, 1888-1920," *Federal Probation* (1988).

Smith, Beverly A. "Murder in a Rural Setting: Logan County Homicides, 1865-1900," *Western Illinois Regional Studies* 13 (1990).

Smith, Beverly A. "Homicide in a Nineteenth Century Rural Community: The Talbott/Bell Case of 1879," *Deviant Behavior* 11 (1990).

Smith, Beverly A. "The Murder of Zura Burns, 1883: A Case of Homicide in Lincoln," *Illinois Historical Journal* 44 (1991).

Smith, Beverly A. "An Incest Case in an Early 20th Century Rural Community," *Deviant Behavior* 13 (1992).

Smith, Beverly A. "'Divine is Doomed, AND SO ARE HIGH PRICES': The Hanging of Patsey Devine in Clinton, 1882," *Illinois Historical Journal* 91 (1998).

Smith, Beverly A. "'Mt Pulaski's Horror', 1882: Murder and the Rural Underclass," *Journal of Illinois History* 4 (2001).

Sterling, David L. "The Federal Government v. The Appeal to Reason," *Kansas History* 9 (1986).

Sullivan, Robert B. "The Birth of the Prison: The Case of Benjamin Rush," *Eighteenth Century Studies* 31 (1998).

Sutter, Kelly A. "Illinois First State Prison," *Illinois History* 41 (1987).

Takagi, Paul. "The Walnut Street Jail: A Penal Reform to Centralize the Power of the State," *Federal Probation* 39 (1975).

Thibaut, Jacqueline. "'To Pave the Way To Penitence': Prisoners and Discipline at the Eastern State Penitentiary, 1829-1835," *The Pennsylvania Magazine of History and Biography* (1982).

Urban, William. "Monmouth College in the Civil War," *Journal of the Illinois State Historical Society,* 71 (1978).

Zuckerman, Michael. "The Nursery Tales of Horatio Alger," *American Quarterly* 24 (1972).

Unpublished Dissertations

Dodge, L. Mara. "Her Life Has Been An Improper One": Women, Crime, and Prisons in Illinois, 1835-1933. (unpublished dissertation at University of Illinois at Chicago, 1998).

Falcone, David. John Peter Altgeld: Progressive Apologist for Social Injustice (unpublished dissertation at Saint Louis University, 1989).

Kammerling, Henry Douglas. "Too Much Time For The Crime I Done": Race, Ethnicity, and Politics of Punishment in Illinois and South Carolina, 1865-1900. (unpublished dissertation at University of Illinois, 1998.)

Phelps, Margaret Dorsey. Idle Outside, Over Worked Inside: The Political Economy of Prison Labor During the Depression in Chicago, 1871-1897. (unpublished dissertation at University of Iowa, 1992.)

Sanders, Wiley Britton. The History and Administration of the State Prisons of Illinois (unpublished dissertation at the University of Chicago, 1929.)

Wish, Harvey. The Administration of Governor John Peter Altgeld of Illinois, 1892-1897 (unpublished dissertation at Northwestern University, 1936).

Index

Breinigsville, PA USA
18 December 2010
251721BV00001B/1/P

9 780761 853008